Innovative Governance in the European Union

Studies on the European Polity

BRENT NELSEN, SERIES EDITOR

The Europeans:
Political Identity in an Emerging Polity
David Michael Green

Sustaining European Monetary Union:
Confronting the Cost of Diversity
Tal Sadeh

Innovative Governance in the European Union:
The Politics of Multilevel Policymaking
edited by Ingeborg Tömmel
and Amy Verdun

Europe and the Middle East:
In the Shadow of September 11
Richard Youngs

Innovative Governance
in the
European Union

The Politics of Multilevel Policymaking

edited by
Ingeborg Tömmel
Amy Verdun

LYNNE
RIENNER
PUBLISHERS

BOULDER
LONDON

Published in the United States of America in 2009 by
Lynne Rienner Publishers, Inc.
1800 30th Street, Boulder, Colorado 80301
www.rienner.com

and in the United Kingdom by
Lynne Rienner Publishers, Inc.
3 Henrietta Street, Covent Garden, London WC2E 8LU

Library of Congress Cataloging-in-Publication Data
Innovative governance in the European Union : the politics of multilevel
  policymaking / Ingeborg Tömmel and Amy Verdun, editors.
    p. cm.
Includes bibliographical references and index.
  ISBN 978-1-58826-639-2 (hardcover : alk. paper)
  ISBN 978-1-58826-614-9 (pbk. : alk. paper)
  1. European Union countries—Politics and government. 2. Political
planning—European Union countries. 3. Organizational change—European
Union countries. I. Tömmel, Ingeborg. II. Verdun, Amy, 1968–
  JN30.I522 2009
  341.242'2—dc22
                                                            2008033569

British Cataloguing in Publication Data
A Cataloguing in Publication record for this book
is available from the British Library.

Printed and bound in the United States of America

 The paper used in this publication meets the requirements
of the American National Standard for Permanence of
Paper for Printed Library Materials Z39.48-1992.

5 4 3 2 1

Contents

Preface

The European Union (EU) has witnessed a growth in innovative governance in recent years, much of which is not well understood. This book offers a comprehensive account of what characterizes the modes of governance in various areas of EU policymaking. From the outset the project aimed at being more ambitious than most, asking what the specific characteristics of European modes of governance across policy areas are and how EU governance and policymaking differ from those at the national level. To embark on such an ambitious study obviously required major preparation. As editors and authors, we are indebted to institutions and people for the support we received along the way.

The book is the product of half a decade of collaboration. We first met in 2003 at the Max Planck Institute for the Study of Societies in Cologne, Germany, where we were both visiting fellows on sabbatical leave. It was then that we started to think about working together on a major project. In 2004 we designed a research study in which we could identify the nature of EU governance and policymaking. We applied for and received research support from the Canada Council for the Arts and the Social Sciences and Humanities Research Council of Canada (SSHRC) that enabled Ingeborg Tömmel to spend the academic year 2005–2006 at the University of Victoria as holder of the Diefenbaker Award. During this time we developed the analytical and theoretical framework of the research and also held a conference in Victoria in March 2006 with scholars from both sides of the Atlantic. The conference was aided by a general SSHRC grant (646-2005-1135). We gratefully acknowledge additional financial support by the University of Victoria and the British and German consulates.

We owe a debt of gratitude to Lynne Rienner, who was from the outset as excited as we were about the idea of publishing this book and who, along the way, provided numerous suggestions for improvement. We are also grateful for useful comments on the entire manuscript from three anonymous referees, as well as from Brent Nelsen, the series editor.

The broader research project, "Jean Monnet Transnational Research Group on Governance and Policy-Making in the European Union" (W06/0054), which would eventually culminate in this book, benefited from a grant from the Jean Monnet Action Budget and support from both our universities. Earlier versions of chapters of the book were presented at various scholarly conferences, and we held a closed workshop in Osnabrück in which chapters were presented and discussed. We thank participants in all of these conferences and workshops for their comments and suggestions.

We thank Umut Certel, Christina Hamer, Can Mutlu, Melissa Padfield, and Carina Sprungk for providing conference assistance at the University of Victoria and Susanne Pihs and Astrid Bothmann for providing conference assistance in Osnabrück. We also thank Susanne Pihs, Assem Dandashly, and Emma Pullman for their assistance in the final stage of preparation of the manuscript. Finally, we are particularly grateful to Carina Sprungk for her assistance throughout, in particular her insightful comments on and proposals for revision of the chapters of the book.

—*Ingeborg Tömmel,*
Amy Verdun

1

Innovative Governance in the European Union

Ingeborg Tömmel and Amy Verdun

Policymaking in the European Union (EU) has been an important area of research since the foundation of the European Communities. Yet, in the early years of integration, European policies were limited in scope and substance. Certain powers regarding the creation of a Common Market and adjacent policy areas (i.e., competition policy and agricultural policy) were transferred to the European level, whereas the bulk of policymaking clearly remained the responsibility of the member states.

This situation changed slowly in the 1970s and rapidly in the 1980s. Together with the launch of the single market project, EU policymaking evolved in a broad range of areas. Today, nearly all possible policy areas are covered by the EU, either based on exclusive or—more often—shared competences or merely on a coordinative role at the European level.

It was in particular the increased use of coordinative procedures and practices in European policymaking that gave rise to alternative analytical concepts and interpretations. The focus of analysis shifted from a state-centric view of European policymaking to concentrate on (1) the highly diversified EU procedures and practices, combining formalized modes of rule setting with informal practices of negotiation, cooperation, and consensus building; (2) the multilevel and multi-actor structure underlying these procedures and practices, and, not least, (3) the diverging patterns of implementation under a common umbrella. The analytical concept best suited to capture these specific aspects of EU policymaking was the governance approach.

The governance approach was initially developed to analyze alternative modes of political steering within states and in the international system. Viewed from a governance perspective, policymaking was no longer seen as merely public intervention in the economic and societal sphere but rather as a complex interaction among a wide variety of actors: governments, other public institutions, international organizations, private actors, and representatives

1

of civil society. The governance approach not only investigates how and why certain policies are made but also analyzes the institutional setting, the actor constellation, and the ensuing process of coordination among actors. Public order is assumed to be the result of interactions of divergent political forces and societal actors, all pursuing their respective interests but striving, at the same time, for coordination of behavior and action. As a consequence, the boundary between the public and the private sphere, between state and economy, and between state and society is increasingly blurred.

These insights generated by the governance approach were particularly suited for application to the most recent developments in European policy-making. In particular the "invention" of the open method of coordination (OMC), which spread rapidly across a range of European policy areas, gave rise to many studies on the issue. The OMC is a procedure for defining policy objectives at the European level while leaving member states discretion to determine their own policy objectives and practices. In the literature, the OMC and other similar approaches to policymaking are often labeled "new modes of governance." This term refers to both a recent change in governance and new forms of governance, using in particular "soft" or nonhierarchical means to achieve policy objectives.

In spite of a rapidly and increasingly diversified literature on (new) modes of governance in EU policymaking, theoretical reflection and empirical research have not resulted in a clear conceptualization of the governance approach, let alone in a stringent methodology for its application to the analysis of new forms of policymaking (Kohler-Koch and Rittberger 2006). A wide variety of competing concepts, interpretations, and perceptions of the term *governance* and its meaning coexists in the literature. In empirical research, we see an even greater variety in the use of the governance concept in general and that of new modes of governance in particular.

In the context of this book, we prefer to speak of *innovative modes of governance* in the EU. We capture under this term not only the recently established coordinative procedures such as the OMC, but all forms of governance in the EU that transcend the classic forms of state intervention based on legislation and/or financial incentives. Such a broader and more open terminology implies that these forms of innovative governance have not just recently started to emerge. Instead, we assume that they were present in the EU in one policy area or another since its foundation. It is only with the enormous proliferation of EU policymaking—its rapid spread into areas that hitherto were seen as highly sensitive to the member states striving to preserve their autonomy—that coordinative procedures and practices have started to play a major role and come more visibly to the fore as new or, in our terminology, innovative forms of governance.

In this book we pursue four main objectives. First, we aim to clarify further the governance approach and its application to EU research. Second, we seek to identify the nature of European governance and in particular its innovative dimension in a number of European policymaking areas. In selected areas of policymaking we assess what specific forms of governance prevail, the ways to coordinate the behavior of a wide variety of actors, and how the institutional setting affects the behavior of actors. Third, we strive to compare these case studies so as to identify common characteristics of, as well as divergences between, the different areas of European policymaking and the respective forms of governance. In addition, we seek to spell out the similarities and differences between European modes of governance and policymaking and the corresponding modes at the national level. Fourth, we aim at generating insights into the interrelation between European modes of governance and the institutional structure of the EU.

In the next section we outline the distinctive features of European policymaking and provide a first insight into why innovative modes of governance might play such an important role in the EU. In the last section of this introductory chapter, we provide a brief overview of the chapters of the book.

The Distinctive Features of European Policymaking

European policymaking is characterized by specific features that distinguish it from policymaking at national level. These features are linked to the institutional structure of the EU and its role vis-à-vis the member states.

First, European policymaking is usually not directed at its final addressees or target groups. Rather it focuses on intermediary actors—national and partly regional or local governments as well as private or nongovernmental actors—so as to direct their behavior toward regulating or influencing economic processes or social change.

Second, the EU is not sovereign in determining the realm and scope of its competences. These limits on autonomous action imply that European policymaking needs to include specific strategies for creating competences at the European level or else to establish specific procedures so as to circumvent or to substitute for the lack of competences.

Third, the EU is not simply superimposed onto the member states so that it can rule over national governments or other actors directly. In order to achieve its policy objectives, it often has to develop strategies that mobilize governments or other actors to cooperate with EU institutions. Furthermore, the EU has to institutionalize stable relationships with national (regional, local) governments and nonstate actors in order to address the lack of clearly defined hierarchical relationships.

Fourth, the EU itself has no competences to implement policies directly. The implications are that the EU is dependent on national (regional, local) governments and increasingly on private and nonstate actors for policy implementation. Therefore, European policymaking often entails strategies and procedures that direct the behavior of decentralized actors on due implementation.

In this book we give particular attention to four aspects of European governance and policymaking. One is the modes and procedures for generating new policy competences or widening the scope of action at the European level; the second is the modes and procedures for generating the goals and substance of European policymaking. A third aspect is the mobilization of actors for cooperation in policy formulation and implementation. Fourth is the structuring and restructuring of relationships between government levels and between public and private or nongovernmental actors.

We focus on these four aspects of European governance and policymaking not only because they allow for highlighting the specific patterns and procedures of European policymaking but also because we regard them as paradigmatic for elaborating on the emergence of innovative modes of governance in the European context. In other words, the characteristics of European policymaking lead us to expect innovative governance to play a major role in the EU so that it can deal with the complexity of the multi-level and the multi-actor structure of the system.

The book contains fourteen case studies that cover a wide range of policymaking areas—in particular those in which we observe innovative modes of governance. Based on these case studies we seek to find answers to a number of questions. Are there common features across different policy areas characterizing governance and policymaking of the EU? Are there specific features of EU governance and policymaking in different fields that distinguish it from governance and policymaking at the national level?

The Chapters of This Book

Chapter 2, by Ingeborg Tömmel, provides a conceptual framework for the analysis of the case studies. The chapter discusses the emergence of the governance approach and its application to EU research. Furthermore, it presents four basic modes of governance—hierarchy, negotiation, competition, and cooperation—serving to analyze the distinctive forms and combinations of modes of governance in the various policy areas. Finally, it elaborates on the relationship between European modes of governance and the institutional structure of the EU, discussing incentives and constraints for the use of various modes of governance.

The chapters in Part 1 start with a reflection on combined modes of governance and then continue with case studies that examine particular shifts in modes of governance. Chapter 3, by Arthur Benz, takes the framework set out in Chapter 2 a step further by investigating how combinations of modes of governance operate and evolve in the context of the multilevel system of the EU. Depending on the mechanisms generating collective action and the way they are coupled (tight or loose), modes of governance can be positively or negatively linked. Benz shows how combinations of modes of governance can either reinforce actors' willingness or ability to coordinate their policies or cause conflicts.

Chapter 4 deals with environmental policy. In this chapter, Katharina Holzinger, Christoph Knill, and Andrea Lenschow stress that although hierarchy has traditionally been the dominant mode of governance in this policy area, in recent years innovative modes of governance have emerged. Thus, environmental policy is increasingly characterized by a mix of modes of governance, even though hierarchy still clearly dominates this area and competition is being used only to a limited extent.

In Chapter 5, Claudio M. Radaelli and Ulrike S. Kraemer provide an analysis of direct taxation policy by examining various arenas (harmful tax competition, corporate tax reform, and the tax arena dominated by the European Court of Justice [ECJ]). They conclude that there is no single actor dominating all arenas. Furthermore, they identify shifts in modes of governance in the area of direct tax policy, but they do not observe a linear trend over time from hard to soft governance or vice versa. Instead, they have found that different modes of governance dominate in different arenas of direct taxation policy.

Chapter 6, by Amy Verdun, examines economic and monetary policymaking and finds an intricate development of soft and hard modes of governance. First, soft modes of governance emerged in the area of economic and monetary policymaking prior to what is generally assumed in the literature (i.e., they were already used in the 1960s). Second, soft modes of governance can turn out to have harder impacts than the hard measures that are based on hierarchical means of steering. The opposite can also be the case: hard modes of governance can be evaded or watered down by member states, as is the case with the softening up of the Stability and Growth Pact (SGP). Third, resistance of national governments to one mode of governance fostered the emergence of other, less controversial ones, leading to a complex mix of governance modes.

In Chapter 7, Laura Cram finds that in the area of EU social policy, the member states are the dominant actors, whereas the Commission has found itself needing to act with institutional creativity to find a role to play. That role is one of "steering" or "governing" the direction of EU social policy by indirect means, which increasingly serves as a model for the spread of innovative modes of governance to other sensitive policy areas. The Commission has also actively incorporated actors from civil society in the development of this policy.

The chapters in Part 2 deal with those policy areas in which hierarchy plays the role of catalyst for other governance modes to emerge. Chapter 8, by Dirk Lehmkuhl, focuses on competition policy. It shows that although initially clearly governed by hierarchy, this policy area recently underwent major transformations, so that now a number of alternative modes of governance coexist.

Both the competition commissioner and European courts play important roles in promoting soft law instruments. Other important actors are European competition agencies and private actors. Here we find that hierarchy and cooperation are used in tandem in ways that enable soft modes of governance to have "harder" effects than may initially appear.

Chapter 9, by Susanne K. Schmidt, looks at single market policies, in particular the role of mutual recognition as a new mode of governance. Schmidt argues that the single market program took off with the implementation of the principle of mutual recognition following the 1979 *Cassis de Dijon* ruling of the ECJ. Mutual recognition as an alternative governance form, however, transfers the transaction costs of dealing with heterogeneity from the decisionmaking stage to the implementation stage. Therefore, the Commission has built up institutional support structures that absorb the resulting transaction costs. In addition, it has made national administrations responsible for reacting to demands from other member states. The Commission has also strengthened transnational networks so as to free up the workload of national and EU-level administrations.

Sports are another area in which hierarchy exercised by the ECJ clearly formed a catalyst for the evolution of EU policymaking. In Chapter 10, Osvaldo Croci shows that EU sports policy has developed because of ECJ rulings, defining sports as an economic business. In order to keep sports policy within the rules of EU law and to preserve a "European model of sport," the Commission embarked on negotiations with sport stakeholders to reach mutually satisfying agreements before any cases might be brought before courts.

Chapter 11, by Michelle Egan, highlights the evolution of new modes of governance as an expression of changing ideas about market regulation. It focuses more broadly on the questions related to the restructuring of the state, through the delegation and creation of regulatory agencies, self-regulation, and regulatory competition as well as cooperation and institutional coordination in other cases. Regulatory reforms changed the overall mode of governance and the relative dominance of actors. Governments are but one set of actors; new actors include public-private networks, industry associations, and regulated firms. Nonhierarchical modes of governance have become more prominent in this area of policymaking; there is a growing emphasis on codes, rules, and standards, developed by standards-setting bodies or autonomous agencies.

In Chapter 12, Charles C. Pentland offers an analysis of a rather different area of policymaking: the enlargement process. The first rounds of enlargement were relatively simple: the process was managed by the member states; the Commission's role was technical and advisory. Modes of governance displayed a combination of intergovernmental negotiation and hierarchical regulation. Subsequent enlargements reinforced this pattern, but the political resources available to the Commission gradually expanded. Modes of governance have not become "softer"; on the contrary—conditionality has implied stricter rules and procedures. A further finding is that enlargement policy has revived the use of deliberation among the existing members about the structure and functioning of EU institutions.

The chapters in Part 3 bring together those analyses that focus on cooperation as a mode of governance, partly combined with hierarchy or competition. Chapter 13, by Edgar Grande and Ute Hartenberger, focuses on three of the most important public utilities—telecommunications, electricity, and railways; these all belong to the category of network-based technical infrastructures. The analysis of these three utilities shows that the structuring of a dynamic interaction space within Europe offers a counterperspective to the prevalent emphasis on the formal demarcation and allocation of competences. They find that "regulatory governance" in Europe is organized not in a "regulatory state"—neither nationally nor supranationally—but in new types of cosmopolitan interaction spaces, integrating national and supranational actors and institutions alike in a dynamic manner.

Miriam Hartlapp's Chapter 14, on social policy, shows how the implementation process is a key point of governance and policymaking. In this area of policymaking member states have shown great reluctance in implementing policies correctly and in a timely manner. The European Commission has responded not so much by using more hierarchical modes of governance but rather by using seemingly softer instruments, such as more competitive mechanisms (e.g., benchmarking or whistle-blowing). The Commission has also empowered individuals and organized interests to increase indirect pressure. Hartlapp concludes that implementation politics can be characterized as a specific governance process, in which the European Commission heavily influences national policies with soft means but hard impacts.

Chapter 15, by Burkard Eberlein and Abraham Newman, compares the areas of data privacy and energy so as to examine a particular dimension of governance, namely the role of transgovernmental networks. Such networks also operate in a range of other sectors. In these areas the EU has incorporated organized groups of national regulators through European law into a novel, regulatory process, called by the authors "incorporated transgovernmentalism." Eberlein and Newman also identify this mode of governance as different from "coordination" in that it does not exclusively rely on deliberative mechanisms and peer pressure but can bring delegated authority to bear. In this sense, it is a hybrid form combining hierarchy and cooperation.

Chapter 16, by Sandra Lavenex, examines the Area of Freedom, Security, and Justice (AFSJ). She finds that intensive transgovernmentalism is the dominant mode of governance in this area of policymaking. Its characteristics are a particular division of resources that gives salience to the Council of Ministers and its working groups, limits the use of the Community method, weakens the legislative outputs in terms of substantive scope and legal stringency, and builds on mutual recognition and open coordination. In other words, she sees this mode of governance as privileging integration through the promotion of personal, communicative, and operational linkages between member states' administrations and law enforcement authorities while keeping the role of common hierarchical, supranational rules to a minimum.

Chapter 17 deals with another area of policymaking in which we observe horizontal coordination. Barbara Haskel examines the so-called Bologna Process (cooperation in the area of higher education in Europe). The Bologna Process has been based predominantly on cooperation, but elements of competition (benchmarking) have also been present. The actors in the process have primarily been national governments as well as subnational actors, whereas the Commission officially only becomes a major player at a later stage of the process. Haskel seeks to answer the question of whether these seemingly weak processes can generate strong results. She finds three conditions to be important: a permissive consensus among the states, several parties wanting changes but not being able to generate them by themselves, and a body in a "hub" position that can provide the strategy to bring the others together.

In Part 4, Ingeborg Tömmel and Amy Verdun draw conclusions with regard to the overall outcomes of the research project. First, they give a brief overview of how the objectives formulated in the first section of this chapter were met. Second, they briefly review the case studies and highlight the main governance modes that were used, the combinations that prevailed, and the changes over time that occurred, in particular those toward more innovative modes of governance. Furthermore, they spell out the role of the EU institutions, the Commission and the Council, in advancing or hampering the evolution of certain modes of governance. Third, they discuss the characteristics of European modes of governance: on the one hand, across policy fields, and on the other hand, the features distinguishing European governance from that of the national level. They conclude that European modes of governance do not differ as much from the national level with regard to the *processes* that they entail, but they do differ in the configuration of the *actors* involved as well as in the *institutional setting* underlying this configuration.

2

Modes of Governance and the Institutional Structure of the European Union

Ingeborg Tömmel

In recent years, the governance approach has increasingly raised attention among scholars of policymaking in the European Union (EU). Initially, this approach was developed in response to major political changes regarding the role and performance of the state in shaping and steering society. In the context of public policy at the national level, it was the decline of the intervention state (Jessop 2003a) and the increasing inclusion of nonstate actors in public decision- and policymaking that gave rise to the concept of governance, defined as a more cooperative mode of steering society (Kooiman 1993; Rhodes 1997). In the international realm, intensified cooperation between states as well as between international and nongovernmental organizations triggered the notion of governance as a mode of jointly establishing public order and providing common goods in the absence of government (Rosenau 1992).

Yet to date, no single definition or common understanding of the term *governance* has emerged. Instead the approach, whether referring to national states or the international system, covers a broad range of diverging conceptualizations (see, for example, Pierre 2000; Pierre and Peters 2005; Caporaso and Wittenbrinck 2006; Kohler-Koch and Rittberger 2006). The spectrum reaches from a mainly state-centered view on governance, equating the term more or less with governing or political steering (Treib, Bähr, and Falkner 2007), to a much broader definition focusing on the interactions between a plurality of public and private or societal actors and the institutional patterns structuring their behavior (Kooiman 1993, 2003; Rhodes 1997). It was particularly this broader concept of the governance approach that was widely adopted in research on European policymaking. As the institutional structure of the EU does not allow for a simple "command and control" policy, the EU is to a large degree dependent on the consent and cooperation of member states and other decentralized actors and hence on deliberate coordination of their behavior and actions (Zeitlin 2003; Sabel and Zeitlin 2007).

This chapter aims, first, to give a brief overview of the concept of governance and its application to EU policymaking; second, to clarify the term *governance* and elaborate on a typology of basic modes of governance; third, to highlight the role that different modes of governance play in the EU; and, fourth, to discuss the relationship between modes of governance and the nature of the EU. The typology of modes of governance serves to clarify which modes are being used in the various policymaking areas of the EU and how governance has changed over time. Relating modes of governance to the institutional structure of the EU serves to reflect on the characteristics of European governance and on possible differences as compared to governance within states. Two questions are central to this chapter. First, is the EU characterized by specific modes of governance, and if so, in what way might they differ from modes of governance practiced at the national level? Second, to what extent are European modes of governance shaped by the institutional structure of the EU and its procedures of decisionmaking? In dealing with these issues and questions, a conceptual framework will be provided for the analysis of European governance and policymaking and particularly its innovative dimension.

The Governance Approach:
Its Origins and Application to EU Research

The governance approach had its origins in two different sets of conceptual perspectives. The first, referring to "governance without government," was elaborated by Rosenau and Czempiel (1992; see in particular Rosenau 1992) with regard to international relations or, more specifically, to order in world politics. In his seminal article, Rosenau argued that, although a global public regime, let alone a world government, does not exist, some kind of order is being established. It results from cooperation among states, creating international regimes, and from complex interaction between a plurality of actors, both public and private or nongovernmental, pursuing different objectives, but all contributing to provide common goods and thus to establish order in a globalizing world.

The second conceptual perspective is rooted in research on changes in statehood at the national level (Kooiman 1993, 2003; Rhodes 1997; Benz 2004a). In this context, the emergence of new or alternative modes of governance is seen as a reaction to a declining capacity of the state to direct economic growth and social progress and to solve complex problems of modern societies. Scholars of this approach assume that public regulation and intervention are increasingly being shared with or partly delegated to private or nongovernmental actors. This in turn requires enhanced coordination between different actors, thus shifting modes of governance from hierarchy to cooperation, from regulation to delegated self-regulation, from top-down political steering to horizontal coordination. Both these approaches, whether referring to national political systems or to the international realm, have in common that they contest the exclusive role of the state in providing common goods and shaping public order.

The issues and arguments raised by these approaches are particularly suited for application in an analysis of European policymaking. In comparison to the international system, the EU similarly lacks an institutionalized government or centralized governing authority equivalent to that of a national government. Nevertheless, it is able to establish a dense web of rules and procedures guiding the behavior of member states as well as of other public and private or nongovernmental actors. In contrast to the international system, however, the EU has more authoritative or even coercive means at its disposal for directing the behavior of member states' governments and other actors, so that in this respect it is more comparable to national states.

Compared to national states, the EU is not characterized by a *declining* capacity of intervention but by restrictions on the use of such a capacity. Its competences to intervene directly in the economic and societal spheres of the member states are limited to certain policy areas and issues, particularly those referring to the single market and adjacent problems, that is, to market-making policies (Scharpf 1999). In other areas, particularly those defined as market-correcting policies (Scharpf 1999), the EU shares competences with the member states, if it shares at all, or is restricted to a mere coordinative role. Thus, it can only activate member states to pursue objectives defined at the European level, as is the case, for instance, with the European employment strategy (EES). In addition, since the relationships between the European and national level are not structured along clear hierarchical lines, the EU often relies on coordination of action and cooperation with national and sometimes also the regional levels of government. In a similar vein, its relationships with private or nongovernmental actors are based on cooperative forms of interaction. In sum, because of the characteristics of the EU, its "differentiated polity" (Rhodes 1997), European governance is to a significant degree based on coordination of and cooperation with a wide variety of actors rather than on the use of hierarchical means to direct their behavior. As compared to the intervention state, which until recently was the dominant form of shaping economic development and societal life at the national level (Jessop 2003a), governance in the EU is characterized to a higher degree by seemingly less hierarchical means to achieve its policy objectives.

Thus, by applying both approaches to the EU, they merged into one, focusing on the emergence of governance without government and on alternative modes of governance, characterized by coordination of and cooperation between government levels and other public, private, or nongovernmental actors. These forms of governance were mostly seen as having emerged quite recently, in particular as a reaction to member states' reluctance to further transfer powers and competences to the European level (Zeitlin 2003). Therefore, they were often discussed under the label of new modes of governance (Héritier 2002a), as was in particular the case with the open method of coordination (OMC).

Although there is no clear consensus in the literature, new modes of governance are characterized as nonbinding decisions, voluntary agreements, nonformalized procedures of consensus building, and, in general, relatively open procedures for coordinating the behavior of different actors, both public and private or nongovernmental (Héritier 2002a; Eberlein and Kerwer 2004). In other words, new modes of governance are conceived of as soft modes of governance, since they do not rely primarily on formal powers and authority or on established mechanisms and procedures to enforce compliance and, therefore, have a comparatively softer impact.

Some scholars assume that these new modes of governance characterize only a transitional stage in the integration process until member states are ready to create a more powerful system at the European level. Others claim that cooperative and coordinative modes of governance might characterize the future development of policymaking in the EU (Wallace 2005) and even in other international and national contexts (Sabel and Zeitlin 2007). In this chapter, it is assumed that new or—in our terminology—innovative modes of governance are particularly suited to and inherently linked with the institutional structure of the EU. This argument will be further elaborated on in the following sections.

Modes of Governance: Definitions and a Typology

Following Rosenau (1992) and Mayntz (2002, 2004, 2005; see also Benz 2004b, 2004c), governance is to be defined in broad terms, distinguishing it clearly from governing, or political steering. Whereas the latter terms refer to strategic actions of the state or public authorities in order to intervene in the economic and societal sphere, governance refers to providing common goods or establishing public order as a result of the interactions between various categories of actors and the coordination of their behavior. Governance is based on a system of rule(s), shaping and coordinating the behavior of actors (Rosenau 1992). The term *governance* has two dimensions. On the one hand, it refers to a process; on the other hand, it refers to the underlying regulatory structure (Mayntz 2004; Börzel 2005). Governance as a process encompasses various modes of coordination, whereas governance in its structural dimension refers to the actors involved in the process and thus to an institutional setting underlying and shaping its various forms.

In looking first at the *process* dimension of governance, different categories or modes of governance can be distinguished. In the literature on the issue, a wide variety of proposals on how to categorize modes of governance coexists (see, e.g., Kooiman 2003; Pierre and Peters 2005). The variety refers to the number of categories; to the defining criteria, referring to either the process or the structural dimension of governance or to both; and, in some cases, to the actor constellation or the procedures being used (see, e.g., Scharpf 2001). Moreover, the degree of abstraction varies widely within and between such typologies.

In this chapter, I distinguish between four basic modes of governance, referring primarily to the process dimension of the term and thus to the mode of coordination of an actor's behavior. These are *hierarchy, negotiation, competition,* and *cooperation.*

These four basic modes of governance constitute ideal types. In practice, they are usually combined with each other or used in hybrid forms (see Chapter 3). The extent and the combinations of their use may, however, vary widely in different contexts. Thus, most scholars of the governance approach assume that in recent times a major shift has occurred away from hierarchy as the traditional and most widely used mode of governance toward new or softer modes of governance (Rhodes 1997; Kooiman 2003). The latter are assumed to incorporate nonstate actors into the process of governance to a much higher degree than in the past and to make use of more indirect and less coercive means for directing the behavior of actors. This shift is usually explained as a consequence of a declining capacity of the state to steer economic and social life and to provide public goods in both the national and the international arena.

With regard to the *structural* dimension of governance, it is the institutions and actors involved in the process that form its basic constituents. The state or public authorities play the most prominent role in structuring processes of governance (Pierre and Peters 2005). Private or nonstate actors are increasingly being involved, however. They may also exercise governance without direct interference of the public sphere, thus establishing order through self-regulation (Zürn 2005). The institutional setting structuring the relationships between actors can vary widely according to the level of governance (international, national, or regional/local), the interrelations between those levels, and the relationships among the political, the economic, and the societal sphere. Against this background, it is of particular interest to determine how modes of governance are being used in the institutional setting of the EU, which is characterized by a highly differentiated actor structure and thus an increased demand for coordination of interactions.

Seen in light of the four basic modes of governance presented above, new or soft modes of governance fall primarily—though not exclusively—in the category of cooperation. Yet, negotiation and competition may also entail some forms of softer modes of governance. In practice, soft modes of governance are often combined with harder modes, that is, certain forms of hierarchy, negotiation, or competition (see also Chapter 3).

Modes of Governance in the EU

When looking at the modes of governance characterizing the EU, it is important to note that the four categories presented above all play a significant role. There are, however, substantial variations as compared to the practice of governance within states. First, European modes of governance may differ in both process and structural dimension from the corresponding modes at the national level; second, the mix of modes of governance in the Union may differ from that of the member states.

In this section, I first give a brief overview on how the basic modes of governance are exercised in the context of the EU and then elaborate on some specific characteristics of European governance as compared to governance in national political systems.

Hierarchy as a mode of governance is usually associated with the state, in particular the sovereign state, that exercises power over individual citizens or society as a whole. Hierarchy in modern states is primarily exercised by legislation and rule making or by taking binding decisions, accompanied by powers and action to enforce compliance.

In the context of the EU, hierarchy is primarily exercised through the legislative powers of the Union. Some authors even claim that regulation in the form of legislation is the dominant mode of governance characterizing the EU (Majone 1996, 2005). Hierarchy also plays a role in decisions at the European level, that is, decisions of the Commission, the European Court of Justice, or the European Central Bank (ECB) (Scharpf 1999). Finally, hierarchy in the EU is often exercised at the level of the member states, following decisions jointly agreed upon at the European level.

Negotiation as a mode of governance by contrast supposes the interaction of various types of actors, ranging from exclusively public actors of different government levels and functional sectors to a combination of public and private or nonstate actors as well as to exclusively private or nonstate actors. Negotiation is the preferred mode of governance for accommodating highly divergent interests among the actors involved. Negotiations can result in binding decisions or even in formal contracts, but these are usually not accompanied by hard sanctions to enforce compliance. Negotiation can also be used to achieve compliance with rules or decisions.

In the EU, negotiation characterizes the whole process of decisionmaking. Some authors therefore speak of the EU as a negotiated order (Scharpf 1999). Extensive negotiations not only precede every legislative act but also structure the process of policymaking and implementation. In many policy fields, it is mainly through negotiations and the ensuing decisions and contracts that policy objectives and procedures of implementation are determined (see, e.g., Tömmel 1994; Cram 1997). Negotiations structure the relationships between a wide spectrum of public actors both in the vertical and horizontal direction as well as those between public and private or nongovernmental actors, thus constituting a multilevel and a multi-actor system of governance in the EU (Marks 1993; Marks, Hooghe, and Blank 1996; Grande 2000; Marks and Hooghe 2001; Bache and Flinders 2004; Benz 2005).

Whereas both hierarchy and negotiation refer to processes of decision-making or rule setting, *competition* as a mode of governance refers to a mechanism affecting the decisions and actions of individual actors and thus coordinating their behavior. Competition does not emerge by itself, however, but has to be established and sustained by defining the rules of the game and guaranteeing their validity and effectiveness. This means it is in large part, although behind the scenes, dependent on the government or public authority creating and maintaining the regulatory framework. Compliance, in the framework of competition, is not being enforced but triggered by more or less strong incentives as well as disincentives.

Competition plays a prominent role in the EU, since the core project of European integration, the creation of the single market, focuses on establishing and enhancing competitive relationships between economic actors and also between member states. Competitive mechanisms are crucial in order to induce mutual adaptation and policy convergence among member states (Scharpf 2001; Knill and Lenschow 2005; Schmidt 2007). In addition, competitive mechanisms are being used for structuring the behavior of actors in non-market-driven sectors and spheres. For example, through benchmarking and peer reviews, member states or other institutional actors participating in such procedures are subject to competitive pressures (see Chapter 3). Furthermore, pseudomarket mechanisms providing incentives and disincentives—that is, in the form of subsidies or fines—are established in order to direct the behavior of actors.

Cooperation as a mode of governance for its part encompasses a plurality of actors and a wide variety of measures aimed at guiding or coordinating their behavior. It does not at all rely on coercion but is based on voluntary participation in a cooperative process. This implies that compliance with jointly taken decisions, common agreements, or only jointly held beliefs is also voluntary. Thus compliance is not guaranteed; a larger degree of noncompliance may occur. Cooperation, therefore, is a mode of governance with highly contingent outcomes; its effectiveness may vary according to the actors involved, the degree of their commitment, external circumstances, and specific favoring conditions.

Cooperation plays a major and increasingly important role in the EU. Since it implies voluntarism, it is primarily applied in those cases where the

EU lacks formal competences to legislate or to implement policies. It allows for a certain degree of joint action and thus for circumventing the reluctance of member states to transfer powers to the EU (Zeitlin 2003; Schäfer 2006). To a growing degree, however, it also complements other modes of governance in policy fields where major competences already exist at the European level, that is, competition policy or regional policy (see Chapter 8; Tömmel 2006a). In all those cases, cooperation serves to accommodate divergent policy options and strategies of national governments and other actors involved in a framework of well-defined policy objectives or of more binding modes of governance. Cooperation, because it does not depend on lengthy procedures of formal decisionmaking, is also sought in situations where policymaking needs flexible adaptation to changing demands and circumstances.[1] Finally, through processes of mutual learning and socialization, cooperation serves to foster convergence in perceptions, views, and attitudes of the actors involved, thus improving the conditions for collective action in the EU.

Governance in the EU: Its Characteristics

To what extent does European governance differ from that practiced at the national level? In the literature on the issue, the difference is primarily seen in quantitative terms: the EU is assumed to make use to a much larger degree than national political systems of new or soft modes of governance. Often, the latter are even seen as a specificity of the EU. The EU, because of its limited formal competences and its lack of sovereignty, is thought to be particularly prone to the emergence of such modes of governance. Some authors, however, stress that the EU continues to rely primarily on traditional modes of hierarchical steering (Börzel 2007).

I argue here that European modes of governance, in principle, do not differ in their process dimension from those at the national level. Differences come to the fore, however, with regard to the impact of European governance, which in turn refers to the underlying regulatory structure and also the actor constellation. The deviating impact of European governance becomes particularly obvious in the case of hierarchy, which is usually seen as a hard mode of governance linked to national sovereignty and the monopoly of power of the state. In the context of the EU, hierarchy—that is, legislation and its enforcement—implies a highly interactive process including various public and private actors, and therefore EU rules in the form of legislation are less hierarchical in their impact than those of nation states. The reasons for this difference are manifold.

First, legislation at the European level is precarious, because decisions are dependent on powerful actors with highly diverging interests and preferences, that is, they are dependent on consensus in the Council, which, however, is difficult to achieve (Scharpf 1999). This forms a general constraint on making use of legislation in the EU, and it often leads to vaguely or ambiguously formulated rules (Majone 2005). Second, in most cases, European legislation in the form of directives has to be transposed into national legislation, which implies that it gives member states a certain degree of discretion in the process of transposition (Falkner et al. 2005). As a consequence, it does not have a uniform impact on the whole EU. Third, as mentioned above, European legislation is seldom accompanied by hard sanctions and clear procedures of enforcement, thus lacking the authority of national law (Hartlapp 2005; see also Chapter 14). Fourth, European legislation is often framework legislation, aimed primarily at creating procedures for guiding the behavior of national and sometimes regional government instead of directly intervening in economic or social life. It thus often has only an indirect impact that, again, may vary widely between member states.

When looking not only at legislation but also at European decisions, a similar tendency toward a comparatively less authoritative impact can be discerned. For example, the European Commission has the powers to take binding decisions in competition matters. But in practice, such decisions are only taken after lengthy negotiations with all actors involved—member states' governments and private firms—in search for an accommodation of their diverging interests. Therefore, they often represent a compromise rather than a clear top-down decision.[2] To sum up, hierarchy as a European mode of governance, whether in the form of legislation or decisions, is often reduced in its impact, in particular if compared to hierarchical modes of governance exercised at the national level. This situation, however, should not be seen as a dysfunctional aspect of European governance; on the contrary, it is to be interpreted as a constellation corresponding to the multilevel and multi-actor structure of the Union. The EU has not only to establish common rules but also to accommodate diversity among the member states. In a similar vein, although to different degrees, the other modes of governance also show certain modifications in their impact in the European context as compared to the national level.

Thus negotiation also implies that the ensuing decisions are less binding, in particular because member states and their governments often have to reconcile them with other objectives at the national level. In case of contradictions, they are inclined to follow their national objectives rather than those agreed upon at the European level. Decisions as a result of negotiations are not accompanied by clear sanctions and seldom by other mechanisms of enforcement.

Competition, in contrast, is a mode of governance at the European level that may have a comparatively harder impact on all actors subject to it. Once in place as a mechanism for regulating the market, member states and other actors have hardly a chance to evade, let alone to change, its rules. It is the competitive mechanisms of the enlarged market that sanction or even rule out nonconforming performances. In case of pseudomarket mechanisms, however, setting nonmarket actors under competitive pressure, the impact of this pressure may widely vary. It depends on the incentives and disincentives constituting these mechanisms, whether actors will adapt or seek to realize other options.

Cooperation by nature is based on voluntarism and, therefore, its impact depends on the commitment of actors to the commonly defined objectives and, more so, on the perceived gains (or losses) resulting from participation. On the one hand, the impact of cooperation at the European level might be weaker than at the national level since European voluntary agreements are usually seen as less binding and can be evaded more easily. On the other hand, its impact might be stronger, since gains from transnational cooperation might be larger than those from mere cooperation within states.

Saying that European modes of governance often lack hard mechanisms of ensuring compliance or are less binding on member states or other actors involved does not imply that compliance is not achieved at all. On the contrary, in the longer run, as actors become more sensitive to softer modes of governance and as they sense the advantages linked to them, compliance might improve. Therefore, softer modes of governance are not by definition less effective, but their effectiveness is contingent, that is, it depends on a wide spectrum of influential factors. Moreover, as European modes of governance are not exercised in the form of ideal types, but as combinations or hybrids of different modes of governance, the impact on the behavior of actors will further vary, according to the combinations of sanctions, incentives, and disincentives.

In conclusion, I argue that European modes of governance in principle do not significantly differ from those exercised at the national level insofar as their process dimension is concerned. The impact of these modes of governance on actors' behavior, however, as compared to national political systems, may vary. Thus, in the European context, hierarchy, negotiation, and cooperation seemingly have a less binding impact, whereas competition in the framework of the single market puts increased pressures on actors to adapt. This situation may be explained with the insights of Bartolini (2005), who claims that the EU offers more exit options to actors than national states do. This, however, does not imply that European governance has a weak impact; it rather explains the continuous search for innovative forms of governance, the increasingly complex combination of modes of governance, and the ever more diversified actor structure, which corresponds to an equally diversified institutional structure. In the following section, the structural dimension of European governance will be examined in more detail.

Governance and the Nature of the EU

The most salient issue regarding the structural dimension of European governance is whether and, if so, how European modes of governance are interrelated with the institutional structure of the EU. To answer this question, I take a neoinstitutionalist perspective on the EU and, more precisely, an actor-centered approach to neoinstitutionalism (Mayntz and Scharpf 1995). Based on this perspective, one could hypothesize that the institutional structure of the EU offers actors incentives for and constraints to the use of certain modes of governance. This relationship, however, is not seen as a deterministic one; rather, it is assumed that the EU provides an opportunity structure for actors to foster certain developments in policymaking, whereas other developments are discouraged. No single actor can set the scene, however; rather, the modes of governance emerge from the actions and interactions of divergent institutional actors in the process of policymaking. In this section I will first briefly define the institutional structure of the EU and its specific actor constellation and then highlight how both the incentives and the constraints that the system provides to or imposes on actors foster the use of distinctive modes of governance.

The most prominent characteristic of the EU is its hybrid form, generally described as a combination of intergovernmentalism and supranationalism. These terms however, often used as a dichotomy, are misleading in that they refer to different institutional categories and to contradicting theoretical strands. Therefore, I prefer to characterize the EU as a system reflecting two principles underlying its institutional structure: the European principle and the national principle (Tömmel 2008; see also Beck and Grande 2004, Majone 2005). This constellation finds its institutional expression in both a horizontal fragmentation of power at the European level and a vertical fragmentation of power between the European and the national level.

In the horizontal dimension at the European level, the two principles primarily find their expression in the Commission—representing the Union as a whole—and the Council—representing the member states. Both institutions, forming the core centers of power in the EU, constitute a bicephalous structure, in contrast to national political systems that are more clearly centralized. All other institutions and actors of the system, although taking varying positions in concrete decisionmaking, are structurally related to one or the other side of these centers of power, meaning to the underlying principles in the process of integration. Thus, on the one hand, the Parliament and the Court, although independent actors with far-reaching powers, often act in support of the Commission; that is, they also represent primarily the European principle. On the other hand, the highly differentiated substructures of the Council—the Permanent Representatives Committee (Coreper), various special committees, the Council Secretariat, and the working groups—all act primarily in support of the national principle.

In the vertical dimension, the European principle is represented by the Commission, often supported in this constellation by the Council as a whole, the Court, and Parliament, whereas the national principle is represented by the individual member states. Since the Council makes decisions on policy objectives, legislation, and the overall process of integration, it has an important role vis-à-vis single member states in guiding their behavior. Parliament, in its legislative functions, and the Court, because of its role in infringement procedures against member states, both primarily represent the European principle in this constellation.

The relationship between the institutions and actors of the EU representing contradicting principles is not definitively defined; there is no clear division of powers, let alone an attribution of sovereignty to one side or a clear definition of a structure of shared sovereignty. It is true that member states are sovereign, but only individually and only to the extent that this sovereignty is not constrained by rule making at the European level. In the context of the EU, in order to be able to exercise power, member states have to pool their sovereignty (Keohane and Hoffmann 1991). This pooling, however, is not once and for all established, or delegated to the Commission; it depends on decisionmaking and consensus building in the Council and, therefore, it is precarious.

The European level, and in particular the Commission, has been attributed certain competences, but they do not allow for taking independent action. The Commission, through its monopoly of proposing legislation, can set the agenda and shape the substance of legislation to a far-reaching degree, but, in the end, it is always dependent on the Council's taking the respective decisions. The Council in turn is to a growing degree dependent on Parliament, supporting its decisions or, more often, supporting and at the same time amending the proposals of the Commission. The Court, by using its judicial powers to a maximum, has established its position as final arbiter in the EU but also as a rule maker. As the most recent judgments in competition matters prove, however, it is also sensitive to indirect pressures from the member states. Thus, the distribution of powers in the EU is continuously being structured and restructured through ongoing processes of decisionmaking, consensus building, conflict, and cooperation. The central institutional actors, in particular the Commission and the Council as well as the Commission interacting with individual governments of the member states, are permanently involved in negotiations determining their respective role and influence in every policy field. It is through this constant interaction that European modes of governance evolve and are further modeled and differentiated.

Following this necessarily rough characterization of the EU, we can identify the major incentives and constraints that are set by the institutional structure of the system and provide the context in which actors use specific modes of governance.

Two characteristics of the EU system pose major constraints. First, since the EU is not sovereign, institutional actors are constrained in making use of hierarchy as a mode of governance. Although the EU has far-reaching legislative powers, the extent to which these powers can be used is largely dependent on consent of the Council. Such consent is difficult to achieve because of diversity among member states and because of a general reluctance of all member states to transfer powers and competences to the European level beyond the sphere of market regulation. Second, the EU is constrained in enforcing compliance with its rules. It does not have major competences in rule enforcement, let alone the powers of command and control vis-à-vis the member states. Since member states are sovereign, they have many means and ways at their disposal to resist or even obstruct European rules, binding decisions, and other modes of exercising power by the European level.

The institutional structure of the EU also offers major incentives for the use of certain modes of governance. First, since the EU is characterized by the fragmentation of powers between institutional actors with highly diverging preferences and interests and at the same time, if collective action in an issue area is desired, by a high degree of interdependence between those actors to pool their powers, it offers incentives for both aggregating and transforming diverging interests and preferences. This in turn fosters the emergence of modes of governance based on negotiation, consensus building, and cooperation among different actors. Second, insofar as powers have been transferred to the European level, these powers mostly refer to building and ensuring effectiveness of market mechanisms. Therefore, and in combination with the otherwise limited powers of the EU, the system offers strong incentives for using market mechanisms and competition as modes of governance, also beyond the realm of the real market. Third, since the EU lacks far-reaching powers in many policy fields and, therefore, is highly dependent on external power resources, it offers strong incentives for including a wide variety of actors, both public and private or nongovernmental, in its procedures of decisionmaking and policy implementation. This in turn stimulates the "invention" of procedures for fostering consensus building among the actors involved, leading to convergence of visions, norms, attitudes, and preferences.

In sum, on the one hand, the dependence of the EU on the consent of national governments is the main factor constraining the use of hierarchy as a mode of governance beyond the realm of market regulation. On the other hand, it is precisely the need for searching and building consensus among member states that fosters the emergence of alternative modes of governance based on the use of market mechanisms and competition, negotiation, and cooperation as means of directing the behavior of actors toward achieving jointly defined objectives. This is not to say that the position of member states is the decisive factor determining European governance. Instead, since the member states in many cases also prefer collective action in the framework of the EU, it is the interactions among all actors involved, their mutual interdependency, that finally determines which modes of governance emerge in which combinations. It is through Commission proposals, Parliament's amendments, Court judgments, Council decisions, and, finally, the degree of compliance or noncompliance of the member states (to mention only the roles of the most important actors) that policymaking and modes of governance evolve while accommodating divergence.

The above list of incentives and constraints to the emergence of European modes of governance does not imply that other incentives and constraints do not exist. On the contrary, those mentioned are only the most basic and salient incentives and constraints, and others play a role as well. Furthermore, incentives and constraints have to be looked at in more detail. Thus, for example, the use of hierarchy as a mode of governance is particularly constrained in new policy areas, where thus far competences have not been transferred to the European level. Hierarchy is also more constrained when legislation refers to the substance of policymaking, whereas it is much less constrained when used for determining procedures, in particular ones that provide for extensive participation of national actors in European policymaking. Therefore, it is primarily an empirical question to determine the impact of incentives and constraints, resulting from the institutional and the actor structure in the EU, on processes of governance.

Conclusion

Against the background of the analytical framework as outlined above, some conclusions can be formulated with regard to (innovative) modes of governance in the EU. First, European modes of governance do not emerge by design of single actors but are the result of the process of policymaking, evolving through the interactions between different institutional actors at the European level, between the European and national (and sometimes regional) government level and the actors representing them, and finally between public and nonstate actors. In sum, they result from cooperative *and* conflicting relationships between them. Second, European modes of governance in their process dimension do not significantly differ from those practiced at the national level. They differ in their impact, however, since the multilevel system of the EU offers more opportunities for actors to choose an exit option. Third, European modes of governance are shaped and modeled according to the incentives and constraints that the institutional structure of the EU and the corresponding actor constellation set to their emergence and evolution. The structure of the system implies, on the one hand, a comparatively higher demand for negotiation, cooperation, and competition and, on the other, a higher degree of constraints for taking recourse to hierarchy as a mode of governance.

Notes

1. This is particularly important for the EU, since formal decisions are always dependent on the consensus between member states, which is often hard to achieve.

2. It is true that the European Court of Justice takes binding, authoritative decisions without compromising with the parties involved. Appealing to the Court implies cumbersome and costly procedures, however, so that only a limited number of infringement cases are being brought before the Court (Hartlapp 2005). Moreover, in most cases, the Court can only express a verdict; it seldom has sanctions at hand so that compliance is not guaranteed.

PART 1

Shifting Modes of Governance

3

Combined Modes of Governance in EU Policymaking

Arthur Benz

In research on policymaking in the European Union (EU), the governance concept has received a substantial boost over the past two decades. Among the concepts used to characterize the particulars of European structures and processes of policymaking, "multilevel governance" (Hooghe and Marks 2001; Benz 2003; Bache and Flinders 2004) and "network governance" (Eising and Kohler-Koch 1999) have attracted attention. In addition, scholars have emphasized changes of governance in the EU and have identified "new modes of governance" (Héritier 2002a; Eberlein and Kerwer 2004; Kohler-Koch and Rittberger 2006; Treib, Bähr, and Falkner 2007). In this context, a number of typologies have been proposed, which have been applied in empirical research on European policymaking and on coordination in the multilevel polity of the EU (Eising and Lenschow, 2007; see also Chapter 2).

It goes without saying that all these efforts to elaborate categories for policy and governance research are helpful, if not necessary, and so are all proposals for more precise definitions. In any case they can contribute to sharpening our understanding of governance and turn the concept into an analytical tool for empirical research. In this way we can overcome a serious conceptual deficit in European studies, in particular in research on European policymaking. In a recent review article, Beate Kohler-Koch and Berthold Rittberger rightly characterized this deficit as follows: "Despite the omnipresence of 'governance' in the study of the EU, governance is still ambiguous and under-specified as a concept, let alone as a theory" (Kohler-Koch and Rittberger 2006: 42–43). Nonetheless, this statement does not imply that the debate about governance leads into a dead end. In fact, it can provide us with useful conceptual lenses when coping with the complexity of policymaking in the EU. This chapter outlines how the concept of governance can be applied as an analytical basis to better explain the operation and evolution of multilevel governance.

The term *governance,* as applied in this chapter, covers modes of coordination, that is, particular patterns of interrelated structures and processes that imply mechanisms of collective action (Lange and Schimank 2004; Benz et al. 2007a; Schimank 2007). Coordinated collective action is possible without individual actors' being guided by rules entrenched in institutions. With governance we usually mean collective action in institutions, however, with the latter enabling and regulating individual actions and social interactions. It is the interplay of institutions and interactions that determines how governance works and how it changes. By setting rules, institutions control the behavior of actors and define the patterns of interaction. But they also constitute a framework in which modes of governance emerge and evolve.

Many scholars tend to apply a narrower notion of governance as meaning a new way of governing in networklike settings. This implies that regulation and control in a hierarchical structure have come to their limits with the EU's extension of its powers. The broader term refers to the fact that not only hierarchy but all ways of governing and collective action have their deficits regarding the functions ascribed to them. Discussions about state failure, market failure, deficits in democratic procedures, or, more generally, dilemmas of collective action indicate this. Against this background, the governance concept provides a framework for comparing the relative effectiveness and deficits of different modes of collective action. As its core, such a framework requires a typology of governance modes. For analyzing policymaking in political systems, we can start with distinguishing hierarchy, networks, negotiation, and competition, which should cover the relevant modes of governance (Benz 2006) and for which basic theoretical models are available (Schimank 2003). Real policymaking, in particular multilevel governance of the EU, results, however, from a combination of these basic modes of governance, and for these complex configurations hardly any theoretical models are available. Therefore policy researchers have to identify the mechanisms of collective action and try to understand how they interact. Even though theoretical models of basic governance modes can serve as kinds of "modules" (Scharpf 1997a) in analyzing governance, it is only empirical research on policymaking in complex settings that can lead us to theories of governance in the EU.

In the following sections, I will illustrate this perspective by focusing on the development and operation of so-called new modes of multilevel governance in the EU, that is, the coordination among the European, national, and subnational actors by agreement, voluntary compliance with goals, or mutual adjustment without the application of formal power. The invention of these modes has enabled European policymakers to influence and control policies of the member states even when they cannot dispose of formal powers. Nonetheless, it is misleading to label them as "soft" or regard them as merely working with agreement or deliberation. More often than not they are embedded in or connected with control in a hierarchy. As a rule they combine different basic modes of interaction and different mechanisms of coordination. How they work and whether they are effective or not depends on the specific combination of mechanisms. The next four sections apply this analytical perspective to the most important governance modes in the EU.

From a functionalist point of view, the emergence of new modes can be explained by a growing mismatch between responsibilities assigned to the EU and the limited competences of European institutions. This imbalance of the European federation is the result of an integration process that started with market creation, deregulation, and reregulation and is now ingrained in the particular sharing of powers between the EU and its member state governments. What a functionalist reasoning cannot explain is why and how actors react to these institutional problems. Indeed, European policymakers have to cope with the consequences, but the way they do this depends on their interests and powers. I will sketch very preliminary ideas on how the evolution and dynamics of governance in the EU can be explained.

Regulation of the Common Market: Coordination by Hierarchy?

The term *governance* appeared in the literature and in official papers of the EU at a time when nonhierarchical modes of coordination had gained in importance in policymaking. Scholars working with a broad concept of governance have labeled these as new modes, thus distinguishing them from traditional modes of regulation and implementation of the law. The latter have been identified with a traditional command-compliance model of politics and have been linked to the institutions of the modern state that are legitimized to enforce decisions against the will of individual citizens or groups (Caporaso and Wittenbrinck 2006). Apparently the EU lacks this power of the modern state.

Nonetheless, it should not be ignored that the Common Market was created by European law, which ranks superior to national law and can be enforced against disobedient member states. Thus European regulation constituted a hierarchical order of multilevel governance. The legislative acts are to be implemented by member states or, if passed in the form of directives, are to be transposed by their parliaments into national law. Indeed the member states' governments maintained the power of the use of physical force, and the EU cannot refer to such instruments against governments when they persistently break the rules. The Commission is entitled to initiate proceedings, however, if it observes infringement of European law, and they can end with sanctions against the respective member state.

Governance through law conformed to the liberal policy approach of the Common Market project. By deregulating state interventions favoring national firms and branches, abolishing tariff barriers, and implementing a joint currency and monetary policy, the EU acted in accordance with the concept of liberal state theories (Eberlein and Grande 2003). Regarding policy instruments, this approach has led to a predominance of law that supported the prominent role of the European Court of Justice (ECJ). Moreover, the hierarchical approach of governance has been revealed in the institutions of independent regulatory agencies (Majone 1999).

This development raises doubt as to whether the categories of "old" (hierarchical) and "new" (nonhierarchical) modes of governance really help to describe the evolution of governance in the EU. First of all, it has to be emphasized that regulation cannot be identified with governance if the power of the member states is restricted to implementing European law. Hierarchical governance means that actors subject to law have influence on lawmaking either in the legislative process or, indirectly, by way of implementing the law. In the regulatory policy of the EU, these patterns of mutual adjustment are characteristic of the work of regulatory agencies or committees deciding on the elaboration or implementation of legislative acts. In these institutions, the asymmetry of power between the European and the national level remains in the background when representatives of the Commission or of agencies, of member state governments, and of private interests negotiate (Young 2005). Hierarchy prevails in regulatory policy aiming at the market creation. But in EU regulation the well-known problems of information asymmetries and conflicts of interests are reinforced by veto powers of member state governments in the multilevel process of legislation, by the weakness of enforcement powers of European institutions, and by the influence of powerful private interests.

This has caused adjustments of governance in at least two respects. First, regulative programs are usually specified in negotiations between experts from national and European administrations and from associations. The institutional basis for these negotiations is provided by the comitology system. Outside this institutional setting, these processes have been stabilized by networks (Eberlein and Grande 2003: 433–438). Worth being mentioned in this context is the European Competition Network, which was established by the Commission with the intention of generating a common culture of regulation in competition policy, not by issuing binding rules but by recommendations and communication (Ehlermann and Atanasiu 2004). Second, the program to introduce a general Common Market, started in the 1980s, revealed the complex task of deregulation that brought the hierarchical mode of governance to its limits. The EU therefore tried to induce processes of mutual adjustment in regulatory competition among member states. The shadow of hierarchy and economic competition should motivate governments to harmonize their regulation. Both developments led to a variable combination of governance modes. The particular patterns, which include negotiations, networking, and competition as well as their operation, are still not adequately understood, and there is obvious need for further research.

"Network Governance":
Negotiations in Networks and Hierarchy

As empirical studies on policymaking in the EU have shown, conflicts between institutions and actors from different levels or sectors often are dealt with in negotiations. In many cases these include actors from the private sector that continuously cooperate with representatives of the Commission or of national governments in networks. Emphasizing these patterns of policymaking, some scholars have characterized governance in the EU as "network governance" (Eising and Kohler-Koch 1999: 5–6; Schout and Jordan 2005). This concept should not only underscore the particulars of European legislation in view of the fact that the Commission regularly formulates initiatives after negotiating with national, regional, or private actors. It should also draw attention to the multitude of working groups in the implementation of law and to partnerships between the Commission and associations of private interest groups. In cases where these groups have persisted over a longer time span, there are good reasons to categorize them as networks. They constitute stable patterns of interactions between independent actors linked by mutual trust and interested in a joint solution of problems (Kappelhoff 2000: 25–29). In other cases, which we find in committees of the Council and the Commission, it would be better to speak about institutionalized systems of negotiation in order to comprehend the effective mechanisms of collective action.

Networks support the coordination of independent actors' policies without the intervention of an external authority and without formal decision rules. When it comes to a specific decision, they set the framework for negotiations. Continuous interactions and mutual trust prevent actors from strategically using their bargaining power and from making tactical moves that cause uncertainty and conflicts and increase the probability of negotiation failure. The "bargaining dilemma" (Lax and Sebenius 1986: 38–39; Scharpf 1992a) caused by the mixed motives of negotiation partners—whether to use bargaining power or to cooperate—can be avoided if negotiations are embedded in iterated relations of communication. Networks emerging from such communicative practices generate mutual trust among participants, common understandings of situations and problems, shared information, and normative guidelines for behavior. All these factors make solutions in negotiations and coordinated actions highly probable. The necessary density of communicative relations and trust usually does not link all actors in a network, however, but only includes a core group; actors at the periphery are more loosely integrated. Therefore networks have to be regarded as differentiated configurations of structures and processes. The patterns of interactions reflect effective disparities of power and influence between actors involved (Jansen 2006: 230–231). For this reason agreements and policy outcomes produced by actors in the core network can always be opposed by peripheral actors.

This differentiation of center and periphery can be observed in European governance when representatives of national executives negotiate with representatives of private interests. These two groups often maintain intense contacts and tend to negotiate in the "arguing" mode. These actors are included in wider patterns of interactions, however, in particular when they speak for a national or regional government or for private organizations. These relations constitute the periphery of European networks. If partners in the core network are committed to institutions or actors in the "periphery," the processes of arguing are less likely or may be interrupted by external interventions. Such interference is likely to surface if actors in European policymaking intensely communicate on issues at stake while at the same time hardly any contacts exist between the organizations represented. Under such conditions, policymakers are members of different, weakly connected networks and work at the interface of different arenas. If policies made in these arenas confront them with diverging demands or expectations, coordination in network governance can turn out to be rather problematic.

Moreover, multilevel governance by networks or negotiations is doomed to fail if representatives of governments or private organizations are strongly influenced by rules of interactions in their national or regional organization that make them behave in a way not compatible with network relations. Governments have to find the support of their parliaments, which can be uncertain depending on the structure of party competition. Ministers and their civil servants have to take into consideration procedures of interdepartmental coordination. Representatives of interest groups can be constrained in their communication with public actors by fluctuating majorities or factions in their association. If actors are committed to complying with rules constraining their discretion, even negotiations embedded in stable networks can end in a deadlock. Only a loose coupling between the different levels, which allows a sequential solution of conflicts in different arenas and shields negotiations from immediate repercussions from outside, can prevent such problems, as is revealed, for example, by governance of the EU structural funds (Auel 2003; Benz 2003: 333–340).

More often than not, negotiations in the EU operate in the context of formal institutions. If actors fail to come to an agreement, a decision can be made by a legitimized authority or can be passed by majority rule. In this case the looming intervention of an external body motivates actors to find a solution in negotiations—irrespective of their individual interests (Scharpf 1993a). Decisions in formal institutions are unattractive for partners in negotiations because they deprive them of their influence on the outcome and can leave them worse off than the status quo or any compromise. As a consequence they feel compelled simply by the "shadow of hierarchy" to find a solution in negotiations. Such a governance mix can be found, for example, in social policy, where the EU has the competence to regulate minimum standards. In this case, directives are to be negotiated in the social dialogue among employers and unions. If the dialogue fails, the Commission can initiate the formal process of legislation. Uncertainty about the outcome of this process as well as their interest in maintaining power over the policy puts the social partners under pressure to find a compromise (Falkner 2000: 287). Thus in principle, this governance configuration proves effective. The fact that social regulation in the EU is still not well developed does not have to do with the governance mode. It can be explained by the limited legislative competences of the EU in this policy field and by the decision rules in the Council, which has to decide by unanimity if it decides on standards trespassing a minimal threshold. Both institutional rules limit the shadow of hierarchy. Furthermore, constraints of social regulation are caused by the dualistic cleavage structure in the social dialogue, which gives rise to distrust among actors and fosters bargaining instead of arguing (Smismans 2006b: 124–126). Finally, the asymmetry in power relations among actors makes negotiations difficult, because employers can credibly threaten to end negotiations whereas unions are not able to counteract by mobilizing protest at the European level (Streeck 1998: 394).

In a similar manner, the shadow of hierarchy is institutionalized in regulation committees that implement European law. When they consult on issues of regulation, they are integrated in the interplay between the Commission and the Council of Ministers. If such a comitology committee votes against a proposal of the Commission or does not come to a decision, the issue can be submitted to the Council. As all members of a committee usually regard this as a rather unattractive solution of conflicts, they make all efforts to find a consensus. The deliberative mode of interaction, which has been discovered in studies on committees (Joerges and Neyer 1997), results from this combination of networks and institutions.

In policy areas in which—due to the lack of EU competences—there is no shadow of hierarchy, effective network governance and negotiations can emerge because governments or interest groups are confronted with competition and the prospect of an unpleasant "race to the bottom." If the expected costs and benefits of competition clearly discriminates among states, regions, or social groups, joint decision in negotiations is less likely. This is the reason why most efforts to harmonize taxes regularly have failed. Sectoral or regional networks can arise and work effectively, however, if they promise to shield particular interests against the negative consequences of competition with other sectors or regions. This explains, for example, the evolution of a network of national ministries and authorities responsible for spatial planning and environment during the 1990s (Faludi and Waterhout 2002). By coordinating their policies at the European level, they had hoped to prevent the incremental downgrading of their positions at the national level. Once more this is a case revealing that it is not only the trust among partners in the network but the relationship between modes of interaction in different arenas and at different levels that explains how "network governance" works.

Thus when trying to understand "network governance" in the EU, we have to consider the differentiated structures and the multilevel character of networks, the influence of decisions and rules in different arenas on actors' behavior, and the way networks are embedded in institutions or competition. The term *network* conceals variations in governance patterns. Moreover, networks do not always provide solutions but may also produce problems when they burden governance with negative interferences of different modes. Policy networks in the EU can cause strong commitments of actors and can make processes opaque. As a consequence, conflicts can arise at the national level when it comes to control of executives by parliaments or to implementation of policies. Finally, in order to explain outcomes, we have to take into consideration that the communication in networks mostly constitutes a background for explicit negotiation that often takes place in the shadow of hierarchy or competition.

Mutual Adjustment by Competition on Regulation

During the 1980s, after the decision to implement the Common Market, the European Community (EC) was confronted with the difficult task of harmonizing a multitude of national regulations of products and services. It turned out to be impossible to simply replace national law with European law. Not only would this have overburdened the European legislative institutions, it also implied the risk of failure in view of the veto players in decisionmaking and implementation. In this situation the Commission found an escape route when it took up the idea of harmonization of law by mutual recognition (see Schmidt 2004a), the principle defined by the ECJ in its famous decision on the *Cassis de Dijon* case. By adopting it, the Commission initiated European legislation only for those issues that required uniformity of law in the whole Community. And even in these cases legislative acts only set minimum standards for the production of goods and services.

In this framework, the member states are expected to recognize rules of another state as equivalent to their own law and to decide on the permission of goods and services according to the rules set by the home country of the supplier. At face value, mutual recognition implies forgoing coordination and relying on the willingness of governments to implement law of other states.

The genuine aim of the new governance approach, however, was to induce member state governments to mutually adjust their laws. The driving force motivating them to coordinate their regulatory policies was the market. In a competition on goods and services traded according to different national terms, two outcomes are possible. On the one hand, products conforming to ·high standards will prevail if consumers demand goods and services of a particular quality and regard high regulation as a "benchmark." On the other hand, competition is likely to end with low standards if consumers compare the price of goods and services and prefer those produced at low costs. In any case governments of member states that have to realize disadvantages in the market are motivated to adjust their regulation to the standards in successful national economies.

For two reasons, competition on regulation cannot work without minimum standards. First, only similar rules will be mutually accepted by national governments. If there is too much divergence, the market does not lead to an efficient result. Second, European regulation has to prevent an unlimited "race to the bottom," as in the case of negative social consequences, when citizens blame their government for not adequately controlling the free market. Therefore a central institution, in this case the EU, has to define a regulatory framework that supports coordination by mutual adjustment in intergovernmental competition.

Following from this, governance by competition generated by the rule of mutual recognition has to be embedded in a hierarchical structure. Alternatively it can be supplemented by bilateral negotiation and cooperation between governments of the member states concerned. In either case, mutual recognition in fact constitutes a complex combination of basic modes of governance. If standards defined and enforced by central institutions serve to stimulate and support mutual adjustment among governments at the lower level, this combination of hierarchy and competition works effectively. Negative inferences can occur as well, however. This is the case if standards or regulation set at the central level go beyond de facto abolishment of the market as a driving mechanism. In the EU, this outcome is not very likely. More realistic is the second scenario of a blockade in policymaking. It occurs when regulatory competition causes redistributive effects for the member states, which stir conflicts at the national level. As not only interests of national governments but also particular interests of branches of the economy are affected, cleavages can turn out to be rather complicated and may mutually reinforce each other. Under such conditions, not only mutual recognition but also European regulation can be blocked if governments or a coalition of governments feel compelled to exploit their veto power to defend economic interests. As Susanne Schmidt has shown for the service sector, this can produce significant insecurity for all public and private actors concerned (Schmidt 2003, 2004a).

The Open Method of Coordination:
Deliberation in Networks or Competition

As mentioned above, the rise of new modes of multilevel governance, which attracted attention in recent studies on policymaking in the EU, can be interpreted as attempts of the Council and the Commission to manage the constraints of an imbalanced allocation of powers between the EU and its member states. When the project of a Common Market no longer appeared sufficient to legitimize European integration, when the European economy was challenged by global competition, and when the projects of a political and social union came on the agenda, policymakers had to find ways to overcome the obstacle of constrained competences concerning matters of "positive integration." In view of the likely vetoes against a centralization of powers, the Council and the Commission resorted to mechanisms of "horizontal" coordination between member states (Caporaso and Wittenbrinck 2006). This mode of governance should not curtail the formal competences and responsibilities of national or regional governments. Yet, processes should be initiated that are designed to promote performance and innovation in the member states and in their subnational units in those policies essential for achieving the political, economic, and social targets of the EU.

In publications, these new modes are usually characterized as "soft law" or as negotiated decisionmaking with the participation of private actors (Héritier 2002a: 187; Caporaso and Wittenbrinck 2006: 473; Kohler-Koch and Rittberger 2006: 36–37). Bargaining or deliberation, the diffusion of ideas, and collective learning are identified as mechanisms of interaction. In fact, the different policy fields reveal a broad variety of mixed modes of governance. Some scholars regard "network governance" and mutual recognition as new modes. This denomination emerged with the introduction of the open method of coordination (OMC), however. In contrast to governance modes applied so far, this method focuses on those policies concerning public welfare and service delivery. In these fields, European policymaking cannot work with compulsory tools or incentives but has to motivate the governments of the member states to implement reforms. It was this objective for which the OMC was invented. And this method provides an excellent example for the complexity and dynamics of new modes of governance.

The OMC was invented as a means of achieving greater convergence of member states' policies necessary to turn Europe into "the most competitive and dynamic knowledge-based economy in the world capable of sustainable growth with more and better jobs and greater social cohesion" (European Council 2000: 2, point 5). Considering the diversity of relevant instruments, the complexity of the matter, and the fact that implementation of this aim requires innovative activities at the national and the subnational level, the Council introduced a new mode of multilevel governance. It involves the following elements:

- guidelines for the Union combined with specific timetables for achieving the goals in short, medium, and long terms
- qualitative or quantitative indicators and benchmarks as a means of comparing best practice, defined regarding to the highest standards in the world and tailored to the needs of different member states and sectors
- specific targets for national and regional policies and measures, taking into account national and regional differences
- monitoring, evaluation, and peer review aiming at mutual learning (European Council 2000: 12, point 37)

In line with the principle of subsidiarity, the member state governments or their regional and local levels should coordinate their activities according to guidelines without the Council or the Commission taking over powers to regulate and without binding agreements in joint decisions (Hodson and Maher 2001; Radaelli 2003a; Laffan and Shaw 2005; Zeitlin, Pochet, and Magnusson 2005).

The broad framework demarcated by the Council left leeway for variation in the application of the OMC (Radaelli 2003a: 31–38; Borrás and Jacobsson 2004; Laffan and Shaw 2005: 329–336). In fact different procedures have emerged in a number of policy fields (Laffan and Shaw 2005), and this renders it difficult to understand the mechanism of coordination and to categorize this mode of governance. Not by coincidence, scholars disagree on the nature of the method (Trubek and Trubek 2005). Usually, the mechanisms of interaction that should coordinate policies of the member states are characterized as deliberation and social learning in networks. This ignores the fact that with competition for best practices, the OMC includes a quite different mechanism. And it was this mode that the Commission intended to implement from the outset.

In fact the definition of the OMC by the European Council covers different mechanisms of coordination. On the one hand, periodic monitoring, evaluation, and peer review are introduced as means to stimulate mutual learning by deliberation among responsible organizations in national or subnational governments. On the other hand, the Council decision mentioned benchmarking as a means for defining best practices, with the intention of introducing comparative evaluation of member states' policies according to their quality. This method can be applied in order to achieve an exchange of experience and to diffuse innovation in a communicative process ("cooperative benchmarking"). It can also be used to stimulate policy competition, however, if practices of member states are compared and ranked in "scoreboards" ("competitive benchmarking"). Thus beyond elements of a top-down mode of coordination (guidelines, targets, timetables, monitoring) and bottom-up processes of innovation and diffusion of policies, the OMC can be implemented either as a deliberative process of exchange of experiences and learning or as a policy competition among decentralized governments determined to trigger cycles of innovation (Kerber and Eckardt 2005).

Both types of the OMC cannot be adequately comprehended, however, if one assumes that coordination is only achieved either by deliberation or competition. These mechanisms make up the core of the governance mode but it is linked to other mechanisms. The process of coordination starts with negotiations among governments and experts determined to define targets for a policy. They should elaborate and finally agree on criteria or indicators for evaluating or ranking of national policies. Evaluations and rankings are elaborated by experts cooperating in professional networks. National or subnational policies should be influenced by persuasion in the deliberative mode and by incentives to achieve higher ranks in the competitive mode. Whether these mechanisms of horizontal coordination among governments of the member states work or not depends to a large degree, however, on modes of governance that predominate in intragovernmental policymaking in the national or subnational institutional settings. At these levels, party competition plays a significant role in parliamentary systems and also in negotiations in consensus democracies or in patterns of corporatist intermediation between governments and interest groups. Moreover, these modes of governance may vary from policy to policy (see Figure 3.1).

In this mixed mode of multilevel governance, deliberative procedures have been revealed as not very effective and as extremely prone to being affected by interference by other mechanisms. Arguably, deliberation (or "arguing" as a mode of negotiation) is not unlikely to develop among experts or in networks of European, national, or regional bureaucrats, when these actors exchange experience or seek solutions to joint problems. The

Figure 3.1 Governance Modes of the Open Method of Coordination

	Deliberative Mode	Competitive Mode
Coordination between member states	• *negotiations:* definition of common goals • *networks* of experts: evaluation of (sub)national programs and projects • *networks:* diffusion of best practices	• *negotiations:* definition of common goals • *networks* of experts: indicators and rankings ("scoreboards") • *competition:* imitation and innovation
National (subnational) governance	*party competition—negotiation* *intranational/interregional networks*	

solutions elaborated in these processes have to be accepted, however, and transposed into formal decisions in national governments or parliaments. In these arenas, not only experts but also executives, competing parties, or interest groups have to be convinced of a proposed policy, and they usually are not impressed by best-practice models arising out of expert meetings at the European level if they do not confirm their interests or ideologies. Party competition and the logics of bargaining between governments and interest groups usually solidify positions on policies, which can hardly be dissolved by new information or persuasion. Discourses of experts, shielded from political pressure, can generate innovation, but it is another situation to implement innovative policies in the member states in processes subject to different mechanisms at the national or subnational levels. For this reason it is hardly surprising that empirical studies have so far not justified high expectations as regards effectiveness and democratic quality (De la Porte and Nanz 2004; Zeitlin, Pochet, and Magnusson 2005).

Although the competitive mode of the OMC was part of the original framework decided at the Lisbon Council meeting, so far it has been applied only in rare cases. Empirical studies are not available, but theoretical reasoning (Benz et al. 2007a) supports the assumption that this mode gives stronger incentives for national or subnational governments to adjust their policy to European standards than does the deliberative mode. Governments succeeding in European policy contests can profit from this in national party competition for voters' approval. Governments ranked low in a comparative evaluation of policies come under pressure from opposition parties in parliaments or in public discussions. To be sure, competitive benchmarking will not compel governments simply to imitate a highly ranked policy, the more so as examples of policies often cannot be transferred between different national contexts. In combination with party competition, however, policy contests can stimulate open discussion on effectiveness and can generate incentives for a reform leading in the direction of the European targets. In the member states such contests can open a window of opportunity to revitalize blocked negotiations between governments and interest groups or help to break up conservative policy networks.

In order to make this governance mechanism work, a number of conditions have to be fulfilled. First, policies of competing governments or administrations have to be evaluated in approved procedures and according to accepted indicators. Second, governments of member states and the majority parties in national parliaments have to be willing to expose their performance to a contest. Third, the policy concerned has to be salient in the national political process and has to raise the attention of political parties and the public. Fourth, the goals of policy competition have to be approved in the national arena, which is unlikely if they are prone to ideological conflicts or if they imply significant redistribution. Finally, competition procedures of coordination by mutual adjustment require a framework of networks, if standards or indicators cannot be set by a superior institution. Policy competition has to be guided by rules and directives, which in the EU usually are defined in committees of experts, and the diffusion of best practices and the adjustments of national or subnational policies are supported by horizontal networks of executives and experts of the member states. All in all, the existence of these conditions can hardly be taken for granted.

If these conditions are fulfilled, the competitive mode of the OMC has enormous advantages and makes coordination quite effective. The deliberative mode seems to be more compatible with the autonomy of decentralized governments and with the principle of subsidiarity, and it seems to support legitimacy by including participants on an equal footing. Neither argument can be confirmed in an in-depth analysis, however (see Benz et al. 2007a). In fact it is governance by competition that fosters horizontal coordination between member states against top-down governance in EU intergovernmental relations. Policy contests do not compel member state governments or administrations to copy policies emerging as best practices. Competition is based on a comparative evaluation of performance measured by indicators, but it is left to the responsible institutions of the member states to explain the causes of success or failure to their parliament or citizens. To be sure, the intensity of participation and the rationality of negotiation may be higher in the deliberative mode of governance compared to the competitive mode, if only the European level is considered. Such deliberative processes, however, create opportunities for national or subnational executives to shift the blame for decisions and to avoid being held accountable by parliaments. In contrast, the competitive mode between member states can be translated into national party competition, which reinforces transparency of decisionmaking and supports accountability of governance.

Given the advantages of the competitive mode of the OMC regarding effectiveness and legitimacy, one should expect it to be more often applied than the deliberative mode. Actually this is not the case. Member state governments strongly resisted any efforts of the Commission to comparatively evaluate and rank national performance in policy fields. Recently there are indications of a slight shift in favor of the competitive mode. In labor market policy (Hartlapp 2006: 17) and in research and technology policy (Bruno, Jacquot, and Madin 2006), performance of the member states is compared according to quantitative indicators and by "scoreboards," and this stimulates competitive processes. Whether these cases remain exceptions or whether they point to the beginning of a change of the OMC cannot be determined on the basis of available empirical evidence. The examples cited above prove the variability and dynamics of the OMC, however, which are activated by changes of elements of the complex governance configuration. Presumably different varieties are applied in practice at the same time, which in a pragmatic manner can be adjusted to circumstances.

Explaining Dynamics of Governance

When looking at the process of European integration and the evolution of governance in policymaking, it is evident that new modes of governance arose in reaction to institutional constraints of the EU multilevel polity and the legitimacy deficits resulting from these constraints. This argument should not be taken as a functionalist explanation of the evolution of multilevel governance, which would not be compatible with the governance approach (Benz et al. 2007b). The explanation refers to the fact that institutions of the European federation cause problems of effectiveness and legitimacy that vary according to policy fields. In reaction to these problems, modes of governance have to be adjusted. Changes in governance cannot be expected, however, as long as these problems are not salient for actors that can influence decisions on governance modes and as long as existing modes allow them to achieve their aims. The number of actors that are relevant in this context is limited. New modes of governance may include private actors and experts, but decisions about their form ("metagovernance") are made by representatives of member state governments in the Council and by the Commission in cooperation with national executives. Therefore we have to explain why and how these actors have responded to the constraints of the institutional framework with the invention of new modes of governance.

After the project of the Common Market had been accomplished and the reform of the political union had ended with the disappointing Treaty of Nice, the European elites tried to deepen and stabilize the integration process by two strategies. One was the making of a constitution for the EU, which should bring about an institutional reform and should tackle the democratic deficit. With the other strategy, the change of governance, already initiated by the Council and the Commission before the project of a constitutional treaty had been stopped by the French and Dutch referenda, the EU should be strengthened in policy fields remaining under the control of national governments but requiring coordination with regard to basic targets of the Union. This should be achieved by new modes of governance promising to cope with the dilemmas entrenched in the institutions of the European federation. It was quite in accordance with the Commission's interests to improve governability in the EU. In the same way, it conformed to the "mixed motives" of the member state governments, which have an interest in the EU's taking over responsibility for market failure but are not willing to accept a transfer of powers to the European level, as long as a majority of national citizens remains skeptical about the legitimacy of European politics.

These strategies and interests cannot fully explain the forms and dynamics of governance that finally came to the fore. They resulted from a kind of "endogenous" development of governance because the final choice on the combination of hierarchy, negotiation, networks, and competition is made by those actors participating in governance. As regards the variations of the OMC, we have to explain why and to what extent the deliberative or the competitive modes have been adopted. We can assume that the following constellation of interests has been decisive. For the Commission the competitive mode seems rather attractive, as it guarantees higher effectiveness of coordination. Lacking formal powers in the policy fields concerned, the Commission is not able, however, to compel member state governments into policy competition without the risk of having them block necessary negotiations on the targets, standards, and rules. National governments prefer "soft" modes of governance, that is, a combination of negotiations on policies and the implementation of policies in networks or by the diffusion of innovation without pressure of competition. This way, governments can justify policies in their parliaments and in public but cannot be compelled to pursue a particular policy.

There is some empirical evidence, however, that, under certain conditions, member state governments participate in comparative evaluation and ranking of their policies and thus accept a competitive mode of governance. Apparently this mode of coordination in multilevel governance is applied when the pressure on governments to change policies is high or when the repercussions of the Common Market are an important topic in national public debates. In both cases national governments profit from impulses for change triggered by the EU, in particular if they have to deal with powerful veto players. This can only be expected, however, if governments and a majority in national parliaments agree with the basic direction of change initiated by the EU. Policy competition is also probable if member states not participating in policy contests risk falling behind in the competition for capital and investments. Moreover, when subnational governments have the competence, the national government can use European governance to induce pressure for change without being responsible for or affected by the outcome of decisions. Policy competition can also help governments to evade commitments in corporatist settings that impede policy reforms. Therefore it is no coincidence that the competitive mode of governance is applied in regional policies and in labor market and technology policy.

Multilevel governance by deliberative negotiations and networks requires that actors agree on basic norms and goals, but the effective outcome of policy coordination is determined in processes of collective learning. In contrast, policy competition is only possible if the direction of change and indicators for comparative policy evaluation are approved. Furthermore, member state or subnational governments participating in competition are in fact compelled to adjust to best practices. For these reasons it is not very likely that the competitive mode of governance will spread into many policy fields, given that the EU lacks the necessary formal competences for coordination. Nonetheless, with the consent of the member state governments, the option of this mode is available, and it can be used if deliberative processes fail. Thus the dynamics of complex governance, that is, the opportunity to shift between a more deliberative and a more competitive mode, can contribute to more effective multilevel coordination.

Conclusion

Despite the conceptual problems mentioned in the introduction of this chapter, the governance concept provides a useful analytical toolbox for policy research. It focuses the attention of researchers on a variety of mechanisms of collective action and coordination among public and private actors that are participating in policymaking. It also allows consideration of the dynamic interplay of interaction and institutions. In the European multilevel polity, actors are subject to different rule systems and are guided by different mechanisms of collective action. This combination of rules and mechanisms can cause serious role conflicts that policymakers have to deal with, but it also implies opportunities to adjust governance to new challenges and to allow actors to find escape routes when coordination ends in a stalemate. This is the reason for an "endogenous" dynamics of governance that can be facilitated but not regulated by institutions.

In order to understand this dynamics of multilevel governance in the EU, which strongly influences how policies are made in this complex setting, we have to identify the mechanisms of interaction (Hedström and Swedberg 1998) inherent in the different modes of governance. The term *mechanisms* refers to basic causal relations between structures and processes. They guide actions of individuals and organizations so that collective action can be achieved. The next step of analysis would require looking at the way in which different mechanisms are linked and identifying positive and negative effects of interferences as well as reactions of actors to potential or actual dysfunctions. Such a perspective in policy analysis and the analytical tools provided by the governance approach would help us to better understand and explain the operation and the performance of different modes of multilevel governance in the EU.

With such an approach we could also find explanations for the evolution of European governance. In principle the rise of new modes can be traced back to institutional constraints and dilemmas burdening policymaking in Europe. They result from an institutional development driven by the interplay of intergovernmental and supranational forces toward European integration. In the context of an imbalanced federation resulting from the integration process, the selection of a particular combination of governance mechanisms depends on the interests of those actors who have the power to shape patterns of interaction and who use this power in a strategic way in order to escape looming stalemates in policymaking.

The governance approach by itself does not provide a theory. It does, however, point to a fruitful combination of interaction-oriented and institutionalist theories or at least elements of such theories (Kooiman 1993). Empirical studies on policymaking based on such a framework allow us to find patterns of structures and processes and to improve our typologies of governance. Moreover, they can generate hypotheses or improve available "models" of complex governance. Beyond contributing to advancing our theoretical and empirical knowledge, they have a considerable practical value too. Empirical and theoretical knowledge on governance can enable policymakers to understand the dynamics of mixed modes of governance and to identify the options for strategic action offered by this dynamics.

Note
An extended German version of this chapter appeared in Ingeborg Tömmel (ed.), *Die Europäische Union: Governance und Policy-Making,* PVS-Sonderheft 40 (Wiesbaden: VS Verlag für Sozialwissenschaften, 2007).

4

Governance in
EU Environmental Policy

Katharina Holzinger, Christoph Knill,
and Andrea Lenschow

Environmental policy is one policy field that has been closely associated with the concept of the "regulatory state" attributed to the European Union (EU) by influential authors such as Giandomenico Majone (1996). In coining this term, Majone expresses the dominance of modes of governance that come in the form of binding legislation as the output of EU policymaking. Hierarchy, in other words, appears to be the primary mode of governance exercised in EU environmental policy.

The recent literature on environmental policy in the EU, however, suggests that there has been a transition in modes of governance since the beginning of the 1990s. Some authors are speaking of "new instruments" (Héritier 2002a; Jordan, Wurzel, and Zito 2003; Rittberger and Richardson 2003) when highlighting a departure from uniformly applicable, low discretionary, "command-and-control" modes of governance. The discussion of alternative instruments goes hand in hand with the diagnosis of a "transformation in environmental governance" in the EU (Lenschow 1999: 39), referring to the structural dimension of governance and pointing to the extension of a network-style system that emphasizes the close cooperation of public and private actors in the formulation and implementation of EU environmental policy.

In the terminology of this book (see Chapters 1 and 2), in the past most environmental policy instruments employed at the EU level belonged to the mode of *hierarchy*. This mode is characterized by interventionist instruments, with state actors dominating the processes of decisionmaking as well as implementation and enforcement. Examples are emission standards, prohibitions, or technical specifications. In recent times the three other modes have gained momentum, however. The mode of *competition* has been introduced into EU environmental policy with the so-called economic instruments, such as environmental taxes and subsidies. EU policymakers define the rules of the game within the regulatory framework of the system. Yet the individual addressees are induced to comply with these rules not through active enforcement but by incentives. In the mode of *cooperation,* governance relies on the voluntary participation and voluntary compliance of various state and nonstate actors; the processes of defining the goals and of implementing them often merge into one. Information rights, voluntary coordination of member states' policies, or certification instruments, such as the Eco label, fall in the cooperation category. Finally, the mode of *negotiation* is reflected in voluntary agreements between the European Commission and certain industrial sectors, with industrial peak associations acting on behalf of their members. Voluntary agreements are contractually binding, but in the absence of legal enforcement, a sanctioning of noncompliance occurs only indirectly in the form of legislative measures threatening to replace the agreements.

If one considers the various environmental action programs (EAPs) that define the strategic orientation of the EU environmental policy for the middle term, a relatively sound finding regarding the prevailing regulatory ideas becomes apparent. The political demands for nonhierarchical modes of governance are clearly reflected in the three most recent EAPs. They call for a stronger cooperative spirit and "shared responsibility" of a wide range of public and private actors in producing public decisions. An explicit paradigm change in regulatory policy was expressed in formulations about "new governance approaches." This change in governance ideas, however, seems only partially expressed in changes of the concrete instruments introduced in EU environmental policy (cf. Rittberger and Richardson 2003). We will show that this gap between political declarations in the action programs and actual policy is closing gradually. But the hierarchical mode of governance still constitutes the dominant form of environmental policy in the EU—although the modes of coming to such policy decisions may have grown increasingly cooperative (see Chapter 2). We will investigate what the limits are of nonhierarchical modes of governance in the political system of the European Union and the policy output produced by these modes of governance.

This chapter proceeds in the following way. In the next section, we first analyze the reception of new governance ideas in the various environmental policy action programs and investigate what may have caused these wide-reaching changes. In the following section we explore whether and, if so, to what extent, changes in ideas have affected the choice and the allocation of modes of governance. Then in the next section we explain the empirical findings. The general outcomes resulting from this analysis are summarized in the conclusion.

The Call for New Modes of Governance

EU environmental policy developed as a policy area in its own right from the early 1970s onward. Initial policies of the Community were primarily command and control instruments, implying a highly interventionist approach (Rehbinder and Stewart 1985: chap. 4). Since the mid-1980s, however, new governance ideas have appeared. Two strands are to be differentiated: beginning in the mid-1980s the EU Commission advocated "economic incentive instruments," such as environmental taxes, tradable permits, or risk liability schemes. At the beginning of the 1990s, primarily "context-oriented instruments" were suggested. These instruments aim in part at enhancing the cooperative mode of lawmaking, for instance by opening administrative procedures and including the policy addressees in policy formulation and implementation. Hence, they soften the hierarchical steering of the EU. A second group of context-oriented instruments provides a framework for cooperative decisionmaking, that is, by confronting the member states with targets rather than standards or by supporting cooperative processes through infrastructure, information, or rules of procedure. From the governance perspective, economic incentive instruments correspond to the competition mode in subjecting environmental polluters to market conditions that account for environmental costs and by offering incentives to improve environmental performance. Context-oriented instruments either modify the hierarchical mode by allowing the addressees, especially, an earlier voice in the process, or they can be subsumed under the mode of cooperation, implying that participation and compliance are voluntary for the addressees.

Within both strands of discussion voluntary agreements were proposed. Voluntary agreements were grouped in the economic instruments category, as they imply the incentive to regulate one's own affairs for private—typically industrial—actors in negotiations with public policymakers. They were also grouped in the context-oriented instruments category, as compliance is voluntary, that is, there is considerable leeway for reaction. In the terminology of this book, voluntary agreements are a typical representative of the mode of negotiation, and we will thus treat them separately in the empirical section. In this section, however, they will be dealt with as part of both discursive strands.

Competition: Governance by Economic Incentives

The introduction of economic instruments was first proposed in the third environmental action program of the Community (1982–1986).[1] The fourth action program (1987–1992) dealt in detail with economic instruments.[2] Emission taxes, emissions certificates, state aid, negotiable deposit permits, voluntary agreements with the polluters, and stricter liability laws were specified as modes of governance relying on the market mechanism. How did this new orientation in the use of instruments come about, and which ideas are behind the mentioned instruments?

Instruments such as environmental taxes, tradable permits, subsidies, and voluntary agreements are among the measures in the "classical canon" proposed by environmental economics as superior forms of regulation, especially when compared to hierarchical intervention (Binder 1999). The discussion about economic instruments was especially intense between 1975 and 1985. In the second half of the 1980s this canon was expanded to include risk liability schemes and fund solutions to compensate for environmental damages (Endres 2000).

There are primarily three expectations connected with economic instruments. First, these instruments correspond to the polluter-pays principle, that is, the normative distribution principle stating that the polluters have to bear the costs of the pollution they have caused. Economic instruments implement the polluter-pays principle in a much more encompassing way than is the case for interventionist measures. The only exception is a subsidy: although subsidies are classified as economic instruments, they are not in accord with the polluter-pays principle but rather follow the common cost principle. Second, economic instruments are suited to guarantee the optimal allocation of environmental resources (Frey 1972; Siebert 1976; Endres 2000). For regulatory standards, in contrast, allocation is not efficient. Third, economic instruments are dynamically efficient. The fact that the residual pollution still has to be paid for gives those addressed by the provisions an incentive to be innovative. Regulatory standards do not give rise to this incentive unless the standards are regularly reviewed and adjusted to technological development (e.g., inside the comitology procedures).

In the mid-1980s the first two expectations in particular impressed the European Commission in its thinking about the future of environmental policymaking and its emphasis on two policy principles, namely the polluter-pays principle and the principle of compatibility between ecology and the economy. Although these principles arguably already featured in the first action program,[3] they were emphasized more strongly in the third action program.[4] Against the background of worsened global economic conditions, the Commission feared cutbacks in environmental policy. Hence, by introducing the third action program the Commission argued that it is important to achieve the optimal allocation of the resources "in the broadest sense of the term." It proposed applying a stricter form of the polluter-pays principle,[5] specifically in employing "new instruments," including in particular environmental taxes and charges, liability, and funding schemes as well as international agreements (Ifo-Institute for Economic Research 1989: 5). In the fourth action program, the same instruments are listed, expanded to include state aid, tradable permits, and negotiated agreements with polluters.[6]

Which changes in regulatory conditions prompted the Commission to expand the range of environmental policy instruments? Most important in this respect are the changes in the legal framework and political and ideological developments outside of the Community as well as a changed problem structure and new environmental priorities in the Community.

First, the polluter-pays principle was integrated into the European treaties with the Single European Act. The Community was thus bound, without restrictions, to the polluter-pays principle. Second, in the mid-1980s, the polluter-pays principle was also intensively discussed in other international organizations, especially within the framework of the Organization for Economic Cooperation and Development (OECD). Various studies on its development were carried out (OECD 1981a, 1981b, 1994; Opschoor and Vos 1989). Third, in the 1980s there was a global shift in macroeconomic philosophies: liberalization, deregulation, and a "return to the market" were the new catchwords. This created a climate in which the plea for cost-effective and market-conforming instruments fitted well. Fourth, environmental problems of the early 1970s were different from those at the end of the 1980s. To finance the elimination of hazardous waste, contaminated land, and pollution from diffuse sources, fund solutions and liability schemes became popular in the United States and some European states. The Commission was very responsive to these developments.

Cooperation: Governance by Voluntary Participation

The fifth action program (1993–2000) marks a second reorientation in EU environmental regulation.[7] On the one hand, instead of a problem-oriented perspective we find a primarily governance-related approach (Weale et al. 2000: 61). Central to the latter is the principle of "sustainable and environmentally suited development," on the basis of which economic growth and environmental protection are to be brought into harmony with one another. On the other hand, the ideas developed in the fifth action program reflect a major departure from approaches propagated in earlier programs. Especially hierarchical modes of governance are to be replaced or complemented with new forms of cooperative instruments (Knill and Lenschow 2000). This comprehensive change in the dominant ideas is characterized by various components.

First, effective regulation is to be guaranteed by the intensive and broad collaboration between public and private actors at the various institutional levels during policy formulation and implementation. The rhetoric focuses not so much on the substance of regulative measures but on the integration and consultation with the actors concerned. The "shared responsibility" of all actors is in the foreground; this ought to be achieved by intensive dialogue and cooperation with the addressees and the responsible authorities.[8]

Second, achieving this requires that the involved actors have enough discretion to optimally align compliance with EU rules with the conditions of the specific political, social, and economic contexts that exist at the national, regional, or local levels (Johnson and Corcelle 1989: 17; Knill and Lens-chow 2000). These components "soften the hierarchy" in environmental policymaking.

A third characteristic of regulatory change is the development of "new instruments," which correspond to the cooperative modes of governance specified above. Such instruments leave it to public authorities and private addressees to find suitable ways to achieve substantive results. Although many "new instruments" take the form of binding legislation, their environmental policy objective is to activate rather than regulate; the targeted actors are invited to cooperate through the creation of more hospitable framework conditions. These instruments therefore forgo detailed specifications of contents (such as emission standards). Their emphasis is on defining broad objectives (quality objectives) in order to grant the member states greater scope of action in choosing the means to reach these objectives. Furthermore, they give procedural guidelines to facilitate a change of behavior at the lower level of governance (Héritier, Knill, and Mingers 1996). For instance, the Commission pushed the development of instruments to improve rights to information and participation of a large group of different state and private actors (Mol, Lauber, and Liefferink 2000).[9] Voluntary agreements with (or among) industrial actors and forms of private self-regulation similarly follow the spirit of cooperation.[10]

What background conditions have been favorable to this deep-reaching transition in the regulatory ideas? A first factor favoring these changes refers to the growing politicization of the EU's limited policymaking capacity against the background of an increasing number of transboundary environmental problems. Thus, in the face of diverse national conditions and interest constellations, the detailed specification of regulatory policies underlying the hierarchical approach to governance implied many drawn-out and problematic decisionmaking processes at the European level. Through restricting regulatory requirements to generally defined targets, by contrast, the complexity of the European decisionmaking process was to be reduced (Mol, Lauber, and Liefferink 2000; Héritier 2002a).

The second problem that is to be overcome by the transition from hierarchical to cooperative governance regards the implementation deficit in European environmental policy (Krämer 1996; Jordan 1999). Detailed binding regulations did not always represent the most effective way to achieve the intended policy results (Knill and Lenschow 2000). New regulatory approaches that explicitly aimed to take nationally diverse conditions into consideration were to be used in an attempt to reduce these implementation problems. Beyond that, it was presupposed that participatory forms of policy formulating and implementing would lead to greater acceptance and thus to effective implementation.[11]

A third factor refers to the subsidiarity principle that was laid down not only as an environmental policy principle in the EU but also as a general principle of action within the Maastricht Treaty. With that, hierarchical intervention in national politics increasingly suffered legitimacy problems (Collier 1998). The Molitor report, published in 1995, called for a new approach to environmental regulation, which was intended to provide for a greater scope for the national implementation of European laws and for more flexible and less hierarchical forms of intervention (European Commission 1995).

Fourth, the changes in EU environmental policy resonated well with a more general and global reform wave, characterized by catchwords such as *privatization, liberalization,* the *withdrawal of the state,* and *new public management.* Associated goals regarding the development of less bureaucratic, more flexible, and more effective concepts favored and legitimized the formation of synchronized patterns of context-oriented regulation at the European level (Lenschow 1999: 40–41).

In sum, since the mid-1980s two general lines of development can be observed regarding the development of EU environmental governance. The hierarchical philosophy, which earmarked the EU environmental policy from the beginning of the 1970s, was initially called into question as economic instruments and the competitive mode were accentuated. This questioning was especially evident in the third and fourth action programs. In the fifth action program, at the beginning of the 1990s, we witnessed a new orientation toward ideas of cooperative modes of governance. The focal point was cooperation between public and private actors in formulating and implementing European environmental policy as well as the flexible development of policies against the background of diverging conditions at the national and subnational levels. The sixth action program from 2002 continues in this spirit.

Changes in Modes of Governance:
EU Environmental Policy from 1967 Through 2005

Although changes in regulatory ideas in the respective action programs of the EU can be clearly understood and substantiated, this does not necessarily imply that this transition is reflected in empirically observable changes in policy instruments. The environmental action programs of the EU are merely declarations of political intentions, in which general guidelines and goals are defined. The existence of these programs by no means, however, gives rise to the legal obligation of actually passing such measures. Against this background, the following section will investigate more closely whether, and if so to what extent, changes in ideas have been accompanied by corresponding shifts in modes of governance.

Data Basis
We studied the development of the use of instruments in EU environmental policy from 1967 through 2005. These years were chosen because 1967

marked the year in which the first environmental policies were passed, and 2005 falls in the early period of implementing the sixth environmental action plan. All measures that follow explicit environmental policy objectives were investigated. The basis for the data is the systematic compilation of EU environmental law by Haigh (2005). This collection is not entirely complete, but it includes most—and all of the important—EU legal activities with regard to the environment that were passed in this time period. In addition, the Commission was also consulted (especially for obtaining information on voluntary agreements that are not all published and carefully documented, given their nonlegal status). The legal sources themselves were checked in order to classify the instruments in terms of governance modes.

A simple listing of the measures implies that they are weighted equally. Differences in the relevance of the individual measures are not apprehended in this way. Yet, this procedure is justified given the difficulties in finding clear criteria for determining their relevance. Problems arise in the choice of criteria; for instance, should the basis be the number of actors affected, the benefits for the environment, the initial adoption of a measure, or the continuation of one? The process of evaluating the criteria also presents problems. Nevertheless, we acknowledge that the equal weighting is likely to introduce a "conservative" bias, in the sense that especially cooperative means of governance tend to have a large scope and can be expected in only small numbers.

The legal acts were classified according to the central types of instruments (standards, financial aid, right to information, etc.) and the governance mode implied in their employment (hierarchy, competition, cooperation, negotiation). This procedure implies that accompanying measures and supplementary provisions are not listed. The number of such secondary measures per legal act varies considerably. They are largely related to the procedural specifications of hierarchical measures, for instance, the specification of information rights of the Commission.

Empirical Findings

To determine whether and to what extent the changes in governance ideas resulted in concrete changes of policy, we classified all EU environmental acts that were passed in the time period under study in accordance with their implied central policy instrument. These we sorted along the lines of the four modes of governance (see Table 4.1).

The hierarchical mode refers to instruments that are based on the compliance of the addressees with specified goals and objectives that are enforced through the power of legal sanctions. They encompass not only emission and quality standards but also technical specifications, prohibitions, and other restrictions and obligations.

The competition mode guides the application of economic instruments, that is, financial incentives or disincentives. Whereas in some cases member

Table 4.1 Modes of Governance and Instruments in EU Environmental Policy

Governance Mode	Absolute Numbers, 2000	Share (%), 2000	Absolute Numbers, 2005	Share (%), 2005
Hierarchical mode				
Emission standards	51	19.5	54	16.8
Quality standards	34	13.0	38	11.8
Technical specifications	14	5.4	16	5.0
Prohibitions	38	14.6	43	13.4
Production and trade restrictions	17	6.5	21	6.5
Declaration obligations	8	3.1	9	2.8
Preventive obligations	5	1.9	9	2.8
Information and data inquiry obligations	54	20.7	63	19.6
Sum hierarchy	*221*	*84.7*	*253*	*78.7*
Competition mode				
Financial aid	11	4.2	15	4.7
Emission trade			1	0.3
Liability rules			2	0.6
Taxes, fees			1	0.3
Licences			1	0.3
Sum competition	*11*	*4.2*	*20*	*6.2*
Cooperative mode				
Quality targets	8	3.1	10	3.1
Certification	2	0.8	4	1.2
Information rights	2	0.8	3	0.9
Coordination of member state policies	4	1.5	7	2.2
Campaigns, appeals	3	1.1	4	1.2
Sum cooperation	*19*	*7.3*	*28*	*8.6*
Negotiation mode				
Voluntary agreements	10	3.8	21	6.5
Sum negotiation	*10*	*3.8*	*21*	*6.5*

states may have the legally enforceable obligation to put these instruments into place, policy effectiveness follows from economic (not legal) incentives for the addressees. Until 2000, economic instruments appeared at the European level only in the form of financial assistance. This overlooks the fact that some directives that were classified as hierarchical, such as the ones on car emissions or on the disposal of used oil, explicitly authorized the member states to introduce economic incentives (e.g., tax reductions). In other words, some EU measures invite member states to follow a competition mode of governance. Yet, at the EU level the hierarchical mode, focusing on emission or technical standards, prevailed. After 2000, however, we see the slow emergence of European taxes, fees, liability rules, and so on.

Under the cooperation mode, we sort instruments that aim at voluntary participation and compliance of individual addressees, such as quality targets, certifications, rights to information, campaigns, and appeals. Again, most of these instruments require the legal transposition of the directive or regulation in the member states (i.e., hierarchy), but the governance logic employed for achieving environmental objectives relies on the voluntary cooperation of private or economic actors.

Voluntary agreements, finally, are representative of the negotiation mode of governance. Typically, voluntary agreements are negotiated between the Commission and industrial peak associations at the EU level; the latter in turn reach an agreement among their members. There are no legal sanctions if agreements are broken, although their effectiveness is often linked to the *shadow* of hierarchy in form of the Commission's threat to propose legally binding standards or procedures. Between 2000 and 2005 the use of policy instruments based on cooperation or negotiation increased in most categories; we observe an especially large jump in voluntary agreements (from ten to twenty-one).

The data demonstrate that the hierarchical mode of governance still plays the dominant role. Although the action programs strongly emphasized the need to introduce economic instruments, competition still forms the least common governance mode at the EU level. Economic instruments took off with a slow start. Most markedly, the planned introduction of a CO_2/energy tax failed in the early 1990s because of the resistance of several member states. This is true even though the intensive debate on climate change (both the fifth and the sixth EAP dedicate important chapters to this theme) and the adoption of the Kyoto Protocol seemed to create a more favorable framework for economic instruments especially focusing on issues of energy efficiency and the reduction of CO_2 emissions. But this policy window was used to extend the negotiation mode of governance. Notably, most voluntary agreements that have been adopted in the last few years deal with energy-related issues (cf. Lenschow and Rottmann 2005). Hence public (European Commission)–private (industry) negotiations compensated for the failure to explore the competition mode more widely at the EU level.

The share of instruments relying on the cooperation and negotiation modes may not fully reflect the rhetoric during the negotiations of the fifth action program, which suggested a comprehensive overhaul and the expansion of such governance modes. Nevertheless, we witness quite a remarkable increase in the numbers. With respect to voluntary agreements, there is even some evidence of a multiplication effect from one product category to others; yet not all industrial sectors lend themselves to the effective conduct of such public-private negotiations. Besides this quantitative analysis, following the announcements in the fifth action program there may have been a "softening" of hierarchical governance due to the creation of a more participatory and cooperative policy framework at the EU level more generally, which is not reflected in the nature of the policy instruments, and hence ignored in this chapter.

Although the overall share of policy instruments relying on competition, cooperation, or negotiation as governance modes is still limited, this does not necessarily mean that the development of these new governance ideas is of little significance for the allocation of environmental instruments in the EU. The influence of new ideas becomes apparent insofar as the share of these less hierarchical modes increased over time. Table 4.2 makes this relationship even clearer by summarizing the governance evolution for the time periods of the EAPs.

In fact, we see that before the adoption of the fourth action program, EU environmental policy basically relied upon the mode of hierarchy. Certain deviations from this pattern were only observed during the second action program, when 12 percent of the measures were quality targets and information campaigns, that is, classified as cooperation mode. The competition mode was first employed during the period of the fourth action program. The increase in its use during the fifth action program was merely a matter of financial assistance, as is made clear in Table 4.1. Since the adoption of the sixth action program, however, the proportion of economic instruments has significantly increased and the specific measures have diversified. Cooperation and negotiation significantly increased as modes of governance during the reign of the fourth, fifth, and sixth action programs. Notably, although the four voluntary agreements adopted during the period of the fourth EAP were all later replaced by regulation, this has not (yet) been the case for the fourteen agreements adopted between 1993 and 2001 (although some have

Table 4.2 Share of Governance Modes in EAP-Defined Time Periods (percentage)

Time Period	Hierarchy	Competition	Cooperation	Negotiation
1967–1972	100.0	0.0	0.0	0.0
1973–1976 (1st EAP)	100.0	0.0	0.0	0.0
1977–1981 (2nd EAP)	88.0	0.0	12.0	0.0
1982–1986 (3rd EAP)	100.0	0.0	0.0	0.0
1987–1992 (4th EAP)	82.4	2.9	8.8	5.9
1993–2001 (5th EAP)[a]	71.6	7.5	11.2	9.7
2002–2005 (6th EAP)[b]	69.0	16.7	7.1	7.1

Notes: a. The fifth EAP formally ended in 2000, but as the sixth EAP did not start until 2002, the intermediate year was added to the fifth EAP.
   b. The sixth EAP runs until 2012.

been terminated or were of limited duration from the start) (Lenschow and Rottmann 2005: annex). During the last period (lasting only three years), cooperative and negotiation instruments have been overtaken by economic instruments, though mostly by financial aid instruments that may not fully represent the "new" philosophy of governance through competition.

As a whole, since the mid-1980s there has been a notable reduction in the relative use of hierarchical governance tools. This development cannot be exclusively connected to the respective political declarations in the action programs. This is demonstrated by the fact that the reliance on the cooperation mode had already increased during the fourth action program, although corresponding ideas were only introduced with the fifth program. The reorientation of ideas with the fifth and sixths action programs may thus be understood as a confirmation of a development that was already under way.

Explaining the Patterns of Governance Change

The analysis of EU environmental policy from 1967 through 2005 suggests that albeit changes in forms of governance took place, they were not only less pronounced than the discussion on new governance ideas might lead us to expect, but they were also introduced with different speed and scope. We can thus indeed observe considerable change in the composition of the relative mix of different governance approaches, with a relative decrease of hierarchical regulation, whereas the relative share of governance by competition, cooperation, and negotiation is increasing. Nevertheless, hierarchy still constitutes by far the dominant mode; the emergence of new forms of governance has to be interpreted as a complementary development rather than as a substitution for hierarchical governance. What is more, until very recently, cooperative forms of governance played a more important role in this process than governance by competition or by negotiation. What are the factors that explain these patterns in the development of EU environmental governance?

Why Is Hierarchy Still the Dominant Mode?

A first factor explaining the still unchallenged dominance of hierarchical governance in EU environmental policy rests on functional arguments, emphasizing that there is only limited room for replacement of hierarchy by competition, cooperation, or negotiation. With respect to the suitability of cooperation or negotiation as substitutes, important restrictions emerge from the objective of harmonization underlying many environmental policies at the European level. As cooperative regulation explicitly emphasizes discretion for national adjustment and the definition of domestic regulatory requirements within rather broad objectives and guidelines, it is hardly appropriate for achieving harmonized levels of national regulation. It is rather the basic objective of cooperative regulation to allow for regulatory variety. Equally, negotiated agreements allow for flexible solutions and, not least, due to their voluntary character they cannot guarantee harmonization for all relevant parties.

Why does harmonization constitute such a central motivation of EU environmental policy? Harmonization arguments are particularly pronounced in the case of environmental product standards (e.g., emission standards for cars). The establishment of the internal market requires the harmonization of standards in order to avoid trade barriers and distortion of competition. The trade-oriented rationale was especially dominant as long as there was no explicit legal basis for the development of EU environmental policy. Environmental measures had to be legitimated by economic rather than environmental objectives—a constellation that changed only with the treaty revisions established in the 1987 Single European Act. Moreover, national industries typically have a common interest in harmonizing product standards, as the adjustment of product characteristics to different national standards would increase production costs. As a result, industry in both high-regulating and low-regulating countries benefits from uniform product standards (Scharpf 1997b; Holzinger 2002).

As regards process standards, high-regulating countries, in many instances, display a strong interest in the harmonization of environmental standards for production processes (e.g., emissions form large combustion plants). They want to avoid economic disadvantages for their industries subject to competition from their counterparts in low-regulating countries. Although the low-regulating member states might strongly resist such efforts (given the implied loss of competitive advantages), the EU has adopted a considerable number of environmental process standards. This result, which departs from more skeptical expectations of theories of regulatory competition (Scharpf 1997b; Holzinger 2002), can be understood against the background of the particular dynamics underlying EU environmental policymaking. These dynamics include, in particular, compensation payments to potential harmonization losers and package deals[12] as well as first-mover advantages for member states seeking to establish innovative regulatory approaches at the European level (Héritier, Knill, and Mingers 1996). Taken together, these aspects might explain why high-regulating member states to a considerable extent succeeded in establishing harmonized process standards at the EU level.

From the measures falling under the hierarchy mode investigated in this chapter, product and process standards constitute by far the largest part of EU environmental policy (134 measures out of a total of 253 hierarchal regulations in 2005, including emission standards, production and trade restrictions, technical specifications, and prohibitions). It is only for the remaining policies that regulation by cooperation or negotiation constitutes a feasible alternative, whereas for most of the existing policies these new forms of governance interfere with underlying harmonization goals, with substitution offering no functionally equivalent option.

Certain restrictions also exist for the substitution of competition for hierarchy. In the literature, it is generally argued that the comparative advantage of economic instruments over hierarchical regulation is confined to specific constellations in which instruments are characterized by the common objective of reducing or stabilizing maximum emission levels for a given region (Endres 2000: 117). The total of emissions of all polluters in a region shall be restricted to a certain limit. The whole academic discussion on potential benefits of economic instruments rests on the assumption that they are applied in this specific context. As a consequence, economic instruments constitute a viable alternative to hierarchical regulation only in cases in which environmental regulations are directed at the achievements of clearly defined objectives concerning emission or environmental quality standards for a certain region.

Following the classification of environmental instruments in Table 4.1, this constellation applies to 92 (54 emission standards and 38 quality standards) of the 253 hierarchical policies investigated (numbers for 2005). Hence, around 36 percent of the hierarchical measures can be adequately replaced by economic instruments, whereas economic instruments such as environmental taxes or tradable emission licenses cannot replace other types of hierarchical regulation, such as technical specifications, prohibitions, production and trade restrictions, declaration obligations, or information obligations.

In sum, there are important functional restrictions on the replacement of hierarchical regulation by cooperation, competition, or negotiation. Indeed, we observe an absolute increase of all policy instruments, that is, evidence of differentiation rather than substitution. Notably, the cooperative mode, which suffers from rather serious limits with regards to substitution, has been introduced first and most frequently among the new modes. In the following, we therefore need to look for additional factors that might account for this development.

Lack of Political Support for Competition and Negotiation

Environmental economists have proposed economic instruments since the 1960s. Until the beginning of the 1990s, however, economic instruments were actually introduced in only a few instances in the OECD world. Prominent early examples are the introduction of the so-called emissions trading in the US Clean Air Act of 1977 or the introduction of the German wastewater tax in 1978. During the 1970s and 1980s some more environmental taxes were implemented in Europe, in particular in Scandinavian countries and the Netherlands, as well as in the United States, Canada, and Japan. In sum, however, there was no clear shift toward economic instruments.

Lack of support on the side of almost all actors explains this hesitant uptake of economic instruments. Environmental economists propose several reasons why industry can be expected to reject tradable permits and taxes: compared to standards, both permits and taxes are more expensive for industry, because it must also pay for the residual pollution. Moreover, individual standards can often be negotiated with the administration, whereas permits and taxes cannot be influenced. Voluntary agreements form a different category in this respect, as industry typically prefers them to less predictable and usually uniform legislative measures.

Governments and politicians hesitate for two reasons. First, on electoral grounds, governments do not like to impose clearly visible costs on industry as is implied in environmental taxes and licenses. Second, for politicians it is important that the benefit of a political measure can be attributed to them. This is not (or only indirectly) the case with economic instruments and even less so with voluntary agreements. For the environmental administration, economic and voluntary instruments mean a loss of competences and power because the instruments work either automatically after introduction or because (in the case of voluntary agreements) the administration merely plays a facilitating role.

Finally, environmental organizations and the general public may resist economic instruments. First, these groups worry that there is lack of information and comprehension of the functioning of economic instruments. Second, economic instruments imply the explicit allocation of rights to pollute, which offends the values of the environmental movement (e.g., Frey 1972: chap. 8; Binder 1999: 187ff). Moreover, there is the issue of adequate control over self-regulating industrial actors. Moving from abstract conjectures to empirical evidence, a study by Holzinger shows that during the 1980s, governments, the environmental administration, industry, environmental organizations, and political parties all preferred hierarchical regulation by classical standard setting to other forms of regulation (Holzinger 1987: chaps. 6 and 7).

This situation of general lack of support seems to have changed during the 1990s, when the use of economic instruments considerably increased, especially in OECD countries (OECD 1997, 1999). An important background for this is the fact that the green movement began to accept economic instruments as a means of achieving higher environmental quality. This became evident when environmental nongovernmental organizations (NGOs) supported the international emissions trading system for CO_2 negotiated at the Kyoto conference and its follow-ups. A second factor is surely that the OECD has actively promoted the use of economic instruments. Whereas the use of economic instruments, and especially of environmental taxes and charges, has clearly grown at the national level of European OECD countries, economic instruments at the EU level were late in catching up.

Reasons for this delay are related to the decisionmaking structure in the EU for fiscal measures. In tax matters, unlike in most other environmental policy, the treaties still require unanimity in the Council. So far only one proposal for a European tax with a clear environmental objective has been developed by the Commission and negotiated in the Council from 1991 to 1993, namely the combined CO_2/energy tax. The proposal failed because the required unanimity of member states could not be achieved given fierce resistance of concerned national industries. Other projects for environmental taxes developed by Commission officials never reached the level of official negotiations within the Council.[13] Tax matters are very sensitive, because they are related to the notion of national sovereignty. Anticipating difficult and cumbersome decisionmaking processes, the Commission and member states hesitate to come up with such proposals—especially after the failure in the CO_2/energy case.

Similar structural limitations do not apply to the negotiation of voluntary agreements, however. Although the Council and the European Parliament are robbed of their decisionmaking powers, and hence try to argue against a large-scale shift to the negotiated instruments, such agreements depend on the favorable constellation of industrial actors and active industrial peak associations rather than formal decisionmaking structures in the EU. Hence, the increasing acceptance of the OECD rhetoric among political and industrial actors did lead to a rise of voluntary instruments negotiated at the EU level.

The explanations given here have been developed inductively. They are an attempt to understand why we find few economic instruments apart from subsidies at the EU level, although the Commission intended to promote them, although they are often a practicable alternative to emission standards, and although the political support for these instruments has obviously increased during the last decade. Negotiated agreements, by contrast, suffer from fewer structural constraints but face the limits of substitution.

Conclusion

Hierarchical intervention has become an increasingly controversial practice in EU regulatory policy. In this chapter, we investigated the extent to which three nonhierarchical forms of governance (competition, cooperation, and negotiation) have actually found their way into EU environmental policy. Our empirical evidence suggests a mixed answer.

There is indeed a decrease in the relative importance of hierarchical governance. These measures today amount to less than 80 percent of all environmental policy, which is less than in the year 2000 (approximately 85 percent) or prior to the mid-1980s, when this governance form was the only category in Brussels-made environmental policy. Even though hierarchical governance clearly remains the dominant approach in EU environmental governance, it is complemented by competition, cooperation, or negotiation modes. The introduction of these new modes has been characterized by uneven speed and scope, partially lagging behind the respective political discussions about their introduction.

We have argued that these patterns can be explained by several factors. There are important functional restrictions to the replacement of hierarchy by other governance forms. Additional problems can be identified for the introduction of economic instruments, in particular for environmental taxes, which interfere with the fiscal sovereignty of the member states. Such institutional constraints continue to be effective even as member state resistance to economic instruments is declining (as OECD data on the use of economic instruments at the domestic level indicate).

Considering the serious limits to substitutability, the partial shift toward new forms of governance seems to be more remarkable than the numbers suggest at first sight. EU environmental policy is increasingly characterized by a mixed repertoire of instruments reflecting the willingness to let softer competitive, cooperative, and negotiation governance modes complement the traditionally hierarchical, interventionist patterns. This diversification has been a response to the constraints of the EU governance system with its known difficulties in enforcing compliance (see Chapter 2). The spread of responsibility (cooperative and negotiated instruments) and the use of the sanctioning power of markets (economic instruments) are two ways of dealing with this systemic deficit. But all new instruments rely heavily on the acceptance of environmental objectives among national, societal, and economic actors and are vulnerable to political upturns and downturns; hence they are no panacea.

Notes

1. *Official Journal of the European Communities* (OJ C) 46, 17.02.1983.
2. OJ C 328, 7.12.1987.
3. OJ C 112, 20.12.1973; cf. European Commission (1984: 15) and Lenschow (2002).
4. OJ C 46, 17.02.1983, 4–5.
5. OJ C 46, 17.02.1983, 8.
6. OJ C 328, 7.12.1987.
7. OJ C 138, 17.5.1993.
8. OJ C 138, 17.5.1993, 17.
9. OJ C 328, 7.12.1987.
10. OJ C 138, 17.5.1993, 14.
11. OJ C 138, 17.5.1993, 17.
12. Note that these deals and compromises emerge from the "negotiated order" that characterized the EU as a decisionmaking system (see Chapter 1 in this volume; Scharpf 1999).
13. Personal communication with Commission official, 25 June 2007.

5

Modes of Governance in EU Tax Policy

Claudio M. Radaelli and Ulrike S. Kraemer

Direct tax policy is a traditional domain of the nation state, at the heart of state sovereignty. Taxation determines the capacity of the state to fund its policies and redistribute resources. Developments in welfare state policies and other redistributive programs can be explained by looking at the tax system (Steinmo 1993). Although in a common market some forms of coordination of indirect taxes provide efficiency gains, one would not expect delegation of direct taxes to the supranational level. It is therefore not surprising that there are no specific treaty provisions for dealing with direct taxation at the European Union (EU) level.

Of course, this does not mean that there are no externalities to deal with. Suffice it to mention the problems created by the taxation of certain types of income generated by cross-border enterprises. As will be shown in this chapter, over the years, several studies, committees of inquiry, and policy initiatives have brought to the surface the externalities created by the single market without direct tax coordination. Recently, the academic and political debate has focused on whether some forms of international tax competition generate externalities and, if so, what kind of efficiency gains could be made by cooperating at the international level—at the EU level or in organizations with a wider membership, such as the Organization for Economic Cooperation and Development (OECD) or the United Nations (UN).

Nevertheless, for the EU to intervene in this area, the presence of externalities is a necessary though not sufficient condition. The obstacles are of both political and legal nature. Politically, there is no consensus on the major aims of tax governance at the EU level. Should it aim at reducing harmful tax competition? Or should it deal with the preconditions for a single market without tax frontiers? What is the appropriate role of the European Court of Justice (ECJ) in reviewing the direct tax laws of the member states? How much initiative should be left to the Commission and how much to intergovernmental negotiation outside the Community method? On each and every question, there are profound divisions among the member states.

The European Community (EC) Treaty leaves very few options for the development of secondary legislation in this area. Essentially, the only option is to draw on single market provisions—in which unanimity in the Council still applies. Intergovernmental cooperation (but not Community action—the EC Treaty refers to "negotiations") is envisaged for the abolition of double taxation within the Community (Article 220, Article 293 of the consolidated version). Alternatively, initiatives have to be developed outside the Community method. Given the heterogeneity of member states' interests in tax policy, often portrayed as a classical prisoner's dilemma,[1] it is not surprising that the requirement of unanimity has been a serious obstacle for EU tax cooperation.

Notwithstanding the above observations, over the years some forms of governance have emerged. This invites an exploration of the main issues aired in this book, specifically the following questions. First, what modes of governance are dominant in this policy area and how have they changed over time? Second, who are the actors involved in the construction of governance, and what do they get from cooperation at the EU level? Third, how do dominant actors and modes of governance match, and over time, is there any shift in modes of governance and dominant actors?

To answer these questions, we look at direct tax policy as a set of governance arenas rather than a single entity. The major actors are the member states, the European Commission, the ECJ, and the business community. The European Parliament has played a minor role in some areas of direct taxation, but it is not examined in this chapter. Civil society organizations promote campaigns for fiscal justice, but they are definitively policy outsiders in Brussels.

We explain modes of governance by looking at how actors balance power relations across arenas. We argue that there is no actor dominating all arenas. The Commission has orchestrated the creation of two different governance arenas to balance the power relations among Brussels, the member states, and the business community. We call one arena "harmful tax competition" and the other "corporate tax reform." For Brussels it is vital to secure a process goal, that is, making sure that there is progress on EU direct tax policy. Revenue authorities are the dominant actor in one arena, whereas in the other both member states and the business community play an important political role. But neither the Commission nor the member states have controlled the emergence of a third arena dominated by the ECJ.

Turning to shifts in modes of governance, the selection of one mode or another takes place within the individual governance arena. There is no linear trend from hard to soft governance over time. Moreover, in the "harmful tax competition" arena a code of conduct has been negotiated in the context of a tax package including directives and the regulation of state aids with a fiscal component. The Commission has used state aids rules to convince the recalcitrant governments to abide by the code of conduct—a classic example of soft governance in the shadow of hard governance.

The arena of corporate tax reform, on the other hand, shows a clearer preference for soft governance. This in turn is explained by the technical complexity of the exercise, the exploratory nature of this arena, and the political hesitation of the member states to make progress with directives. The emerging third arena dominated by the ECJ is characterized by hard governance. The Commission has tried to steer the reaction of the governments to the ECJ jurisprudence by producing communications and recommendations on how to coordinate the response, but the reaction of revenue authorities has been lukewarm. Finance ministers have also tried to react to the ECJ jurisprudence via soft intergovernmental cooperation, but this has produced more discussions than concrete results.

In the remainder of this chapter, we first sketch the evolution of EU direct tax cooperation. We find indeed, as Ingeborg Tömmel states in Chapter 2, that modes of governance "do not emerge by design of single actors but are the result of the process of policymaking, evolving through the interaction between different institutional actors at the European level, between the European and national (and sometimes regional) government level and the actors representing them, and finally between public and nonstate actors. . . . [They] are shaped and modeled according to the incentives and constraints that the institutional structure of the EU and the corresponding actor constellations set to their emergence and evolution." Looking at the member states, the Commission, and the business community, we then show the emergence of governance arenas and the different logics they are based on. We discuss the interplay of different modes inside arenas and how they relate to the preferences of the actors. In the conclusion we go back to the research questions mentioned above, briefly discuss the efficiency of tax governance, and present our thoughts on the institutionalization of governance arenas.

The Evolution of Governance

As mentioned, legal resources for harmonizing corporate taxes are scarce in the treaties. Important general principles such as free movement of people, freedom of establishment, free provision of services, and free movement of capital can be used by the ECJ, however, which in fact has recently turned out to be a major driving force in this area since its landmark judgment in the *Avoir Fiscal* case in 1985.[2] This judgment reaffirmed the principle that direct taxes should remain with the competence of the member states, but this competence has to be exercised consistently with the EC Treaty.[3] The

Court has attacked both overt and covert discrimination (between a resident and a nonresident company, provided that they are objectively comparable) contained in domestic tax systems. It has also embarked on a mission to strike down the tax barriers to the exercise of freedoms in the single market—derogations are possible only to protect the public interest. The latter has been conceptualized by the Court as the need to safeguard the cohesion of the tax system, to protect the efficiency of fiscal supervision, and to prevent tax evasion. Revenue authorities have to demonstrate, however, that the tax measures used to protect the public interest are appropriate, necessary, least onerous, and proportionate (Gammie 2003: 93).

The pressure of ECJ jurisprudence on revenue authorities is often felt in terms of revenue losses. This is why over the past few years there has been a debate on whether the ECJ should take into account how its decisions may derail the budget of a member state. Recent decisions confirm that the Court is aware of this problem, although it is too early to speak of a trend. Another obvious pressure concerns the overall aims of tax legislation. If the Court strikes down one element of the tax system, this may affect the overall balance between different taxes or the overall redistributive stance within a single tax. Lawyers working for national revenue authorities have complained that the Court cannot pursue the implementation of abstract principles by drilling holes in the tax systems in a random fashion.

Turning to the Commission, the limited treaty base has not prevented the Tax Directorate from making proposals. Direct taxation is championed by a commissioner, with tax competences split between two (direct and indirect taxation), at some stages even three, different Directorates General (DGs). Currently, there is a commissioner for taxation supported by one single DG, called Taxation and Customs Union (TAXUD). In the past, direct taxation was part of the portfolio of the commissioner for the single market. This was at times an asset for direct tax policy, as single market commissioners are important players in the college, but on other occasions it was a liability—a commissioner for the single market can always decide not to make taxation a priority.

The distortionary influence of domestic tax measures on the establishment and functioning of the common market was recognized soon after the conclusion of the Treaty of Rome. On 5 April 1960, the Commission set up a Fiscal and Financial Committee chaired by Fritz Neumark; it produced what is known as the Neumark report. "It must be studied," the Neumark report stated, "if, how and to what extent the abolition of Customs frontiers could also lead to the abolition of 'tax frontiers.' Another clear objective of integration is the avoidance of all taxation and other discrimination based on nationality or tax domicile" (EEC 1963: 101).

It soon became clear that, for EU governance to emerge in this policy domain, a sense of purpose was needed. The Neumark report showed one direction—the creation of a single market without frontiers. Consequently, the Commission set up working parties to look into this issue (Farmer and Lyal 1994: 19). But there was also the option of being more ambitious and, instead of focusing on specific externalities, of making proposals for a single set of rates, a Community-harmonized tax base, and a single system for the taxation of profits.

The Commission was never entirely clear on whether a final fiscal system was justified in terms of externalities (specifically, the need to limit tax competition and avoid races to the bottom) or was the means to the end of promoting more European integration and increasing the power of EU institutions (Radaelli 1997, 1999). As shown by Majone (2005), the confusion between sound economic reasons for EU action and political aims has led to a legitimacy crisis in several areas of EU regulation. Taxation is no exception to this trend. As the reasons for the creation of specific governance structures in direct taxation were not clarified and discussed, and obviously not agreed upon, the member states maintained their skeptical attitude toward the proposals of the Commission.

The uncertainty between an economic and a political approach continued during the 1960s and the 1970s. In 1969, the Commission presented proposals for two directives limited in scope and justified in terms of externalities— these directives were approved in 1990. At the same time, Brussels tried to exploit the momentum for European integration created by the 1970 Werner report on monetary coordination with grandiose plans for the harmonization of the tax base, cooperation among revenue authorities against tax evasion, and the approximation of tax rates in the Community. These proposals reflected the belief that strengthening European integration is a desirable aim in itself, rather than being the logical complement to the single market.

But these political aims were frustrated. A Council resolution dated 21 March 1972 promised that the proposals for fiscal harmonization would be given priority. Once placed on the Council's agenda—the resolution stated— proposals from the Commission would receive a decision within six months. The Commission presented an ambitious set of proposals for company taxation in 1975. But the dynamism of the Council was short-lived—by 1975 the promise to take action on direct tax policy was long forgotten (Radaelli 1997).

As mentioned, the proposals of the Commission leaned toward the choice of a final or "ideal" fiscal system based on robust doses of hard governance—such as directives on compulsory ranges of tax rates and the choice of a single European system for the treatment of profits. The Commission's approach came to be perceived as oriented toward fiscal centralization. Even incremental proposals (the 1969 draft directives, for instance) were damaged by this image of centralization surrounding the Commission.

The Commission redirected its political strategy in 1989–1990, however, banning the word *harmonization* and choosing to focus on a set of specific draft corporate tax directives for the completion of the single market. This time the Commission found it was not alone. The business community showed appreciation for the single market orientation of the new strategy. The ambiguity between integration by stealth (in the sense of Majone 2005) and the economic justification of proposals was dissolved.

Revenue authorities did not play ball, however. Although two directives and one convention were agreed upon in 1990, the Council of Ministers of Economic and Financial Affairs (ECOFIN) became increasingly reluctant to process direct tax proposals. Commissioner Christine Scrivener launched a high-profile committee of independent experts in 1992, the Ruding Committee. Several members of the committee were business leaders. Their proposals were considered unrealistic by the revenue authorities (Radaelli 1997). Momentum for EU direct tax governance was at its minimum level in 1995, when a new commissioner, Mario Monti, changed strategy one more time. This time the commissioner pressed the button of politicization again, but with a twist that changed the direction of the political relations among Brussels, the member states, and the business community. The key concept behind this shift was harmful tax competition.

Externalities created by harmful tax competition—Brussels has reasoned since 1996—are inefficient and damage the welfare state and employment levels (via the depletion of the revenue base in countries that do not engage in harmful tax competition and via higher taxes on labor to compensate for the drop in capital taxation). For the first time, the Council's policymakers from countries such as Germany and France saw tax coordination proposals not as measures needed to complete the ideal (but abstract) design of the single market (with companies as main beneficiaries), but as tools to re-establish policy autonomy at home and to govern the welfare state. Other member states, such as the United Kingdom (UK), Ireland, Luxembourg, and the Netherlands, were less than enthusiastic about this redirection. They successfully resisted the idea of using EU governance to limit tax competition across the board. But they agreed that tax regimes created with the sole purpose of attracting a foreign tax base were not defensible in a common market. Most important, they agreed on the need to protect the revenue base and policy autonomy at home. In 1997, all member states agreed on the specific criteria defining undesirable tax competition.

Turning to the research questions behind this chapter, the emergence of governance can be explained by the shift in the strategy of the Commission and by the fact that the narrative of harmful tax competition is a means to the revenue authorities' end of guarding the revenue base. Other variables played a role, too, namely the increasing pressure on revenue authorities created by integrated financial markets across the globe and the support of the OECD, which initiated its own campaign to mitigate the harmful consequences of tax competition in the same period (OECD 1998; Radaelli 1999).

The swing of the political pendulum toward containing harmful tax competition was not just a reshuffle of ideas, it was also a recombination of dominant actors. The preferences of the business community were well represented in the Ruding Committee and in the draft directives presented by Scrivener, less so in relation to the 1997 agreement of the finance ministers. In order to roll back harmful tax regimes and prevent governments from introducing new beggar-thy-neighbor tax provisions, ECOFIN adopted a code of conduct for business taxation on 1 December 1997.[4] The code is a nonbinding instrument managed by a high-level group of tax policymakers. It is based on peer review of potentially harmful tax regimes and specific guidelines provided by the group itself. The definition of harmful tax competition is contained in the 1997 ECOFIN agreement.

The 1997 agreement goes beyond soft governance, however. The code is included in a tax policy package comprising a directive on the taxation of savings and a directive on cross-border payments of interests and royalties. There was no switch from hard to soft governance in 1997. The tax package, eventually finalized in 2003, is an example of hybrid modes of governance.

Since the launch of the harmful tax competition campaign, the scene has changed. On the one hand, the tax package has remained a fundamental component of the strategy pursued by the EU institutions. On the other hand, another governance arena has emerged, alongside the "harmful tax competition" arena. This more recent arena deals with corporate tax reform and is closer to the preferences of the business community. Its emergence has been orchestrated by the Commission, with a view to re-entering multinational business in the tax governance game, this time via the door of new, soft modes of governance. To understand how this has happened, and why different modes of governance have been selected in the two different arenas, we need to take a closer look at the political logic of institution building.

Arenas, Power, and Modes of Governance

Institutions (in our case, arenas based on different modes of governance) can be examined as dependent variables arising out of political interaction rather than as independent variables (Moe 2005). Of course, most institutionalists would choose the alternative option of using institutions as independent variables—and measure their effects on policy change and other variables (Steinmo 1993). Our choice is dictated by the particular problem at hand, that is, to explain why the EU selects different modes of governance across time and arenas.

As mentioned, the Commission has a process goal, that is, to formulate policy and make sure that political discussion among actors with different interests ends with an agreement. The Commission has changed strategy on several occasions since the early days of the Community. The strategies pursued in the 1990s by Brussels were characteristically unbalanced in terms of power relations. Scrivener's approach based on tax neutrality in the single market was biased toward the interests of the multinationals. Monti's strategy was more sophisticated. It revolved around a two-step approach, based on the elimination of beggar-thy-neighbor, harmful tax practices in the first stage and then on the completion of a single market without tax barriers. The first stage dominated the scene up until the end of the 1990s, during which the relation between the Commission and the revenue authorities became quite close. In consequence, the process goal of the Commission has become to avoid this type of sui generis capture and to secure legitimacy for direct tax policy both from the member states and from the business community.[5] The lesson that the tax policymakers working at the Commission have learned is that no progress can be made if power relations are too unbalanced toward the interests of one of the key actors.

True, interests and power could in principle be balanced via a body looking at all tax issues synoptically. There has not been any agreement on comprehensive institutional solutions, however (the creation of a special tax body within ECOFIN has always been rejected). Thus, the sui generis capture problem has been compounded by the lack of systemic venues for tax coordination. The pragmatic solution has been to orchestrate the construction of two functionally differentiated tax governance arenas. Preferences are accommodated, and the capture problem of the Commission is eased, across arenas, rather than within individual arenas. These arenas provide distinct rules for the selection of participants, modes of interaction, and decisionmaking. They follow different political logics and therefore empower actors differently. They differ in important dimensions concerning the "quality" of governance, such as participation, problem-solving efficiency, accountability, and transparency. They also allow actors to select their own policy problems (specifically corporate tax reforms and harmful tax competition) and, most important, their own modes of governance. The choice of modes of governance takes place at this (subsystemic) level.

The first arena can be called harmful tax competition. Here the main actors are the member states and the Commission. This arena contains a code of conduct, the directive on the taxation of savings, and the provision for fiscal aids contemplated in the 1997 tax package. In terms of mode of governance, there is a combination of hard and soft modes, often to the benefit of the Commission.

The procedure against state aids with a tax component has been used successfully to put pressure on member states in the context of the negotiation of savings and the rollback process of the code. In July 2001, the Commission launched the state aid procedure against fifteen fiscal aid regimes. The idea was to increase pressure on member states to finalize the tax package and implement the code of conduct by using the state aid procedure. The

Commission noted in its 2004 report on state aids relating to business taxation: "The Commission's state aid work, carried out in parallel with the code of conduct work, has to some extent helped to facilitate the conclusion of an agreement on the code of conduct" (Commission 2004c: 19).

There has been socialization, practices informed by the open method of coordination, and consensus-based deliberation within the code of conduct group (see evidence in Radaelli 2003b) but harder modes of governance in state aid and savings. The selection of modes of governance is therefore politically contingent. There is no clear preference for one mode of governance over another. What matters is the political result of combining different modes. Further to the release of a list of EU citizens with savings in Liechtenstein in spring 2008,[6] political determination to tighten up rules against tax evasion has increased. ECOFIN asked the Commission to accelerate the review of the directive of savings. The Commission presented some preliminary proposals on how to refine the directive in April 2008 (European Commission 2008).

The second arena of corporate tax reform deals with an agenda that entered the stage at the end of the 1990s. The main actors in this arena are the business community, the Commission, and, often but not always reluctantly, the member states. The competitiveness agenda launched at Lisbon in 2000 and its redefinition in 2005 as a "growth and jobs" agenda have provided momentum (European Commission 2005a), although the catalog of problems and policy solutions that characterizes this arena has been developed independently from Lisbon. The dominant style of interaction is facilitated coordination based on benchmarking, technical exercises on the creation of a common tax base in Europe, and agreements on best practice. Although some member states are concerned that too much "technical" work on a common consolidated EU tax base may lead to "political" decisions to carry on with harmonization of both rates and base, so far there has been no evidence of hard modes of governance in this arena. The choice of soft governance is the result of the political logic prevalent in this domain. It is a logic based on exploration, pragmatic solutions, and, as mentioned, the concern of more than one member state that any deviation from soft exploratory governance could be used to start planning directives for the harmonization of tax rates (see Ruding 2005 on the position of different member states).

This arena emerged in 2001. As soon as the Commission felt that some progress was being made in the harmful tax competition arena, it released a communication that stated: "Now that the work on the tax package seems to be progressing satisfactorily, increased attention must be paid to the removal of these obstacles. It is high time to put much more emphasis on the concerns of the EU tax payers" (European Commission 2001a: 20).[7] In October 2001 the Commission published the results of a comprehensive study in the communication "Towards an Internal Market Without Tax Obstacles" (European

Commission 2001b). The study included an economic analysis of taxation and the results of a panel of business experts on the key tax obstacles to the single market.

Since then, the Commission has launched several initiatives for corporate tax reform (on transfer pricing and on a common consolidated tax base) that all fall outside the classical Community method. On the one hand, this arena scores well on transparency and participation, at least looking at the Transfer Pricing Forum and the consultation process for the pilot project on home state taxation. On the other hand, the Common Consolidated Corporate Tax Base (CCCTB) Working Group refused to allow such experts other than those sent by governments to be members of the group, although they agreed on building an expert group that can be consulted on request. Some members of the group even wanted to keep meeting records unpublished until informed by Commission services that there is an obligation imposed by the Council and the European Parliament to disclose working documents, the same as for the meetings of the Joint Transfer Pricing Forum.[8]

The Commission has somewhat balanced power relations across the two arenas described above but has not exercised control on a third arena, dominated by the ECJ. DG TAXUD has sought to use the ECJ decisions to coordinate reforms in the member states. The message is simple: given that the ECJ jurisprudence has highlighted the areas in need of reform, member states should agree on a common position in the working parties orchestrated by the Commission. In its 2003 communication, the Commission proposed the adoption of soft governance, especially recommendations to provide guidance and "pro-active coordination of those features of member states' tax systems that are or are likely to be in conflict with EU law" (European Commission 2003: 7). Along the same line, the Commission issued communications on the tax treatment of occupational pensions, investment funds, and dividend taxation (European Commission 2001c, 2000a, 2003).

The reaction of the member states has been reluctant so far. There is hesitation as to whether the Commission should be given a specific role in this delicate area, where the lawyers working for the Commission tend to concur with the ECJ's negative opinion about the compatibility of national tax provisions with the treaty freedoms. During the British Presidency of 2005, there was an attempt to kick off an intergovernmental, soft approach to devise a common position across the member states in relation to ECJ matters. The Commission was kept outside this exercise. But we have not found evidence that intergovernmental cooperation is producing specific governance structures or arrangements. One partial innovation concerns ECJ hearings. Even though ECJ cases target one specific tax provision or a given member state, revenue authorities from more than one country show up at the hearings, addressing different points, and thus defending the tax legislation of the government under ECJ attack from different perspectives.

This may well be a first result of more cooperation across member states on ECJ matters.

Conclusion

This chapter has described the evolution of EU direct tax policy and the emergence of functionally differentiated governance arenas. Thinking of the lines of inquiry suggested by the editors in Chapter 1 of this book and of the classification proposed in Chapter 2, our evidence suggests the following conclusions.

There is no dominant mode of governance in the policy domain examined in this chapter—neither across time nor across arenas. Over time, however, there has been an intensification of activities, with the result that soft governance, although not new, has cropped up in several places.

Modes vary across arenas. In the harmful tax competition arena, we have found hierarchy (the state aid provisions used for fiscal aids are among the hardest provisions in the treaty), negotiation (in the saga of the directive on savings taxation), and cooperation (in the code of conduct against harmful tax competition). There is more reliance on cooperation in the corporate tax reform arena. In the third arena there is predominantly hierarchy and a few attempts (so far failed or limited) to create cooperation.

The main actors involved in these modes of governance are the member states, the Commission, the ECJ, and the business community. They gain different things from coordination at the EU level. The member states gain increased domestic policy autonomy via the protection of the revenue base in the harmful tax competition arena, the pressure groups manage to probe solutions to the tax problems of multinational business in the single market in the corporate tax reform arena, and the Commission pursues a process goal by balancing power relations between the first and the second arena. In the third arena, both member states and the Commission would definitively gain from coordination and the use of a cooperative mode of governance, but the member states insist that cooperation should be exclusively intergovernmental whereas the Commission would like to use its recommendations to steer the process and control the agenda. So Brussels vetoes the creation of a tax body within ECOFIN, and the governments do not want to engage in cooperative governance with the Commission in the pilot's seat. The result is that both the member states and the Commission are losing in the third arena, and pressure groups often win. So far the jurisprudence of the ECJ has favored the taxpayer, but future decisions may be more erratic.

Notes

Research for this chapter was carried out at the University of Exeter in the context of Integrated Project "New Modes of Governance" (www.eu-newgov.org), financially supported by the European Union under the Sixth Framework program (Contract No. CIT1-CT-2004-506392). The authors would like to thank Amy Verdun, Ingeborg Tömmel, and the participants of the conferences in Victoria, BC, March 2006, and Osnabrück, Germany, November 2006, for their comments and advice on earlier drafts of this chapter.

1. See for example Gordon (1992), Hallerberg (1996), and Genschel and Pluemper (1997).

2. ECJ 28 January 1986, Case 270/83, *Avoir Fiscal* (Commission v. France), 1986, ECR 273.

3. Since then the ECJ has struck down national law in more than fifty cases, forcing national governments to redesign their tax systems in order to prevent further rules from being struck down (for a full list of cases see the Taxation and Customs Union, legal proceedings, available at http://ec.europa.eu/taxation_customs/index_en.htm).

4. "Conclusions of the ECOFIN Council Meeting on 1 December 1997 Concerning Taxation Policy," *Official Journal of the European Communities,* OJ C 002, 06/01/1998, pp. 1–6.

5. We say sui generis because real capture would have eroded the capacity of the Commission to elaborate autonomous strategies and to pursue its process goals.

6. See the story and comments by Willem Buiter in *Financial Times,* "Blockade the Tax Havens," 20 February 2008, at http://blogs.ft.com/maverecon/2008/02/blockade-the-tax-havens/.

7. The point was reiterated in a 2005 document, arguing that the elimination of harmful tax regimes was meant to re-establish the integrity of the tax base in the interest of the fiscal authorities. Having eliminated the main elements of fiscal degradation, the EU should eliminate the main fiscal obstacles to economic cross-national activity and turn to the preoccupations of European taxpayers. See Aujean et al. (2005: 12–13).

8. See the minutes of the first meeting of the CCCBT Working Group, 23 November 2004, at http://ec.europa.eu/taxation_customs/taxation/company_tax/common_tax_base/article_2336_en.htm.

6

Regulation and Cooperation in Economic and Monetary Policy

Amy Verdun

Governance in economic and monetary policymaking has progressed through various stages since 1998. Following the framework developed in this book, we see that all four modes of governance or ideal types—hierarchy, negotiation, competition, and cooperation—have been applicable, either singly or in a combination of two or more, over time.

These ideal types are spelled out in more detail in Chapter 2. Some of these ideas can also be found in other parts of the literature (e.g., Mayntz and Scharpf 1995; Pierre 2000; Jachtenfuchs 2001; Mayntz 2002, 2004, 2005; Benz 2004b, 2005; Pierre and Peters 2005). In the case of economic and monetary integration, it is the member states or public authorities that play the most prominent role in this policymaking area. Nonstate actors may also exercise governance without interference from the public sphere, thus establishing order through self-regulation. In the case of economic and monetary policy, however, most of the actors are public actors, many of them bureaucrats or other experts who contribute to the development of policies and to governance. Their interaction, and who the most important actor is for any given development of economic and monetary policymaking, differs considerably over time, however (see Chapter 2).

This chapter has a twofold aim. First, it seeks to describe and evaluate the governance concept as adopted in this analysis. Second, it offers an analysis of how modes of governance emerge in the process of economic and monetary policymaking by examining four stages of such policymaking.

Economic and monetary policymaking in the European Union (EU) has made major progress throughout its development. One might even go so far as to say that it is one of the areas of policymaking in which the EU has come from behind and has gone the furthest in obtaining deep integration. It started off from no cooperation and has ended with the creation of a single currency and a single supranational authority making monetary policies for the entire eurozone area (Dyson and Featherstone 1999). The modes of governance that were used throughout differed. Sometimes—and regarding some aspects of economic and monetary policymaking—they are more hierarchical; at other times they are softer and more informal.

In terms of this development one can differentiate four important stages. The first stage (1958–1970) starts at the Rome Treaty and lasts until the launching of the Werner Report. The second period (1971–1992) covers the years in which the so-called snake European exchange rate mechanism took place. It also includes the dark years from the initial euphoria until the moderate exchange rate mechanism of the European Monetary System (EMS) was adopted. Finally this period ends with the signing of the Maastricht Treaty. The third stage (1993–1998) involves the run-up to the creation of the Economic and Monetary Union (EMU). The final stage (1999–) is the period that starts with EMU and continues today. In each of these stages a different mode of governance was dominant, although usually more than one mode of governance was occurring during any single stage.

The following four subsections examine these four stages and identify the modes of governance at work. They also look at how those modes of governance evolved in this policymaking area. In general the first stage was characterized by cooperation. During the second stage competition and negotiation emerged as the dominant modes of governance. Both competition and the onset of hierarchy can be noted during the third stage. We mostly observe a combination of competition and cooperation during the fourth stage. An analysis of economic and monetary policymaking throughout the decades follows the stage-by-stage discussions. The conclusion examines the various modes of governance that have been adopted throughout these periods and how we can categorize them.

Economic and Monetary Policymaking in the European Economic Community, 1958–1970: Cooperation from Rome to Werner

Economic and monetary policymaking in the European Economic Community (EEC) was not at all based on hierarchy as is the case with the European Central Bank (ECB) today. Instead, economic and monetary policymaking was firmly based on softer modes of governance, in particular on cooperation. The 1957 Treaty of Rome mentioned economic and monetary policy coordination in Articles 103–109, treating these policies as "a matter of common concern" (Verdun 2000a). In Articles 103–109, economic policy referred broadly to budgetary and fiscal policies, whereas monetary policy referred to exchange rate policies. In these early years economic and monetary policy coordination took place in a number of committees. The EEC Treaty called for a Monetary Committee as an advisory organ. In the early 1960s, based on Commission proposals, numerous other committees were created to assist in coordination. After initial hesitation of the Council, the following committees were created in 1964: the Committee of Central Bank Governors, a Budgetary Policy Committee, and a Medium-Term Policy Committee. Together with the Short-Term Policy Committee that already existed, the Community now had five coordinating committees (Rosenthal 1975). The work that was done in the 1960s took place in these committees; they had a hybrid form. The committee members represented the member states but worked together toward cooperation as a semi-Community-oriented institution. The mechanism of cooperation in these committees was that of discussing policy objectives and exchanging views. This mode of governance fits best in the category of "cooperation."

By the late 1960s, the leaders of the European Communities agreed that it was necessary to move on toward further economic and monetary unification. By now the customs union was completed, and other areas of policy-making (agriculture) would benefit from having stability in exchange rates (Tsoukalis 1977). The customs union had created a zone of free movement of goods and services among the member states. There were no longer internal barriers, and there was a common external tariff toward the outside world. This far-reaching degree of collaboration on trade issues enabled the member states to be ready to take a next bold step in economic integration (Kruse 1980).

At the Hague Summit in December 1969, the proposal to create an EMU was given approval, and a plan was to be made in 1970 to lay out the steps toward that goal. What became known as the Werner Plan set out a proposal to create EMU in stages by 1980 (Council-Commission of the European Communities [Werner Report] 1970). The members of the Werner Committee represented the chairs of the various economic and monetary committees mentioned above. These persons had a vast experience with economic and monetary cooperation, which they had obtained through their deliberations over the years. Thus when they drafted a proposal for EMU, it was firmly based on that background experience. The eventual plan was presented in 1970 and adopted in 1971 but ultimately failed to be implemented. This period is predominantly characterized by negotiation. Many of the actors involved represented the member states. Some of them had been "socialized" through their work in Community committees to include some of the norms and practices of the Community (Verdun 1999, 2000a). The plan was weak in transfer of sovereignty in the first stages. But eventually EMU would transfer sovereignty over monetary policy to a new supranational monetary authority and would create a center for decisionmaking that would coordinate economic policies. The vision of economic and monetary policies in the European Community that had been created here was a mix of hierarchy regarding monetary policy and a slightly softer mix of hierarchy and cooperation regarding economic policy. Monetary policy included setting of interest rates and the control of the money supply. Economic policy included coordinating budgetary deficits. It was as yet unclear if there was a necessity to coordinate fiscal policies (in particular common taxes and a collective budget that could be used for redistribution to settle any imbalances related to creating an EMU).

From Exchange Rate Cooperation to EMU: Competition and Negotiation

In the 1970s progress in the area of economic and monetary integration was mainly by seeking cooperation in the field of monetary policy (exchange rate policy), first through the so-called snake (exchange rate arrangement) and, as of 1979, the so-called EMS (Ludlow 1982). The snake mechanism was the predecessor of the EMS—a system of fixed but adjustable exchange rates in which most currencies could not fluctuate more than 2.25 percent from an agreed upon parity. Owing to the turbulent economic circumstances of the time, the system broke down because of its voluntary characteristic. Any member state that did not manage to keep its currency within the agreed parity just dropped out of the system, leaving the snake participants as a group of countries in which some were EEC member states and others were not. Some larger member states were outside. The cooperation in the EMS was based on seeking to target exchange rate objectives. Even so, most member states agreed to keep their currencies within the narrow band of 2.25 percent. Any rearrangements of the agreed upon exchange rate parities were discussed and decided on in the Monetary Committee. The process in the EMS had become a little harder and was more based on negotiation (especially the Monetary Committee, which had to determine whether or not to change the agreed upon parities between currencies). During the 1980s the policies of member states were often reflected on and committees discussed "best practices" (well before those words were used to describe the process). In the case of monetary policy cooperation, policymakers looked to the best performing country/countries and sought to follow the policies of the best performer(s) (notably: the Federal Republic of Germany [see De Grauwe 1991]). This mechanism is mostly characterized by cooperation but to some extent also follows the principles of the mode of governance of competition.

In the 1970s and early 1980s, in the area of macroeconomic cooperation, there was not much success in formal Community policy development. What did happen, however, was the use of the modes of governance of cooperation and negotiation to advance the development of European policies in this area. This increased the awareness that budgetary and fiscal policies had an important effect on monetary policies (exchange rates) and therefore benefited from successful cooperation.

By the late 1980s, the EMS turned out to be quite a bit more successful than it had been in its early years. The main reason was the commitment by each of the participating member states to keeping the exchange rates of its national currency within the agreed upon parities. It was a political decision to put much weight on that arrangement, and other policies were sought to be put in line with them. These policies were made by national monetary authorities and, as said, were based on negotiation, best practices, policy learning, and informal coordination as well as discussions. Here we see a combination of modes of governance rather than one mode dominating.

The resurgence in the late 1980s of the plan to create EMU was triggered by the wording in the Single European Act and the enthusiasm surrounding the idea to "complete the single market" by the end of 1992. The content of these plans as well as the hype around these two European integration resurrection initiatives subsequently led to an increased desire to try again to take the next step in economic and monetary unification, now also building on the success in the EMS that was managing to keep exchange rates stable. The Treaty on European Union incorporated into its structure a detailed blueprint for EMU. The blueprint was based on the earlier Delors Report, which in turn had been written by the national central bank presidents, two EU commissioners, and a few independent experts (Committee for the Study of Economic and Monetary Union [Delors Report] 1989). Very much like the Werner Committee, the Delors Committee represented member states but also the experts, who were speaking in their own capacity. By choosing central bankers, experts, and commissioners, a mix of state and nonstate actors was involved in the planning stage. Of course these central bankers were fully aware of the political limits of what might be feasible in the area of creating EMU, yet they were also writing up an "experts" plan, assuming that national government leaders would still make many changes. They were, in fact, surprised that so much of what they had agreed to eventually was incorporated into the treaty.

The EMU model was characterized by a transfer of European monetary policy to a new supranational central bank, whereas budgetary and fiscal policies remained at the level of member states, and cooperation would take place by targeting objectives. Even though many of the factors were originally conceptualized in the Delors Committee, the run-up to the creation of Economic and Monetary Union in the EU should be characterized as being based on the "negotiation" mode of governance (see Moravcsik 1998). In particular, because of the skepticism of the United Kingdom, the deals that needed to be made to keep EMU firmly based in the Treaty on European Union implied serious negotiation.

The Run-up to the Creation of EMU: Competition and Hierarchy

After the 1992 Treaty on European Union entered into force on 1 November 1993, the time schedule for EMU took off. There were three stages to full EMU. The first stage (that had already started on 1 July 1990) included the liberalization of capital markets and the completion of the internal market. Although neither of these two programs would be completed, that first stage of EMU was considered to have been entered. The second stage included the creation of the European Monetary Institute (EMI), which occurred on 1 January 1994. The main task of the EMI was to implement the commitment to EMU. This predecessor of the European Central Bank, though supranational in nature, did not have sovereignty over monetary policy. It was merely an institution that would pave the way for the later creation of the ECB. It was transformed (that is, abolished) into the ECB at the start of stage three of EMU on 1 January 1999.

On the part of the member states, much needed to be done before entering into the final stage of EMU. The member states had to meet the so-called convergence criteria. These consisted of maxima on interest rates, long-term interest rates, exchange rate performance, budgetary deficits, and public debts. The mode of governance that was prominent here was competition: member states who wanted to be ready to join EMU from the first possible date needed to perform well according to the convergence criteria. Only those that came sufficiently close to these criteria could join by the latest time for stage three, in order to start with the countries that were ready, which was 1 January 1999. The treaty also stipulated that if at least half of the member states met the convergence criteria before this date, EMU could start sooner. It is this last provision in particular that signals the "competition" mode of governance prominent in this stage of economic and monetary policymaking.

In addition to the policy objectives that member states were trying to reach, there were other policies that had to be transferred to enter into the final stage of EMU. Monetary policy was to be transferred to a supranational body that would be above the national central banks. Once that occurred (which took place on 1 January 1999), that new supranational institution was given the authority to set interest rates for all the member states who were part of the euro zone. With this step the EU had made the hierarchical mode of governance the prevailing one in monetary policy. The EU now started to resemble more the characteristics of a "state" in this policymaking area, in part owing to the hierarchical mode of governance.

The institutions that were related to the European Central Bank (the national central banks) became "branches" of the broader European System of Central Banks (ESCB) (Howarth and Loedel 2003). The ESCB performs the function of the European supranational authority. Even though formally the national central banks have ceased to be the authority in the national setting, a part of their behavior still seeks to determine what role there is for them to play in the context of this institutional structure in which the ECB has the authority and the national banks are subordinate.

In the area of budgetary and fiscal policies, the situation is quite different. Sovereignty over these policies has remained with national authorities, even though subject to rules (for example on budgetary deficits). In this area we see a variety of different modes of governance at work. The process of ensuring low deficits includes a soft part (benchmarking, best practices, peer pressure) as well as a hard part (sanctions). One could say that in this area of policymaking we see elements of all four modes of governance at work: hierarchy, negotiation, competition, and cooperation. The prominence of this combination of modes of governance comes more to the surface in the next stage.

EMU in Action: Hierarchy, Negotiation, Competition, and Cooperation

The role of the European Central Bank and its mode of governance have been undisputed and clear since the start of EMU in 1999. The ECB has set monetary policy for the whole area, and once it sets it, it takes effect immediately. Here we see a hierarchical mode of governance. As was touched upon in the previous section, where the situation became messy was in the area of economic policies.

The period of the 1990s and the start of the 2000s was characterized in this policy area by many interactions between the Commission and the member states regarding the performance of the member states on economic performance indicators and targets of budgetary deficits and public debt. The Commission played an important role in facilitating the cooperation. As part of this aim, so-called Broad Economic Policy Guidelines (BEPG) were set up, in which the Commission has to alert member states when their policies or macroeconomic performances are getting out of line. The modes of governance here are competition and cooperation. Member states are supposed to perform according to the targets set out, and the Commission offers feedback about their performance. That this soft mode of governance can also potentially have a "hard" effect should be clear. An example will serve to clarify.

The first time a so-called early warning was issued was in 2001 in the case of Ireland. Based on a proposal of the Commission, the Council adopted a recommendation that stated that the budgetary policy of Ireland in 2001 was out of line with the objectives (Council Opinion of 12 February 2001 of Ireland's Stability Program 2001–03 [OJ C 77, 9 March 2001]). Even though Ireland was running a budgetary surplus of about 4.7 percent of gross domestic product (GDP) and had a low public debt, the concern was about the strong economic activity and hence the accompanying inflationary tendencies. The Council stated that Irish fiscal policy should be focused on reducing the risk of further overheating and thus inflation (Council Recommendation to Ireland Under Article 99[4] of the EC Treaty). Thus the Commission and Council aimed at forcing the Irish government to change its macroeconomic policies even though its economy was growing fast. This forceful behavior of the Commission and Council can be seen as a "hard effect." Needless to say, the Irish government was unhappy with this verdict, as the Irish economy was growing faster than that of other member states and thus should not be unnecessarily penalized for that good performance (for a discussion and criticism of this era, see Hodson and Maher 2001).

Details of trying to enforce collaboration in the area of budgetary deficits and public debt were set out in the Stability and Growth Pact (SGP) (Heipertz and Verdun 2004, 2005). Here, too, the Commission plays an important role in giving member states an early warning and in following the steps of the agreement. The Commission analyzes the financial and budgetary situation of each of the member states and provides its assessment of how the member state is doing and whether it needs to consider dealing with expenditure reduction or increasing government revenue. These arrangements have both a soft and a hard part. The soft part consists of exchanging best practice experiences, informal collaboration, and nonhierarchical sets of relationships in seeking to meet the end objectives. The actors involved in policy coordination in the area of budgetary and fiscal policies are member states, the Commission, and the Council, including advisory committees. One idiosyncratic body that plays an important role in this context is the so-called Eurogroup. It consists of the ministers of finance of the countries that are in the euro area. They meet informally before the ECOFIN council meets and are a crucial body to be reckoned with. Uwe Puetter characterizes this group as engaging in deliberative intergovernmentalism, as they negotiate their way through (Puetter 2006). Reflecting on our modes of governance, this type of interaction would be characterized as a mix of negotiation and cooperation. Finally, an important role is also played by the policy community that provides input into the types of policies and EU arrangements that are being considered.

That these modes of governance in the area of monetary policy also have hard components is made clear by some elements of the Treaty on European Union, further elaborated on in the Stability and Growth Pact. There are provisions in both that stipulate that the member state that is repeatedly violating the 3 percent annual budgetary deficit ceiling as a percentage of GDP may face sanctions. These pecuniary sanctions would first take the shape of a loan and later a penalty. These are hard measures based on an incremental violation of the deficit ceiling. As is reported in great detail elsewhere (Grimwade 2005), the process could give rise to a member state's being confronted with the next step in the excessive deficit procedure, leading to sanctions. When France and Germany were confronted with the next steps in the procedures in November 2003, however, they persuaded enough member states not to apply the rules to them so they were not held to the procedure. The result is that what was designed to be a hierarchical mode of governance with "hard" rules turned out to be much softer than originally envisaged. So the mode of governance that seemed clearly "hierarchical" (imposing the next steps that would bring these countries closer to sanctions) was watered down in a process of negotiation (bargaining in the Council over the interpretation of the rules). As such it was no longer quite as hierarchical as before.

Following the November 2003 Council decision that de facto put the SGP in abeyance, EU member states decided to reform the SGP. The rules-based, relatively hierarchical mode of governance was considered questionable in comparison with a system that was looser and would give more room for negotiation and competition. In spring 2005 a new Stability and Growth Pact was adopted that allowed member states more room for maneuver and would not lead to sanctions as quickly as the old regime had. Furthermore, if any sanctions were to take place, a member state would under the new rules have an easier time seeking to clarify that some of the conditions were unfavorable and that thus no sanctions should be imposed.

These arrangements all consider the budgetary policies. It is remarkable, perhaps, that monetary policy, during all this time, remained the core responsibility of the ECB. This particular mode of governance for monetary policy has not received great criticism or scrutiny. The focus of attention has been on budgetary policies, and in that area of policymaking the mode of governance has been watered down to more competition and negotiation rather than hierarchy. At the same time, as discussed, monetary policy is clearly hierarchical. In earlier work I have referred to the different development in economic and monetary policymaking as "asymmetrical" (Verdun 1996; see also Verdun 2000a). In the area of monetary policy there is a clear transfer of sovereignty and a willingness by the member states to accept that hierarchy is the dominant mode of governance.

Analysis and Reflection on the Various Modes of Governance in Economic and Monetary Policymaking

Going over the historical development in this area of policymaking, it should be clear that the modes of governance have from the outset included facets of what in the literature is referred to as "new modes of governance" (see, for example, Caporaso and Wittenbrinck 2006; Héritier 2002a). Examples of these new modes of governance include informal exchanges of ideas, development in areas of policymaking in which the mandate in the treaty is not clear, creation of informal advisory bodies to facilitate cooperation, and hybrid functions for these informal bodies (they represent member states yet seek to aim at Community coordination) (see also Eberlein and

Kerwer 2004). Yet, it should also have become clear that using best practices, benchmarking, and similar procedures was part of the policy process well before those words were introduced in EU jargon in the late 1990s or at the Lisbon Council in 2000. Furthermore, it should be clear from the above examples that "soft cooperation"—through committees, informal targets, and, often, self-discipline—has been quite successful in creating real convergence in policies, which in turn has provided a solid basis for taking the next step in institutional change (take the example of the success of the EMS, which contributed to the desire to create EMU, and EMU in turn being put firmly in the treaty). It is noteworthy, however, to point to the fact that from the outset there was a lot of competition behind the scenes for being among the first group of countries ready to join stage three of EMU. In recent years these modes of governance have been formalized and put in the language of the treaty. But in fact, as so often in European integration, the procedures and practices preceded their formalization. In the area of budgetary and fiscal policies there was insufficient desire to transfer the policy competence to the supranational level and thus the choice was made to keep it at the level of nation states and have national governments try to meet such targets. The details of how to implement such a policymaking procedure have been at the heart of the development of the Broad Economic Policy Guidelines and the Stability and Growth Pact.

What has also been made clear is that the different modes of governance have different effects in leading to closer integration in the area of economic and monetary policymaking. At some times the softer modes of governance (cooperation) have been quite successful (1960s), whereas when times were tough (1970s) cooperation did not produce the desired result. In the 1970s some of the cooperation was extended to become a little harder with more negotiation playing a role. By the late 1980s and early 1990s some parts of the areas of policymaking were transferred to supranational bodies or put in the context of hard rules. Since the late 1990s we have seen clarity in the mode of governance in monetary policy (hierarchy) but signs of all four modes of governance in the economic area (negotiation, competition, and cooperation as well). Thus, we see varying degrees of success of both soft and hard modes of governance.

It is worth noting that part of the reason for not transferring powers over budgetary and fiscal policies to a supranational EU institution is a fundamental distrust in what an EU supranational budgetary and fiscal policy would look like or what its mandate would be. Member states want to stay involved in this area of policymaking. Thus the collaboration represents a mix of the various institutions: the Commission, the Council, and the member states (with the bulk of the work done in advisory committees). The outcome of this form of policymaking has been quite far-reaching and is having a lasting impact. Over the years, critics of EMU have argued that without firm authority or firm rules EMU would not be able to survive. To date it appears that these modes of governance have been able to substantiate this development with quite some success.

Conclusion

This chapter set out to assess four basic modes of governance in relation to economic and monetary policymaking in the European Union. I analyzed the case of economic and monetary policy and looked in particular at how modes of governance emerge in the process of policymaking through the interaction between all institutional actors involved. In regard to the interaction between two actors, the Commission and the member states, it was the times when it was unclear how to integrate further that gave rise to the emergence of the softer modes of governance. When there is a lack of consensus about the need to transfer sovereignty to a supranational institution, the Commission tends to push for more competences at the European level whereas the member states are often reluctant to transfer such competences. The case study of economic and monetary policy suggests that nonhierarchical modes of governance are at the heart of the evolution of EU policymaking.

To sum up, we can learn three lessons from developments in economic and monetary policymaking as part of our overall study on governance and policymaking in the EU. The first is that new, that is, *soft* modes of governance emerged in the area of economic and monetary policymaking considerably prior to what is generally assumed in the literature. In the case of economic and monetary policymaking, they had already emerged in the 1960s. They were, however, recently pushed more vigorously to the forefront in the area of macroeconomic policy coordination (in particular the Broad Economic Policy Guidelines). Benchmarking and best practices are at the heart of trying to coordinate macroeconomic policies, and thus these soft modes of governance are used to produce some level of cooperation among member states in this area of policymaking.

Second, these soft modes of governance can turn out to have harder impacts than the so-called hard measures that are based on hierarchical means of steering. In the case of economic policymaking, this is the result of member states' holding the formal powers in this field and their willingness to take responsibility for due implementation. But the opposite can also be the case. Hard modes of governance can be evaded or watered down by member states, as the case of softening up the Stability and Growth Pact in monetary policy shows.

Third, all modes of governance emerged through interaction between institutional actors. Resistance of important actors, mostly national governments, to one mode of governance fostered the emergence of others that were more promising or less controversial. On the whole, this tended to give rise to ever softer modes of governance, which can, however, sometimes have harder or more far-reaching impacts than what is usually assumed. Likewise, institutionalizing hard modes of governance would not necessarily imply a guaranteed track to that mode's being implemented that way (as the case of the SGP shows).

7

From "Integration by Stealth" to "Good Governance" in EU Social Policy

Laura Cram

The rise of new modes of governance has variously been associated with a shift away from the traditional "Community method" or traditional regulatory approaches to a more flexible "open method," a shift from hard law to soft law, and a shift in the balance of power away from supranational top-down edicts toward shared solutions reached through participation with a range of actors from different policy levels within the intergovernmental domain. Analysis of this shift has also been accompanied, in some cases, by a rather strong normative element in support of such new approaches to governance in the European Union (EU), even, as Caporaso and Wittenbrinck (2006: 476) note, "going so far as suggesting that they represent the leading edge of a thoroughly modern form of deliberative problem-solving" or, as Idema and Kelemen (2006: 116) note, being presented as "well suited to addressing 'democratic deficit' concerns." The rise in profile of civil society involvement in the policy process has been similarly accorded a strong degree of support as a democratizing and legitimizing force (Smismans 2006a: 5).

There is considerable academic debate concerning the relationship between governance and democracy: for example, "this shift from 'government' to 'governance' is associated with the consolidation of new technologies of government, on the one hand, and with profound restructuring of the parameters of political democracy on the other, leading to a substantial democratic deficit" (Swyngedouw 2005: 1991). Yet, in the EU context, the "new modes of governance" based on "voluntarism, subsidiarity, flexibility, participation, policy integration, and multi-level integration" (Borrás and Jacobsson 2004: 189) have been widely portrayed, particularly by the Commission, as ushering in a new (improved) era in the EU policy process.

Any understanding of the extent to which the emergence of new forms of governance has taken place requires, however, some understanding of what the old *methods* were, the relative roles of the *actors* involved, and the *context* in which current practices developed. In the area of EU social policy, the Commission has capitalized upon and encouraged the enthusiasm for "new modes of governance" and their purported association with improved democracy and legitimacy, to create a central role for itself in previously untouchable preserves of the member states while also generating a constituency of support for further action in these areas. Whereas in the past, the technique of drawing in unelected societal actors to pressure elected national executives into adopting the preferred proposals of the unelected Commission was viewed as "integration by stealth" (Majone 2005), today the incorporation of a wide number of actors through new policy instruments is increasingly presented, not least by the Commission, as a model of "good governance."

EU Social Policy: From "Integration by Stealth" to "Good Governance"?

The starting point for the study of EU social policy must be the very limited legal basis for action bestowed by the founding treaties (Teague 1989; Hantrais 1995; Shaw 2000). Member states have always limited the involvement of the Commission in sensitive policy areas such as employment, social protection, pensions, and health care. Within this constrained environment, however, the Commission has not simply applied itself to the areas of equal opportunities in the workplace or health and safety policy, where it was given stronger grounds for action, but has consistently sought to use the limited means available to it to expand its room for maneuver (Majone 1992; Cram 1993, 1997; Leibfried and Pierson 1995). Institutionally driven creativity in the face of member state opposition has always been at the heart of the development of EU social policy. The introduction of new policy instruments can be seen as part of this process. The open method of coordination (OMC), for example, rather than marking a shift away from supranational influence in the area of social policy, has in fact provided a unique opportunity for the Commission to participate in hitherto forbidden policy preserves of the member states. Indeed, far from undermining the Commission's role, "the OMC has allowed the Commission to take initiatives and to expand cooperation to new areas belonging to the legal competences of the member states; hence, it has been able to bypass the subsidiarity principle. It is thus not obvious that the OMC has weakened the Commission" (Borrás and Jacobsson 2004: 198).

The European employment strategy (EES, or the Luxembourg Process) was the flagship project for the open method of coordination (Mosher and Trubek 2003). The OMC was extended to the areas of social protection and inclusion (from 2000 onward) and, for example, pensions (from 2002 onward) and health and long-term care (from 2006 on) as well as being rolled out across a wide range of policy areas beyond EU social policy. There has also been extensive involvement of "civil society" in the area of EU social policy, championed by both the Commission and the Economic and Social Committee (ECOSOC). This is exemplified by the high profile of the European Social Platform and its role in constituting the Civil Society Contact Group. In its 2005 communication on the "social agenda," the Commission identified a "partnership for change" (Commission of the European Communities 2005a: 3) among public authorities at the local, regional, and national levels; employer and worker representatives; and nongovernmental organizations (NGOs) as a key condition for successful policy implementation. It is little wonder, then, that EU social policy has been the subject of much scholarly interest in the operation, effectiveness, and implications of "new modes of governance" not only in relation to EU social policy but to EU policymaking more generally.

The Directorate General (DG) for Employment, Social Affairs, and Equal Opportunities (DG EMPL, or DG V as it was formerly designated) has enjoyed a long and fruitful relationship with civil society organizations. The origins of this relationship were largely instrumental. Central to this development has been the role of the Commission and its constituent DGs, although more recently, ECOSOC (see Smismans 2003) has also sought to reinvent itself by donning the mantle of champion of the civil society cause. As Mazey and Richardson (1994: 178) noted, lobbyists seeking to influence the Commission often found themselves knocking at an open door. Particularly in such areas as social policy, in which the Commission lacked formal competences, consultation was often a surrogate for action. At the same time, however, the consultation process sought to create a "constituency of support" (Mazey and Richardson 1993) for future actions. While initially, the consultation as surrogate for action model was largely the preserve of the weaker DGs (especially for example, DG EMPL and DG Environment), more recently this model has increasingly been "mainstreamed" throughout the Commission.

"Integration by Stealth"
The legal competence of the Commission in the area of social policy has always been limited.[1] DG EMPL has long made use of its limited competences in a creative manner, however. The practice of establishing action programs and nonbinding guidelines for action in the social field goes back as far as 1962. Indeed, the effectiveness of this incremental, low-key approach was established in the early years of the Coal and Steel Community: "As the High Authority has demonstrated in the social field, the power to enquire, to collect facts, and to make proposals, is often a most effective way of promoting action" (the Commission as cited in Collins 1975: 189–190). The establishment of action programs in sensitive policy areas was often, in turn, used as a means for claiming that the Commission now had some competence in that particular field. For example, although member states could

not agree on a role for the EU in social protection issues, having established the Poverty Program in 1975, the Commission justified its recommendations on social protection (92/441/EEC and 92/442/EEC) on the grounds that it had already created a role for itself in this area (COM [91] 511 Final). DG EMPL also became skilled at utilizing the rhetoric of member states as a rationalization for Commission action. As a senior Commission official argued, Council conclusions "give you a knock out blow in negotiations. If you can cite a European Council conclusion in a debate you're away" (cited in Peterson 1995: 72). By holding member states up for ransom over their stated commitment to the social dimension, the Commission often claimed that it had legitimacy to act in the social field (Cram 1997: 107–109). All of these tactics, of course, are weapons of the weak, resorted to only because more sturdy instruments were unavailable and were vulnerable to the changing intensity of member state oversight. One of the key weapons of the weak has always been the involvement of a wider range of interests able to provide information upon which proposals might be based, to legitimize proposals on the grounds that there was a broad range of support, and to mobilize in support of DG EMPL when its powers were under threat.

From its very early days the Commission sought to utilize the support of wider interests to promote its preferred interpretation of the treaties, for example, on the harmonization of social systems. There was no consensus among member states concerning the necessity of harmonization, rather than coordination, in this field at all (Holloway 1981: 17–27). Yet, on the initiative of the Commission, trade unions, employers associations, and member governments participated in ad hoc committees to examine "ways and means of attaining these ends" (Commission of the European Communities 1962: 180). Member states began to recognize that "such moves by the Commission suggested that governments might be bypassed and action encouraged which was unwelcome to them" (Collins 1975: 191). In December 1962, for example, the Commission organized a European Conference on Social Security aimed at drawing a range of public and private bodies into the discussion on the harmonization of social systems (Commission 1963a: 51–52). Significantly, the member states refused to participate, other than as observers (Holloway 1981: 53). Nevertheless, in October 1963, the Commission issued a preliminary draft program for the harmonization of social security schemes on the basis of the conclusion of the conference (Commission 1963b: 36). Ultimately, member states signaled their discontent by refusing to cooperate with the Commission, and no meetings of the Council of Ministers for Social Affairs were held between October 1964 and December 1966 (Collins 1975: 195; Holloway 1981: 54). In effect, the Commission had had its wings clipped and had to seek out a less confrontational approach. Central to this approach, however, continued to be the process of drawing a wide range of actors into the policy process.

Throughout the 1970s and early 1980s, DG EMPL, enjoying only limited legislative powers, concentrated on developing small-scale catalytic research activities and promoting the institutional development of EU social policy. During this period, for example, the Poverty Program (OJ L 199, 30.7.1975) and the Action Program for Health and Safety (OJ C 13, 12.2.1974) were established and entered their second phases (OJ L 2, 3.1.1985 and OJ C 67, 27.2.1984). A number of EU organizations and committees in the social field were also established, for example, the Standing Committee on Employment (1970), the European Foundation for the Improvement of Living and Working Conditions (Regulation 1365/75), the Social Problems of Agricultural Workers (74/442/EEC), and Equal Opportunities for Men and Women (82/43/EEC).

By establishing research projects and small-scale social programs, issuing communications, and drawing a range of actors into the policy process (whether formally or informally), the Commission engaged in a "softening up" process (cf. Kingdon 1984; Majone 1992) in readiness for the emergence of a policy window.

The 1980s was a period of mixed fortune for DG EMPL. The Single European Act (SEA) gave a marginally increased legal competence, particularly in the area of health and safety, but the enthusiastic embrace of these new powers by DG EMPL quickly led to problems, in particular, in relation to the government of the United Kingdom (UK). Alarmed by the expansive use made by the Commission of its power to use qualified majority voting as a basis for legislation relating to health and safety issues, the UK government—led by Margaret Thatcher—chose to "opt-out" of the social chapter and later, under John Major, to refuse to be party to the Social Protocol of the Maastricht Treaty in 1992. Once again, the legitimacy of Commission activism on the legislative front was under challenge and once again the response of the Commission was to continue its less overtly threatening activities in the form of its action programs and consultation activities.

There was no significant shift in power to the EU in the area of social policy. Yet, by 1992 more than 100 networks of voluntary or community organization were identified in Europe (Harvey 1992: 277). A wide variety of collective forums emerged in the area of EU social policy. Some of these, of course, were completely independent of the EU. A number, however, were independent networks and organizations sponsored by DG EMPL, such as the European Anti-Poverty Network (EAPN), which emerged out of the Poverty Program; the European Disability Forum, which emerged from the activities of the Handicapped People in the EC Living Independently in an Open Society (HELIOS) program; the European Women's Lobby (EWL); and the Migrants' Forum. Others were networks initiated by the EU but coordinated by other organizations, such as the network on older people in poverty and the network on older workers and age discrimination, which were coordinated for DG EMPL by Eurolink Age. Likewise, a number of organizations developed that were initially sparked off by Commission-funded initiatives. The European Federation of National Organizations Working with Homeless (FEANTSA), for example, initially emerged from a DG EMPL–funded conference on homelessness held in Dublin in 1985 (Harvey 1992: 181). Meanwhile, the various programs that DG EMPL ran, such as HELIOS, Community Network of Demonstration Projects on Vocational Training for Women (IRIS), and the Poverty Program, often awarded up to 50 percent of the operation costs for transnational collaborative activities of the actors involved. DG EMPL also funded a number of "observatories" to investigate the issues of, for example, social exclusion, homelessness, and unemployment in the fourteen member states, thus bringing together the relevant actors. Often coordination of these observatories was a crucial source of funding for the Eurogroups. FEANTSA's principal project in 1993, for example, was the European Observatory on Homelessness (FEANTSA 1993). In all of these bodies, national organizations worked collectively at the EU level when they might not otherwise have done so. DG EMPL also established a number of forums in which Eurogroups might jointly participate in the EU policy process. Thus, in the liaison groups concerned, for example, with social inclusion, older people, and education, representatives from the various Eurogroups concerned with the issue in question were brought together. In this way, DG EMPL can be said to have played an important role as "catalyst to collective action" in the social field (Cram 1997: 128–130).

In the difficult context of the early 1990s, with the UK opt-out, the prospects for legislative progress in the social field looked slim. In this context, DG EMPL stepped up its tried and tested method of consultation in an attempt to legitimate its next offering: the consultative Green Paper "European Social Policy: Options for the Union" (Commission of the European Communities 1993). This elicited more than five hundred responses from a wide variety of actors (Commission of the European Communities 1994). Indeed, in the associated action program, reference to support from consultative partners was accorded almost equal status with references to, for example, Council conclusions. Thus, a "wide-ranging consultative process highlighted a broad agreement on a number of key themes which underpin this action programme" (Commission of the European Communities 1995: 8). The consultative method became all the more central to the activities of DG EMPL when in 1994 the Council of Ministers refused to sanction the latest phase of the Poverty Program, in part on the grounds raised by the German Presidency that "by choosing Article 235 as legal basis for its proposal, the European Commission itself clearly showed that there is no Community competence in the fight against poverty" (Agence Europe 1994: 14). After almost twenty years of utilizing small-scale catalytic programs to pursue its goals in the social field, DG EMPL lost one of its preferred instruments. In this context, the consultation of key interests, whether preexisting or engineered, became all the more central to the work of DG EMPL.

Mainstreaming "Good Governance"
Through "Civil Dialogue"

The Maastricht Treaty was a great disappointment to DG EMPL and the various Euro interests active in the social field. Declaration 23, which stressed the importance of cooperation between the EU and "charitable associations and foundations as institutions responsible for social welfare establishments and services," provided the first formal basis for interaction between DG EMPL and the relevant interests in the social field, however. This was quickly seized upon by DG EMPL as providing a rationale for the launch of the Social Policy Forums and for the establishment, in 1997, of a new budget heading (B3-401) for "cooperation with charitable associations and with NGOs and associations dealing with the interests of the elderly" (European Social Policy Forum 1998: 8).

The first Social Policy Forum was held 27–30 March 1996. Around 1,000 people representing NGOs, the social partners, and the Commission met in Brussels. The aim of the forum was to "broaden the scope of interaction between the Commission (together with other EU institutions) and those involved at grassroots level in the field of economic and social action and social cohesion as well as social partners, involved in the social dialogue" (Commission of the European Communities 1996: 1). In 1995 the Social Platform, funded by the Commission, was created to act as interlocutor for the social actors with the Commission at the Social Policy Forum. The origins of the cooperation among the members of the platform had its roots, however, in the consultation process that had emerged following the issue of the 1993 Green Paper. The various organizations, many of which were heavily dependent on the Commission for their emergence and continued existence—such as EAPN, FEANTSA, the Migrants' Forum, EWL, and the Disability Forum—discovered that working together allowed them a stronger voice in negotiations.

From its very first intervention in the 1996 Social Policy Forum, the Social Platform sought to expand the notion of NGO participation at the EU level: "NGOs in the social sector are playing a vital role in expressing, revealing and considering people's needs—and particularly the needs of the most vulnerable members of society—and guaranteeing rights. They are contributing to solidarity among citizens, to the acceptance of responsibility and, therefore, to democracy" (Commission of the European Communities 1996: 15). The forum was considered by the Commission and NGOs to have been a great success, and it was said to "have acted as the starting point for what is known as the European 'civil dialogue'—a relatively new concept with its immediate roots in the 1992 Maastricht Treaty and the Commission's 1993 Green Paper on social policy" (European Social Policy Forum 1998: 4). The Social Platform continued its joint endeavors and "led the way in demanding a Treaty Article," which would provide "a legal underpinning to civil dialogue and would guarantee it is no longer . . . a question of grace and favour" (Beger 2004: 5). Although the Amsterdam Treaty of 1997 was something of a disappointment to DG EMPL and the Social Platform, a new declaration (no. 38) annexed to the treaty did recognize "the important contribution made by voluntary service activities to developing social solidarity" and stated that "the Community will encourage the European dimension of voluntary organisations with particular emphasis on the exchange of information and experiences as well as on the participation of the young and the elderly in voluntary work."

By the time of the second Social Policy Forum in 1998, the agenda had been somewhat overtaken by a budgetary problem that had led to the Commission's closing down a number of its budget lines for NGO and voluntary sector activities. Once again, one of the only instruments available to the Commission was under attack. The UK and Germany had raised questions about the competence of the Commission to fund projects aimed at combating social exclusion. On 12 May 1998, the European Court of Justice (ECJ) had ruled that only "non-significant" actions could be financed without prior adoption of a legal basis. The Court had also stated that a small amount of money or a short duration of funding did not in itself constitute "non-significant." As a result, the Commission had suspended a number of important budget lines related to NGO activities while it reviewed the implications of this ruling. In response, "the NGOs involved in social issues, human rights, development and the environment went into action and created a strong alliance between themselves and the European Trade Union Confederation (ETUC). They also discovered that they could mobilize their members in the capitals to create a strong lobby." In the end the issue was resolved "but not before the NGOs had learnt the importance of alliance building between each other and of coordinating lobbying actions in Brussels with those in the capitals" (Beger 2004: 4).

The objectives of the second Social Policy Forum held 24–26 June 1998 included promoting the idea of a "participative, inclusive and interdependent" European society, strengthening the "civil dialogue," and encouraging the "exchange of concrete examples, demonstrating the wealth of civil society" (European Social Policy Forum 1998: 14). This broad-based agenda was reinforced by Commissioner Pádraig Flynn in his opening speech: "Citizenship is a process of belonging, and of ownership, not an administrative label. It is about people participating in change, not just being recipients of institutional recipes for the future" (European Social Policy Forum 1998:

16). Commission President Jacques Santer, echoing the demand of Willy Brandt in 1972 for a "human face" for Europe, expressed a deeper concern: "It is projects like yours which contribute to making Europe accepted and loved. I would like to salute here the important work that you, the protagonists of civil society, perform at local level. You make Europe a tangible reality" (European Social Policy Forum 1998: 17). This second Social Policy Forum ran in three parallel sessions, one of which was entitled "Promoting Participation and Citizenship." This session concluded: "To this end, it is considered vital that *new modes of governance* be promoted and there should be strengthening of social dialogue, civil dialogue and partnership at all stages of the preparation and implementation of social policy" (European Social Policy Forum 1998: 36; emphasis added).

In strictly legal terms, DG EMPL should never have funded the Poverty Program. The 1997 budget debacle revealed that it might not have had legal competence to fund organizations such as EAPN, whose members emerged from the Poverty Program; EWL; FEANTSA; or the Migrants' Forum and the Disability Forum, some of which went on to become key members of the Social Platform. A weak DG used small pockets of (perhaps illegitimate) money to catalyze organizations and activities at the EU level, and these organizations, when threatened with the loss of their financial support, immediately mobilized to argue for its reinstatement, thus enhancing the competence of the Commission. In the meantime, these organizations, along with many others involved in the civil dialogue, went on to develop and propound a shared discourse concerning the role of NGOs in the civil dialogue and the place of the civil dialogue in promoting democracy and participation.

It was not, of course, only DG EMPL that was struggling in the early 1990s. The appearance of the various "opt-outs" in the Maastricht Treaty and the narrow approval of the treaty in the French referendum had left both the Commission and the member states troubled about the role that the EU institutions ought to play and how they were being perceived at the national level. One of the solutions grasped by the Commission was the notion of "civil dialogue" as a means of improving the so-called democratic deficit at the EU level.

Although the case of DG EMPL is the focus here, the process observed is not unique to the area of social policy. DG Environment, for example, has a long history of involving relevant actors, particularly when it enjoyed no legal basis for action prior to the SEA: "The environment NGOs were probably the most advanced in terms of civil dialogue. Recognized in a Council regulation and enjoying since many years a solid base of core funding, they held regular consultations with the Environment Directorate General and commissioner, and were also regularly consulted in over fifty Commission Committees of Experts" (Beger 2004: 4). Indeed, the creation of the European

Environment Bureau (EEB) in 1974 occurred "when the European Commission started its coordinating role in environmental policies. The Commission did not, however, have much of a mandate, until the Single Act in 1987" (EEB 2004: 8). (It should be noted that the EEB continues to be heavily funded by the Commission, receiving 929,954 euros of its 1,869,736 euro income in 2005 from that body [EEB 2005: annex 1].) Other "Cinderella" sectors, such as development and human rights, have similarly well-developed, though not always well-structured, traditions of civil dialogue between NGOs and the Commission.

DG EMPL has undoubtedly played an important role in the institutionalization of a formal structure for civil dialogue, however, in particular through its role in the establishment of the Social Platform in 1995. The Social Platform played an important role in this "mainstreaming" of the civil dialogue model throughout the Commission: "The Platform has played a significant role in the development of a dialogue between DG Trade and NGOs concerning trade issues, and the World Trade Organization (WTO), in particular. A structured dialogue has now been established between civil society and DG Trade, with regular meetings at which the Platform is represented, and specific 'issues groups' where NGO experts—including Platform members—discuss technical aspects of trade policy with the Commission" (Platform of European Social NGOs 1999–2000: 10). This structured dialogue in DG Trade, as well as the relationship between DG EMPL and the Social Platform, continues to inform other attempts at civil dialogue, as is evidenced in the annex to the recent Green Paper on the role of civil society in drugs policy in the European Union (Commission of the European Communities 2006a).

Although the Social Platform became an independent legal entity in 2001, it continues to be funded by a grant from the European Commission to support its running costs (see www.social-platform.org). Meanwhile, to ensure a coordinated response from civil society organizations to the convention drawing up the Constitutional Treaty, for example, the Civil Society Contact Group (CSCG) was established to bring together the voices of the various NGO sectors. Its membership includes the European NGO Confederation for Relief and Development (CONCORD), representing development NGOs; Green 10, representing environmental NGOs; the EU Human Rights and Democratization Contact Group (HRDN), representing human rights NGOs; the European Forum for Arts and Heritage (EFAH/FEAP), representing culture NGOs; the European Public Health Alliance (EPHA), representing public health NGOs; EWL, representing women's NGOs; and the Social Platform, representing social NGOs. The roots of cooperation for these organizations came in part from their earlier joint action in relation to the Commission's suspension of budget lines in 1997; however, within this grouping, "leadership has come from the Platform" (Jarre 2005).[2]

European Social Policy and "New Modes of Governance" in Historical Perspective

The Commission, acting as a "purposeful-opportunist" (Cram 1993, 1997) in the area of EU social policy, has developed a number of key skills over time.

1. One skill is the ability to *select appropriate policy instruments* in response to the emergence of policy windows and to *package policies* in ways least likely to engender the opposition of member states by *rationalizing interventions* in terms of popular rhetoric or previous council commitments. "Demonstrating that there is a problem which can be attacked by one's favourite instrument is a very real preoccupation of participants in the policy process" (Majone 1989: 117). In a similar vein, Mosher and Trubek (2003: 67) have noted, in relation to the introduction of the EES, how in response to the new policy window (created by the employment crisis in Europe during a period of slow economic growth and exacerbated by the commitment of member states to the "stability and growth pact"), "deft lobbying and manoeuvring by the Commission put subtle pressure on member states to use the EU to respond to the crisis." Creative interpretation of its delegated powers has also allowed the Commission to create precedents for its role in a particular policy area, in much the same way as it has been argued that the Commission has sought to increase its standing within the EES "by establishing and conscientiously upholding a fictitious sole right of initiative within the field of employment policy" (Deganis 2006: 21).

2. The Commission also engaged in what Majone (1992: 6–7), building on Kingdon (1984), called a *"softening up process"*: paving the way for the Commission's preferred course of action should a "policy window" open up (Cram 1997: 37–38). Creating a precedent for action in a particular field has included funding small-scale action programs, creating committees or observatories, and initiating research. It should be noted, for example, that the Mutual Information System on Employment Policies (MISEP) was created in 1982, followed by the Community System of Documentation on Employment (SYSDEM) in 1989. Building upon these, the European Employment Observatory (EEO) was formally created in 1989 with the aim of developing a "network between member states and the Commission to exchange information through the provision of comparative data and research on employment policies and labour market trends" and was a direct predecessor to the EES.[3]

3. *Facilitating the emergence of a policy window* is an additional skill. From its early days, the Commission sought to create a constituency of support for its actions in areas where it lacked legal competence. Particularly in areas where its powers were limited, the involvement of a broad range of actors was used to identify salient issues and to generate grounds to push for the extension of the Commission's competence (Cram 1993, 1997). Indeed,

playing the role of *"catalyst to collective action"* (Cram 1994, 1997) in the area of social policy, DG EMPL was not averse to creating a relevant group at the European level when one could not be found. By encouraging groups to voice the need for new policies at the EU level, the Commission also sought to create opportunities for future action.

Idema and Kelemen's (2006: 117–118) interpretation of the application of the open method of coordination to the field of EU social policy fits rather neatly with the analysis presented above:

> Advocates of a strong EU role in social policy find themselves hamstrung by the EU's lack of competence to regulate in this area. While they might wish to impose binding EU law in this field via the traditional community method, opponents of a powerful role in social policy will not permit this. Opponents of a powerful "social Europe" have, however, been willing to allow the operation of the OMC in this field, as they see the OMC as a rather innocuous exercise that entails no binding commitments. Advocates of EU social policy hope that OMC—even where it fails to produce concrete effects in the short run—may prepare the ground for more codified, legally binding initiatives in the long run. . . . For advocates of European social policy focusing on the *long durée,* the immediate effectiveness of the OMC is secondary. The OMC will be a success simply if it contributes to the development of a "coordination reflex" that helps move social policy from the periphery of EU policymaking to the core and sets the stage for more ambitious initiatives in the future.

Conclusion

In the area of EU social policy, the relationship between the key *actors* remains broadly the same. Member states retain the upper hand, and the Commission is forced to act with institutional creativity to carve out a role for itself. The *methods* employed by the Commission and its attempts to draw a wider range of actors into the policy process also remain broadly the same. The Commission has continued to play a role in "steering" or "governing" the direction of EU social policy, which increasingly serves as a model for the spread of "new modes of governance" to other sensitive areas of EU policymaking. The *context* in which these actors operate and these methods are employed has altered dramatically, however. The methods elaborated above traditionally formed part of what Majone (2005) described as "integration by stealth" or what Margaret Thatcher decried, at the 1990 Conservative Party conference, as "socialism through the back Delors." The rise of discourses (often encouraged and mainstreamed by the Commission) concerning the role of "civil society" in contributing to participatory democracy or to the development of a "European Public Space" has created a context, however, in which instead of being unaccountable "integration by stealth," the incorporation of a wide number of actors through new policy methods is increasingly viewed as a model of "good governance."

Notes

1. This early historical section draws upon Cram (1997).

2. Indeed, Marie-Françoise Wilkinson, who set up EAPN, became the first director of the Social Platform and was one of the speakers for the CSCG at the convention hearing. Similarly, the EWL, which was created on the initiative of the Women's Information Unit of the Commission in September 1990, now occupies a controversial position. EWL is a member of the CSCG by virtue of its membership in the Social Platform as well as being an individual member of the CSCG. The EWL was also represented directly by its director, Mary MacPhail, at the convention hearing (European Convention 2002).

3. See http://europa.eu/scadplus/leg/en/cha/c10205.htm.

PART 2

Hierarchy as a Catalyst for Experiments in Governance

8

Cooperation and Hierarchy in EU Competition Policy

Dirk Lehmkuhl

Since the overhaul of its enforcement provisions in 2004, European competition policy displays some interesting governance features that allow for quite different interpretations. One is very much in line with Tömmel's observation in Chapter 2 that cooperation as a mode of governance plays an increasing role in the European Union system. It highlights the emergence of soft modes of governance such as the Commission's increasing reference to guidelines, notices, and interpretations in the areas of state aid, antitrust, and merger control policy. A further indicator of this interpretation is the devolution of enforcement competences leading to a constellation in which the music of European competition law will in future be performed by an orchestra of national competition authorities plus the European Commission rather than by the Commission as a soloist. Furthermore, the incorporation of national competition authorities and the Commission into the network of European competition authorities institutionalizes the shift from hierarchy to cooperation (see Chapter 15). In a similar vein, the new system emphasizes private enforcement of European competition provisions and decisions. The new enforcement policy no longer counts exclusively on action of competition authorities but encourages actions of private parties to detect breaches of competition rules. As will be shown, the move to private enforcement goes even beyond the alternative of litigation in national courts and involves private arbitration as a mode to resolve conflicts arising, for instance, from suspected abuses of dominant market positions.

The second interpretation acknowledges the existence of elements that are usually associated with cooperation as a dominant mode of governance. In contrast to the first, however, it delves deeper into the actual practices and the operational side of interactions. The closer look reveals that cooperation operates much more in the shadow of hierarchy than is obvious at first glance. It is emphasized that the European Commission's practice of taking recourse to legally nonbinding modes of cooperation allows for bypassing both the Council and the European Parliament. By following that path, the Commission's sectoral policy guidelines not only exercise pressure on market actors but also achieve a significant authority with respect to both national competition authorities and national courts. The basic check of the way in which the Commission exercises its discretion derives from judicial review by European courts rather than from control of the member states.

To substantiate the finding of a coexistence of alternative modes of governance and to answer the question of how this observation relates to systemic features of the European Union (EU), the chapter proceeds in three steps. In a first approach, it presents basic features of European competition policy. An overview then identifies the relationship between European courts and the Commission, the reference to soft law instruments by the Commission, the European network of competition agencies, and the move to private enforcement of competition provision as areas in which it is possible to trace the ambiguities in the modes of governance. The final section interprets the findings with respect to both the systemic features of EU governance and to the institutional balance in the EU's multilevel governance.

Basic Developments in European Community Competition Policy

The objective of competition policy is to fight monopolies, oligopolies, cartels, and market-sharing arrangements as well as subsidies and state protection. Most generally, it is a means of achieving a more efficient allocation of resources, a promotion of innovation, lower consumer prices, and by means of all that, an overall increase of societal welfare. As these objectives more or less describe the purpose of the economic integration in Europe, the delegation of competences to the European level was only a logical step. The signatories of the European Community (EC) Treaty were however more restrictive in delegating competences to the Commission than the signatories of the Treaty of Paris that granted the High Authority of the European Coal and Steel Community (ECSC) with more encompassing competences (Allen 1996; McGowan and Cini 1998; Wilks and Bartle 2002; Wilks 2005a).

Nevertheless, the inclusion into the Treaty of the European Economic Community (EEC) was an important starting point for competition policy-making. The respective articles in the treaty that referred to restrictive practices (Article 85–94 EEC, designated since the Treaty of Amsterdam as Article 81–90 Treaty Establishing the European Community [or TEC]) and Regulation 17/1962 as the procedural regulation to these articles provided the European Commission with a very strong position over companies. Furthermore, it provided the European Commission with the monopoly to grant exemption for otherwise prohibited behavior.

The actual development of Commission activities in the different dimensions of EC competition policy was quite uneven. For instance, before the late 1980s there was no substantial control of state aid, and liberalization of utilities began only in the late 1990s (Wilks 2005b: 117). At the same time, control of mergers and acquisitions, the realm that tends to attract most visibility and media attention because of the frequent involvement of well-known companies, was omitted in the Treaty of Rome, basically because it was not thought of as a matter of priority.

In contrast to the signatories of the Treaty of Rome, the Commission conceived of mergers, acquisitions, and joint ventures as a potential source of anticompetitive behavior. Given the omission of merger provisions in the treaty, it tried in the 1970s and 1980s to use Articles 85 and 86 EEC (today, respectively, Articles 81 and 82 TEC) as instruments to challenge certain mergers that it considered to be restrictive of competition. In its efforts, it was on several occasions backed by judgments of the European Court of Justice (ECJ) (McGowan and Cini 1999: 179; OECD 2005: 13). Yet, by the mid-1980s there was a substantial degree of legal uncertainty that raised a critique from both industry and some member states.

The German and British criticism concerning a potentially too lax and politicized merger control policy culminated in the call for an independent European merger control agency in the 1990s. At the same time, the Commission faced additional difficulties. Its move to address state aids and state monopolies in the realm of public utilities was not welcomed by the member states, and at the same time a lack of precision and stringency in the interpretation of the concept of market position made both the European Court of Justice and the Court of First Instance (CFI) override Commission decisions on several occasions (McGowan and Wilks 1995: 150; Morgan 1998; McGowan and Cini 1999: 181).

In combination, the chastisement of Commission decisions by European courts and the criticism of the member states fueled "protracted and often passionate negotiations" (McGowan and Cini 1999: 180) that led to a new merger control regulation in 1990 (Council Regulation 4064/89). The intensity of the debate was to some extent due to conflicts about the interpretation of the principle of subsidiarity, that is, over the relationship between the competences of the European Commission and the national level in addressing merger cases. In particular, those countries with well-established control agencies, such as Germany and the United Kingdom, were opposing too strong a dominance of the European Commission. The final compromise established absolute turnover thresholds allowing for a "necessarily arbitrary" determinant of either the Commission's or a member state's jurisdiction on a case-by-case basis (Morgan 2001: 456).

With the new merger control regulation, the European Commission was for the first time equipped with proper control competences in the realm of merger and acquisition. The reality of an increasing workload made the situation precarious again, however, from the early 1990s onward. The Commission continued its practice of using bloc exemptions (granting approval to an entire class of cases according to Article 81[3] TEC) and so-called comfort letters (interim measures relieving companies from future fines in case of a negative decision by the Commission) to meet the deadlines.

In this situation, decentralization became an ever more appealing option for the Commission. *Decentralization* became the word of the year in 1993, and the Commission's "Notice on the Co-operation Between National Courts and Commission"[1] must be seen against this background (McGowan and Wilks 1995: 168n43). In full awareness that its long-time "procedural bible" (Regulation 17/1962) was more and more inadequate in an environment that had already changed significantly and that with the prospect of an enlargement the EU was going to change dramatically, the European Commission has pursued a fundamental overhaul of its antitrust policy. Following the issuing of a Green and White Paper on merger control and an interim amendment of the 1989 merger regulation in 1997, the Council of Ministers adopted a new legal framework for the enforcement of Articles 81 and 82 TEC in 2002.[2]

Entering into force in May 2004, the new legal framework of Regulation 1/2003 replaced the forty-year-old system of Regulation 17/1962. The regulation, with its new approach to the implementation of the antitrust and merger control policy of Articles 81 and 82 TEC, can be summarized as follows. The prior ex ante notification control is being replaced by a system of ex post control. Alongside this replacement came two important changes. Rather than awaiting a formal (positive or negative) clearance by the Commission, companies now bear the burden of proof, as the merging units have to self-assess the merger's market impact (and to suggest remedies if necessary). What is more, under the new regime, the ex post control of the actual market impact of a merger or acquisition is now exercised by either the European Commission or national competition authorities and national courts. This implies that the right to grant exemptions according to Article 81(3) TEC is no longer a monopoly of the Commission but may also be exerted by national competition authorities and national courts. In order to guarantee coherence and consistency in the implementation of competition provisions and in the jurisprudence on European and national authorities, a couple of safeguards have been introduced. To start with, Regulation 1/2003 imposes European competition law in place of national competition law for all restrictive agreements when potentially affecting trade between member states. Furthermore, the new regulatory regime implies close cooperation between the European Commission and national competition authorities. To this end, the regulation entails provisions that should ensure an exchange of documents and evidence both vertically between the European and national administrative competition units and horizontally from one state to another.

The decentralized enforcement of the European competition provisions is tailored around the concept of the emerging European Competition Network (ECN), comprising the national competition authorities and the European Commission. In addition to its function as infrastructure for the mandatory exchange of information and for consultation and debate, the ECN has the crucial task of allocating cases to either the Commission or national authorities. Although national courts will not be part of the ECN, they may request procedural, legal, and economic information from the European Commission. At the same time, both the Commission and national competition authorities may submit written observations to national courts. Finally, the very fact that national courts come into play is related to the importance assigned to private enforcement. The European Commission explicitly aimed at encouraging actions before national courts by any undertaking or final consumer suffering from an infringement of EC provisions or Commission decisions.

Cooperation and Hierarchy in EC Competition Policy

The rough review of basic developments provides ample evidence that supports the importance of cooperation as a dominant mode of governance in various realms of competition policy in Europe. The concept of decentralization and the creation of a network of competition agencies are only two examples. At the same time, it is necessary to link these findings with the observation that the strong role of the Commission and European courts as two supranational institutions confirms the characterization of competition policy as being the "first supranational policy" (McGowan and Wilks 1995). Taking into account the supremacy of European law and the strong position of the Commission, or even more precisely, the powerful role of the Directorate General for Competition (DG Comp) in the protection of competition and the promotion of realizing the internal market, an overwhelmingly strong emphasis on cooperation and voluntary compliance is at least questionable. In what follows, I will account for the ambivalent observations by looking at four important areas of competition policy: the interaction between the Commission and European courts, the use of soft law instruments in state aid, merger, and antitrust policies; the European network of competition agencies; and the private enforcement of competition provisions.

The Relevance of Court-Commission Interactions

As has been intimated above, the regulatory framework of European competition policy has been made up both of what was in the Treaty of Rome *and* what was not. On the one hand, primary and secondary legislation in Article 85–94 EEC (Article 81–90 TEC) and Regulation 17/1962 equipped the Commission with a significant authority to develop European competition policy over time into one of the most influential policies that cuts across sectors and addresses states, substate units, and private undertakings alike. On the other hand, the treaty provisions were neither precise nor the actual numbers of directives or regulations extensive. On the contrary, it can be argued that treaty provisions necessarily remained limited with respect to both precision and depth, and, moreover, secondary legislation played only a minor role in the design of rules governing competition policy. Take, for instance, the case of state aid control; it was not until 1998 that the member states agreed to adopt the first official regulations. Or look at the case of control of mergers and acquisitions, an area that was deliberately not included in the Treaty of Rome and one in which the legislation that the member states finally managed to issue by the late 1980s was already inadequate when it entered into force.

The case of merger control policy provides a good starting point to elaborate on how the interaction between the Commission and European courts contributed in a specific way to the development of competition policy in Europe. Basically, two patterns can be distinguished: (1) judicial review of Commission decisions and (2) the Commission's reference to court judgments in its guidelines and notices. I will start with the issue of court review of Commission decisions.

From the very beginning, the Commission perceived the omission of merger control in the Treaty of Rome as a severe handicap for its capacity to procedurally and substantially exert control over mergers and acquisitions. Although acknowledging that Article 85 EEC (Article 81 TEC) did not cover issues of concentration, DG Comp thought of Article 86 EEC (Article 82 TEC) as a venue in which to probe the issue—although this venue bore the risk of a ruling by the ECJ (Goyder 2003: 335–336). Indeed, the ECJ had to decide in a number of cases on Commission decisions. Two cases of court review of Commission decisions contributed particularly to an expansion of the Commission's jurisdiction in merger cases. In the *Continental Can* ruling (case 6/72 [1973]), the ECJ sanctioned the Commission's action to regulate concentration with Article 86 EEC (82 TEC) on abuse of dominant position. Furthermore, in the tobacco industry judgment on Philip Morris (cases 142 and 156/84 [1987]), the ECJ stated that Article 85 EEC (81 TEC) refers not only to restrictive market practices but may also be applied to mergers. With its judgment, the Court shared the Commission's approach of giving effect to the spirit of primary legislation and ensuring consistency between treaty provisions. The shared teleological approach of Commission decisions and court rulings specifies which general treaty provisions helped to provide EC competition policy with contours. At the same time, it also contributed to a certain degree of uncertainty for both member states and companies (Goyder 2003: 339).

Uncertainty and discontent of both member states and European companies related to a too lax and politicized control policy and to shortcomings in the economic quality of Commission decisions. One pattern of reaction was the call by some member states, in particular by Germany and the United Kingdom (UK), for a specialized European competition authority that would take over a substantial share of DG Comp's functions (McGowan and Wilks 1995). A second pattern of reaction was the number of appeals against Commission decisions. In this respect, the Court of First Instance, which was established in 1989, not only doubled the judicial capacity of the Community but also provided a practical venue for complaints (OECD 2005: 13). As of September 2007, the CFI had issued thirty-one judgments under the EC Merger Regulation and had overruled almost ten Commission decisions (Bailey 2007: 114). In 2002 alone, the CFI issued three annulments that left their mark because they questioned the Commission's ability to adequately assess the economic consequences of envisaged mergers between undertakings.[3] As mentioned above, the Commission's response to these problems was the formulation of a proposal for a new merger control package and the creation of a special economic unit including the position of a chief economist (OECD 2005: 13).

To sum up, the first pattern of governance relates more to the ideal type of hierarchy than to any other mode of governance. On the one hand, it has been the Commission that established itself at the center of EC competition policy, and its decisions have had an increasing impact on states in the area of state aids and on companies in the areas of mergers and antitrust. On the other hand, it is not possible to tell the story of EC competition policy without emphasizing the role of European courts. Even though both the ECJ and the CFI have frequently supported the Commission in its approach to make competition policy the prime instrument for implementing a liberalized single market in Europe, judicial review by European courts has also been a strong—perhaps the strongest—means to control the Commission. What is true for Commission decisions also holds for the Commission's policy to govern competition policy matters by soft law instruments.

The Use of Nonbinding Instruments

One way of dealing with uncertainties in the interpretation of the regulatory framework would have been to enact less ambiguous secondary legislation. Indeed, a first draft of a merger regulation was issued a few months after the *Continental Can* ruling of the ECJ in 1973. The member states could not agree on a common position, however. Only after the ECJ stated that Article 85 EEC refers not only to restrictive market practices but also may be applied to mergers (cases 142 and 156/84) did the member states accept the necessity of issuing a proper merger regulation. Faced with the long-lasting political resistance of the member states to the issuance of new secondary legislation, the Commission made use of more than just decisions in individual cases to demonstrate its concrete understanding of general rules. In addition, to guide its policies on state aid, merger, and antitrust, it opted for the application of legally nonbinding instruments as an alternative that would overcome uncertainties resulting from a limited scope and precision in the regulatory framework of EC competition policy.

In the area of state aid policy, it was as early as 1971 that the Commission, in a letter to the member states, laid down some principles on its strategy to deal with state aids in the clothing and textile industries. Since then, the Commission has established a practice of applying legally nonbinding instruments over the years. For instance, it has done so for interpreting treaty provisions, for clarifying procedural questions, for explaining its own or the case law of European courts, or for providing information on its future policy objectives. The form of these instruments may be that of guidelines, notices, communications, recommendations, and, as just mentioned, even letters (Aldestam 2004: 14). Complementing its regulations, for example, on bloc exemption on small and medium enterprises, the Commission issued notices and guidelines to clarify, among others, its policies about aid for regional development, research and development or environmental protection, and corporate rescue and restructuring (OECD 2005: 33). What is more, to improve compliance with the regulatory framework as set out by hard and soft measures on state aid, the Commission does not rely only on case-related enforcement. Rather, since 2002 the Commission has written a biannual state aid scoreboard that replaces its prior annual surveys and is meant to make the granting of state aid by the member states transparent and to indicate general developments.

In the field of control of mergers and acquisitions under antitrust provisions, it is possible to trace a substantial reference to "nonregulatory documents" in the form of notices, guidelines, and so on.[4] For instance, the Commission's first notice on agreements of minor importance that are expected not to restrict competition under Article 81(1) TEC ("de minimis Notice") was published in 1986 and has been revised several times since. Also, "comfort letters" were used as a quick and informal means that allowed the Commission to decide on cases by communicating to companies that their agreement does not infringe on Article 81(1) TEC. Over time, the Commission's experience, experiments, and habits with the merger control regulation of 1989 have evolved into "efficient 'best practices,' which are now the subject of extensive soft-law guidance" (OECD 2005: 67). This practice has continued since the new merger regulation of 2003. The regulation provides for a new approach to the implementation and enforcement of the antitrust and merger control policy of Articles 81 and 82 TEC. It only provides the skeleton of the new regulatory regime, however, leaving some important questions open; including, for instance, the scope of exemption provisions according to Article 81(3) TEC, the clarification of criteria for case allocation, or measures to ensure a harmonized application of European provisions by national competition authorities (e.g., leniency provisions). The Commission has put flesh to the bones of the new regulation by adopting an implementation regulation, and by June 2007 had issued more than twenty notices and guidelines to address these questions and to provide guidance in various aspects of the enforcement of Articles 81 and 82 TEC.[5]

As has been mentioned, cooperation via legally nonbinding instruments is a means for the Commission to cope with ambiguities und uncertainties in the regulatory framework of EC competition policy. Of course, many of the objectives could have also been accomplished by regulations. Yet, from the perspective of the Commission, soft law instruments had the advantage of combining time effectiveness, flexibility, policy stability, and credibility—in addition to providing the Commission with the highest possible level of discretion (Cini 2001: 199). Sometimes the term *policy framework* is used as a generic term to describe the function of legally nonbinding instruments issued by the Commission (Aldestam 2004). There are two specific features of these instruments outside of Article 249 TEC that shed additional light on these modes of governance. On the one hand, none of these measures requires consultation or approval of the Council or the European Parliament. As such, administrative rule making provides the Commission with a substantial degree of discretion (Hoffmann 2006). On the other hand, soft modes of governance add to the predictability of policy implementation, as they not only provide guidance about Commission policies but also bind the Commission itself to its practices. In 2006 the ECJ stated that although guidelines "may not be regarded as rules of law which [the Commission] is always bound to observe, they nevertheless form rules of practice from which [the Commission] may not depart in an individual case without giving reasons that are compatible with the principle of equal treatment."[6]

The European Network of Competition Agencies

Cooperation as a form of governance is of particular importance under the new regulatory framework of merger control. According to the new framework, not only the Commission but also national competition authorities and courts have the competence to fully apply European competition provisions. Although the decentralization of competences is in line with the general concept of subsidiarity, it poses a challenge to a consistent and coherent application of European competition provisions. To mitigate this challenge, cooperation between relevant authorities (i.e., not European or national courts) has been institutionalized within the ECN. With the objective of achieving an effective and coherent enforcement of European provisions in the system of parallel, that is, national and European, competences, the ECN concentrates on issues such as an efficient division of cases within the network, a coherent and consistent application of provisions by all members of the network, and finally, an efficient fact-finding through cooperation, assistance, and confidential exchange of information. The organizational structure of the ECN should ensure that these policy objectives are realized in the day-to-day practices. There are basically four forums within the ECN: at the highest level there is the biannual meeting of general directors of all network members in which major policy issues are discussed; the ECN Plenary involves the officials acting as liaisons with the network and national competition authorities and the ECN unit of the Commission's DG Comp; plenary meetings are usually prepared by working groups that explore specific issues such as leniency programs, sanctions, or horizontal procedural issues; finally, there are sector-specific subgroups involving experts on issues such as railways or energy.

Both European and national competition authority officials assess the achievements of the ECN in very positive terms. In particular, the dynamism within "the network, the commitment, the professionalism, and the cooperative spirit of all ECN members" (Lowe 2005: 4) and the "willingness to understand one another, to overcome difficulties, and to reach compromises where compromises are necessary" (ABA 2005: 6) have been highlighted. These observations closely match the broader finding that the existence of a "network strengthens incentives for jurisdictions to seek convergence because convergence allows for deeper and broader cooperation" (Raustiala 2002: 68).

In this respect, the ECN is part of a broader international and European pattern of policy cooperation via networks. At the international level, informal networks have gained attention as means of peer-to-peer ties between domestic officials and their foreign counterparts in loosely structured interactions that allow for exchanging information and harmonizing implementation practices (Raustiala 2002; Slaughter 2004a; Slaughter and Zaring 2007). In Europe, the concept of networks has been used to describe quite different observations. According to a broader interpretation, "network governance" has been identified as a characteristic feature of policymaking in Europe's vertically and horizontally segmented polity (Kohler-Koch and Eising 1999). In a more restricted sense we find the concept of networks related to the characterization of the EU as a regulatory state, with regulatory networks involving the "full set of actors, institutions, norms and rules that are of importance for the process and the outcome of public regulation in a given sector" (Eberlein and Grande 2005: 91). The existence of European networks of regulatory agencies is interpreted either as a new step of delegation (from member states to independent national regulators and then to networks of European regulators) or as a reaction to incomplete vertical delegation, that is, the unwillingness of member states to create a European regulator (Coen and Thatcher 2008; Eberlein and Newman 2008).

Given the assessment of the dynamics within the network, the ECN also matches the framework of this book, which relates modes of governance to systemic features of the European Union. In this regard, the emergence of the ECN is an expression of the shift away from hierarchy toward cooperation. At the same time, however, this interpretation is questioned by more skeptical voices that point to centralizing rather than decentralizing tendencies related to the implementation of Regulation 1/2003 in general and the role of the Commission in the ECN in particular. The arguments of these skeptical voices can be summarized as follows.

A first aspect relates to the observation that although the ECN is an informal forum of cooperation, it involves a formalization of prior forms of cooperation between competition authorities in Europe. Prior to the new regulatory framework, competition authorities met and discussed the application of competition rules in the Association of European Competition Authorities. Similar to the ECN, this forum also had working groups on specific themes of general interest such as multijurisdictional mergers and economic exchanges (Smith-Hillman 2006: 42). With the provisions leading to the inauguration of the ECN, the voluntary basis of this information exchange has been transformed into a mandatory form of cooperation, now including the European Commission.

A second aspect relates to the special role and position of the European Commission in the ECN. Although in theory the Commission is but one member of the "European family of competition authorities," de facto DG Comp may at least be seen as a primus inter pares and, according to an even more dramatic interpretation, dominates policies within the network in a de facto hierarchical manner. The primus inter pares interpretation largely relates to the information advantage of DG Comp. DG Comp gathers information from experts and interest groups via hearings and comments on its drafting of papers, it has jurisdiction for the most important multijurisdictional cases, and it scores high in terms of budget and other resources in relation to other competition authorities. The latter point is anything but trivial, as it stresses the importance of asymmetries among the partners of the ECN. Given the economic and legal complexity of cases, to be a full-fledged member of the European family of competition authorities largely depends on the endowment with appropriate powers of surveillance, investigation, and enforcement. At the moment, however, there seem to be different classes of family membership, with some first-rate members in terms of budget and case load, including the British, French, German, and Italian agencies in addition to DG Comp, and a majority of other family members lagging behind (Riley 2003a: 658; Wilks 2007: 5).

In a context in which there are information and resource asymmetries, the Commission's practice of issuing notices, guidelines, and other forms of nonbinding rules strengthens its position in procedural and substantial terms vis-à-vis national competition authorities and in relation to national courts. For instance, in a frequently cited case from the area of social policy (occupational diseases), the ECJ stated that "national courts are bound to take recommendations into consideration in order to decide disputes submitted to them, in particular where they cast light on the interpretation of national measures adopted in order to implement them or where they are designed to supplement binding Community provisions" (Case C-322/88, 18). It is this combination of the Commission's ability to set out policy frameworks via nonbinding instruments on the one hand and its formal competences—for instance, to decide which cases have a European dimension—on the other hand that cast doubt on an interpretation of the ECN as a pure form of co-operation. Rather, the complexity of competences and interactions within the network has inspired somewhat contradictory interpretations such as "directed networks" or "hierarchical networks" (Wilks 2007: 6).

Private Enforcement

An important feature of cooperation as a mode of governance is the extension of participants beyond the executives of member states. In particular, the inclusion of nonstate actors is frequently regarded as a strong indicator for new modes of governance in action (Eberlein and Kerwer 2004; Treib, Bähr, and Falkner 2005). Given this indicator, the concept of private enforcement that has been introduced by the merger control regime seems to be an example of the mode of cooperation in EU competition policy. Similar to the discussion about the ECN, I will address this new feature with the intention of elaborating on a more balanced interpretation of the modes of governance involved. To do so, the following features will be addressed: the new systems of approving mergers, the concept of private enforcement, and the role of national courts and of private dispute settlement.

A first aspect that requires some attention refers to the abolishment of the old notification regime according to which a positive or negative ex ante clearance of the Commission provided the necessary legal backdrop for companies' cross-border activities. As mentioned above, the system of prior notification had put stress on the Commission's working capacity almost throughout its fifty years of existence (OECD 2005). The Commission's way of handling the intensive workload was to operate with bloc exemptions, comfort letters, and other instruments that helped to live up to deadlines. The situation has changed significantly under the new system. Basically, the burden of proof for market-distorting effects of an envisaged merger or cross-border economic activities has been shifted from the Commission to the private parties involved. According to the new practice, companies have to assess themselves whether their planned activities impact negatively on the respective markets, and, moreover, they are required to make proposals of how to remedy negative effects.

The shift from a German-style system of ex ante notification to a French format of ex post control is reminiscent of the original discussions of EC competition provisions in which German and French negotiators had advocated their respective model (Quack and Djelic 2005). What is more, the new system basically operates according to the practice that has long been used to apply French competition law.

A second important innovation in EU competition policy is less reminiscent of earlier European discussions and practices; instead it resembles much more a mimicking of US antitrust enforcement practices. Although the influence of fundamental principles of US antitrust regulation on EC competition provisions has always been very strong (Quack and Djelic 2005: 266), the encouragement of private enforcement by activities of companies before national courts has significantly been inspired by the US experience. About 90 percent of US competition enforcement is by private actions before courts. The general goal of an enforcement system is to influence the incentives to comply with competition laws by detecting and sanctioning violations. Whereas in a public enforcement system public authorities (i.e., the Commission at the EU level and the national competition authorities at the member state level) investigate suspected misconduct, a private enforcement scheme is characterized by private parties' seeking civil action before national courts.

A system based on private enforcement is associated with attributes of lower costs of detecting violations and gathering information and of better information on industry practice and behavior. "Competitors and takeover targets are ideal litigants in terms of litigation capability because they are likely to have the skill, knowledge of the industry, financial resources, legal sophistication, and motivation to mount a powerful case with the speed and precision necessary in merger injunctions" (Brodley 1995: 36). At the same time, a private enforcement system may also be used strategically when firms seek to "win in the courts what they were unable to win in honest competition with their rivals" (McAfee, Mialon, and Mialon 2006: 1; see also Segal and Whinston 2006: 9–11). In its "Green Paper: Damages Actions for Breach of the EC Antitrust Rules" (COM[2005] 672), the Commission hailed private law enforcement as a powerful policy instrument. At the same time, the Commission was not naive about the conditions under which private parties can bring actions for alleged breaches of the Community antitrust rules before the national courts of the member states. On the one hand, private enforcement in Europe operates in a different legal environment with damage compensation or class action and so on. On the other hand, then Competition Commissioner Monti referred to the dark side of private enforcement when the social costs of litigation outweigh its benefits. As a consequence, he called for an approach that should avoid falling "into the excesses that we have seen in other legal systems" (Monti 2004a: 5). The new control regime seeks to achieve this objective both by building pillars of enforcement and, at the same time, by improving the awareness and acceptance of private litigation by companies and courts of the member states alike.

The latter point brings us to the third aspect of our discussion of private enforcement and its relevance as a mode of governance. Private enforcement is enforcement by means of legal action before a court brought by an affected party of a breach of European competition rules. Important to note is that it is national rather than European courts that take the responsibility of administering these actions. The flipside of the devolution of enforcement competences is the risk of an inconsistent and incoherent application of European laws in courts of the member states. To address this risk and to prepare national judges for the expected development, the Commission has put into place programs to improve the training of judges in EC competition law, "which are being attended well" (Monti 2004a: 4). In addition, the Commission strengthens its efforts to ensure a harmonized application of EC competition provisions before national courts and by national competition authorities by setting up a database of EC competition cases in the member states. And finally, there is the Commission notice on the cooperation with national courts that sets the framework for the interaction between the Commission and national courts.[7] It remains to be seen whether all these measures will suffice to render obsolete the impression that under the new merger control regime, national courts will be degraded to become *"'Erfüllungsgehilfen' der Kommission"* (servants to the Commission).[8] Although the Commission is convinced that the situation is going to develop positively in the long run, the historical experience with the Commission's 1993 notice on the cooperation between the European Commission and national courts is sobering: there was almost a complete absence of national courts asking for help (Riley 2003b).

A final aspect refers to the observation that the new approach of private enforcement is not limited to litigation in national courts but also involves the encouragement of private arbitration. Arbitration is a means of private dispute settlement that has gained significance in resolving disputes in transnational economic activities since the 1970s. Advantages of arbitration are traditionally seen in its neutrality, flexibility, confidentiality, time and cost efficiency, technical expertise, and the binding character of its awards (Dezalay and Garth 1996; Lehmkuhl 2003; Mattli 2001).

Traditionally, the European Commission as well as the European Court of Justice had a rather skeptical stance toward arbitration. In the area of competition law, this critical position derives, for instance, from the practice of a prominent Swedish arbitration center's actively marketing its "off shore" services to settle disputes without intervention of the Commission (Dolmans and Grierson 2003: 38) Yet, the situation has shifted "from distrust to embrace" (Komninos 2001: 214), basically for two reasons. Arbitration centers and arbitrators have discovered EC antitrust policy as a new market. For instance, the International Chamber of Commerce in Paris, which with its International Court of Arbitration hosts the most prominent international arbitration institution, has set up a Task Force on Arbitrating Competition Law Issues to follow the work of the European Commission on private enforcement.[9] At the same time, the Commission now recognizes the advantages of arbitration with its broad acceptance by the business community as a "particularly quick and efficient way of bringing to an end any possible infringement and providing legal certainty" (Dolmans and Grierson 2003: 38). Today, the Commission not only accepts arbitration in competition matters but also incorporates private dispute resolution in its decisions on mergers and acquisitions (Blanke 2006; Lehmkuhl 2007).

In this respect, private arbitration fits perfectly in the Commission's strategy of decentralizing the implementation and enforcement of EC antitrust policies. The incorporation of arbitration into the private enforcement policy of European competition policy may also serve as another example either for coordinated governance by the incorporation of private actors or even for the private regulation of business conduct through private enforcement (Wigger and Nölke 2007: 494). Yet, a different interpretation is also possible. In practice, the Commission increasingly takes recourse to arbitration as a credible procedural remedy in antitrust and merger control issues of Articles 81 and 82 TEC. In this regard, the incorporation of arbitration reflects the Commission's practice not to accept the companies' own proposals to prevent market-distorting effects of cross-border activities but to settle problematic activities by modifying the original proposal. Here, it is important to highlight the difference between private enforcement by litigation in courts and arbitration, where it is the Commission that largely determines the mandate of the arbitral tribunal. This capacity grants the Commission a much stronger control over the implementation and enforcement than before national courts that can only be addressed by soft means such as notices or training seminars (Lehmkuhl 2007).

The Hardness of Soft Governance

Against the backdrop of the information presented in this chapter, it seems adequate to describe competition policy in Europe as being in transition. There are, however, different interpretations with respect to the direction of this transition. For some the direction is best described as Americanization, characterized by a shift of Rhenish capitalism toward its Anglo-Saxon counterpart (Wigger and Nölke 2007). Others see competition policy in Europe as being reshaped in terms of economic principles as the Commission bases its decisions increasingly on economic reasoning and analysis (OECD 2005: 12). Still another interpretation emphasizes the closer cooperation of competition-enforcing agencies that has given rise to a legal epistemic competition community involving Community experts of DG Comp, experts of national competition authorities, legal scholars, and lawyers of big law firms from both sides of the Atlantic (Van Waarden and Drahos 2002; Wilks 2005a). Most recently, efforts to theorize on the development of European competition policy have emphasized the explanatory potential of traditional or revised neo-functionalism (Büthe 2007; McGowan 2007). Although for most of the time the European competition policy was the realm of a few specialists, these interpretations indicate an increasing interest in the complexities of a policy field that due to its strong supranational competences differs from many other areas of European policymaking.

This outstanding character provides an important point that helps to answer the question of how to interpret the finding of a coexistence of hierarchy and cooperation as dominant modes of governance. Competition policy is a special case, with very strong regulatory competences of the Commission. Neither more critical periods, in which the member states seemed less willing to follow the Commission's impetus to address market-distorting behavior, nor the fact that "competition is a means and not an objective of the Community"[10] prevented the companionship between the European Commission and European courts from being quite successful in fighting restrictions or distortions of competition in Europe's internal market.

In combination, the supremacy of European law, the incorporation of competition provisions into the founding document of the European integration project, and the entrepreneurship of committed competition commissioners have made the hierarchical mode of governance in European competition policymaking much more prominent than in most other European policies. Neither the significant reference to legally nonbinding instruments such as notices and guidelines nor the decentralization of the policing of anticompetitive behavior and handling of complaints to national competition authorities, national courts, and private arbitral tribunals seems to have changed the situation significantly. Rather, the analysis confirmed that there is a difference between governance *in* networks, that is, a perspective that emphasizes the dispersion of power and competences in horizontal patterns of interactions, and governance *with* networks, a perspective that takes into account the importance of institutional politics, power asymmetries, and a shadow of hierarchy (Börzel 2005: 87; Héritier and Lehmkuhl 2008). As elaborated by Arthur Benz in Chapter 3, dynamics in patterns of interaction may be related to the way in which different modes of governance are coupled. In the present case, hierarchy and cooperation are coupled in a way that renders soft modes of governance harder than they may seem at first glance.

Notes

I would like to thank the editors and Carina Sprungk for their very helpful comments on earlier versions of this chapter.

    1. OJ C93/6 (13 February 1993).

    2. "Council Regulation (EC) No. 1/2003 of 16 December 2002, on the Implementation of the Rules on Competition Laid Down in Articles 81 and 82 of the Treaty" (OJ 2003, No. L 1/1, C 101/43, 4 January 2003).

3. The three cases in which the CFI issued annulments were Case T-342/99, *Airtours v. Commission (Airtours),* (2002) E.C.R. II-2585; Case T-310/01, *Schneider Electric v. Commission* (2002) E.C.R. II-4071; and Case T-5/02, *Tetra Laval v. Commission* (2002) E.C.R. II-4381.

4. See http://ec.europa.eu/comm/competition/antitrust/legislation/legislation .html (accessed 12 June 2007).

5. See http://europa.eu.int/comm/competition/mergers/legislation/index_new .html (accessed 17 June 2006).

6. Judgment of the Court of Justice of 18 May 2006 in Case C-397/03 P, *Archer Daniels Midland v. Commission* (Amino acids), of the European Union 15.7.2006; quoted in Wils 2007: 203.

7. "Commission Notice on the Cooperation Between the Commission and the Courts of the EU Member States in the Application of Articles 81 and 82 TEC" (OJ C 101, 27.04.2004, 54–64).

8. The then president of the Federal Constitutional Court in Germany, quoted in Blessing 2003: 24n13.

9. See http://www.iccwbo.org/policy/arbitration/id1784/index.html (accessed 12 June 2007).

10. Michel Petite, director general of the Commission of the European Communities' legal service, in a letter to the *Financial Times,* 27 June 2007, p. 10.

9

Single Market Policies: From Mutual Recognition to Institution Building

Susanne K. Schmidt

The single market program was the major initiative in the mid-1980s; it reinvigorated European integration and remains one of the most important policy fields in the Union. The single market program took off with the invention of a new mode of governance—the principle of mutual recognition that built on the case law of the European Court of Justice (ECJ) (the *Cassis de Dijon* case). Whereas previously the common market had relied on harmonization, that is, the agreement of common rules through the Community method, mutual recognition establishes that member states have to recognize their different regulations as equivalent—if there are no good reasons to demand an exemption. Mutual recognition is thus an alternative way of achieving governance functions, a new mode of governance (Schmidt 2007).

Yet, when the debate on new modes of governance came up in the mid- to late 1990s—particularly as related to the need of economic policy coordination in view of monetary integration—mutual recognition was no longer at the center of attention. "The most important of Europe's institutional innovations is hardly mentioned any longer in the debates on the so-called 'new modes of governance'" (Joerges and Godt 2005: 95). Instead, the open method of coordination has been the focus of much political science research. It is with the spread of mutual recognition to other policy fields, notably Justice and Home Affairs (JHA), interestingly, that this principle has drawn attention in the debate on new modes of governance. In general, political scientists seem to show little interest for single market issues. "Somewhat paradoxically, the growing emphasis upon the need for effective 'political' direction or governance within Europe may thus be argued to have distracted attention from what is, at one and the same time, the root cause of Europe's putative 'democracy deficit' and the primary arena of continuing European integration: i.e. the Internal Market" (Everson 2002: 155).

By making it possible to achieve integration without engaging in cumbersome negotiations and decisionmaking processes on harmonization, mutual recognition offers a "you can have your cake and eat it too" solution to integration. The aim of the single market can be achieved without the agreement costs that are associated with integration. For mutual recognition to work, however, important preconditions exist. Member states, because they are the ones who are politically responsible should regulation be insufficient, are not prepared to agree unconditionally on accepting each other's regulations. Thus, they reserve the right to enforce their own regulations if this should be necessary because of "general interest" considerations (Tison 2002: 323). This caveat raises difficult questions of when national rules apply and when products regulated in other member states have to be accepted. Although national rules should be relevant only as an exception, for administrators and business to know when this exception applies—and when not—requires supporting institutional structures.

This chapter analyzes the specifics of mutual recognition as a new mode of governance and gives particular attention to its impact on institution building. Its starting point is the argument that mutual recognition implies a transfer of transaction costs from the decisionmaking to the implementation stage (Nicolaïdis 1993: 352). Even though the European Union (EU) lacks the legitimacy to build effective decisionmaking structures, the high transaction costs of implementing mutual recognition require supporting institutions. These include the need for standard-setting institutions, in order to provide a basis for the exchange of goods, and for increased cooperation of member states' administrations. With the new services directive requiring national administrations to cooperate, the latter are slowly being transformed from national into (partly) Community institutions. It remains to be seen whether the legitimacy problems that hinder a more effective system of decisionmaking in the EU can be dealt with more easily at this implementation stage. I proceed as follows. After explaining how mutual recognition works and what its benefits and disadvantages are, I analyze how mutual recognition works in the three areas of goods, services, and JHA. Although mutual recognition presents many advantages over harmonization, the chapter shows that these benefits have significant preconditions in terms of an institutional support structure, and thus institution building.

Mutual Recognition as a New Mode of Governance

Member states are obliged to recognize each other's regulations through the principle of mutual recognition. This obligation follows from the four freedoms (of goods, services, capital, and people) of the treaty, which are constitutive of the single market. For mutual recognition to enter the Community, an important innovation of the ECJ's case law was necessary. When included in the Treaty of Rome, the four freedoms simply required that member states abstain from discrimination against one another. Thus, member states were free to regulate their markets. They only had to assure that goods, services, or businesses from other member states would not have to face other rules than their own domestic goods, services, or businesses. As is well known, a change of interpretation occurred with the rulings of the ECJ in the *Dassonville* and *Cassis de Dijon* cases. In *Cassis de Dijon,* Germany was told that it could not restrict the trade of this French liqueur simply because it did not conform to German standards of alcohol content. Rather it had to accept the French regulation as equivalent because there were no justifications not to do so (Alter and Meunier-Aitsahalia 1994). Thus, first for goods, the ECJ decided that the market freedoms did not require merely nondiscrimination. Rather, member states were not allowed to impose disproportionate burdens on their markets, which would hinder the use of the fundamental market freedoms.[1] With this change of interpretation from a "prohibition of discrimination" to a "prohibition of restrictions," the Commission and the ECJ received a mandate to examine national regulations. As the four freedoms constitute fundamental rights, member states may not restrict them disproportionately.[2]

It is important to note that an interpretation of the fundamental freedoms as a prohibition of restrictions leads to the obligation of mutual recognition. As member states have to honor the fundamental freedoms and not merely ensure that they do not discriminate, it becomes important for them to know how other member states regulate their goods, services, and businesses. Any duplication of controls would be disproportionate. Member states therefore have to recognize each other's regulations and controls. In other words, if member state A aims to achieve the same regulatory goals with a rule, albeit with other means than member state B, member state B has to accept the products of member state A. It is only if member state B can raise objections rooted in considerations of the general good that it may impose additional regulatory burdens on products or businesses of member state A. Originally, the free movement of goods of Article 28 was only constrained by Article 30, which allowed member states exceptions for reasons of public security and order. Simultaneously with broadening the scope of the freedom of goods in *Cassis,* the Court improved the possibilities for member states to claim exceptions by introducing "mandatory requirements," which refers to regulations member states may impose. These "overriding requirements of general public importance," as they are also called, constitute an open list for which the Court has so far recognized consumer protection, the prevention of unfair competition, tax evasion, the improvement of working conditions and of the environment, the freedom of the press, and the preservation of the financial balance of the social security system (Oliver 1999: 804). Whether a member state rightly claims exceptions under the mandatory requirements is judged by applying the proportionality principle, meaning that the measures have to be necessary and proportionate for achieving the regulatory goals and cannot be attained by any lesser means.

With mutual recognition, markets can be integrated by simply recognizing each other's regulations, rather than attempting to formulate a common position to regulation through harmonization. Compared to harmonization, negotiation and implementation costs of new regulations can be evaded. At the same time, markets can be entered without having to adapt to the regulation of the importing state, as is the case with national treatment (i.e., nondiscrimination). As member states accept regulations of other member states as equivalent to their own, however, they do not know anymore which regulations apply in their own territory. Similarly, consumers cannot be certain anymore if the products they consume conform to their domestic rules or to those of another member state. Consequently, this far-reaching horizontal transfer of sovereignty is only acceptable if member states can claim exceptions, given that in cases of regulatory failure they are the ones that are ultimately being held politically responsible (Nicolaïdis 1993: 488–491). Accordingly, with the introduction of mandatory requirements the possibility of claiming exceptions was broadened.

With the introduction of mutual recognition, the previous need to rely on harmonization as a precondition for the single market lapsed. Harmonization was now only needed in those instances in which member states could otherwise claim exceptions and thereby fragment the market. With the move of the single market program to establish the market via mutual recognition, the Commission introduced the concept of minimum harmonization to define a common ground where member states would otherwise seek exceptions from market freedoms. Member states would be generally free to subject their own nationals to further restrictions, going beyond the minimum harmonization threshold.

Mutual recognition is thus a significant institutional innovation. It is a substitution for the need to harmonize, although it can also often be complementary to it. Member states will only agree to recognize each other's regulations within a context of some harmonization. In addition, for some exceptions, national treatment prevails. Nicolaïdis uses the term *managed mutual recognition*, to show that mutual recognition is not unconditional but embedded in certain rules (Nicolaïdis 1996). Fundamental to mutual recognition is the significant amount of trust that member states need to integrate markets this way (Majone 1994a).

Why could mutual recognition be regarded as a new mode of governance (Schmidt 2007)? First of all, new modes of governance—or governance in general[3]—are normally juxtaposed to government, implying the capacity of hierarchical steering. Mutual recognition is characterized by a horizontal transfer of sovereignty (Nicolaïdis 1993: 490–494), in the sense that the legitimate rules of one member state apply in another member state, although they were not adopted by its sovereign. The transfer of sovereignty explains why trust is so crucial for mutual recognition: Member states have to trust that the rules adopted by one sovereign are acceptable to another one. Moreover, they have to trust that compliance with rules is monitored and enforced regardless of whether the behavior concerns domestic activities or other member states. If we follow another definition of new modes of governance, the classification becomes even clearer: if new modes are those replacing the classic Community method (i.e., the adoption of directives and regulations by the Council and the Parliament based on proposals from the Commission) (Scott and Trubek 2002: 1; Eberlein and Kerwer 2004: 122), mutual recognition is a new mode given that in many ways it compensates for the need of harmonization.

Nevertheless, for our context the definitional issue is of marginal importance. More important in this regard is that mutual recognition is a central feature of the single market as one of the major pillars of European integration. By being an alternative and complement to harmonization (in the sense that minimum harmonization and mutual recognition rely on each other), mutual recognition fulfills governance functions just as harmonization does. From its successful adoption in the single market, mutual recognition is being transferred to another important area, that of JHA. Given the specific features of mutual recognition, the following parts of this chapter will inquire into the impact on institution building that the choice of mutual recognition entails.

The Origin: Mutual Recognition in Goods Markets

The working of mutual recognition in goods markets is a story often told, so only the features of the regime shall be recapped here (Egan 2001). Such a summary seems necessary, as the institutional underpinnings of the single market for goods are complicated enough that there is not much knowledge of how mutual recognition in goods markets actually works. Mutual recognition in the single market for goods is embedded in a context of minimum harmonization, assuring member states that mutual recognition will not lead to a situation of insufficient regulation (a race to the bottom). The system builds on the general expectation that all member states regulate their market in a similar way: There might be different regulations, but as member states pursue similar policy goals, these regulations are in general equivalent. Therefore, it is not necessary to harmonize them, but it is possible to mutually recognize them. Member states have to have good reasons not to simply accept goods regulated differently (the "general good" exceptions), and these are then the areas where minimum harmonization is needed, in order to overcome such market fragmentation.

In order to facilitate harmonization, which was previously very cumbersome as all product details were agreed upon and enshrined, two innovations took place. One was the move to minimum harmonization, allowing member states at the same time to adopt more stringent regulation in their country. This option facilitated agreement as member states retained more possibilities for regulating their domestic economy. The other innovation was the "new approach" to technical harmonization, defined in a Council resolution in 1985 (see Chapter 11). Following this innovation, member states only agreed to directives on a set of "essential requirements"—for instance, those relating to health and safety—that goods would have to meet. The responsibility of defining the technical specifications necessary to meet these essential requirements was then delegated to the European standards bodies such as the European Committee for Standardization (CEN), the European Committee for Electro-technical Standardization (CENELEC), and the European Telecommunications Standards Institute (ETSI). Standards bodies represent concerned parties, public and private, mainly the producers of products, agreeing on joint technical specifications. Thus, with the new approach, part of the necessary work for building the single market for goods was delegated to standards bodies and private parties, which is notable in terms of institution building (Pelkmans 2007).

The previous cumbersome full harmonization detailing the specifications of tractor seats or the ingredients of chocolate was thus replaced by a more complex regime: the general presumption of equivalence of regulation among the member states with the mutual recognition of different regulations, the agreement on essential requirements in directives of minimum harmonization in those areas where an equivalence of regulation was lacking, and the delegation of the translation of these essential requirements into standards to specialized bodies, which relieved the Community process of significant decisionmaking costs. Thus, harmonization as a mode of governance was replaced with mutual recognition, as the former proved unable to keep up the necessary pace for integration.

If we consider the workings of this regime in practice (Pelkmans 2007), it appears that trade is much more difficult in cases where Community standards are absent and member states (should) mutually recognize their national regulations as equivalent. In these cases, exporting companies as well as inspectors controlling goods face the difficulty of deciding whether goods are in fact equivalent to domestic (mainly health and safety) requirements or whether the member state can claim an exception from the freedom of goods and require imports to meet the domestic specifications. For mutual recognition to work, institutional support structures are required. Even though the regime has been in place since the late 1980s, it was only in 2002 that a new institutional layer was added: the SOLVIT network. Previously, if member states failed to respect their obligations under the mutual recognition regime, or if there was a conflict between exporting companies and member states as to the scope of mutual recognition, the Commission had to become involved through a complaint, starting the formal infringement procedure, leading ultimately to a ruling of the ECJ. Now, the SOLVIT network can attempt to find a solution before this formal process starts. Every member state has designated a SOLVIT center, which in Germany, for instance, is located in the Federal Ministry of Economics and Technology. Companies having problems with the single market can contact these centers, which are obliged to aim for a solution within ten weeks. A central Internet platform[4] gives information about contact points and the type of problems dealt with, which need to be of a transborder nature and concern conflicts between private parties and public authority. If a company has a complaint and addresses the SOLVIT center in its country, the latter will contact the responsible SOLVIT center in the member state whose administration has given rise to the complaint. Both SOLVIT centers will try to solve the matter in cooperation. At the same time, the SOLVIT website gives examples of solved cases, thereby raising awareness among private and public actors of their respective rights and duties under Community law.

As Pelkmans (2007) shows, there is another important institutional feature of the mutual recognition regime for goods. The aspects discussed so far all relate to existing national regulations. But regulation of markets changes rapidly with technical innovations. For the single market to work, it is therefore of utmost importance to ensure that member states do not add to existing heterogeneity with new regulations. The Community tackled this problem early on and included a notification system for member states to inform each other and the Commission of planned technical standards and regulations in directive 83/189/EEC (replaced by directive 98/34/EC). Following this procedure, member states are obliged to notify the committee established by this directive of all planned technical standards and regulations. All national regulations have to include clauses on mutual recognition and equivalence to pass this procedure. If objections are raised against the plans of a member state within three months, there is a waiting period of up to eighteen months during which the national regulation is suspended. In this way, between 1988 and 1998 the committee was notified of 5,000 regulations (see Pelkmans 2007). With the help of this regime, the obligation of mutual recognition has become much more firmly enshrined into member states' daily practices than would have happened otherwise. By having to notify certain domestic regulatory plans, member states moreover are held to be faithful to the Community when drawing up domestic plans.

Mutual Recognition and Services

Trade in services is more cumbersome than trade in goods, as most services do not travel independently of their production. Only so-called correspondence services cross borders, typically with the help of telecommunications, television signals, or the Internet. The trade of other services is dissimilar to the trade of goods, as either the producer (active freedom of services) or the consumer (passive freedom of services) has to cross the border for services delivery to take place (Roth 1988). What does this mean for mutual recognition? Whereas for the trade of goods, product specifications are relevant but the details of the production process is normally of no concern to importing countries (the prohibition of child or forced labor is a notable exception), the case is more difficult with services. If service providers move, in order to deliver their products, it becomes questionable whether they should adhere to the rules of their home or their host country. Although for goods it is no question that labor costs and regulations have to be observed in the country where production takes place, for services this issue is much more difficult to decide. If all the rules for services provision of the host country have to be adhered to, services trade is effectively hindered. If in contrast all the process standards of the home country remain valid, not only would there be a significant pressure on high-wage countries but also consumer protection or environmental goals could be endangered if production processes were used that would be illegal under host-country rule.

In the EU, the services freedom does not cover the whole tertiary sector but relates only to the temporary cross-border delivery of services that is remunerated (Roth 1988). If service delivery takes place on a permanent basis, normally the freedom of establishment applies, and with it, the rules of the country where the services activity takes place become relevant. Because the services freedom is normally used on a temporary basis, the ECJ has ruled that too many requirements of the host state would render it prohibitive. Due to the temporary nature, regulations of the home state normally have to be recognized. In its judgment *Rush Portuguesa* (C-113/89), however, the ECJ ruled that the host state could apply its minimum wages and labor law also to service providers temporarily in the country. The ECJ saw this exception from the home-country rules as covered by the general interest, as member states would otherwise have problems safeguarding their labor regulation. In addition, workers could benefit from being treated under the host-country rule. The posting of a workers' directive, which was enacted following upon this case, gives member states the possibility of enforcing their labor market rules vis-à-vis EU nationals.

Compared to the extensive reach of home-country rules in the trade of goods, the ECJ left much more room for host-country rules in the area of services. In addition, it had also established in the *Van Binsbergen* case (C-33/74) that companies could not rely on the services freedom just to circumvent their national laws. It is only recently that the situation seems to be changing so that the significant scope that services trade offers for arbitrage indeed becomes a danger. Several developments are responsible for the change. First, the case law of the ECJ has changed. Beginning with its rulings on the freedom of establishment, which introduced the right of business to pick the least restrictive regulatory environment (*Centros* [C-212/97], *Überseering* [C-208/00], and *Inspire Art* [C-167/01]), the ECJ also loosened its case law on services, allowing more room for home-country rules (Hatzopoulos and Do 2006). In addition, it has changed its case law on the abuse of Community law, increasingly accepting that national law is being circumvented by using European law, thereby departing from its earlier *Van Binsbergen* judgment (Engsig 2006: 444). Second, the eastern enlargement increased the economic heterogeneity among the member states significantly and with it the scope to use European law for arbitrage. Finally, the European Commission has renewed its efforts to tackle the single market for services, given that services account for an increasing percentage of economic growth, which is not yet matched by services trade in the Union. To complete the services single market has become a central issue of the Lisbon agenda, which was agreed on in 2000 by the heads of state and strives for the EU to become "the most competitive and dynamic knowledge-driven economy by 2010."[5]

In January 2004, the Commission published its proposal for a services directive. It proposed to follow a horizontal approach for realizing the services market, spanning across almost all services sectors, after the attempts with sector-specific directives, for instance for financial services, had proven cumbersome, lengthy, and only partly successful. Thus, this directive was to liberalize about half of all economic activity of the member states. The directive, aiming at realizing the freedom of services and of establishment, largely followed the principle of home-country control, seeking to minimize the possibilities of member states resorting to imposing host-country rules under the general interest. With this proposal the Commission went far beyond the case law of the ECJ, radicalizing it by limiting the possibility of imposing host-country rules to very few exceptions. Accordingly, the reactions to the draft directive were vivid. The Bolkestein directive, as it became known after the responsible commissioner (at the time) for the single market, was the first example of a single market directive that roused significant political debate—albeit in a mostly negative and critical sense. In the course of the discussion, the EU Constitutional Treaty was voted down in the Netherlands and France, owing much to the impression of neoliberal European integration that the services directive was offering. As Commissioner Frits Bolkestein said when presenting his proposal, "Some of the national restrictions are archaic, overly burdensome and break EU law. Those have simply got to go. A much longer list of differing national rules needs sweeping regulatory reform."[6]

But the conflict about the services directive not only exhibited different approaches to the regulation of markets and a communication failure on the part of the Commission. The conflict most of all showed how the specifics of services trade, generally requiring the presence of the service provider, raised difficult issues for home-country control and mutual recognition, for which the Union lacked sufficient answers. As mentioned, the Union (much in the form of the rulings of the ECJ) has decided for services trade neither to opt for full home-country control (and thereby maximum scope for arbitrage) nor for full host-country control (which would stifle services trade). Instead, there is a difficult balance between both principles, and even though the services directive aims at restricting the regulatory means of the host country, the posting of the workers' directive and the related case law of the ECJ imply that minimum wages and working conditions of the host state are relevant.

Although in view of the different development (and wage) levels among the member states, such a mixture between host- and home-country principles is the only acceptable way to strengthen services trade, it is very difficult to enact. Home-country control means that host-country authorities are not allowed to check on companies from other member states. Yet, with service providers being present in their countries and having to adhere to some of their rules, they are normally the only ones that could assure adherence. Home-country authorities, in contrast, are neither in a position to know the rules applicable under host-country control from all other twenty-six member states, nor can they be generally assumed to be interested in their implementation. In so far as these rules impose further costs on their business, there is even an incentive not to follow them, particularly as costs from insufficient regulation are borne by the host country and not by the home country. "While for the trade of goods, the necessary trust relates to the quality of home-country regulations and their enforcement, for services it also extends to the trust that interest in competitive advantages will not lead to strategic non-enforcement of foreign rules, given that the costs of non-enforcement exclusively fall upon another territory while the benefits can be accrued at home" (Nicolaïdis and Schmidt 2007).

The case of Germany serves to illustrate these problems, given that it borders the new member states, does not have a general minimum wage, and is a high-wage country. Therefore Germany has been experiencing much of the difficulties of controlling this mixture of host- and home-country rules after enlargement. As there is only a minimum wage in the construction industry, which was moreover exempted from the services freedom (along with exemptions from the free movement of labor), service providers from Eastern Europe can normally profit in Germany from their low-wage level. They do have to adhere to the stricter German working conditions and to the limitation of the services freedom to temporary activities, however; social security has to be paid in the home country, and the company has to be active in its home country—mere letter-box companies established exclusively for posting workers are illegal. Moreover, posted workers may not be fully integrated into the German company's work process, because in this case the service character of the activity would be lost.[7]

Although companies can benefit from the wage differential, a wide array of illegal activities has been found. Violations include the temporariness of service provision, the exclusion of certain branches, the working conditions of the host country, and the need to pay social security expenses in the home country as well as obligations under the posted workers directive. Many companies are only established for posting workers, but it is difficult for the host country to detect whether they do not follow regular economic activity in their home country or do not dispense social security contributions. Moreover, it is unclear under what conditions a company can legally post workers: How many persons have to be active in the home country in relation to the host country, for instance, or what part of the turnover may be achieved in the host country?[8]

For the freedom of services to work under conditions of heterogeneous membership, member state administrations thus have to cooperate closely. If not, the balance between gains from services trade and protection from rule arbitrage cannot be achieved. In this respect, the services directive brings an improvement, as Chapter VI on administrative cooperation (Articles 28–36) details the responsibilities of the administrations in the home and the host country. In the final version of the directive, it was agreed that host-country authorities would be responsible for controlling those rules that they might impose (Article 31). Generally, home-country authorities are the ones legally responsible for oversight. Both authorities have to cooperate, since home-country authorities cannot become active in the host country but have to request the responsible authorities to act. The directive establishes a duty to cooperate among the member states' administrations, an important procedure that has not existed before.[9] Thus, Article 28 (8) foresees that the Commission will start an infringement procedure if member states fail to comply with their duties:

> Member States shall communicate to the Commission information on cases where other Member States do not fulfil their obligations of mutual assistance. Where necessary, the Commission shall take appropriate steps, including proceedings provided for in Article 226 of the Treaty, in order to ensure that the Member States concerned comply with their obligations of mutual assistance. The Commission shall periodically inform Member States about the functioning of the mutual assistance provisions.[10]

In order to facilitate cooperation across the language barriers, the Commission is promoting an information system that provides for automatic translation of specific standardized paragraphs.

Thus, the services directive lays the root for administrations' operating transnationally. Instead of simply following the instructions given in the national hierarchy of command, with the minister on top being ultimately politically responsible, administrations now also have to comply with horizontal demands, coming from administrations from other member states. By instituting a new line of duties, administrations are unbound from their exclusive national obligations and start to be similarly dedicated to the needs of other member states in the context of the Community cause. In terms of institution building, this is a significant development, possibly laying the root for a network of nationally based administrations pursuing European objectives, rather than segmented national authorities pursuing domestic goals.

Mutual Recognition in Justice and Home Affairs

Mutual recognition in JHA similarly espouses the significant cooperation demands inherent to this principle. The application of mutual recognition in JHA bears similarities to the single market. With the opening of borders through the single market, member states perceived an increased demand to cooperate in home affairs. The first introduction of mutual recognition occurred with Schengen and the agreement in 1990 to mutually recognize decisions on asylum to prevent "forum shopping" by asylum seekers. The next major step was decided upon in the Tampere Council in 1999. Here, mutual recognition was formally adopted as the approach to answer the perceived need of strengthening integration in JHA. The mutual recognition of arrest warrants was the first, and until now the only concrete, measure to be agreed upon. For this measure to work, the Council of Ministers adopted a framework decision in mid-2002. Mutual recognition of arrest warrants replaces the previous system of extradition. With the latter, member state A demands extradition of member state B. Whether member state B responds is a decision of foreign policy that allows for much discretion. Part of the consideration would be whether the offense is judged as a criminal act (double criminality); part may also be other diplomatic considerations. Thus, extradition corresponds to national treatment in goods (Sievers 2006). With the switch to mutual recognition, police and judicial authorities are supposed to act on the principle of equivalence and should react automatically. A European arrest warrant may be issued by a national court if someone is accused of an offense for which the penalty would be more than a year in prison or if there has already been a prison sentence of at least four months. The removal of the traditional double-criminality requirement was agreed on for thirty-two types of offense. Once a court in member state A issues such a warrant, member state B where the person happens to be has to arrest him or her and is supposed to act without any further controls as to the standards of procedure and the kind of punishment. Thus, mutual recognition implies that judicial decisions by member state A are implemented by member state B, and member state A can borrow the authorities of member state B for its goals, regardless of whether these are fully shared in member state B (Lavenex 2007; see also Chapter 16).

Part of the decision of mutual recognition for arrest warrants is that member states now have to surrender their own nationals to other member states and cannot save them from prosecution there. This requirement in particular has given rise to objections by national courts, who partly regard the implementation of the European arrest warrant as conflicting with their national constitution. The German constitutional court has thus ruled against the domestic implementation of the European arrest warrant, arguing that another interpretation of the European framework decision would have corresponded more closely to the obligations of Germany's Basic Law. Similar developments can be noted for some other member states. Because of the difficulty of accepting equivalence without previous agreement on common minimum standards, some member states have insisted on the implementation of requirements going beyond the prescriptions of the European arrest warrant (Lavenex 2007).

Mutual recognition in JHA has fostered cooperation among national police and judicial authorities, as shown by the significant number of arrest warrants that have been issued. In order to strengthen cooperation, a number of support structures have been established. Thus, Eurojust is a group of twenty-seven EU prosecutors, one nominated by each member state, that coordinates cross-border investigations and prosecutions, improves information, and offers mutual legal assistance. The European Judicial Network consists of almost 250 national contact points throughout the member states, providing information as a support for requests for judicial cooperation. Finally, liaison magistrates are exchanged among member states, in order to establish direct links between judicial authorities and to promote the mutual understanding of the different legal systems. Nevertheless, it is apparent that mutual recognition in JHA so far lacks the necessary support structure to function as well as mutual recognition in the trade of goods does. As some member states have declined to respond to demands for arrest warrants of others, the latter have decided to play "tit for tat," putting at risk the whole cooperation (Lavenex 2007).[11] As the problems of mutual recognition have not altered the perception of the need to cooperate, it remains to be seen whether increased harmonization or other supporting structures will be invoked to foster mutual recognition in JHA. In general, however, one can expect that mutual recognition faces more obstacles in JHA than in goods markets. In JHA, mutual recognition requires member states to assume an equivalence of laws that concern personal liberty rights, which in general fall under the sovereignty of Parliament. In contrast, in goods markets we often deal with standards that are delegated to professional bodies at the national level. With norms that require less legitimation, it should be easier to assume equivalence.

Conclusion: A Double Transfer

Compared to harmonization, mutual recognition builds on a double transfer: sovereignty is transferred not to the supranational level but horizontally to other member states, and the transaction costs of overcoming heterogeneity among member states are transferred from the decisionmaking stage to implementation. The institutions of the European political system—as well as its legitimacy—are too weak to surmount significant heterogeneity of interests and of institutional solutions among member states, mostly because of the requirement of unanimous or qualified majority voting. Given the weak legitimacy of the system, binding decisions require qualified majorities, similar to constitutional amendments at the national level. Although at the European level qualified majority voting is already an achievement (some areas, particularly in JHA, remain to be decided unanimously), decisionmaking remains much more cumbersome than at the domestic level. Even though decision rules are less effective, the range of different interests and institutional solutions is much greater in the EU than domestically.

If in this situation the need is perceived to achieve integration despite heterogeneity, mutual recognition seems to be a very elegant solution. As an institutional innovation, I have argued, it can be seen as an example of a new mode of governance. Member states can keep their heterogeneous solutions and their sovereignty, but they have to agree to a horizontal transfer of the latter and recognize each other's approaches as equivalent. Thus, joint action and integration can be achieved, be it in markets for goods, services, or criminal and asylum matters. Integration comes at the price of high transaction costs in the implementation stage, however. In fact, surprisingly little is known about the day-to-day cooperation of member states' administrations in the implementation of mutual recognition. How do member state authorities know whether goods, regulated to different national standards, should be regarded as equivalent? The system becomes even more complicated when not only goods are exchanged but service providers cross borders or the home office of one member state implements judicial decisions of another.

Why is this situation so complicated? For services, if production takes place in the host country, but under home-country rules and control, it is not only the question of whether the services product is equivalent but also of whether the production process is regulated and controlled as it should be. Although products are regulated at the domestic level, regardless of whether they will be exported or not, the control of production processes in services can be assumed to differ depending on whether it takes place at the domestic level or in another member state. For trade in goods, member states only need to trust each other to protect their populations in an equivalent way, but for trade in services further trust is required. In this case, it extends to an interest to protect the population of other member states, for instance from certain production processes (think of detergents in cleaning services) or from imbalances in labor relations. Member states can be assumed to have an interest domestically in minimum labor conditions and fairness, but this is likely to be less the case when services are delivered abroad. With domestic regulation, excessively low labor standards have a detrimental effect on the whole economy as conditions in all sectors are pulled down. In the case of services trade, this downward pressure is exerted on the economy of another member state. At the same time, individual benefits can be accrued, particularly in times of high unemployment, when domestic constraints relating to social security contributions or working time are loosened for service providers active in other member states.

Mutual recognition in JHA presents yet other problems. Here, several areas are affected—the rule of law and civil rights, standards of a fair trial, and standards of punishments of different offenses, for which each society has reached different decisions, which are democratically legitimated. To simply interchange these agreements with those reached in other member states and to subject citizens of the domestic polity to the standards of another member state is much harder to accept than mutual recognition in goods and services trade.

Thus, different degrees of trust are necessary for mutual recognition to function in the three areas discussed. Trust is not merely necessary at the level of governments deciding on whether to install a mutual recognition regime; it is also needed in the day-to-day practice of administrators controlling goods and services markets and being involved in police and judicial cooperation. Instead of dealing with heterogeneity at the decisionmaking stage within a relatively closed group of decisionmakers, mutual recognition diffuses the confrontation with heterogeneity to numerous administrators. Thus, this transfer of transaction costs, involving not only administrators but also consumers, who often can no longer know to which country specification goods and services are being regulated, requires an institutional support structure.

For the trade of goods, this support structure can be found in standardization committees, in the embedding of mutual recognition in agreed standards,[12] in the 98/34/EC committee reducing regulatory heterogeneity among member states, in the exchange of administrators, and in the recent establishment of the SOLVIT network, increasing awareness of the obligation of member states with regard to the freedom of goods (and services). The Commission has also held a series of sector-specific roundtables of administrators and business.[13] For services, mutual recognition increases demands on cooperation, as authorities of the host state, when detecting fraud, cannot investigate themselves but have to rely on the home-state authorities. Thus, the services directive establishes for the first time the duty of member state administrations to cooperate and supports this with an electronic communication and translation system. For JHA, experiences with mutual recognition seem too recent to have yet led to a significant support structure that reaches beyond transnational administrative cooperation.

It is thus very interesting to analyze mutual recognition from an institution-building perspective. In view of significant heterogeneity, the European political system proves unable to achieve agreement on harmonization. Mutual recognition as an alternative governance form, however, transfers the transaction costs of dealing with heterogeneity from the decisionmaking stage to the implementation stage. Confronted with the problems of putting mutual recognition to work, the Commission has mounted efforts to devise and construct institutional support structures that absorb the resulting transaction costs and foster the necessary trust for mutual recognition to work. By making administrations responsible for also reacting to horizontal demands from other member states, transnational networks are strengthened and national administrations are partly liberated from their national chain of control. It remains to be seen whether the legitimacy problems that hinder a more effective system of decisionmaking in the EU can be dealt with more easily at this implementation stage.

Notes

I would like to thank the participants of the workshop in Osnabrück for helpful comments, most of all my discussant, Edgar Grande. Thanks are also due to Julia Sievers for updating me on Justice and Home Affairs and most of all to the editors, Ingeborg Tömmel and Amy Verdun, for all their comments and editorial support. Research for this chapter was partly done at the Max Planck Institute for the Study of Societies, Cologne, and within the Integrated Project "New Modes of Governance" (see the website www.eu-newgov.org). Funding provided by the 6th Framework Program of the European Union (Contract No CIT1-CT-2004-506392) is gratefully acknowledged.

1. Later the ECJ interpreted the other freedoms similarly, so that there has been a considerable convergence of interpretation (Oliver and Roth 2004: 440).

2. Note that this only relates to market participants of other member states. Member states remain free to regulate their markets as they wish; however, it may violate national nondiscrimination rules if EU nationals are regulated less stringently than nationals.

3. The debate about new modes of governance has shown that the attribute "new" is quite tricky. Even though the open method of coordination is new to the EU, it is very similar to the intergovernmental coordination the Organization for Economic Cooperation and Development (OECD) has used all along (Schäfer 2006). Independent regulatory authorities are another example, because even though they are now being included in the European discussion, they are already firmly established in the United States.

4. The SOLVIT website is http://ec.europa.eu/solvit/site/index_en.htm.

5. See the summary of the Lisbon agenda at http://www.euractiv.com/en/agenda2004/lisbon-agenda/article-117510.

6. Quoted in "Services: Commission Proposes Directive to Cut Red Tape that Stifles Europe's Competitiveness" IP/04/37 Date: 13/01/2004. http://europa.eu/rapid/pressReleasesAction.do?reference=IP/04/37&format=HTML&aged=1&language=EN&guiLanguage=en (accessed 18 October 2006).

7. *Fleischwirtschaft,* 12 May 2005, 10.

8. *Frankfurter Rundschau,* 23 July 2003, 12.

9. Interview, European Commission, DG Internal Market, 27 September 2005.

10. Available at http://eur-lex.europa.eu/LexUriServ/LexUriServ.do?uri=CELEX: 32006L0123:en:html (accessed 26 January 2007).

11. Spain has responded to Germany in this way. The Spanish parliament decided to no longer follow up on German requests, after a Spanish request to extradite a German to Spain was denied following the ruling of the German constitutional court in July 2005 (Lavenex 2007).

12. With this harmonization, mutual recognition merely concerns the certification process.

13. See http://ec.europa.eu/enterprise/regulation/goods/mutrec_en.htm#roundtable.

10

Taking the Field: The European Union and Sport Governance

Osvaldo Croci

Since the mid-1970s, European sport has undergone a number of significant changes. Most of them are the result of sport's having resolved its longstanding ambiguous attitude toward money, as symbolized by the decision of the International Olympic Committee (IOC) to abolish the distinction between amateur and professional sport and have the Olympic Games commercially sponsored. Aided also by the liberalization of the telecommunication sector, sport has itself become big business.[1] This transformation has also changed the way sport is regulated. The rules of sport, the organization of national and international competitions, and the administration of sport justice have traditionally been the responsibility of autonomous sport organizations. As sport has turned into a full-fledged economic activity, however, political authorities, and the European Union (EU) in particular, have begun to challenge some of the rules devised and enforced by these autonomous bodies. EU intervention in the field of sport is somewhat peculiar because it occurred at a time when public authorities were retreating from an increasing number of spheres of social and economic activity (Strange 1996). The EU, in other words, has become involved in sport at a time when the trend for political institutions was to relinquish to independent agencies even those responsibilities that were traditionally and indisputably seen as their own.

This chapter will first explore the reasons why the EU intervened in sport and its policy goals. It will then examine the nature and evolution of EU involvement, focusing on the identity and roles of the various actors participating in the regulation of European sport. Finally, the chapter will conceptualize the nature of such involvement as being one of governance characterized by negotiation and, to a lesser extent, by competition and cooperation.

The EU Takes the Field

Sport has traditionally been regulated in all its aspects by a set of autonomous organizations relating to each other vertically, as in a pyramid. In football (often referred to in North America as soccer), for instance, clubs are organized in various national leagues (professional, semiprofessional, amateur). Leagues, as well as national professional associations (e.g., players, coaches, and referees), are part of national football federations, which are the constituent members of six continental confederations as well as of a worldwide federation (Fédération Internationale de Football Association, or FIFA). Leagues, national federations, continental confederations, and FIFA are all responsible for the regulation of football, each in its own geographical/functional sphere of competence and, theoretically at least, according to the principle of "subsidiarity."[2] Briefly, sport was an independent sphere of activity. States and other political actors hardly played any role in it, except for the granting of subsidies and the attempt to use it to promote nationalism and the ruling political regime, as was the case especially with fascism and communism.

This situation began to change in the late 1970s when political authorities, the EU in particular, entered the field of sport, ironically at a time when the trend was for them to abandon the regulation of various spheres of social and economic activity. This involvement, or encroachment for some, has been justified in terms of the "rapid [economic] development of sport, especially professional sport, and the important place occupied by sport in society" (European Commission 1998a: 3). Such a statement captures very well the two different, and difficult to reconcile, objectives that the EU has set for itself in the field of sport. On the one hand, the common or single market is an area where people, goods, services, and capital should move freely under conditions of free competition, and this is supposed to apply also to sport. On the other hand, albeit most professional sports have indeed become a form of business, sport also remains a social, cultural, health, and educational activity. Hence, EU institutions need to find a proper balance between safeguarding EU basic principles and recognizing that sport, even when an economic activity, has peculiar characteristics that need to be preserved, especially since the EU itself has recognized sport as an important tool in the construction of a "people's Europe."

Technically speaking, there is no such a thing as EU sport law or policy, since sport is not a Community competence. The EU has become involved in sport as a result of the need to uphold its basic principles, mainly free movement of people and nondiscrimination on the basis of nationality, as well as to achieve objectives in other policy areas. Hence, it is competition policy, for instance, that can have an impact on sport, or social policy that can occasionally harness sport to some of its ends. EU interventions can be divided into "hard" and "soft." The first type is represented by rulings of the

European Court of Justice (ECJ). The second is represented by declarations of the European Council. The actions of the Commission fall somewhere in between, since they can be considered "hard" in terms of the impact of the positions the Commission takes but "soft" concerning the process through which it takes those positions. What follows is a brief historical excursus of EU intervention in sport. It focuses on the rulings of the ECJ, the reactions of sport stakeholders, and the role of the European Commission.

EU involvement in sport began in the mid-1970s and was at first exclusively juridical, that is, the ECJ was called upon to provide preliminary rulings on a number of cases referred by national courts and concerning the principles of free movement of people and nondiscrimination on the basis of nationality (Miège 2001). In both the *Walrave and Koch* and the *Donà* cases,[3] the ECJ declared that the rules of sporting organizations fell within treaty provisions to the extent that sport constituted an economic activity and except for those rules that were only of sporting interest. The difficulty for national courts would be to determine in each case which rules could be considered of exclusive sporting interest and which could not, because there is no clear-cut basis to distinguish between the two.[4] In the *Heylens* case, which was referred to the ECJ in the mid-1980s, the Court provided some guidance to its early ruling by suggesting that professional football was an economic activity and professional coaches and athletes were laborers and that any restriction on their free movement for sporting reasons had to be properly motivated.[5]

The case that brought media and popular attention to EU involvement in sport was referred to the ECJ in the early 1990s. Belgian football player Marc Bosman, encouraged and supported by the Fédération Internationales des Associations de Footballeurs Professionels (FIFPro), initiated action against the Belgian football federation, the Union of European Football Associations (UEFA), and FIFA. He claimed that their transfer rules, in particular the provision that a new employing club had to pay a fee to the old one, had prevented him from moving to a French club after his contract with his club in Belgium had expired. Besides reaffirming that professional sport was an economic activity and athletes were laborers, the *Bosman* ruling also established that transfer fees for players out of contract were an impediment to free movement and that restrictions on the number of nationals from other member states that a club could field were a form of discrimination on the basis of nationality.[6]

In two separate rulings rendered in April 2000 as well as in a third one rendered in 2006, the ECJ provided examples of some sporting federations' rules that, even if appearing prima facie to be a restriction on the fundamental principles guaranteed by the treaty, were nevertheless justifiable because necessary to the organization of the sport qua sport. The *Deliège* case concerned limitations on the number of athletes admitted to participate in international competitions. The ECJ considered that the limitation imposed by the Belgian judo federation on the number of Belgian athletes who could participate in an international competition did not infringe on the fundamental freedom to provide services, as argued by Belgian judoka Christelle Deliège, because such a limitation is an integral and inevitable part of the way international sport competitions are organized and the criteria of selection are a responsibility solely of sporting organizations. The *Lehtonen* case concerned the compatibility of transfer deadlines with Community laws. Jyri Lehtonen, a Finnish basketball player, complained about the Belgian basketball federation's refusal to ratify his transfer to a Belgian team because such a transfer had taken place after the date the federation had set as a deadline. Although the rule could be considered an infringement on the principle of free movement, the ECJ accepted the argument that such a rule was necessary for the fair organization of the championship. The 2006 ruling concerned doping-related bans. The ECJ rejected the complaint lodged by swimmers David Meca-Medina and Igor Majcen against a two-year ban imposed by the international swimming federation for use of a prohibited substance. The two swimmers had argued that such a ban constituted a restraint on their freedom to exercise their activity.[7]

Finally, the ECJ is currently considering a case concerning the obligation imposed by FIFA on football clubs to release players selected for their national teams. Action was initiated by the Belgian club Charleroi, which had one of its players seriously injured while playing for his national team, and is supported by the G-14 (the association of the most wealthy football clubs in Europe). Charleroi's argument is that the FIFA rule constitutes an abuse of dominant position, since FIFA profits by organizing competitions for national teams such as the World Cup, and the suit requests that FIFA should provide adequate compensation to the clubs, especially in the event of injury. The ECJ has yet to render its ruling, but FIFA has already announced that it will introduce an insurance program for players on international duty. UEFA has gone even further and, besides providing insurance, will pay the clubs a daily fee for each player released to the national team.[8]

The reactions of sport organizations, fans, and member states to the *Bosman* ruling in particular were very negative.[9] Perhaps as a lingering consequence of sport's original amateur status, sporting organizations have always felt invested with the noble mission of the promotion of an activity that is supposed to unite humankind. This view, moreover, is shared by the population in general. In fact, according to a recent survey ("Les Citoyens de l'Union Européenne et le Sport" 2003: 5), 81 percent of the people interviewed thought of sport as promoting cross-cultural understanding and 59 percent regarded it also as a means of combating discrimination. Because of the almost mystical character of such a mission, moreover, sporting organizations have traditionally felt above the reach of nation states and their laws.[10]

Hence, national football federations, UEFA, and FIFA regarded the *Bosman* ruling as undue meddling by political authorities. FIFA, for instance, argued that its status as a global organization placed it above a mere regional body such as the EU: "In FIFA's view, it is clear that a small group of countries cannot be granted an exemption from sport regulations which are effective in all parts of the world and which operate successfully and efficiently and for the benefit of football at all levels" (Sugden and Tomlinson 1998: 50). Member state politicians also reacted rather skeptically. Belgian prime minister Jean-Luc Dehaene, for instance, argued that although one should not disregard the principle of free movement of labor, one should also be sensitive to the needs of sport. The challenge was to find a way to reconcile EU rules with the continuing viability of sport. Similar remarks came from the French and Italian governments. Some national politicians also lamented the excesses of a Union that gave too much power to jurists, and at least one member of the European Parliament denounced the *Bosman* ruling as the result of "pro-European legal delirium."[11]

Such a reaction was not due simply to the desires of national politicians to appear to be in tune with the feelings of the public. Another important reason had to do directly with the process of European integration. At its 1984 Fontainebleau meeting, the European Council had recognized the need to build a "people's Europe" and had set up a committee to study ways in which this process could be encouraged.[12] The report of the Committee on a People's Europe recognized that sport was "an important forum for communication among peoples" and that it should be harnessed to the construction of a "people's Europe."[13] The Council then charged the Commission and the member states "to take the necessary implementing measures . . . aimed at involving the citizens of Europe more determinedly in the construction of the Community."[14] Member states' politicians were well aware in 1995, as they undoubtedly also were ten years earlier, that a "people's Europe" could not be built by alienating the feelings of football fans (i.e., most, if not all, Europeans), who are a highly sensitive, opinionated, and conservative group. Hence, the 1997 Amsterdam Treaty contained an annex called "Declaration on Sport" that emphasized "the social significance of sport, in particular its role in forging identity and bringing people together" and called "on the bodies of the European Union to listen to sports associations when important questions affecting sport [would be] at issue."[15] Since then, similar declarations have found their way in the final communiqué of almost every European Council meeting. Finally, the 2007 Lisbon Treaty explicitly incorporated the principles guiding EU action in the sporting field in Article 149, which states that "the Union shall contribute to the promotion of European sporting issues, while taking account of the specific nature of sport, its structures based on voluntary activity and its social and educational function."[16]

Because of its role of "guardian of the treaties" and its duty to act upon the recommendations of the Council, the Commission faced the difficult task of having to reconcile two conflicting objectives: to make sure that the rules of sporting organizations would not contradict treaties' provisions while at the same time working closely with these organizations in order to protect and enhance the social significance of sport. Following the 1976 ECJ ruling on the *Donà* case, the Commission signaled to sporting organizations the need to modify their sporting rules that violated treaty provisions. UEFA, for instance, was notified of the necessity of abolishing the rule that put a limit on the number of foreign players a European football club could hire, which at the time was fixed at two. Such a restriction was justified in terms of the need to avoid allowing the richest club be able to recruit all the best players, to maintain a minimum of national identity, and to give more playing opportunities to young players and thus enhance the competitiveness of their national teams.[17] UEFA attempted to resist what it regarded as undue interference in its sporting domain but eventually agreed to revise such a rule. In 1991—fifteen years after the *Donà* ruling—UEFA adopted the so-called 3+2 rule, whereby a European football team could field three "foreign" players (regardless of whether they hailed from an EU member state or not) plus two "assimilated players" (i.e., foreign players who had played in the country of the relevant national football association for an uninterrupted period of at least five years). UEFA left national federations free to adopt, if they so wished, an even more liberal approach for their national leagues, which the English Football Association, for instance, did.

The *Bosman* ruling made it clear that the 3+2 rule, although a small improvement, still violated Article 48 of the Rome Treaty, at least in those cases in which the adjective "foreign" referred to other EU nationals and the transfer involved two clubs belonging to two different national football federations within the EU. The ECJ, moreover, had also pointed out that the justifications for the transfer fees put forward by the football organizations (i.e., they served to maintain a financial and competitive balance between smaller and poorer clubs, which were usually the sellers, and richer ones, which were usually the buyers, and to support the development of young players) were not convincing since such objectives could be achieved by other means not impeding the free movement of players. The ECJ had chosen not to pronounce itself on Articles 85 and 86 of the Rome Treaty, even if the referral for a preliminary ruling had asked about the compatibility of the transfer fee with competition policy, since the violation of Article 48 was sufficient to make UEFA rules invalid. The Commission chose, however, to adopt a slightly more robust approach. In January 1996, it formally notified UEFA and FIFA that their transfer system needed to come in line with treaty provisions, including Article 85 of the treaty as well as Article 53 of the Agreement on the European Economic Area (EEA). Provisions of treaties moreover applied not only when transfers occurred between clubs located within two different EEA states but also in the case of transfers within the same member state, or between a member state and a third, non-EEA country. The Commission requested the two football organizations to inform it of the steps they intended to take to comply with the ECJ ruling (Van Miert 1996). At the same time, national tribunals began to strike down national sport federations' restrictions on players coming from countries with which the EU had concluded association agreements (Husting 2001: 21; De La Rochefoucauld n.d.; McAuley 2002).

In June of the same year, the Commission, dissatisfied with the pace of progress and wishing to close its file on the transfer system, informed FIFA and UEFA that if by the end of the year the issue had not been settled, it would commence legal action. In September, FIFA and UEFA agreed to a thorough revision of the transfer system lest the Commission act on its threat and "throw the European game into chaos" (*Financial Times,* 1 September 2000). In March of 1997, after lengthy negotiations, the Commission declared itself willing to accept as compatible with competition laws an agreement that at least one legal scholar has defined as a "legally ambiguous compromise" (Weatherhill 2003: 68). The new international transfer system, which underwent further minor modifications in 2005, specifies minimum and maximum length of contracts (one to five years), imposes sanctions for their unilateral rescission, limits to two per year the time periods during which transfers can occur, puts strict conditions on international transfers of players under eighteen, and provides for compensation for training costs in the form of objectively calculable fees but limited to the transfer of players under twenty-three. It also sets up a solidarity mechanism for the redistribution of income among clubs and creates an international Independent Court for Football Arbitration (ICFA), with members chosen in equal numbers by players and clubs. Arbitration by ICFA is voluntary, and it does not, moreover, prevent recourse to national civil courts.[18]

Meanwhile, soon after the 1997 Amsterdam Council's "Declaration on Sport," the Commission developed a consultation document entitled "The European Model of Sport" in which it argued that European sport was characterized by its cultural, educational, and social relevance; its pyramidal structure in which "high-performance sport and popular sport are brought together within sporting associations and treated as related and complementary areas"; and the promotion and relegation principle (Reding 2001: 6). These latter two aspects in particular distinguish the European model from the US model, which has multiple competing leagues, admittance into which depends on financial capacity as opposed to results (European Commission 1998b; Reding 2001). Then, in its "Helsinki Report on Sport," presented to the Helsinki European Council, the Commission committed itself to preserve such a model (Commission of the European Communities 1999a).

At the same time, and mostly as a result of investigating complaints lodged with it, the Commission has also issued so-called comfort letters, adopted decisions, and reached informal agreements that clarify how EU competition rules are to be applied to sport. It has determined, for instance, that the 1998 World Cup organizing committee was in breach of competition rules when it made a large number of tickets available only to residents of France. It has decided that some sponsorship deals, especially by equipment manufacturers, contravene competition rules (e.g., designations such as "official supplier" and "official ball" cannot be used). It has established that the Fédération Internationale d'Automobile (FIA) cannot act both as regulator and commercial exploiter of Formula One and has to stop some anticompetitive practices such as forbidding circuit owners hosting Formula One races from staging other events or obliging broadcasters with rights to Formula One not to telecast other car races. The Commission has not lost sight, however, of sport's peculiarities as a business. Thus, although deciding that "the broadcasting of sporting events, and in particular, the sale of exclusive broadcasting rights is a commercial activity and subject to Community legislation governing competition," member states are allowed to draw up a list of major sporting events that must be broadcast unencrypted even if their broadcasting rights belong to a pay-television station, as reflected in the 1997 "Television Without Frontiers" directive.[19] It has found that UEFA's "blocking rule," that is, the power that national football federations have to prohibit the broadcasting of league matches on their national territory while they are being played, do not appreciably restrict competition. It has decided that the rule of most sport organizations preventing clubs with the same owner from participating in the same competitions is justified on sporting grounds since it aims at ensuring the uncertainty of the result of the competition. It has accepted the rule that football players can only employ agents licensed by FIFA as long as the latter keeps access to the profession open and nondiscriminatory. It has rejected a complaint by a Belgian football team that was prevented by UEFA from playing a UEFA Cup tie home match in a nearby larger stadium located on French territory by arguing that such a rule was a necessary part of the organization of the competition (Weatherhill 2003). Finally, the Commission has also integrated sport into various Community policies because it considers it a good vehicle for some policies (e.g., public health, educational and vocational training, and the fight against racism and xenophobia) and has given a substantial contribution (14.25 million euros between 2002 and 2007) to the World Anti-Doping Agency (European Commission 1998a; Reding 2001: 21).[20]

Yet to be resolved is the question of whether the collective selling of broadcasting rights is legal under competition rules. At the European level, acting upon the prompting of the Commission, UEFA has modified its selling policy by splitting all the media rights into fourteen smaller packages, some of which are exploited only by UEFA and some of which are coexploited by both UEFA and the individual clubs. The Commission has expressed satisfaction with this compromise modification.[21] At the national level, the Commission seems to be reluctant to decide an issue that from a legal point of view falls to member states' legislation concerning the ownership of property (Pons 1999: 16) and on which national legislatures have taken rather different positions (Cave and Crandall 2001: 17; Van den Brink 2000). Some have suggested that the Commission might be ready to accept a compromise whereby collective selling would be allowed if the additional revenues it generates would go to increase financial solidarity between clubs or between professional and amateur sports (Weatherhill 2003: 78–79). Such a compromise, however, would have little or no basis in competition law. It would certainly enable the Commission to claim that it is upholding the European sport model it has engaged to defend and promote in the Helsinki report but might also expose it to legal challenges for overstepping its competences.

The EU and Sport Governance

EU involvement in sport has so far been analyzed from a policymaking point of view only by Parrish (2003). He has argued that EU choices have been the result of a dispute between two "policy advocacy coalitions" (Sabatier 1998). The first, which Parrish calls the "Single Market coalition," includes the ECJ, the Commission, and some special interest groups such as the G-14, FIFPro, and some Brussels-based lawyers. This coalition tends to regard sport as being primarily an economic activity and hence subject to the rules of the single market. The second coalition, which Parrish calls "the socio-cultural coalition," includes sporting organizations and EU member states (and hence also the European Council). This coalition tends to regard sport primarily as a sociocultural activity deserving a special consideration. Parrish argues that EU sport policies until the *Bosman* ruling reflected the beliefs of the first coalition, and more precisely its faith in "liberalization."[22] Concern with what was regarded as "excessive liberalization" brought together the second coalition, which stopped the momentum of the first and tried, unsuccessfully, to find a more permanent check in an official treaty-based recognition of sport as a sector needing special exemptions.

Such an interpretation is enticing but does not stand up well to close scrutiny. That the ECJ and the Commission, for instance, were at first ideologically committed to liberalization and then backtracked because of the rise of the "socio-cultural coalition" is unconvincing. The ECJ was very cautious all along. In the *Walrave* and *Donà* cases, the ECJ established that sport was a legitimate area of EU intervention when it also constituted an economic activity. At the same time, however, it left the field open for "certain exceptions" from Community rules without specifying either the principle or the scope of such "exceptions" (Blanpain 1996: 265). In the *Bosman* case the ECJ based its ruling on the principles of free movement and nondiscrimination on the basis of nationality as it had done in the *Walrave* and *Donà* cases. It carefully avoided pronouncing itself on the issue of whether the transfer system also contravened competition rules, even if the referral had asked the question (Advocate General Carl Otto Lenz had stated that in his opinion it did so). The *Deliège* and *Lehtonen* rulings are not necessarily evidence, as argued by Parrish, of the ECJ's taking a step backward to find a more equitable balance between EU intervention and autonomy of sport organizations. Rather, whereas the first four cases were central to the principles of free movement and discrimination on the basis of nationality, the last two were more far-fetched legal challenges probing the more peripheral aspects of such principles. The rulings in these two cases cannot therefore be considered evidence of backtracking, especially since, albeit ruling against Deliège, the ECJ pointed out that the notions of economic activity and provision of services cannot be interpreted narrowly since they define the field of application of one of the fundamental freedoms guaranteed by the treaties. In *Lehtonen,* the ECJ—while accepting deadlines on transfers as necessary to the proper functioning of a sport league—ruled that there could not be two different deadlines, one applying to nationals and one to foreigners. In the *Meca-Medina* case, the ECJ again ruled against the claimant but at the same time suggested that even doping rules could come under the provisions of the treaties. Certainly the ruling did not please the members of the sociocultural coalition. UEFA, for instance, criticized the ECJ for missing an opportunity to clarify "the scope and nature of the specific sporting rules that fall outside the scope of EU law" and claimed that the *Meca-Medina* ruling was a "step backwards for the European Sports Model and the specificity of sport" (Infantino 2006).

The Commission, for its part, recognized long before the *Bosman* ruling and not only after it, as suggested by Parrish, that ECJ "judgments c[ould] not under any circumstances be seen as warranting any action by the Community in relation to sport which disregard[ed] the prerogatives of the relevant authorities" and that any Community action should "show proper regard for the principle of subsidiarity in relation both to the official authorities and to the organizations responsible for sport." Indeed, the Commission framed its early interventions in sport as a service it was rendering to sporting organizations, namely giving them "a better grasp of the opportunities which the . . . single market w[ould] offer them and where necessary help them adjust the rules governing sport in line with Community law as smoothly as possible" (Commission of the European Communities 1991b: 1–2).

EU involvement in sport can be better conceptualized as an example of a complex system of governance, the latter being defined as a sustained process of competition and coordination, conducted through both formal structures and informal practices, by various actors—private and public, economic and political, national and transnational—in order to regulate a specific sphere of collective activity. In the absence of specific treaty-based competences, EU involvement in sport began as a result of legal action undertaken by private actors who demanded that the EU uphold the principles of free movement and nondiscrimination on the basis of nationality as well as competition rules in the sport sphere as elsewhere. The ECJ established that treaty rules were applicable to sport when the latter could be considered an economic activity. Although the task of deciding when this was the case was left to national courts, the Commission became involved for two reasons. First, following the ECJ rulings, it was its duty, as "guardian of the treaties," to make sure that the fundamental freedoms enshrined in them were upheld. Second, it had to investigate the complaints it received. For these reasons, the Commission has come to be at the center of what can be regarded as a complex system of European sport governance.

A governance system must rely on an effective communication network capable of institutionalizing stable relationships with nonstate actors as well as national and subnational public actors to compensate for the lack of clearly defined relationships among all stakeholders. The Commission, or more precisely the Sport Unit within the Directorate General for Education and Culture, is at the center of this sport communication network. The Sport Unit is responsible for the coordination of sport affairs within the Commission (e.g., between the Directorate General for Education and Culture and those for Competition and for Employment, Social Affairs, and Equal Opportunities) as well as coordination between the Commission and the other EU institutions. It also represents the Commission on all the forums in which European sport authorities meet, including the Council of Europe (meetings of ministers for sport and of the Sport Development Committee) and the Association of National Olympic Committees. The Commission has also set up the European Sport Forum, which provides a permanent "lightweight facility" (Commission of the European Communities 1991b: 12) for mutual information and discussion among the Commission, members of the European Parliament, and officials from national ministries and nongovernmental organizations as well as representatives of European and national sport federations. In May 1999, the Commission also organized a European Conference on Sport, which was held in Greece. Finally, national ministers responsible for sport or top civil servants within departments with some sport responsibilities (also known as sport directors) have repeatedly met at the behest of the Council Presidency.

Because sport is not a treaty-based competence, the mode of European sport governance is primarily that of negotiation. The Commission is the central actor because of its role, that is, what it does, and not because of what it is, that is, it is not at the top of a hierarchy. Hence, the Commission is constantly negotiating with all sport stakeholders in order to reconcile their diverging interests within the somewhat ambiguous and hence flexible parameters set by the ECJ rulings (i.e., sporting rules fall within the provisions of the treaties to the extent that sport is an economic activity and they cannot be justified exclusively on sporting grounds). The first goal of the Commission is to try to bring sporting rules within, or as close as possible to, those parameters. The second is to defend and promote the European sport model, which means that the parameters established by the ECJ are to be interpreted rather flexibly. As stated in its "Helsinki Report," the Commission is convinced that only a "partnership between sporting associations, [national] governments, and the Community institutions [can] maintain the particular identity of European sport and prevent it from becoming exclusively commercial" (Reding 2001: 7). Thus, the Commission limits itself to pointing in the general direction indicated by the ECJ and waiting for all the other actors to move along, now gently prodding the recalcitrant ones, now discreetly restraining those who would like to push too far ahead too fast. An example will suffice to make this point.

After the ECJ rulings on the *Walrave* and *Donà* cases, the Commission had to act with respect to the rules of football organizations' restricting the employment of "foreigners," since football is both the most important and most commercialized sport in Europe. It did not force the issue, however, but chose to engage in negotiations with football organizations. The UEFA 3+2 rule that resulted from the negotiations was a compromise, or as the Commission itself put it, "a pragmatic transitional agreement *increasing the mobility* of professional footballers" (Commission of the European Communities 1991b: 4 [emphasis added]; Dupont 1996: 69–70). The Commission could have invoked Article 169 of the Rome Treaty and warned (and, if necessary, also brought before the ECJ) member states for condoning rules of a private juridical order (that of UEFA and national football federations) contrary to Community law. Such a procedure would have been politically unwise, however, because the extent to which sport could be considered an economic activity had not been well clarified by the ECJ and any hasty decision by the Commission might have led to serious national backlashes. UEFA in fact justified its rules on sporting grounds, and some member states were very sympathetic to this position (Demaret 1996: 12–13). France, for instance, began trying to convince other member states to insert a protocol in the treaties recognizing sport as a sector with special needs and hence deserving exemptions. Aware of the resistance it was likely to encounter, the Commission was very cautious in the way it moved. As explained by then Competition Commissioner Karel Van Miert, the Commission wished to perform its duty as the authority responsible for competition policy but preferred to leave the task of safeguarding individual rights to national jurisdictions and thus limited itself to signaling to football authorities that they needed to adjust their rules (Van Miert 1996: 6–7).

The Commission behaved the same way after the *Bosman* ruling, albeit the signal it sent this time was a bit stronger. UEFA had in fact argued in the *Bosman* case that nationality restrictions, that is, the 3+2 rule, had been sanctioned by the Commission, and the ECJ had replied that the Commission did not possess the power to authorize practices that went against the treaty (Parrish 2003: 97), which could be interpreted as a mild rebuke to the Commission for having taken a soft approach to making sure that the principles established in the *Walrave* and *Donà* rulings were applied. FIFA and UEFA responded to the solicitation sent by the Commission first by announcing that the nationality clause would be suspended at least for what concerned UEFA-organized club competitions and then by setting up a working group that included representatives from national federations and leagues as well as FIFPro to find a suitable alternative to the existing transfer system. The group went about its work while keeping up a constant dialogue with the Commission. Member state politicians, including Tony Blair and Gerhard Schröder, also entered the field in favor of the retention of some kind of transfer fee. The interests, and hence the views, of all these actors were rather diverse, and thus negotiations were long-drawn and heated. The Commission, however, limited itself to acting, to use the apt definition developed by Alberta Sbragia (2000), as a "coxswain," that is, it simply and gently guided sporting actors in the desired direction by restructuring their interests and, consequently, their behavior.[23] In its public rhetoric the Commission was even more self-effacing and described its role as that of a "consultant" or "facilitator" who was trying "to give European sport organizations an opportunity to benefit more from Community activities" and "help them in adapting their structures to the new political, economic and social framework created by the action of the EU" (European Commission 1998a: 15). Thus, with respect to football transfer rules, the Commission argued that it was "available at all times to assist sport organizations to find ways compatible with Community legislation to encourage the recruitment and training of young players and ensure that the equilibrium between clubs [was] maintained" (European Commission 1998a: 5).

After the Commission and FIFA and UEFA had reached an agreement on a new transfer system, Competition Commissioner Mario Monti openly recognized that it had been the result of the adoption by the Commission of the "modern rules of governance" and referred to his role in the negotiations as that of a "referee" explaining "the ground rules and how they [were to be] applied" (Monti 2001). FIFA president Joseph Blatter went even further and described the Commission as if it had been a consultant hired by FIFA itself to improve its rules: "The discussions we have had with the Commission," he wrote to Monti, "have been most valuable to determine how the adapted rule could fit in with the EU Treaty and recent EU legal developments, and I thank you and your colleagues for your fine and constructive input" (Blatter 2001).

The fact that the prevailing mode of governance is that of negotiation is also shown by the fact that almost all agreements reached so far are based on compromises and have little or no legal standing except that they are acceptable to all stakeholders. Thus, the 2005 agreement on football transfers would probably not survive "the scrutiny of the courts" (Drolet 2006: 73), but of course it will not come under such scrutiny as long as it is acceptable to all stakeholders. Such a soft approach has also been adopted when sporting organizations have been found to be in violation of existing rules. Thus, for instance, the 1998 World Cup organizing committee was fined only the symbolic sum of 1,000 euros for its restrictive tickets sale arrangement that violated competition laws (Weatherhill 2003: 64–65).

The Commission did not have a hard task in making international sporting organizations realize that pursuing EU objectives was also in their own interest. This was not only because, as already mentioned, the Commission portrayed itself as a kind of consultant to sporting organizations to help them adjust to a new, more challenging, economic environment. The task of the Commission was also facilitated by an element of "competition" within the prevailing mode of "governance by negotiation." The Commission could in fact rely on other sporting actors to take legal initiatives that would put internal pressure on sporting organizations to modify the rules that violated Community law. Following the *Bosman* ruling, in fact, players, individually or collectively as FIFPro, and clubs that would stand to benefit from its application to areas that the ruling itself had not directly addressed could be expected to take legal initiatives to have the *Bosman* ruling clarified and extended. Since it was based on the principles of free movement and nondiscrimination on the basis of nationality and not on rules concerning competition, the *Bosman* ruling did not address, for instance, transfers within the same member state, transfers of players hailing from European Free Trade Association (EFTA) countries or other countries with which the EU had an association agreement, and transfers between clubs in the EU and third countries. And indeed, soon after the *Bosman* ruling, the Commission began receiving complaints against sporting organizations on the basis of Articles 81 and 82 (formerly 85 and 86) concerning restrictive practices and abuse of dominant position by undertakings. By 1998, the Commission had received fifty-five of them (European Commission 1998a: 1; Crespo Pérez 1998).

The case receiving most attention was that of Media Partners, a private business group linked to the Fininvest conglomerate that owns the Italian football club AC Milan. In 1998, Media Partners launched a proposal to set up a European Football Super League that would compete with the European-wide competitions organized by UEFA. Media Partners lured the best European football clubs by promising them a higher financial reward. UEFA, supported by FIFA, reacted by threatening to ban the players of the clubs that would join the proposed Super League from all other football competitions, including those for national teams. Media Partners then filed a complaint with the Commission arguing that UEFA's attempt to stop them from organizing and marketing football in Europe was an abuse of its dominant position. In the end the clubs that were supposed to join the Super League decided instead to pressure UEFA to change the format of its European competitions and secure for themselves a higher share of the financial returns they generate. Thus, in the end, neither Media Partners nor any of the other complainants went as far as bringing their cases to the ECJ, because all of them were settled by means of compromise. Sporting organizations, however, could expect similar cases to continue to be brought to the attention of the Commission, and possibly also to the ECJ, which put pressure on them to adopt rules that would be acceptable to the Commission.

Pressure on sporting organizations to move along the road indicated by the Commission came also from the so-called passport scandal, that is, the sudden increase in the numbers of extracommunitarian players who acquired a European passport, often through illegal means.[24] The situation became so serious—more than 360 cases were investigated in Italy alone—that in order to avoid the involvement of ordinary justice, some national federations decided to scrap the nationality rule altogether. The International Basketball Federation (FIBA), for instance, announced in December 1998 that as of the 2000–2001 season there would be free movement of players in regard to international competitions for which it was directly responsible. FIBA left national federations free to decide whether or not to adopt the same rule for national championships.

To summarize, competition also characterizes the mode of governance of European sport. Different stakeholders have different interests and are prepared to take different risks to pursue them. This fact pushes all of them collectively, and the international organizations at the top of each sport pyramid in particular, to move toward the general position indicated by the Commission. They do so in order to preempt legal challenges to their preferred position mounted by stakeholders having different interests and to avoid the scrutiny of ordinary courts. Indeed, after *Bosman* at least, an increasing number of cases that had been referred to courts were withdrawn before the courts could issue a ruling, after the disputing parties reached a mutually satisfactory agreement.

Finally, one should also mention the existence of an element of "governance by cooperation." International sporting organizations, albeit reluctant to accept publicly that they no longer have a monopoly over the regulation of their sport, also realize that becoming part of the sport governance network, despite constraining their field of action, contributes to solving their "legitimacy problem" (Croci and Forster 2005). The latter derives from the fact that most international sporting organizations are not representative bodies whose executive officers are clearly responsible and accountable to a democratically elected policymaking assembly composed of representatives of the subordinate organizations. The National Olympic Committees (NOC), for example, are not represented on the IOC. Rather, the IOC appoints the heads of the NOC, who are considered IOC representatives to their own country. The governing function belongs to international sporting organizations by recognition and not as a legal right. Hence, without legitimacy, that function is challengeable, that is, new organizations could make a claim for it and exercise it either in parallel or in competition. Such challenges are even more likely to come now that most sports offer considerable financial rewards. The development of an international sporting governance system means that public authorities recognize existing international sporting organizations as the central stakeholder in a given sport and thus legitimize, and hence also protect, their role and position from likely challengers. Thus, notwithstanding their publicly reluctant attitude, international sporting organizations have a strong incentive to share their regulatory role with public authorities.

Sport organizations officials have publicly interpreted the mention of "the specific nature of sport" in the Lisbon Treaty as a prelude to the EU's granting sport a bloc exemption from treaty provisions on the basis of its "specificity." The EU, however, is unlikely to move in this direction. As one EU official has put it, "every issue will have to be judged on its individual merits on a case-by-case basis" (Ennis 2007). As can also be inferred from the Action Plan that "will guide the Commission in its sport-related activities" (Commission of the European Communities 2007c), negotiation and, to a lesser extent, competition and cooperation are likely to remain the standard modes of sport governance in Europe.

Conclusion

This chapter examined the origins, goals, actors, and mode of the EU sport governance system. The first part argued that the EU became involved in sport because of its increasing economic significance and because the ECJ was called upon to provide preliminary rulings on cases concerning the compatibility of sporting rules with EU law. The EU has two main, somewhat contradictory, objectives in the field of sport: first, to reconcile sporting rules with EU law, at least insofar as sport constitutes an economic activity; and, second, to preserve the "European model of sport" so that sport may remain a social, cultural, health, and educational activity. The network of actors—basically all sport stakeholders plus member states and EU institutions—involved in the process of sport regulation has the Commission at its center. The second part of the chapter focused on the characteristics of the regulatory process. A previous analysis of EU involvement in sport had argued that EU actions flowed from the competitive interaction between two policy advocacy coalitions. It had also identified the *Bosman* ruling as the moment in which policy goals changed as a result of change of the relative power of the two coalitions. This chapter argued instead that there has been substantial continuity in the goals and actions of the EU and that the regulatory process can be better portrayed as a process of governance. The chapter also argued that the prevailing mode of governance is that of negotiation, albeit aspects of competition and cooperation can also be detected. The EU will continue to be involved in sport governance but such involvement will cause fewer ripples than in the past and will be even more low key, since most of the ground has already been cleared. In the future, EU interventions will probably also be less frequent, since all stakeholders have learned to reach mutually satisfying agreements before the cases reach the courts or before the latter pronounce their verdict and because most of those cases that will reach the courts are likely to be solved at the national level.

Notes

1. According to a 2006 Austrian study, sport accounts for 3.7 percent of EU gross domestic product (GDP) and employment for 15 million people or 5.4 percent of the labor force (Commission of the European Communities 2007a: 11).

2. In practice, however, because regional confederations and FIFA are responsible for the organization of international competitions at both club and national team levels, the system is skewed in their favor. This is shown, for instance, by the following statement by FIFA president Sepp Blatter: "We [FIFA] have said clearly that, within their own country, they [national federations] can play football and organise it however they like, with whatever rules they like . . . but they cannot expect to go *outside* their country and play in *our* competitions" (quoted in Radnege 2000: 32 [emphasis in original]).

3. The *Walrave and Koch* case concerned two Dutch pacesetters on motorcycles who work in cycle races in which the cyclist, called a "stayer," cycles in the lee of the motorcycle. They felt damaged by a regulation of the Union Cycliste Internationale providing that as of 1973 the pacesetter in world championship races had to be of the same nationality as the "stayer" *(B.N.O. Walrave and L.J.N. Koch v. Union cycliste internationale, Koninklijke Nederlandsche Wielren Unie et Federación Española Ciclismo, C-36/74).* The *Donà* case concerned a talent scout employed by an Italian lower division football club. The club refused to pay some expenses the scout had incurred abroad, since the Italian Football Federation (FIGC) at the time forbade the employment of foreign players. The case went to court, where the scout claimed that the FIGC rule contravened EC Treaty rules *(G. Donà v M. Mantero, C-13/76).*

4. See, for instance, the sporting arguments advanced by Dubey (2002) for maintaining nationality restrictions in football, at least at the higher levels of the club game.

5. The *Heylens* case concerned the refusal by the French association of football trainers to recognize the qualifications of Georges Heylens, a Belgian national hired as coach by the Lille football club, because his training diploma had been issued in Belgium. The ECJ ruled that nonrecognition of a diploma issued in another member state had to be properly motivated and that such a motivation could be challenged under treaty rules *(Union nationale des entraîneurs et cadres techniques professionnels du football [Unectef] v. G. Heylens and others, C-222/86).* Later, following the 1988

directive on the general recognition of higher education diplomas, the Commission clarified that mutual recognition applied also to professional sport.

6. *Union royale belge des sociétés de football association ASBL v. Jean-Marc Bosman, Royal club liégeois SA v. Jean-Marc Bosman and others,* and *Union des associations européennes de football (UEFA) v. Jean-Marc Bosman, C-415/93.*

7. *Christelle Deliège v. Ligue Francophone de Judo et Disciplines Asbl and Others, C-51/96 and C-191/97; Jyri Lehtonen and Others v. Fédération Royale Belge des Sociétés de Basket-ball ASBL (FRBSB), C-176/96;* and *David Meca-Medina and Igor Majcen v. Commission of the European Communities, C-T-313/02.*

8. "FIFA Explore International Player Insurance," *ESPNsoccernet,* 6 December 2006, available at http://soccernet.espn.go.com/news/story?id=394859&cc=5901; "Da Euro 2008, milioni di euro per chi dà i giocatori alle Nazionali," *La Repubblica.it,* 18 January 2008, available at http://www.repubblica.it/2003/h/rubriche/spycalcio/milioni-per-i-club/milioni-per-i-club.html?ref=search.

9. Critics argued that the *Bosman* ruling would destroy football because (1) it would devastate the finances of smaller clubs by depriving them of a major source of revenue and make it almost impossible for them to compete in the bidding for top players; (2) it would lead to a sizable increase in salaries, at least for star players, since clubs could offer in salary what they no longer had to pay in transfer fees; (3) it would remove any incentive to invest in the development of young players; and (4) the national teams of net importer countries would eventually suffer because of the lack of opportunities for young talent to play at a high level. Their claims were probably exaggerated even if the "liberalization" of the transfer system has certainly enabled better players and better teams to claim a bigger share of the football pie than used to be the case.

10. For instance, following the 1985 Brussels Heysel stadium disaster during the final of the European Champions League between Juventus and Liverpool, UEFA was condemned by a Belgian court to pay some of the money allotted to the families of the victims. UEFA refused, claiming that as an association of more than forty national football federations it was above national laws. Only a threat from the Belgian interior minister to bring the issue to the Trevi group (and hence make it European) convinced UEFA to comply with the court order (Dupont 1996: 66). Apparently the lesson had not been learned, since in the *Bosman* case, UEFA tried again to have the case thrown out of court by arguing that as a Swiss legal entity (its headquarters are in Berne) it was beyond the jurisdiction of a Belgian court.

11. "Hearing on Bosman Judgment Confirms Differing Opinions," Reuter Textline Agence Europe, 22 March 1996.

12. "Fontainebleau European Council," *Bulletin of the European Communities,* 6 (1984), 11, available at http://aei.pitt.edu/1448/01/Fountainebleau__june_1994.pdf.

13. More precisely, the committee suggested that sport organizations be encouraged to set up "European Community events such as cycle and running races through European countries" as well as "Community teams for some sport to compete against joint teams from geographical groupings with which the Community has special links." It also suggested "inviting sport teams to wear the Community emblem in addition to their national colours at major sporting events of regional or worldwide interest" (Adonnino Committee 1985: 19).

14. "European Council in Milan," *Bulletin of the European Communities,* 6 (1985), 14, available at http://aei.pitt.edu/1421/01/Milan_June_1995.pdf.

15. OJ C 340, 10 November 1997, 0136, available at http://europa.eu.int/smartapi/cgi/sga_doc?smartapi!celexapi!prod!CELEXnumdoc&numdoc=11997D/AFI/DCL/2 9&model=guichett&lg=en.

16. The text of the Treaty of Lisbon is available at http://www.consilium
.europa.eu/showPage.asp?lang=en&id=1296&mode=g&name=.

17. In Italy, for instance, it is common to blame any poor performance by the
azzurri on the number of foreign players in Serie A, the top Italian professional soccer league. The presence of foreign players, the argument goes, makes it more difficult for promising Italian players to play at a high level and hence acquire experience that would improve their performance on the national team.

18. "Principles for the Amendment of FIFA Rules Regarding International
Transfers," available at http://www.europa-kommissionen.dk/upload/application/
ba42b081/fifi-regler.pdf, and "Regulations for the Status and Transfer of Players,"
available at http://www.thefa.com/NR/rdonlyres/C78670E4-FC3D-4AF2-A526-
59DEA094982E/97945/Regs_StatusTransferPlayers.pdf.

19. "Directive 97/36/EC of the European Parliament and the Council of 13
June 1997," OJ No. L 202, 1997, 60.

20. For a comprehensive view of the Commission activities, see Commission
of the European Communities (2007b).

21. "Commission Welcomes UEFA's New Policy for Selling the Media Rights
to the Champions League," IP/02/806, Brussels, 3 June 2002, available at http://
europa.eu/rapid/pressReleasesAction.do?reference=IP/02/806&format=HTML&
aged=1&language=EN&guiLanguage=en.

22. This argument has also been advanced by Miller and Redhead (1994) and
Wright (1999). For a series of arguments on the benefits that would accrue to all
sport stakeholders from complete liberalization of the sport sector, see Ross (1991).

23. A similar mode of sport governance exists at the national level. According
to an Italian sociologist, for instance, the dynamics of the Italian government's intervention in the domain of sports can be explained as follows: the increase in earnings
generated by television has led some football superclubs to claim for themselves, and
for football in general, a bigger share of the pie. Such "aggressively profit-oriented
philosophy," however, "has difficulty in coexisting with the principle of public support of the sporting movement." Or, put in simpler words, in Italy by means of legal
betting, football provides "public" financial support to many other sports. If football
claims more for itself, inevitably other sports will receive less. Hence, the intervention of the state aims primarily at curbing the "strong powers," that is "checking the
separatist tendencies of spectator football in relation to the wider system of performance sport." The state, in other words, is called upon "to execute a complex role of
both management and mediation." Sport constitutes "a political arena" in which very
concrete interests are at stake and the management of which "demands powers of arbitration." The state can legitimize its "regulatory" intervention through "the very
scope and the social dimension of the football phenomenon" (Porro 1997: 191–192).

24. The *Bosman* ruling established two categories of players, the EU nationals
and the extracommunitarians. The latter and the clubs employing them obviously
could not use Article 48 to circumvent the nationality clause or the transfer rule. (According to some lawyers at least, they could have used other parts of Community law
to try to obtain the same result [Nyssen and Denoël 1996], but this would have been
a long and difficult route to follow.) Hence, players with a non-EU nationality (third
country nationals) and their clubs became busy finding unlikely grandmothers in all
corners of Europe or arranging marriages of convenience.

11

Governing the Single Market: From Private Coordination to Public Regulation

Michelle Egan

The year 1988 marked the beginning of a period of major political, economic, and institutional reform in Europe. With the advent of the single market and monetary union, market integration, in turn, required a number of institutional changes. These included the creation and strengthening of competition and regulatory agencies, the enactment of new legislation to promote fiscal discipline, the creation of new regulatory frameworks, and greater protection of consumer and welfare benefits. The increased openness of the economy to foreign direct investment, the privatization of traditional state-owned enterprises, and the consolidation of market-oriented reforms have transformed economic activity. With the promotion of deeper liberalization in some sectors, domestic firms responded by increasing economies of scale, expanding export markets, and acquiring foreign subsidiaries. The reduction of barriers to trade and investment has generated both institutional adaptation and change, however. The challenges of governing a market in which the tight controls exercised by governments over cross-border flows of goods, capital, and labor have been substantially reduced has resulted in new public institutions to regulate economic activity as well as new responsibilities for private actors to monitor and coordinate the provision of public goods. Increasingly, the regulatory space is occupied by the state and a variety of nonstate players that have transformed the European polity.

As Ingeborg Tömmel and Amy Verdun point out in Chapter 1, there is a rich scholarly literature on the development and impact of new modes of governance within the European Union (EU). At the core of these debates is the implication that the public sector has lost its exclusive monopoly in providing and shaping public policies within states or at the international level (Scott 2002). Yet liberalization of markets has made it necessary for governance structures to enforce market competition and maintain credible market commitments (Scharpf 1999). As such, regional market integration creates both imperatives and incentives for states to relinquish their authority to set and enforce rules. This transfer of sovereignty can be achieved either by pooling their political authority with other states to provide an effective resolution to problems that transcend national boundaries or by delegating authority in terms of policy initiation, dispute resolution, or implementation. European governance has thus shifted from direct economic interventionism to regulation where a myriad of public and private actors seek to use various instruments to achieve certain goals and objectives. The resulting fragmentation of public authority has created new forms of regulatory governance in which a variety of regulatory institutions, mechanisms, and processes has emerged to create and sustain markets. Although described generally in terms of a layered system of governance based on regulation, the recognition of multiple intersecting networks and overlapping jurisdictional arenas has also generated increased attention to the impact of such political practices, institutions, and principles on accountability and legitimacy (Cohen and Sabel 1997; Picciotto 2000; Slaughter 2004b).

This chapter highlights the evolution of new modes of governance as an expression of changing ideas about market governance. As political authority is increasingly distributed across global, regional, and national levels of governance, a number of key questions characterize the governance literature. Who sets the rules? What are the institutional characteristics of such governance regimes? What modes of governance have emerged? How effective and efficient are such governance structures in fostering market liberalization? The core thesis is that the restructuring of the state, through the delegation and creation of regulatory agencies, and the restructuring of business, through internal governance mechanisms and new instruments of self-regulation, involves dynamics of distributional conflicts and regulatory competition in some cases and significant cooperation and institutional coordination in other cases. This thesis fits with recent debates in the governance field that have increasingly focused on institutional performance in terms of understanding how the European Union, with its segmentation and separation of powers, variable policy boundaries, and diffuse policy networks, can effectively promote the smooth functioning of markets.

The chapter is divided into four parts. The next section discusses the processes and instruments of governance that have emerged in fostering market regulation over the past fifty years. It reviews how the institutions that govern the single market have changed and adapted to cope with rapid technological change, increasing international competition, and a host of other problems that affect European markets and societies. The following section looks at the impact of such governance mechanisms that have flourished under the shadow of hierarchy fostered by European supranational institutions. This section illustrates the specific actors involved, their negotiating strategies, and the instruments used in the internal market. Then a further section discusses governance and accountability. Since the wave of regulatory reforms transforming traditional patterns of rule making and rule enforcement (Braithwaite and Drahos 2000; Levi-Faur 2005) has generated new concerns about sustaining market integration without jeopardizing democratic governance, the conclusion assesses the legitimacy of new forms of governance. This highlights the challenges for law and constitutionalism that emerge as a result of the shift in exercise of public power from traditional law-making institutions. More generally, this chapter reflects the interest among scholars of governance in the institutional redesign of the market mechanism, the nesting of markets, their embedding in nonmarket mechanisms, and attempts to improve efficiency and compensate for market failure (Jessop 2003b).

The Transformation of Governance

The Traditional Hierarchical Modes of Governance

For much of the postwar period, the state was the principal source of governance for society in Europe. Government intervention in the economy grew, in part owing to the need to establish economic security and stability, reduce transaction costs, and respond to increased societal pressures and demands. Although the nation state typically played a decisive role in tackling fundamental problems raised by contemporary capitalism, the traditional conception of legal regulation by the state was subsequently transferred to the European level. As market economies integrated, there was a need to foster the supply and demand of policy instruments to support both the creation and maintenance of a single market. Much of the early efforts of European integration was thus premised on the assumption that the public sector would exercise governance through regulatory harmonization. It would foster increased uniformity through top-down mechanisms of governance that would tackle the trade-impeding effects of divergent regulations and standards. In three areas, namely competition policy, trade negotiations, and internal market regulation (to ensure free movement of goods and services), the European Community began in the 1950s and 1960s to play a major role in shaping market behavior. Some areas in the economic field, including regulation of goods and services, industry, transport, energy, and competition, shifted from exclusively national to concurrent competence as market integration sought to abolish both tariff and nontariff barriers. Yet efforts to promote international policy coordination also need to take account of the fact that many of these barriers reflect legitimate differences between countries in terms of administrative culture, risk assessment, and divergent patterns of state-society-economy relations. Although the European polity advocated principles of nondiscrimination, this was qualified in the treaties to allow exemptions from obligations for a range of public policy and security issues. The European Union has thus always permitted what are deemed as legitimate restrictions on trade (Article 28/30).

Traditionally, the process of governance is associated with the central state that sets authoritative rules. The Community followed such a mode of governance in the 1960s and 1970 through harmonization, which sought to eliminate disparities in national regulatory systems and foster convergence through common policy goals (Twitchett 1981).

Harmonization represents a structure of rule-making authority that creates coordination through formal hierarchy, where states negotiate reliable rules of procedure to increase efficiency and reduce transaction costs. Yet harmonization was difficult to achieve even after the old unanimity rule of Article 100 of the EC Treaty was replaced by qualified-majority voting (Article 100[a] as introduced by the Single European Act of 1987) (Egan, 2001; Joerges 2004b). Harmonization was not flexible enough to provide for the changing economic production (e.g., the shift to services and the introduction of greater product diversity at lower cost). Harmonization was increasingly perceived as a barrier for technological innovations and a burden for producers dealing with various products and shorter product cycles in a competitive environment (Egan 2001: 61–82).

Since the traditional pattern of hierarchical governance was incapable of generating sufficient European-wide standards to facilitate market access, such direct economic interventionism can be characterized as a "regulatory mismatch" in which the instruments chosen are ill-suited to dealing with the problem (Breyer 1982). Failure of prior efforts at government coordination through harmonization led to alternative "new governance" mechanisms. Nonstate actors became more closely involved as substitutes for the increasingly overtaxed state, as either self-regulating or co-regulating actors in network constellations including and with the support of the state (Lenschow 2007).

In the face of this dilemma, policymakers cast about for an alternative means to promote regulatory cooperation at the European level. The attempt to adjust the goals and techniques in response to past experience with harmonization has taken different forms, in an effort to stem widespread criticism for excessive burdens on business, stifling flexible production, and public perceptions and opposition to such hierarchical modes of coordination. Although a significant reform of the single market policies, including more flexible modes of governance, was promoted in the early 1960s and 1970s, moving from hierarchy toward self-regulation, these liberalizing effects fell far short of the goals of removing barriers to trade. More important, they failed to keep member states from introducing new national measures impeding market access. Such growing protectionism undermined EU efforts to promote policy coordination through harmonization, as lack of leadership and political will stalled further efforts at market liberalization.

New Approaches to Market Integration:
Delegation and Private Regulatory Governance

Repeated efforts to promote economic revival led to a comprehensive effort to relaunch the single market. Bolstered by the idea of mutual recognition as a new strategy to promote market access, the European Commission sought to develop the ideas implicit in this legal doctrine into a coherent policy option. Through its ambitious White Paper on the Internal Market, the production of rules has increased dramatically since the single market project was revitalized in the 1980s and 1990s. The emphasis on market integration that resulted from the single market was a direct response to problems attributed to globalization, amplified by national vulnerability to trade and financial flows, eroding competitiveness for European firms, and structural unemployment and labor market rigidities (Hooghe 2004: 2). Although the main impetus was liberalization, which was viewed as the removal or reduction of barriers to trade in capital and commodities, the shift toward more open and competitive markets has at the same time resulted in a growth of regulation, much of it coming from the regional or international level (see Egan 1998, 2001; Mattli 2003). Whether it is accounting standards for publicly traded companies, environmental management, data privacy, or consumer product safety, the single market has been faced with addressing the issue of "externalities" and economies of scale of commodities and services trade across national boundaries, on the one hand, and the heterogeneous preferences of public goods provisions on the other (see also Kahler 2004). Under such conditions, the process of restructuring economies has involved the generation of substantive standards and rules governing economic activity with greater reliance on decentralized and flexible bodies responsible for implementing decisions.

As a result, the European Union has created governance mechanisms that incorporate different forms of cooperation as well as different sets of regulations, based on institutionalized cooperation between private nonstate actors focusing on the creation of voluntary norms and rules. Such delegated governance has resulted in new institutions and techniques of regulation within the EU single market that have been designed to better deal with risk (Picciotto 2002). Many of these regulatory matters have been the subject of policy failure under the traditional mode of harmonization.

As the European Commission has found it difficult to reconcile the political interests of member states, it has, in turn, shifted policy responsibility onto standard-setting bodies, namely the European Committee for Standardization (CEN), the European Committee for Electrotechnical Standardization (CENELEC), and the European Telecommunications Standards Institute (ETSI). These European private standards organizations are the collective umbrella of national standards organizations that are predominantly private but may also include parapublic national standards organizations. Although little was known of the European standards organizations until the advent of the single market program, several powerful national standards organizations such as Deutsches Institut für Normung (DIN, the German standards body) and British Standards Institute (BSI, the British standards body) traditionally provided the bulk of product and process standards, placing their domestic firms in a strategic advantage and forcing other domestic firms to copy or emulate them. These national bodies serve as the representative institution at the European level, with much of the technical regulatory frameworks delegated to transnational networks of committees and working groups that include national representatives, mostly from industry, but also from public regulatory agencies and noncommercial interest groups such as consumer and environmental organizations. The European standards bodies also include affiliate members from candidate and potential candidate states as well as associate members representing broad European interest groups such as the European Trade Union Federation, European Chemical Industry, and European Office of Crafts, Trade, and Small and Medium Business Organizations. As states are confronted by the fundamental trade-off between losing their regulatory authority and gaining increased trade opportunities through improved market access, Community policymakers have harnessed these private sector resources to further public policy goals, and the expansion of indirect governance has created a regulatory system that blends the public and private spheres.

At the European level, instead of direct state interventionism and management, public functions have been delegated to semiautonomous bodies that account for a wide range of networks engaged in regulatory coordination.[1] This new approach has several elements. For example, a crucial feature of the EU's effort to address trade barriers was the mutual information provision, a soft law "gentlemen's agreement" that would serve as an early warning system to prevent new nontariff barriers from emerging. It began as a voluntary mode of coordination, however, which meant there was little incentive for member states to comply. States continued to adopt new national regulations without addressing the consequences for the single market. EU regulators then developed more formal legal arrangements for cooperation based on notification, exchange of information, and consultation through the mutual information directive (83/189). This strategy sought to promote "regulatory pre-emption" and included both standards and regulations, thereby exercising some form of obligation on both public and private institutions. Challenging member state implementation through judicial action, the European Union has been able to foster better compliance with the mutual information directive, which makes notification of national regulations directly effective in the area of goods. The disciplining effect of notification and scrutiny of new regulations is absent for services, however, as there is no equivalent of such constraints on national regulatory authorities.

The new policy addressing nontariff barriers was further outlined in the White Paper of 1985 and the so-called new approach, together with a draft model directive establishing a regulatory strategy based on a sharing of functions between the public and private sector. Where possible under the new approach, there was to be mutual recognition of regulations and standards as well as the means of conformity or compliance with them (see Chapter 9). The principle of mutual recognition provides a framework for the moderate regulatory competition between national regulatory regimes (Sun and Pelkmans 1995). States may keep their regulatory standards provided they do not constitute nontariff barriers. Such competition among rules is, however, subject to minimal standards of equivalence so that mutual recognition constrains the dynamics of a race to the bottom. Where necessary, the harmonization of regulations would be restricted to broad general requirements mandatory for all states. More flexible regulatory networks would emerge, however, as the European Union delegated detailed technical issues to experts who could facilitate policy coordination and standardization. The private standards bodies of CEN, CENELEC, and ETSI would thus act as "proxies" for government in the regulatory process. This form of self-regulation within the European single market developed initially in two areas: reference to standards, to flesh out the directives on technical barriers and new approach directives, and the social dialogues (see Chapter 7). Such a shift in governance was gradually extended to other fields through codes of conduct and voluntary agreements in consumer rights, electronic commerce, professional services, and environmental protection.

Standards setting is the making of voluntary, expertise-based regulations that shift the mode of governance from hierarchy to cooperation, from regulation to delegated self-regulation, and from top-down political steering to horizontal coordination (see Chapter 2). Such standard-setting bodies bring together different actor constellations depending on the issue area, so that thousands of large and small firms, as well as labor and trade union organizations, health and safety bodies, and consumer agencies, are involved in consultation, negotiation, and persuasion. Significant barriers face those that seek intermittent participation, however, so that many firms are in fact standards users rather than standards developers. What has emerged has been described by Majone as "a microcosm in which conflicting epistemologies, regulatory philosophies, national traditions, social values and professional attitudes are reflected" (Majone 1984: 20). Such governance institutions are rule-making bodies that have the capacity to guide firm conduct by providing incentives for compliance, even when they lack independent coercive powers.

Such delegation can helpfully be viewed in functionalist terms in which private regulatory governance reduces information and transaction costs, which are effectively internalized by the trade associations or firms involved. This is because standards are requested by Community policymakers for specific framework laws so that in effect European standards fulfill single market obligations. Private interests provide voluntary agreements that would strengthen conformity and compliance with framework laws. As regulatory agents, the standards bodies are characterized by substantial technical expertise and unrivaled access to specialist information—attributes that allow these private organizations to steer policy developments. Through a rationalist lens, the strategic interactions between market players play a crucial role in the process. How nationally based experts render opinions and form alliances and coalitions to render agreement on European standards is not apolitical. Though markets can be an effective mechanism in setting standards, they are sometimes imperfect and institutional frameworks are crucial as alternative coordinating mechanisms. Because consensus is the general decision rule, the result is a "battle of the sexes" problem in which important benefits are dependent on the ability to cooperate. At the same time, cooperation is dependent on resolving conflict over the solution chosen. In other words, getting an agreement may be likely if preferences converge. If not, the end result will be deadlock, as different interests may block agreement or promote agreement on the lowest common denominator.

Since the strategic impact of standards on market share impacts behavior, rational choice approaches view outcomes as determined by relative power and strategic rationality. In such negotiating systems, firms operate in a competitive mode of exchange and compete with each other in promoting their specific industry standards. Under such circumstances, Scharpf argues that high levels of regulation may create a competitive advantage for the firms subjected to them and thus exert a competitive pressure on other governments to raise their own levels of regulation (Scharpf 1997c). These dynamics are also affected by different resource endowments, for example, in information and expertise, leading to efforts to maximize strategic benefits by creating a bandwagon effect to lock-in specific technology and production processes and generate first mover advantage (David 1985). Such coordination may be absent, however, in areas that concern the social conditions and processes of industrial production, such as minimum wages or air pollution, where the mode of governance is shaped by competitive or even conflicting interests, generating regulatory competition and downward pressures on national regulations.

Standard setting is also structured and shaped by norms determining what kinds of practices are acceptable, including the appropriate behavior in times of conflict, influencing the social context in which negotiation and bargaining takes place. As a result, communicative rationality is at least as important as instrumental rationality in understanding the dynamics of standardization processes. Socially cohesive actors influence each other and tend to adopt similar patterns of behavior (Coleman 1988). Thus, standard setting relies significantly on notions of persuasion, argument, and patterns of mutual trust and credibility, with standards developed through bargaining outcomes in which deliberation and credibility affect outcomes. The nature of deliberation in standard setting is based on the principle of consensus, which means that the outcome of standardization depends partly on the pay-off structure but also on the organizational norms, dynamics, and synergies within the policymaking community. Due process, transparency, openness, and balanced interest representation are crucial norms for structuring meaningful social deliberation. As standard setting depends on the self-commitment of member states to implement policies, this deliberation process is a precondition of its success and basis of its legitimacy. Following Braithwaite and Drahos (2000), such forms of governance highlight the degree to which persuasion, normative appeals, voluntary standards, and governance without government are vital elements of regulation across national borders.

Such use of standards in market regulation means that policymaking becomes more diffuse and derived from multiple sources. Because of the collective action problems confronting member states, such reflexive regulation—as Ayres and Braithwaite (1992) term this public-private interaction—relies on conditional delegations of regulatory responsibility to stakeholders, such as public interest groups, trade associations, and industry itself. Yet the growth of private governance regimes has raised considerable questions about the "privatization" of public law and the classic problem in international affairs of how public goods are provided, with the usual focus being on intergovernmental cooperation (Ruggie 1972). As the boundaries between public and private roles are increasingly blurred, the provision of public goods is becoming more fluid. Equally important, such a shift from hierarchical legal norms and administrative practices has generated a substantial debate about delegation that draws together a number of different concerns about private governance in Europe. These include the impact of the delegation of legislative powers, the effective role of judicial review and oversight of standards, and the lack of transparency and accountability of such bodies.

This problem has generated alternative answers about the expectations and outcomes of such decisions. Schepel has argued that there are a number of formal institutional structures and incentives that shape outcomes. These private regulatory networks are generally legitimated by formal legal provisions so that the relationship is contractual (Schepel 2005). As Scharpf concludes, the delegation of governance tasks to lower levels or nonstate actors depends on a credible shadow of hierarchy (Scharpf 1993b). The process relies on traditional Community methods of law and judicial remedies to foster compliance with standards. Both tort law and antitrust law can be used to monitor the process and identify transgressors. In this view, the introduction of framework laws under the new approach does not mean the transformation to more flexible modes of governance. Quite the contrary, the delegation of standards to private bodies is coupled with mandates that are often very detailed. Even though appearing to be more flexible, in some ways the process has moved toward the same administrative and oversight procedures that accompany the delegation of regulatory power to public agencies (Egan 2001; Schepel 2005).

In seeking to ensure the political responsibility of such private agencies, there are a host of both indirect and direct procedural controls available to other actors. The governance structures of standards bodies allow for complaint procedures and other mechanisms to prevent abuse of a dominant position by any individual company over the standard-setting process. Due process, enforced interest group participation to ensure consumer and labor representation, and potential public vetoes are all potential threats (or "police patrols," to use principal-agent language) to monitor private sector deliberations. As Majone suggests, such accountability efforts can be a valuable alternative, as specific procedural mechanisms can be a fair substitute for democratic legitimacy. His argument depends on the distinction, well known from legal theory, between efficiency-oriented and distribution-oriented standards of legitimacy, however, so that delegation to independent institutions is democratically justifiable as a method of achieving credible policy commitments.

New Approaches to Market Integration: Delegation and Public Agency Governance

As European economies have privatized industries, adopted market mechanisms, and deregulated trade and financial regimes, the institutional effects of such policy changes have unfolded over time. The European Commission did not anticipate the administrative and regulatory powers and resources that the administering of the European market project would require. The gap in administrative law has thus generated the growth of agencies in the European Union, with their own legal personality and administrative structure, and has fostered new forms of governance networks based on "regulation by information" that differ from traditional modes of governance. The agencies currently in existence have been set up in three waves, beginning in the 1970s with the European Centre for the Development of Vocational Training (CEDEFOP) and the European Foundation for the Improvement of Living and Working Conditions, which had limited powers. The second wave of agencies started in the early 1990s with the creation of the European Environment Agency (EEA), followed by agencies in social policy and intellectual property rights, then leading to an on-going third wave that created the European Food Safety Authority (EFSA), the European Maritime Safety Authority (EMSA), European Railway Agency, and the European Aviation Safety Authority (EASA) concerned with interoperability and safety issues, as well as the highly contested European Fisheries Agency and a European Chemical Agency.

Although independent regulatory agencies per se are not new, market integration in Europe has been accompanied by new institutions and instruments of regulation that have been designed to either constitute a new competitive order and maintain entry for new competitors in the case of infrastructure and utilities or to deal with transaction costs and negative externalities in the case of environmental protection or with information asymmetries in the case of medical evaluation and controls. Thus a large number of regulatory agencies have emerged in the areas of both social and economic regulation over the past ten years, dealing with internal market issues. The European Medical Evaluation Agency, Food Standards Agency, European Defence Agency, and European Patents and Trademark Protection Agency each address issues of importance to the single market. Like their private sector counterparts, the growth of European regulatory agencies is a response to the legislative growth and complexity in highly technical areas, posing some of the same problems of oversight and control.

Yet delegating regulatory competences to specialized institutions is in part viewed as a means of insulation of decisions from political control and reversal and an enhancing of the credibility of negotiated agreements after market decisions are made (Majone 2000; Gilardi 2005). As privatization has swept through Europe, the resulting creation of independent regulatory agencies at the national level has been replicated at the EU level. As noted earlier, the link between regulation and market integration, argued most forcefully by Majone, is due to the fact that the EU has limited fiscal and redistributive powers, so it must rely on regulation as an essential tool of governance (Majone 1996). As such, regulatory agencies are part of the European regulatory state, and these nonmajoritarian institutions reflect a desire to facilitate the market, whether through market-specific arrangements, maintaining entry for new participants or competitors, or fostering regulatory coordination (see Table 11.1).

Charged with regulation on market entry and exit, or more general informal, policy-informing, information-gathering duties, the new European agencies meet a purely technical demand for market-corrective and sector-specific regulation (Kreher 1997; Chiti 2002; Vos 2005). Though having limited powers in specific areas, regulatory agencies have not spread evenly across sectors and countries (Thatcher 2005). Not only do their institutional features

Table 11.1 Modes of Governance in the Single Market

	Hierarchical	Coordination	Competition	Network
Instrument	Harmonization	Standard setting (product standards)	Mutual recognition	Administrative agencies
		Regulatory agencies	Standard setting (process standards)	

vary, but their powers and responsibilities under public law may differ as well.[2] The European Union agencies are much more limited in functions and scope as a result of the *Meroni* doctrine (see Everson 2005).[3] Under the *Meroni* doctrine, such delegation to regulatory agencies cannot result in discretionary powers and political judgment, as this would jeopardize the balance of powers between the institutions. Wide discretionary powers cannot be delegated that restrict the possibility of instituting European Community (EC)–wide agencies with legislative, executive, and quasi-judicial powers in many liberalized markets, in sharp contrast to national regulatory agencies. Such legal provisions have constrained the influence of EC-wide agencies, which has generated much criticism about the need to improve their effectiveness (Majone 2000; Geradin 2005).

The delegation of such information-gathering and product coordination tasks to European agencies means that some perform monitoring and coordination functions (so-called soft governance) in the context of the single market (for example, observatory roles under the European Environment Agency), or promote cooperation (European Agency for Safety and Health at Work [EU-OSHA]; European Defence Agency [EDA]). Such negotiating systems can also be characterized as network governance, where coordination is based on mutual agreement and mutual resource dependencies. The EU-level regulatory agencies seek to foster trust in national regulatory systems, particularly under conditions of mutual recognition of rules. Yet the fears of regulatory competition and social dumping in many member states have led to increasing difficulties in adopting such a form of governance. Mutual recognition has effectively been coupled with minimal harmonization and other caveats, reducing its scope in various ways and setting up mechanisms of ex post guarantees and monitoring through including the obligation of national authorities to cooperate with each other (see Chapter 9). These regulatory networks were set up to release the burden of the European Commission from market oversight and in many instances—such as public utilities, foodstuffs, and pharmaceuticals—promote "soft" policy solutions to address problems from policy externalities to market failure.

Yet, agencies that have power to enact legal binding decisions or use regulatory instruments on third parties, such as the European Central Bank, or agencies that have influence over the adoption of final decisions by the European Commission, such as the European Food Standards Agency, suggest that delegation can produce more discretionary power and influence. Thus the institutionalized rule structure may result in greater opportunity for hierarchical coordination in monetary and competition policy, for example, through the supervision of mergers and acquisitions, suspected infringements of market power, and setting of interest rates in the euro zone compared to environmental policy or defense policy. In many ways central bank independence is a model of delegation, as it prevents governments from manipulating monetary policies for electoral purposes (Schamis 2006). Yet most agencies have no compulsory review powers and can be challenged legally before the European Court of Justice on the basis of annulment proceedings or can be subject to administrative review procedures by the Commission or other entities (Geradin 2005: 232).

Whether it is the new financial architecture, liberalization of public service monopolies, or defense industry procurement, such market integration has emerged in conjunction with the coordination among national regulatory or supervisory regimes. Eberlein and Grande (2005) conceptualize regulation through EU-level agencies as "transnational regulatory networks."

There is thus a horizontal dimension to network management in which the European Union seeks to coordinate a set of national organizations involved in the delivery and regulation of services. There is no hierarchical relationship among these agencies, however, with an emphasis on developing trust and incentives to facilitate working together across organizational boundaries. Such regulation by networks with different forms of decentralized and disaggregated modes of governance continues the dispersion of governance both functionally and territorially.

In functionalist terms, the major role of such regulatory networks is to reduce uncertainty and resolve problems of coordination. Regulatory agencies can also foster regulatory networks in which domestic adoption of market-oriented reforms or specific regulatory practices is strongly influenced by international pressures of coercion and emulation (Hooghe and Marks 2003). From a rationalist perspective, this implies that multiple jurisdictions allow for jurisdictional competition and promote the prospect of innovation and experimentation as envisaged under the mutual recognition principle (Gray 1973). By contrast, regulatory agencies can also be understood in sociological terms, where the single market requires commitment to and implementation of contractual obligations. This new understanding of regulatory agencies has led many observers to focus on operating norms and the importance of knowledge and persuasion, rather than command and control, as an alternative means of coordination (Majone 2000). Thus the European agencies work through informal information and consultation procedures, cooperate with national counterpart authorities via networks, and resolve conflict through mediation, with the goal of fostering mutually acceptable decisions through negotiation and deliberation (Yataganas 2001; Joerges 2004a). In the agency context, the mode of governance can also result from "institutionalized habit, redefining of interests, complex interdependency, normative commitments," and "capacity building" (Braithwaite and Drahos 2000: 555).

Given the heterogeneity of regulatory agencies, it is also possible to argue that they reflect different modes of governance. Some function as cooperation mechanisms designed to create a partnership among the national agencies, disseminating information and coordinating networks of experts, as in areas such as racism, social dialogue, and vocational training. On the other hand, agencies that serve the functioning of the single market, such as trademark protection and agencies for maritime and food safety, are often more regulatory, resulting in broader hierarchical powers of inspection, approval, and binding certification. These institutional rules and structures shape the modes of interaction and thus the constellations of power inside the various regulatory agencies, an illustration of which is provided in Table 11.1.

Assessing Single Market Governance

In recent years, the expansion of impact assessment and monitoring mechanisms has focused attention on the performance or functioning of the single market (Chatham House 2003; Radaelli 2005; Dierx and Ilzkovitz 2007). Since the Union level of governance does not derive its authority and legitimacy from direct electoral support, the effectiveness and credibility of the single market has meant that market management issues are increasingly salient, and efforts to make the single market work in practice have risen on the political agenda (Metcalfe 1996, 1999, 2000). The Commission has recognized that there is a widespread perception among businesses that European regulation is particularly rigid and burdensome. In particular, substantial problems remain with the slow development of harmonized standards to meet the minimum requirements under the new approach directives. Significant problems continue in new technology sectors, with business reporting uncertainly about the application of mutual recognition in practice (European Commission 2000c; Pelkmans 2006). The implementation of regulatory policies requires a certain level of suitable infrastructure and administrative and legal capacity to implement the range of regulatory instruments that are necessary to support markets for goods and services (Brenton 2001). Yet the gains already realized could have been substantially larger if the removal of most of the remaining cross-border barriers had been achieved.

Continuing problems such as slow or unsatisfactory implementation of directives, the inadequacy of some policy instruments, and persistence of barriers to trade suggest that the competitive and dynamic effects of the single market have not fully materialized (Egan forthcoming). Various guidelines from the Council and Commission have been issued, all with the stated aim of improving the functioning of the single market. Such initiatives include, inter alia, the Regulatory Simplification Initiative, the Action Plan for the single market, and a scoreboard to generate adverse publicity for those member states lagging behind (*European Report,* 28 November 1997). Most recently, the European Commission has sought to generate a better regulatory climate for business, so that new regulatory initiatives remove obstacles to innovation and growth, and also to integrate impact assessment into the

overall goals of the Lisbon agenda.[4] Such performance shortfalls with regard to the single market have generated pressure for further policy change,
particularly as specific member states have sought to accommodate distinct
national approaches by making EU regulation more flexible.

Although soft law measures such as peer pressure, exchanges of information, benchmarking, and best practices have evolved in the single market
context, there has also been a corresponding emphasis on judicial remedies
such as private litigation, infringement proceedings, and the principle of
state damages liability for violations of European law. The emphasis on soft
instruments for governing has opened up new forms of autonomy, with
much attention given to the indirect and informal means in which such regulatory instruments can shape markets (Héritier 1999; Eberlein 2003). Yet
there are also indications of growing legalization and new patterns of jurid-
ification that stress procedural requirements. Although private litigation entails one means of delegated enforcement (Kelemen and Sibbitt 2004; see
also Chapter 8), soft law mechanisms entail some level of legalization and
are often used as a precursor to hard law or as a supplement to binding regulations (Abbott and Snidal 2000).

As Pelkmans, Vos, and Di Mauro (2000) argue, the effectiveness of the
single market in core areas is dependent on both judicial and administrative
enforcement of rules that can be applied in cases of noncompliance. European case law has been instrumental in shaping market integration, expanding its interpretation of the basic freedoms from a prohibition of discrimination to a prohibition of restrictions. By determining what market areas can
be considered related to the public good, member state regulation is subject
to judicial scrutiny to determine whether specific laws can be accepted as legitimate restrictions on the basis of proportionality.[5] The constitutive role of
law is crucial in prompting the consolidation of markets, since the European
judicial system has placed state and local laws under its purview, to include
determinations of the economic relationship between public intervention and
the market and the political relationship between member states and the
Union. By shifting the focus toward creating the context for open markets
and competition, European law has reduced the cost and uncertainty of innovation and entrepreneurship. Such litigation may result from the relative
weakness of bureaucratic alternatives for achieving policy goals, particularly
owing to the constraints that regulatory agencies and other European institutions face in an exceptionally fragmented governing structure.

The functioning of the single market ultimately requires credible commitments, so that the many new modes of governance can operate within
the shadow of hierarchy. The structure of European institutions and the control these institutions exert over member states has generated a highly detailed, judicially enforceable set of legislation (Keleman and Sibbitt 2004).
Since market liberalization and trade increase aggregate economic growth,

intensify economic uncertainty and income inequality, and create economic winners and losers (Rodrik 1997; Garrett 1998), it is not surprising that there has been a corresponding increase in litigation by both public authorities and private parties over the rules of the market. As Pelkmans (2006) argues, companies incur significant information costs, transaction costs, and compliance costs, and the lack of predictable and regularized rules serves to undermine the effective functioning of the single market. The objective is to reduce the risk factor for private investment associated with uncertainty in the legal environment while recognizing that the new context of divided or shared governance generates increased concerns about policy credibility.[6] By focusing on the sustainability of market integration in the face of rent seeking and sectoral protectionism, increased attention has been given to sustaining credible commitments through the strengthening of the rule of law, ensuring that credibility for the traditional Community method of lawmaking remains crucial for the maintenance of the single market, even as the number of regulatory policy instruments expands.

Governance and Accountability

For any democratic political system to function correctly, there must be adequate checks and balances to maintain the accountability of the polity. In theory, accountability implies a form of legal restraint in which there are checks on exercising discretionary authority. At the level of design, the delegation of regulatory governance poses new puzzles in terms of how to regulate for the common good, as reflected in the intellectual debate on the logics of delegation and the wider issue of regulatory accountability. The functional fragmentation of the public sphere with the delegation of specific tasks to specialized bodies, which perform a public role but are autonomous from central government, has been a key feature of the internal market (Picciotto 2002; Egan 1998). For some, the delegated responsibility of agencies and market regulators has rendered traditional parliamentary accountability obsolete (Scott 2002). Others argue that the continued growth of technocracy and rule by experts is part of the changing nature of power and governance, a shift toward the politics of expertise in which the insulation from political conflicts provides its own legitimacy (Radaelli 1999). This position rests on an assumption of rationality, as delegation can reduce transaction costs and ensure credible commitments, for delegation can be viewed as a set of contracts to cope with the problems of collective action (Magnette 2005: 7). For others, delegation raises credibility problems where there is insufficient administrative capacity to regulate the single market (Majone 2000). This is especially the case involving risk regulation, where societies are divided over the merits of specific technologies, leading to contestation over the goals and instruments of regulation. As Majone concludes, "democratically accountable principals can transfer power to non-majoritarian institutions but they cannot transfer their own legitimacy" (Majone 1997b: 13).

The nexus between legitimacy and accountability in relation to the single market has generated considerable debate about the impact of delegation, as states relinquish their monopoly authority to set and enforce rules. The continued efforts to strengthen the single market have primarily focused on the dominance of market-making over market-correcting policies, without accounting for the emergence of new governance structures, including a range of economic interest groups, scientific experts, and advocacy groups that assist in implementing Community legislation. Although most explanations focus on the significant potential of such new modes of governance, bringing about an appropriate mix of responsiveness and accountability is one of the central issues for European governance. Several solutions to this dilemma have been proposed, but the major proposals are delegation, control and oversight, and deliberative democracy. Each of these perspectives on the transformation of governance in Europe proceeds on the basis of different conceptions of democracy.

For Majone, the European Union is a regulatory state aimed at addressing and mitigating the effect of market externalities. Thus, delegation to technical experts insulates policymakers from traditional majoritarian politics. This allows for more efficient decisionmaking outcomes in areas such as health and safety policies and monetary policy, where such regulatory bodies are engaged in regulative and not redistributive functions. Majone also points out that delegation can increase credible commitments (Majone 1995).

For Sabel, the interaction between public and private governance reflects a more deliberative model of democracy that requires an alternative to the hierarchical legitimacy implicit in the unity of state and law (Cohen and Sabel 1997). Reflecting important innovations, such institutional innovations in European administration provide alternative means of procedural democracy and legitimate governance through institutionally dispersed means of decisionmaking. Given the plethora of different institutions, agencies, and committees involved, deliberative decisionmaking is an effective means of addressing complicated regulatory issues, enabling the new institutions and instruments of governance to fill the void left by the deficiencies of traditional modes of governance. It is no coincidence that the idea of legal pluralism has also emerged as a means of addressing the changing nature of governance in Europe, as the traditional hierarchical and unitary conceptions of law accommodate the shared sovereignty and new legal orders that have evolved.

Conclusion: From Hierarchy to Coordinated Governance?

Since the 1986 signing of the Single European Act, which led to widening and deepening the internal market, there have been notable achievements across the goods, services, and capital markets as well as resistance in certain sectors that remain sheltered from further competition. The change in European political economy has resulted in regulatory reforms that have not only shifted the focus away from the traditional model of public management but also changed the overall configuration of the level and scope of regulation. Although Europe has traditionally been associated with the Community method, there has also been a shift toward institutional alternatives encompassing an increased number of policy areas. Even though attention has focused on the open method of coordination, which is widely regarded as fostering a new form of governance, the single market has promoted the development of other instruments of economic coordination. The new approach is generally seen as an important innovation aimed at more flexible regulatory strategies. Yet from the beginning, the single market program suffered from a tension between the stated aim of mutual recognition and the practice of harmonization.

These principles have had a significant impact on case law, to different degrees in goods and services; they have not yielded all expected benefits (Pelkmans 2002). In terms of scope, the single market has produced substantial bodies of regulation that have become part of the acquis (rules, standards, conformity assessment, risk regulation). Yet gaps remain in regulatory governance between the formal legal state of play and what economic agents experience in actual practice (Chatham House 2003; Pelkmans 2006). These gaps show up in services, in the denial of free movement and the hindrance of free establishment; in goods, in the failure of mutual recognition and recourse to derogations; in capital, in the limited impact of mutual recognition in company law and continued market distortions; and in labor, in national restrictions as well as the curtailment of demand via the host-country control principle. Despite efforts to promote market deepening through the introduction of new modes of governance as well as traditional Community methods, national regulations ensure that certain areas are shielded from competitive challenge at the European level.

In terms of regulatory design, the European polity has shifted from a functionally restricted market order, created by the European Community, in which powers and competences were clearly enumerated, to a system in which the expansion of policy competences into fields such as public health and consumer and environmental protection under the guise of internal market legislation has generated a range of committees, agencies, and other advisory bodies that shape market behavior. The term *regulatory governance* has been increasingly used to denote the shift from hierarchy to cooperation, with an increased range of functions delegated to semiautonomous public or private institutions. The international and domestic effects are interrelated, as governing institutions have been transformed, both at the infranational and supranational levels, resulting in a system of multilevel governance in

Europe. Such increasing differentiation of political and economic structures, which is a corollary of the diminishing steering capacity of the state, has generated different modes of governance to foster a fully functioning integrated market.

By relying heavily on self-regulatory organizations and devices, economic regulation in Europe breaks with traditional conceptions of top-heavy, state-backed formal legal regulation. In many areas of transnational regulation, substantial decisionmaking authority has been handed over to nonstate actors as states have had their capacities to exercise monopolistic control diminished owing to the rapid acceleration of globalization. Governance has evolved in the single market and refers to activities backed by shared goals that may or may not derive from legal and formally prescribed responsibilities. The structures of such governance regimes, composed as they are of governments, corporations, and interest groups, are often aimed at promoting forms of cooperative compliance. In other areas, the traditional constitutional framework and Community method remain central to market integration, backed by formal legal powers to ensure the implementation of duly specified rules. Finally, the advent of European administrative agencies, largely without implementation powers of their own, has secured a degree of administrative powers and resources through their networking with national administrators and the scientific and technical advice that they supply to policymakers and industry clients (Everson 1995; Majone 1997a). European integration has not only reformed the institutional architecture of the state but has fundamentally revised the methods of government and generated innovative modes of governance. The changed nature and scope of many markets implies greater differentiation in governance approaches between sectors to enhance competition and deal with the realities of regulatory diversity and the requirement for coherence between different EU and national policies.

In terms of authority, the single market has fostered a more complex set of strategic interactions in which the collective action of governments is one element and public-private networks are another. Little can be gained, however, by depicting the relationship in the dichotomous language of public authority versus private interests (Hancher and Moran 1989: 271). This new public-private interaction, based on limited and conditional delegation of regulatory responsibilities to agencies, industry associations, or even regulated firms themselves, occurs across a variety of policy areas associated with the single market. By focusing on the emergence, evolution, and transformation of different governing modes over time and across policy sectors in the context of the single market, it is clear that a key question is the effectiveness of such new modes of governance. Growing emphasis in the EU is being placed on codes, rules, and standards, developed by standards-setting bodies or autonomous agencies, in which the regulatory and supervisory roles have generated discussion about their institutional effectiveness. Yet the emergence of new patterns of governance also raises questions of public interest, including how it is maintained in the regulatory state. It is clear that one of the central issues in the literature is the growing discussion over how democratic principles and objectives can be realized amid the growing complexity of regulatory governance.

Although the impact of different power-sharing arrangements has been the core focus of studies of European governance, the functioning of the single market magnifies the fundamental problems that face all democratic polities—including concerns about checks and balances, representation and access, and governmental accountability/delegation and control. To some degree, the literature on European governance has assumed that the problems of delegation, institutional design, and democratic outcomes are unique. From monetary policy to administration of justice, many domestic polities as well as the European Union rely on technical expertise of autonomous agencies, on the one hand, and private semiautonomous agencies with significant decisionmaking capacity, on the other. Such delegation—and corresponding bureaucratic discretion—is inevitable in dealing with complex issues but has the risk of reducing accountability and transparency (Armony and Schamis 2005). As such, the emerging forms of governance, particularly in terms of networks of public and private actors, need to offer at least a partial response to new types of accountability and legitimacy concerns raised by the growth of the European regulatory state.

Notes

1. See Chapter 8 and Chapter 13.

2. I would differentiate between procedural and substantive obligations to differentiate these agencies.

3. In the landmark *Meroni* case, the European Court of Justice (ECJ) clarified the conditions under which a delegation of powers could be granted to a new entity.

4. "Communication from the Commission to the Council and the European Parliament: Better Regulation for Growth and Jobs in the European Union," COM (2005) 97 final, Brussels, 16 March 2005.

5. Current case law provides an open-ended list, including protection of the recipient of services; protection of workers, including social protection; consumer protection; preservation of the good reputation of the national financial sector; prevention of fraud; social order; protection of intellectual property; cultural policy; and preservation of the national historical and artistic heritage.

6. Pelkmans (2006) argues that it is not acquis compliance or conformity to single market procedures per se but rather various country-specific domestic regulations that continue to thwart the single market.

12

Enlargement: Expanding the Realm of European Governance

Charles C. Pentland

As an area of European Union (EU) policy, enlargement is a curiosity. On the one hand, it has been a central and continuing preoccupation almost from the outset of the European project in the mid-1950s. On the other hand, only late in the day has it become formally integrated into the EU's policymaking system. The decade-long process culminating in 2004 with the accession of ten new members saw enlargement policy gradually become embedded into the EU's institutional structures. Ironically, this normalization has occurred at a stage in the history of European integration when the rationale and the prospects of future expansion are increasingly in doubt.

As the first section of this chapter will attempt to establish, much of this paradox can be explained by the uniqueness of enlargement as an issue area and by the way in which the expansion narrative unfolded until the mid-1990s. With the institutional embedding of enlargement policy from that point on, however, it becomes apparent in retrospect that there had been normative and structural forces at work for some time to gradually erode the conceptual and practical distinction between enlargement and other areas of EU policy. The second section of the chapter therefore uses the case of enlargement policy to address the question of how new modes of governance can emerge from the gradual, subliminal accumulation of new norms and decisionmaking practices.

The third section explores how EU governance works with respect to enlargement. It describes the central institutions and actors in the process, identifying its dominant quality as a dynamic equilibrium between the formal powers of the member states, working through intergovernmental institutions, and the informal influence of the Commission and the European Parliament. This sets the stage for the fourth section, in which the central concern is to identify the principal mode or modes of governance that characterize the enlargement process. The main finding is that enlargement is a unique combination of negotiation (both horizontal and vertical) and hierarchical forms of governance. A concluding section then revisits the theoretical issues of governance and institution building, which are central to this book, suggesting how the case of enlargement raises issues and questions for further research.

Enlargement as a Unique Policy Area

The EU is not, of course, the only international organization on the global or regional level that has experienced expansion of its membership. The premier global organization, the United Nations, has seen its membership almost quadruple since 1945, and regional groupings such as the Organization of American States (OAS), the Organization of African Unity (OAU; now the African Union), and the Association of South East Asian Nations (ASEAN) have all enlarged to various degrees. Of course, the EU's enlargement over the past dozen or so years has been paralleled by one of similar proportions in the North Atlantic Treaty Organization (NATO), involving most of the same states (Flockhart 1996; Wallace 2000; Schimmelfennig 2003).

The uniqueness of enlargement in the EU stems in part from the expectation, right from the outset, that the "vocation" of European integration was ultimately to embrace all of Europe—that the process would in some sense be incomplete as long as there were European states precluded from membership by economic or political conditions. This is not to say that at any given time all members gave the same priority to enlargement, but simply that at no time was any member opposed to it in principle. Despite not being clearly articulated in any foundational document, the pan-European vocation of the EU (and of the European Economic Community [EEC] and European Community [EC] before it) has long been one of its most deeply held principles.

Enlargement is also unique among EU policy areas. It looks very much like an aspect of foreign policy—indeed, some argue, the most successful manifestation of it—but foreign policy with a difference of both intention and effect. Its recognized implications for existing members, however, give enlargement policy a domestic face as well, different in degree if not always in kind from the domestic aspect of conventional foreign policy.

Enlargement policy is foreign policy in the obvious sense that its primary target is other states outside the ambit of the EU. At first glance, much of what goes on between the EU and these states looks like classic international relations—diplomatic exchanges, trade promotion, various forms of cooperation and conflict, alignment and opposition—in which the object is primarily to influence the orientation of the other state's foreign and security policies. But these are not just any states. They are European, and therefore neighbors, and most have declared EU membership to be their major purpose, perhaps their only significant foreign policy objective. It follows that— in contrast to classic foreign policy—the EU's prime concern becomes the domestic structures and policies of these prospective members of the club. Their economies, their politics, their legal systems, their societies and cultures all come under scrutiny and are subject to pressures for change.

It is important not to exaggerate the contrast. "Classic" foreign policy has not always respected the sovereign sanctity of domestic arrangements (Krasner 1999). The post–Cold War period has seen Western powers in particular adopt explicitly interventionist foreign policy doctrines, whether favoring regime change and democratization or promoting the responsibility to protect vulnerable minorities. That said, the range and pervasiveness of domestic intervention embodied in the EU's enlargement policy is unprecedented, as is the extent to which the applicant governments are complicit with it. Indeed, even the distant prospect of membership for a neighboring state may see EU modes of governance gradually extending into its domestic sphere, well before the accession process even begins.

Enlargement policy also looks like foreign policy in having transformative effects—intended or unintended, positive or negative—on regions bordering the EU. Managing the neighborhood has been an explicit aim of the EU since the end of the Cold War.

In this sense, enlargement policy complements and overlaps other external policies—trade, development, the European Neighborhood Policy, the Common Foreign and Security Policy—as is evident in the EU's complex and overwhelming presence in the Balkans. It has implications for border management, the place where domestic and foreign policies literally meet (Amato and Batt 1999; Bort 2003).

A state's foreign policy is not only shaped by domestic sources but also has domestic consequences—intended or not. In that sense, too, EU enlargement policy is not unlike conventional forms of foreign policy. But there is a major distinction to be drawn nevertheless: whereas the domestic effects of conventional foreign policy are usually by-products of policies and actions directed outward, in the case of enlargement domestic change is understood from the outset to be one of the intended results. Enlargement is, after all, a deliberate effort to change the composition and thus, almost inevitably, the character of the EU. That the stakes for the EU and its member states are generally perceived to be higher than in conventional foreign policy gives the domestic political process an unusual intensity at both the national and the EU levels of decisionmaking.

As every enlargement to date has shown, each existing member state is acutely aware of the likely consequences and undertakes fine calculations of the political and economic costs and benefits both domestically and with respect to its relative standing in the EU. As enlargement moves from broad strategic debate over whether, whom, and when to focused negotiations between the EU and the applicants, it becomes increasingly difficult to separate it as a policy area from the largely domestic issue areas represented by the thirty or more chapters in which the negotiations are framed. Whether preparing for predicted consequences of the negotiations or reacting to unanticipated ones, governments and other domestic political players in the member states generate new political dynamics and, frequently, innovative policy processes, for example, in such fields as agriculture, immigration, and regional development. Enlargement affects these governments at all levels— national, regional, and municipal—and animates a wide range of civil society and other nongovernmental actors who see their interests and activities as potentially affected for good or ill.

Enlargement also affects the strategic and positional calculations of member states' governments in relation to each other. The accession of Greece, Spain, and Portugal in the 1980s was seen in part as a cultural and political rebalancing of the EC's composition in favor of France and Italy, offsetting the first, more "northern" enlargement of 1973.

The enlargement concluded in 2004 saw members promoting neighbors expected to become like-minded allies once in—Finland and Estonia, Italy and Slovenia, Greece and Cyprus—whereas France's lack of enthusiasm for the process derived in large part from its belief that the new members in Central and Eastern Europe would align economically with Germany and politically with Britain. Such examples suggest that, at least with respect to enlargement, traditional balance-of-power considerations have not been banished from the EU's internal diplomacy.

Enlargement is thus unique among the EU's policy areas in how it combines the classic elements of foreign and domestic policy. Its medium-term objective may be to change the domestic character, external behavior, and, ultimately, the institutional affiliation of neighboring states, but it has consequences, both planned and unforeseen, for the domestic politics of member states, for their relations with each other, and for the EU as a whole. As we shall see, this hybrid quality of its effects is mirrored in the way enlargement policy is made. The distinctive pattern that marks the making of enlargement policy was a long time in emerging, revealing many of its features only in the process that culminated in 2004.

The Emergence of Enlargement as a Policy Area

One of the strange ironies of European integration is that even though its "vocation" to eventually embrace all of Europe is an entrenched principle and even though the EU and its predecessors have been almost continually engaged in expansion, enlargement has only very recently been recognized and normalized as an area of policy in its own right. The history of enlargement tends to be written as a series of distinct episodes that from time to time interrupt the normal forward march of the integration process. On every such occasion, concerns are raised as to whether enlargement will hinder further progress—underlining the assumption that forward motion (or deepening) is the norm, expansion (widening) the exception (Wallace 1976; Miles and Redmond 1996; Laurent and Maresceau 1998; Diedrichs and Wessels 2003).

In fact, almost the entire history of European integration from the mid-1950s on is one of continuous deliberation over enlargement. In almost any year since then, the EEC, EC, or EU could be observed receiving applications for membership, considering them, preparing for negotiations with some applicants, conducting them with others, drafting and signing accession agreements, ratifying them by parliamentary decisions or referenda, engaging in postaccession transition periods, or, on occasion, navigating prolonged periods of "renegotiation" (as with the United Kingdom [UK] until 1984). A given year might see several of these things going on at the same time, as enlargement processes overlapped.

In the formative and early years of the EEC, from 1955 to 1961, the issue of what to do about the UK was already on the table, although not yet framed in terms of enlargement. Britain had been briefly present at Messina, absent from Rome two years later, and instrumental in proposing first a broad free-trade area to include the EEC and then in setting up the European Free Trade Association (EFTA) as a rival grouping. The option of Britain's applying for membership, always implicitly there, did not see the light of day until 1961 (Kitzinger 1973). From that point on, the EEC was firmly and continuously in the enlargement business, notwithstanding vetoes from Charles de Gaulle in 1963 and again in 1967. After the accession of the UK, Ireland, and Denmark in 1973, the process was prolonged for another decade, by transition periods but also, more important, by the rolling renegotiation of the terms of entry conducted by successive British governments until the rebate agreement of 1984 (George 1990).

In 1975, even as Britain was conducting what then seemed a definitive referendum on staying in the EEC, a new round of enlargement got under way. Greece, Spain, and Portugal, newly liberated from their authoritarian regimes, applied for membership and kicked off another decade-long process of negotiation (Tsoukalis 1981). By virtue of its 1962 association agreement, Greece had a head start on adjustment to EC conditions and was admitted in 1981, followed five years later by the two Iberian states. In all three cases, subsequent transition periods of up to ten years followed, in such sensitive areas as labor migration. These transition periods extended into the 1990s, by which time Turkey (1987), Cyprus (1990), and Malta (1990) had applied.

The end of the Cold War saw applications by three neutral states: Austria (1989), Sweden (1991), and Finland (1992).[1] Small, wealthy, and stable, they leaped to the head of the queue and were admitted in 1995 (Granell

1995; Friis 1998). In 1993, even as the EU was engaged in these relatively brief and untroubled negotiations, it made the historic strategic decision to embark on an eastward expansion, involving up to ten Central and Eastern European states as well as the three Mediterranean applicants (Maresceau 1997; Mayhew 1998; Redmond and Rosenthal 1998). May 2004 saw ten of those candidates admitted, with the entry of Bulgaria and Romania deferred to 2007; the opening of negotiations with Turkey was delayed until the fall of 2005. As the twelve new members work through their transition periods, accession talks will continue with Turkey as well as Croatia, joined in the near future by the Former Yugoslav Republic of Macedonia. Other potential candidates await, in the western Balkans and the former Soviet Union. "Enlargement fatigue" notwithstanding, then, the EU will be negotiating with prospective new members for at least another decade.

The foregoing account makes it clear that throughout the history of the European project, enlargement has been an important and continuous preoccupation. It is something of a puzzle, therefore, that its normality as an area of policy has until recently gone unrecognized. This blind spot may be explained in part by the general belief—at least until the end of the Cold War—that enlargement would always be piecemeal and opportunistic, limited at various stages by the existence of alternatives (e.g., EFTA), taboos (authoritarian governments), or barriers (the Iron Curtain). Moreover, the perception of enlargement as a distinctive and exceptional business may in itself have discouraged thinking of it as an area of policy akin to, say, competition, agriculture, or trade.

Whatever the reason for those judgments, the post–Cold War period has seen enlargement finally, if gradually, come to look more like a "normal" area of EU policy. In the process, it has become apparent that it brings with it an accumulated legacy of assumptions, principles, norms, rules, and practices developed over its long and seemingly intermittent history. These include the principle—established during the painful early years of the British negotiations—that the burden of adjustment would lie with the applicant state. From this emerged the concept of conditionality—informal but well understood in the negotiations with Greece, Spain, and Portugal and subsequently formalized in the famous "Copenhagen criteria" of 1993.[2] Successive rounds of enlargement also allowed the member states to develop, refine, and, to some extent, routinize their procedures and structures for conducting accession talks. Episodic though the history of enlargement may have seemed, the wheel did not in fact need reinventing each time, although there could be—and were—improvements to the design. By the mid-1990s, it was pretty well understood and agreed what the respective roles of the main EU institutions—the Commission, the Council, the European Parliament—would be. It had also been well established that, despite the centrality of the Commission, the enlargement process retained important intergovernmental elements: member states could in principle exercise a veto at any number of points along the way—over if and when to commence accession talks, over the conclusion of specific chapters, over each accession treaty, and, of course, over its ratification.

The history of enlargement thus supports some of the propositions developed in Chapter 2 with respect to how new modes of governance can emerge. Even if those involved at the time thought of each enlargement as a unique episode raising novel challenges, retrospectively we can see that from the 1960s on they were building on and accumulating principles, norms, structures, and practices that would eventually become formalized in the 1990s. To describe this as "path dependency" may be too strong, but it was certainly not a haphazard, random process.

Enlargement Policy: Institutions and Actors

The EU's conduct of its most recent enlargement, formally launched in 1993 and still in progress, reveals the richness of this historical legacy and the extent to which it has—at last—become integrated with the central structures and processes of policymaking.

The intergovernmental institutions provide a framework in which the member states, as principal actors in the enlargement process, exercise power and pursue their interests, but those institutions—European Council, Council of Ministers, Presidency—are also collective actors in their own right. The supranational institutions—Commission, European Parliament—exhibit a similar duality: internally, each is a political arena in which national and EU-level forces are in play, but each is also an actor whose collective positions carry increasing weight, based on technical and political legitimacy. A survey of the roles of these central EU institutions in shaping enlargement policy shows not only how embedded enlargement has become but also, somewhat paradoxically, how distinctive it remains as an area of policy (Baun 2000; Friis 2003).

The role of the European Council—the regular summits of the member governments—in framing enlargement strategy, in overseeing the progress of negotiations, and in pronouncing on their outcome underlines the formally intergovernmental character of this policy area. In 1961, when Britain's application began the long process of the first enlargement, it was already taken for granted that the matter would be managed and ultimately decided by consensus or unanimity among the governments of the six original members. If there were any doubts on this score, they were removed by President de Gaulle's actions in 1963 and 1967. The famous "vetoes" were not, in fact, votes cast at formal meetings of the EEC's heads of state and government but rather unilateral statements to the media (Beloff 1963). Although the other five governments neither agreed with de Gaulle nor approved of his methods, they accepted the premise that for enlargement to proceed, all member governments had to be on side.

The inauguration of the European Council as a regular EC practice—although above and beyond its institutional framework—coincided in the mid-1970s with the second, or Mediterranean, enlargement. Although there was no Council meeting between 1976 and 1986 at which these negotiations were the dominant theme, issues that emerged in the course of the process did find their way onto the agenda from time to time. The European Council kept a watching brief and provided a venue for occasional high-level resolution of policy questions, and the Council of Ministers managed things between summits. In assessing and pronouncing on the state of negotiations at various points along the way, and in formally marking their conclusion, the European Council provided a collective legitimization of the outcome based on a consensus of the member states.

The most recent enlargement shows the extent to which these summits have solidified their role in defining the strategy, managing the process, and endorsing its outcome. The Maastricht Treaty creating the European Union in 1993 built the European Council into the Union's institutional framework. The Copenhagen European Council in June 1993 confirmed the decision of the then twelve member states to invite applications from the Central and Eastern European countries, laid down the track along which the negotiations would be expected to proceed, and set out the general economic, political, and legal criteria all applicants would have to meet. Subsequent summits, especially those in Amsterdam (1997) and Helsinki (1999), made important decisions about how—or whether—to differentiate among candidate states with respect to commencing accession talks and about how to assess their progress. Another Copenhagen European Council—in December 2002—formalized the conclusion that ten of the twelve candidates had met the requirements of membership. The Accession Treaty, signed in April 2003 in Athens, required ratification by each of the fifteen members and the candidates. That done, the ten were admitted in the spring of 2004.

Regular summits take place two or three times a year.[3] In between, the member states manage the enlargement process at the ministerial level through the Council of Ministers (foreign ministers, in this case, meeting as the General Affairs Council) and at the "deputy" level through their ambassadors to the EU, who constitute the Committee of Permanent Representatives (Coreper). Ministers or deputies meet to deliberate on reports or opinions from the Commission and to develop the EU's collective negotiating position. And they meet with their counterparts from each applicant state to negotiate the terms of accession. The intergovernmental character of this aspect of the enlargement process is evident.

A further expression of intergovernmentalism in the enlargement process has been the emergence of the Presidency as the day-to-day overseer and director of negotiations with applicant states. Although the practice of rotating the presidency of the intergovernmental institutions—principally the European Council, the Council of Ministers, and Coreper—among the member states every six months has its origins in the 1970s, its importance for the enlargement process only became apparent in the 1990s. In the case of enlargement policy, the institution of the Presidency helps resolve an idiosyncratic problem facing the member states: unlike most other policy areas, enlargement is not managed at the national level by dedicated departments. Instead, that task has been assumed by foreign ministries, partly because of enlargement's proximity to foreign policy, partly because of its comprehensive policy content. Foreign ministers meeting as the General Affairs Council of Ministers, underpinned by Coreper, thus provide intergovernmental oversight of accession negotiations. Chairing these meetings, the Presidency fills an institutional vacuum, providing continuity to the member states' collective management of the enlargement processes and bridging the gap between the relatively infrequent summit meetings. In this respect, the Presidency acts as the delegate and, to some extent, the executive, of the European Council.

The Presidency thus has a clearly demarcated role in the enlargement process. For each candidate, the Commission prepares an opinion as to the merits of its application and makes a recommendation to the Council of Ministers. If the Council arrives at a common position and agrees unanimously to proceed, the Presidency is then authorized to manage the accession negotiations. Working with advice and technical support from the Commission, the Presidency chairs and coordinates ministers, deputies, and other member state officials as they negotiate with representatives of each applicant in each of the policy chapters active at that time. Accession negotiations are thus essentially a set of parallel intergovernmental conferences between all the member states and each of the individual applicants (Baun 2000: 13 14). This process makes great demands on the Presidency and is especially challenging for smaller member states with limited technical and diplomatic resources.

The role of the European Council and the emergence of the Presidency as a vertical link from the summit down through the Council of Ministers and Coreper bespeak a degree of institutional creativity on the part of the member states in asserting the intergovernmental aspect of enlargement policy. So, too, does the prominence of the Presidency in managing negotiations during its six months in the limelight. It is, after all, conceivable that the Commission might have assumed the role of negotiator—acting on a Council mandate—much as it has in the field of trade policy. That it so aspired there is little doubt, but the national governments were of one mind to retain their sovereign authority in this area.

The Commission does, nevertheless, play a vital part in the enlargement process. In contrast to the European Council and the Presidency, its power is largely informal, but it is sufficient to considerably compromise the intergovernmental character of enlargement policy. The findings from its extensive investigation of each applicant, embodied in a formal opinion presented to the Council of Ministers, are critical in determining whether and under what conditions accession talks might begin. In the course of negotiations the Commission provides a continuous flow of information and evaluations to the Presidency and Council officials. It makes annual reports to the Council on the progress of each candidate, including estimates of when some chapters are likely to be closed and others should be opened for negotiations. In effect, the Commission keeps a scorecard or progress chart for each applicant; its findings provide ammunition for the member states and incentives to the applicants, who often see themselves as competing with each other. On the face of it, the Commission's role is technical and bureaucratic, but at its core it is deeply political.

The Commission's political influence becomes more apparent if we consider the broader context in which the accession process takes place. In the late 1980s, before the collapse of the Soviet system and well before most member governments were ready to contemplate an eastward expansion, the Commission began to extend economic and technical assistance to the Central and Eastern European states, signing Trade and Cooperation Agreements (TCAs) with them and beginning a "political dialogue." In 1992, it began to upgrade the TCAs to Association (or "Europe") Agreements, creating a political momentum toward expansion that any hesitant member state (and there were a few) would find difficult to resist. The Commission's design of the Copenhagen criteria in advance of the summit itself was another instance of its capacity to frame the issues, set the agenda, and even design the procedures for the accession process before it was formally engaged.

As the accession process unfolded, the Commission continued to exercise political influence, often through seemingly technical means. In 1997 it published *Agenda 2000* that, in addition to assessing the progress of each applicant, laid down the broad lines of a preaccession strategy and specified the extensive changes that the EU itself would have to undertake—most notably in agriculture—to prepare for enlargement (European Union 1997). This was the Commission in its classic political mode, linking the requisites of enlargement to politically sensitive domestic reforms that needed doing for their own sake.

Like the intergovernmental institutions of the EU, the Commission had to make adjustments to cope with the unprecedented scale of this most recent expansion. It became clear in the mid-1990s that, faced with thirteen applications for membership, the Commission could no longer rely on the traditional practice of providing data and assessments from the various Directorates General in a relatively decentralized and uncoordinated way. If the Commission wished to maintain a position of influence over enlargement policy, it would have to restructure itself so as to better manage the flow of information, oversee the process, and, above all, be able to formulate its own policy.

The Prodi Commission, installed in 1999, therefore created a new Directorate General (DG) dedicated to enlargement and headed by a forceful German Commissioner, Günter Verheugen.[4] It quickly became clear that Verheugen would not hesitate to express the Commission's views as to the prospects of the negotiations and the conduct of individual applicants. It could not always be assumed that these views accorded with those of all member governments.

After 2004 the number of parallel accession talks in progress was reduced from twelve to a more manageable four—the endgames with Bulgaria and Romania, and the early stages with Turkey and Croatia. The Barroso Commission has nevertheless retained DG Enlargement, now led by the Finnish Commissioner, Olli Rehn. He has continued Verheugen's tradition of regularly offering blunt assessments of the state of play, in the process maintaining the Commission's claim to at least part ownership of the enlargement process. The institutional embedding of enlargement policy in the Commission is thus based as much on political will as on technical necessity.

The European Parliament has a voice in the enlargement process once negotiations with each applicant have concluded and the Commission has signed off on the results. Along with the member governments, the Parliament must give its formal assent, by an absolute majority, to the accession agreement prior to its ratification by national parliaments or referenda. In addition, however, the Parliament has assumed an increasingly active political role in all phases of enlargement. Its resolutions can influence the selection of candidates and the timing, pace, and agenda of the negotiations. The pronouncements of its party groups or of individual members of the European Parliament (MEPs) contribute in varying degrees to the political climate in which particular applications, or enlargement in general, are debated. In the early 1990s the Parliament was notably more generous with aid and keener to get on with enlargement than were most member states. At the outset of negotiations, between the Amsterdam and Helsinki summits, it persuaded the European Council to negotiate with all twelve applicants at once—not just the six most advanced—and to accept Turkey as a candidate. Since mid-2004 a number of MEPs have pronounced on the need for a moratorium on further expansion, picking up on the "enlargement fatigue" detected in governments and public opinion around the EU (Rettman 2006; Beunderman 2006; Bureau of European Policy Advisors 2006).

This brief overview shows the extent to which, over the past decade or so, enlargement policy has become embedded in the EU's institutional structure and a balance struck between the formal powers of the intergovernmental institutions, on the one hand, and the informal influence of the Commission and the Parliament, on the other.[5] The member states, working through the intergovernmental institutions, have not ceded any of their formal powers over the process; indeed, the institutional innovations emerging in the most recent enlargement—such as the increased role of the Presidency—have strengthened and diversified those powers. But the informal power of the Commission has, if anything, grown even more. This is largely a function of the complexity of the process—the technical complexity of the acquis and the associated regulatory requirements and the political complexity of dealing with many different applicants at once, not to mention the domestic repercussions in the member states. These changes reflect shifts in the balance within the EU more generally. Enlargement is not the sole reason for the accretion of the Commission's (and the Parliament's) power since the Maastricht Treaty came into force in 1993, but it has played an important part in that development.

Enlargement Policy and Modes of Governance

EU enlargement policy is a fertile field in which to explore the four modes of governance identified in Chapter 2: hierarchy, negotiation, competition, and cooperation. To what extent is each mode represented in the process described above? Does the mix of modes characterizing enlargement policy warrant recognition as new or innovative? How does enlargement policy fit, shape, and take its cues from the EU's institutional structure? And to what extent does it conform to the broad conclusions derived from the theoretical framework of this project?

That the dominant mode of governance with respect to enlargement is negotiation is hardly surprising. The heart of the process, after all, is bargaining between the European club and one or more aspiring members. In many respects this resembles classic forms of diplomatic negotiation. Although the EU is not a sovereign state, it acts like one in this context, as it has for decades in matters of trade. The EU's interlocutors, in turn, may be *demandeurs* and, to some extent, decision-takers, but they are nonetheless sovereign states. From initial application to eventual ratification, therefore, the accession process resembles classic diplomatic negotiations.

What is more surprising is the range and variety of other forms of negotiation involved in enlargement policy. Some of this takes place on what Tömmel describes as the horizontal axis linking, in this case, the Commission and the intergovernmental complex of the Presidency and the Council, with the Parliament being an ancillary player (see Chapter 2). The EU's position on enlargement in general, or on specific matters at issue with a particular candidate, is shaped by this horizontal relationship among the principal institutions. But there is, as well, negotiation on the vertical axis that links the EU to institutions and actors at the level of member states: governments, parties, civil society, public opinion. That this relationship is vertical does not make it hierarchical.[6] Directorates General in the Commission exchange information and arguments with sectors of national bureaucracies. The same is true of political parties at the national and European levels. National governments and EU institutions engage in sometimes competitive dialogue with interest groups and public opinion. Such processes can be formal (mandatory consultations, for example) or informal. But they are negotiations all the same, in that they rely on rational argument and material inducements to reach agreement, rather than on the imposition of rule from above.

That said, hierarchy as a mode of governance is not entirely absent from enlargement policy. Obviously, once accession agreements are made and ratified by EU member governments and applicant states, they have political and legal consequences: laws must be made and regulations imposed. Indeed, the gradual application of conditionality in the course of the accession negotiations will have required—at least for the applicants—domestic legal, institutional, economic, and social reforms coming not only from "outside" but also, unavoidably, from the top down in their domestic political orders. The EU gains compliance from candidate governments by the implicit threat to deny or delay accession. Those governments may use similar arguments against domestic opposition to the required reforms but may also, in the last analysis, seek to impose them by law. Whatever the formal diplomatic trappings of the accession talks, then, the inherent asymmetries of power and purpose between the EU and the applicant introduce an element of hierarchical governance to the relationship.

Competition seems to be present in enlargement policy only in a somewhat marginal, if not eccentric, way, and cooperation seems largely absent. It might be argued that a pool of twelve candidates, such as existed from 1996 on, made for competition regardless of anyone's initial intentions. Indeed, applicant governments speedily framed the enlargement process in terms of rivalry, no doubt hoping to enlist national pride in their efforts to persuade their citizens to make the required sacrifices. Brussels obliged by invoking such sporting imagery as the "regatta"—candidate boats being rewarded in turn by membership as they crossed the finish line. This stirring but impractical vision was soon abandoned in favor of the cluster or the "big-bang" accession, in which all who met the standard by a given date would enter together. Competition still drove states to be part of that group, of course, as it drove the two laggards, Romania and Bulgaria, in jockeying for entry by 2007, and as it drives other aspirant members in the Balkans now. But such interstate competition is somewhat at variance with the general sense of the term in the governance literature.

Enlargement policy, then, is mostly governance by negotiation, with a strong supporting role for hierarchy and a minor part at best for competition. As a mix of modes of governance it is certainly both new and unique. But two cautions are in order here. First, it is not entirely clear what, if anything, we can learn from comparing this pattern of policymaking to others in the EU. Perhaps the closest approximation would be to other policy domains with an external orientation and a predominantly "soft-power" content, such as the Neighborhood Policy and some aspects of trade and development policy. Second, some of the qualities we have observed may prove to have been peculiar to the unprecedented scale of the enlargement just completed. From here on, enlargement is likely to revert to the earlier pattern that saw, at most, three or four candidates being considered at the same time. The current negotiations with Turkey, for example, are likely to be sui generis both in their bilateral dynamics and in their domestic political reverberations.

Enlargement policy has a distinctive place in the EU's institutional structure and decision system. First, consider its location on Tömmel's horizontal dimension that describes the fragmentation of power at the "European level" (Tömmel 2007). The fact that the critical decisions at all stages of the process are made by the European Council and the Presidency would seem to place enlargement close to the "Council" end of that axis. The intergovernmental bodies send directions to the Commission and receive information and recommendations in return. The Commission cannot count on either the Parliament or the Court as an ally. On the other hand, its capacity to frame the issues and shape the accession agenda represents a suite of informal powers that offset the formal prerogatives of the member states. The result may well be a pattern of decisionmaking lying somewhere between the Community method of the first pillar and the compromised intergovernmentalism of the second pillar.

Second, on the vertical dimension linking the European and the national levels, matters are more complicated. In the first place, the progress of enlargement is always hostage to the maintenance of consensus among the member states. From the initiation of the process (as at Copenhagen in 1993) to its conclusion when the last accession treaty has been ratified by all, there are many decision points where national vetoes may be wielded or threatened. Threats to veto can slow the process or, as we saw with Austria's strategy in October 2005, extend it through linkage to another state's candidacy.[7] Member states' positions will of course reflect both their macrolevel positional calculations (is this country's accession to our advantage?) and their reading of domestic opinion (will the electorate reward or punish us, and how malleable are its views?).

Member states are acutely aware that the most immediate consequence of enlargement is to change the composition of the EU's principal organs and the balance of power and interests at play in its decisions.

The other complication lies in the relationship between the EU institutions and the governments and societies of the applicant states. As noted earlier, although those relations have the formal character of negotiations between sovereign states, the asymmetry of power and purpose between the "ins" and the "outs" introduces a strong element of hierarchy. Conditionality obliges applicant governments to undertake far-reaching changes to their economic and legal systems, adopting the acquis communautaire and, under close monitoring by EU institutions, bringing their domestic and foreign policies into line with EU norms. This extension of the EU's legislative and normative reach beyond its boundaries—the gradual "Europeanization" (Cowles, Caporaso, and Risse 2001; Featherstone and Radaelli 2003) of the candidate states—involves a mix of two-level bargaining and domestic regulation by their governments. This relationship is both horizontal, because it involves diplomatic negotiations between the EU and the applicant states, and vertical, because the inherent asymmetry of the EU-applicant relationship compounds the hierarchical order through which applicants implement the required domestic reforms.

Conclusion

Tömmel observes that the new modes of governance are not in fact recent innovations but have been part of the European system from the outset, albeit in a less visible way than now (see Chapter 2). This is certainly true for enlargement policy, in how it incorporates and combines these new modes. In the early years of European integration, enlargement was a relatively simple process. The first enlargement saw a six-member EEC negotiating with four applicants, three of which were eventually admitted. Although governments—especially the British—were sensitive to domestic pressures and cleavages, they could treat the accession talks as a variant of classic international commercial negotiations among equals. Although the EEC had achieved a great deal in establishing the customs union, the Common Agricultural Policy, and free movement of labor, there was not yet much of an acquis. Moreover, each applicant believed—rightly or wrongly—that it could afford to walk away from the table and had a skeptical or divided public to give that position some credibility.

Even so, by the end of those first negotiations a pattern had been established: the process would be managed by the members, each of which could exercise a veto at any decision point; the Commission's role was technical and advisory; and it was for the members, not the applicants, to set conditions. In short, in a simpler form the unique mix of intergovernmental negotiation and hierarchical regulation was already visible.

Subsequent enlargements reinforced this pattern, not least because the asymmetries of power and purpose between the "ins" and the "outs" became more obvious and because the acquis had expanded as the EC/EU acquired new competences. These developments did, however, expand the political resources available to the Commission.

In general, then, the experience of enlargement policy supports Töm-mel's first conclusion. The forms of governance associated with it have be-come more visible, largely because of the experience of the last ten years or so, which saw them used more and also given official status in EU deci-sions and documents (for example, the Copenhagen criteria). One exception is that governance in this area has not necessarily become "softer." Condi-tionality may technically belong to the realm of soft power, but in this con-text it has acquired a strict, "take-it-or-leave-it" quality that moves it closer to the coercive end of the "hard-soft" spectrum. Arguably, its workings are not well captured by the conventional notions of hard or soft power.

The experience of enlargement certainly reinforces Tömmel's second conclusion, that European modes of governance are the product not of de-sign but of evolution and are linked to the systemic structure of the EU. The first three enlargements were managed in a largely reactive manner, in keep-ing with the assumption that each "widening" was a distinct episode, an in-terruption in the forward march of "deepening" integration. Nevertheless, principles, norms, and institutional innovations developed for each round of enlargement were resurrected and refined at the next: examples are condi-tionality and the use of transition periods to resolve deadlocks. The unprece-dented scope and political import of the most recent enlargement, however, almost overwhelmed this accumulated inheritance. Although the core princi-ples governing the conduct of policy could be maintained, the institutions and processes required reform if they were to cope with the complexities of twelve parallel candidacies. Hence the emergence of the Presidency as the prime coordinator and negotiator, the creation of the DG for Enlargement by the Commission, and the formal structuring of negotiations into the famous thirty-one chapters. All three were institutional innovations, but each was an evolutionary adaptation of existing practice to a novel challenge.

To what extent, finally, has the mix of modes of governance associated with enlargement further shaped the structure of the EU system? Paradoxi-cally, the embedding of enlargement as a "normal" sphere of policy in the EU's institutional framework seems to have had little systemic impact. The innovations to which it has given rise have not spread to other areas of pol-icy. As a policy process with an associated set of structures, enlargement has thus become both integrated and quarantined.

This is not, of course, to say that the enlargement process does not have transformative consequences for the EU system. But they are of a dif-ferent order from the effects of other policy processes. First, the anticipa-tion of new members—particularly in large numbers—tends to revive de-liberations among the existing members about the structure and functioning of the European-level institutions. Much of the impetus for the Treaty of Nice and the ill-fated Constitutional Treaty lay in the recognition that the EU system would have difficulty coping with twenty-five or more member states. In fact, since the Nice Treaty's institutional provisions are designed for twenty-seven members, there may be legal obstacles to extending enlargement beyond the 2007 accession of Bulgaria and Romania (Lobjakas 2006). Never before has the link between enlargement and institutional design been quite so apparent.

Second, the enlargement process activates internal negotiations, both on the horizontal Council-Commission axis and on the vertical EU–member government axis, aimed at reform in major areas of substantive policy. Notably, the prospect of eastward expansion provided a powerful additional incentive to change the long-standing principles and practices of the Common Agricultural Policy. In combination with other factors it has also forced member governments to rethink their collective management of the EU's external borders. Such substantive policy changes can, in turn, feed back into modes of governance, altering the balance between the Commission and national governments. For example, Common Agriculture Program reform is likely to see a diminution of the Commission's financial and regulatory role relative to national governments, whereas a common EU border regime would, at the very least, imply a *droit de regard* for Brussels over the customs and immigration practices of "frontier" states such as Poland (Zielonka 2001).

The primary impact of enlargement policy on the EU system has thus come neither from its embedding in EU structures nor from its idiosyncratic mix of modes of governance. Two other effects have, at least to this point, been more important. First, as we are likely to be reminded increasingly over the next few years, there is a direct, two-way link between prospective increases in membership and proposed constitutional change. And second, there is a strong, if indirect, link between enlargement and relations between governing institutions—Commission and Council on the horizontal axis and EU institutions and national governments on the vertical axis—mediated through policy areas such as agriculture. Enlargement shapes the structure of the EU system, therefore, both directly, by confronting its member states with the need for institutional reform, and indirectly, by challenging its established modes of governing other areas of policy.

Notes

1. Norway, a NATO member, also applied but, as in the case of its earlier application alongside the United Kingdom, its electorate rejected the terms of accession in a referendum.

2. The Copenhagen criteria are (1) stability of institutions guaranteeing democracy, the rule of law, human rights, and respect for and protection of minorities; (2) the existence of a functioning market economy and the capacity to cope with competitive pressures and market forces within the Union; (3) the ability to take on the obligations of membership, including adherence to the aims of political, economic, and monetary union; and (4) the EU itself must have the capacity to absorb new

members without endangering the momentum of European integration. The last condition, which is of course the only one beyond the control of the applicants, lay dormant throughout the eastward enlargement and has only recently been resurrected as the mantra of those afflicted with "enlargement fatigue."

3. On occasion, when enlargement is the dominant issue on the summit's agenda, the member states may be joined by the current applicants. This was the case, for example, at Athens in the spring of 2003.

4. Prior to this, enlargement policy had been primarily the responsibility of DG 1A (external relations) headed by Commissioner Hans van den Broek.

5. It is worth adding that the European Court of Justice has heard almost fifty cases concerning enlargement since 1997, although the issues have all been narrowly technical and commercial. For details, see http://www.curia.europa.eu/jurisp/cgi-bin/form.pl.

6. As a recent illustration of this ongoing process of vertical negotiation, note the demands of the German Bundestag for a say on when and under what conditions negotiations with applicants are opened, not just on ratification of treaties of accession once concluded (Mahoney 2006).

7. In effect, although not officially, Austria linked its consent to opening accession talks with Turkey in October 2005 with the opening of negotiations with Croatia, despite other members' concerns about Zagreb's cooperation with the war-crimes tribunal in The Hague (Beunderman 2005).

PART 3

Emergent Patterns of Cooperation

13

Establishing Multilevel Governance in the European Union: Regulating Public Utilities

Edgar Grande and Ute Hartenberger

There is considerable consensus among scholars of European politics that governance in the European Union (EU) proceeds in a dynamic multilevel system—European governance is multilevel governance (see Marks et al. 1996; Jachtenfuchs and Kohler-Koch 1996; Scharpf 1999, 2001; Grande and Jachtenfuchs 2000; Hooghe and Marks 2001, 2003; Jachtenfuchs 2001; Benz 2000, 2003; Bache and Flinders 2004; Tömmel 2006b; for a summary see Kohler-Koch and Rittberger 2006). In analyzing this multilevel system, conceptual efforts as well as the enormous wealth of empirical studies have to a very large extent been concentrated on institutional and material aspects of policymaking and on problems of democratic legitimacy of European politics. In comparison, the *dynamic* aspect of governance in the European multilevel system has hitherto been underestimated or even entirely neglected.[1] This applies to both the external dynamics of the European space of political authority and the internal dynamics of the EU's multilevel system.

This chapter deals with the latter aspect, that is, the structuring of a *dynamic interaction space* within Europe that integrates several levels and arenas of political action.[2] Thus, our analysis does not deal with the (often conflicting) horizontal interactions between supranational and intergovernmental mechanisms of integration on the European level; rather, it highlights the vertical interaction of supranational and national actors in the European policy process. We will demonstrate that the inclusion of vertical multilevel dynamics is indispensable for an understanding of governance and policymaking in the European Union. In our empirical analysis, we concentrate on a particular type of European governance, that is, regulatory governance, and we examine this policy in a specific regulatory field, the regulation of public utilities. The case of public utilities is particularly well suited for our purpose. In this area, in fact, contrary to what was initially expected (see mainly Majone 1994b, 1996, 1997a), there was only very limited transfer of legal competences from the national to the European level and no constitution or extension of supranational institutions (Levi-Faur 1999; Eberlein and Grande 2003, 2005). In short, the liberalization and privatization of public utilities indeed resulted in an increase of regulatory activities but not in the constitution of a European regulatory state. Thus, the regulation of public utilities differs strikingly from the highly heterogeneous area of social regulation (e.g., health, environment) in which an almost inflationary surge of European agencies became evident in recent years.

Nevertheless, as we will show later, the EU plays an increasingly important role in utility regulation. The main argument of this chapter is that the emergence of a multidimensional, dynamic interaction space is characteristic for the regulation of public utilities in Europe. This interaction space is not defined by formal institutions and competences; rather, it is constituted by the interactions and internal dynamics of the European multilevel system of governance. Against this background, we will inquire how the EU managed to gain its influence, and, moreover, we will examine the consequences of this noticeable shift of power for policymaking in the field of regulative policy.

This analysis contributes to the ongoing debates on European governance and policymaking in at least two respects. On the one hand, it shifts the focus toward an aspect of European policymaking that had been neglected by political scientists in previous years. On the other hand, it offers a counterperspective to the prevalent discussion on integration and constitutionalization with its emphasis on the formal demarcation and allocation of competences. Our analysis will show that the process of Europeanization is indeed structured by formal allocations of competences, but in practice it proceeds far beyond such systems of legal competences. Regulatory governance in Europe is not organized in a regulatory state—neither nationally nor supranationally—but in new types of *cosmopolitan* interaction spaces, integrating national and supranational actors and institutions alike in a dynamic manner.[3]

In this chapter, we will develop this argument in three steps. In a first step, we will examine the institutional architecture of regulatory governance in Europe, as it was constituted after the privatization and liberalization of public infrastructures. The outcome of this process of institution building will be defined by us, following David Levi-Faur (1999: 201), as a state-centered, multilevel system of governance. In a second step, we will then show the EU's importance in this field of European policymaking as well as the mechanisms of empowerment by which the EU has increased its influence. Finally, we will describe the dynamics of interaction in this multilevel system and the effectiveness and efficiency of governance in this area. This empirical analysis will focus on three of the most important public utilities: telecommunications, electricity, and railways. They all belong in the category of network-based technical infrastructures, and they have all been objects of far-reaching regulatory changes since 1983. In the following, the regulation of these three sectors will be examined by us on both the European and the national level, concentrating on the three largest EU member states: Germany, France, and the United Kingdom.[4]

The Institutional Architecture of Regulatory Policy in European Public Utilities

European countries have witnessed several waves of liberalization and privatization since the 1980s. This trend has included public utilities such as telecommunications, railways, electricity, and water, which in most countries for most of the time have been the exclusive domain of the state (Schneider and Tenbücken 2004). Hence, the liberalization and privatization of public infrastructures have been among the most significant aspects of a comprehensive transformation of the state and its functions during the past decades (Sorensen 2004). The liberalization and privatization of public infrastructures have not yet resulted in a full-scale "retreat of the state" (Müller and Wright 1994; Strange 1996); rather, they have generated a complex functional transformation of public authority. Following the work of Harold Seidman and Robert Gilmour (1986) on the history of US government in the twentieth century, this functional transformation can be understood as a transition "from the positive state to the regulatory state" (see Grande, 1993, 1994, 1997; Majone 1994b, 1996, 1997a; Moran 2002). The positive state was a state directly providing public goods and services, whereas the regulatory state aims to achieve the same objectives indirectly, by regulating private actors and markets. As a consequence, the liberalization and privatization of public infrastructures have not yet resulted in a downsizing of public functions. Rather, these activities have created a "regulatory paradox": the "deregulation" of public services has triggered efforts to meet public expectations and demands by new means, that of regulation (Majone 1990; see also Vogel 1996; König and Benz 1997; Gusy 1998; Grande and Eberlein 1999; Jordana and Levi-Faur 2004; Schneider and Tenbücken 2004; Coen and Héritier 2006). The most likely results of this transformation, then, are "freer markets *and* more rules," a phrase coined by Steven Vogel.

In Western Europe, this transformation of state functions coincided with an intensified process of European integration. The establishment of a single European market in the late 1980s led to a remarkable upgrading of the supranational level. In view of this constellation, one of the key questions is how these two transformation processes, the functional and the territorial reconfiguration of political authority, have interacted in Europe. Which institutional form has the regulatory state adopted within a vertically differentiated system of political authority? More precisely, how have regulatory competences been institutionalized in the European system of multilevel governance? And, finally, how does the specific institutional architecture of the regulatory state affect its efficiency and effectiveness? Giandomenico Majone (1994b, 1996, 1997a) at the time forcefully argued that as a result of the coincidence of liberalization, privatization, and Europeanization, the regulatory state would be established in particular at the European level, exhibiting strong supranational features. In Europe, the regulatory state would be institutionalized as a European regulatory state, and its institutions would, for good reasons, take on a nonmajoritarian form, that is, one removed from the influence of parliaments and the governments of member states.

As is generally known, historical developments have not yet verified this assumption (see, in an explicit dispute with Majone's thesis, Eberlein and Grande 2003, 2005). The regulation of public infrastructures has hitherto successfully resisted the trend toward supranational integration. Moreover, as we will show in the following, it also differs markedly from the general pattern in the development of state structures and public functions as described in the governance literature (Pierre and Peters 2000; Benz 2004a; Kjaer 2004; Schuppert 2005; see also Chapter 2). This holds in particular for (1) the (remarkable) importance of nation states in infrastructure regulation, (2) the (weak) role of private actors, and (3) the astonishingly limited formal competences of the EU. Taken together, the transition from the positive state to the regulatory state in Europe has resulted in the emergence of a new type of state-centered, transnational regulatory regime that differs significantly from the forms of public regulation as we know them, for example, from the United States (see Grande 2006b).

The Rise of the National Regulatory State in Europe

The new regulatory regimes in the area of public infrastructures are *state-centered* in two respects. In this section we discuss the first of these, the essential fact that they are all nation state–centered. We have not found a transfer of explicit regulatory competences from the member states to the European level (or even beyond) in any of the sectors we examined, and regulatory authorities have not been established on a European level (or elsewhere beyond the nation state) in any of these sectors. The process of institution building, that is, the establishment of regulatory agencies, in particular, has remained completely constricted to the member states. In the course of privatization and liberalization, a process of state-centered institution building has set in and it has generated a multitude of different institutional forms.

In order to organize these forms analytically, we will, in a first step, establish a typology of regulatory institutions based on two distinctions. First, regulatory institutions may be distinguished concerning the scope of their autonomy. In this regard, it is of particular importance whether they are organized in the form of an independent agency (agency model) or whether regulatory functions are assigned to a ministry (ministry model). Both forms

differ significantly with respect to the possibilities of directly exercising political influence on regulatory decisions. These two models may furthermore
be distinguished with regard to the scope of their authority. Here, the distinction between a sector-specific and a cross-sectoral regulatory institution is of
particular importance. On the basis of these two distinctions, we can identify
four different basic types of institutionalization of regulatory competences.
Table 13.1 presents this typology, including organizational examples. The
first type, the most widespread in Europe, is the sector-specific agency
model, which is characteristic of US regulation and which has been established in the United Kingdom (UK) in the course of the privatization of
telecommunications, electricity, railways, and other sectors.[5] In Germany,
this sector-specific agency model can be found in railway regulation (Federal Railway Authority) and in the regulation of public broadcasting. A second variety of an institutionalization of regulatory competences is represented by the sector-specific ministry model, according to which a ministry,
exclusively responsible for a particular sector, has regulatory competence
(the German Federal Ministry of Post and Telecommunications given as an
example was dissolved as of 1 January 1998). A third type is the cross-
sectoral agency model. The German Federal Network Agency is a typical (if
rare) example. A fourth alternative, finally, is the cross-sectoral ministry

Table 13.1 Typology of Regulatory Institutions

Scope of Competences	Organizational Type	
	Agency	Ministry
Sector-specific	(1) Sector-specific regulatory agency (examples: Office of Telecommunications, Office of Electricity Regulation, Office of the Rail Regulator in the UK; Autorité de la Régulation des Télé-communications in France; Federal Railway Authority in Germany)	(2) Sector-specific ministry (example: Federal Ministry of Post and Telecommunications in Germany)
Cross-sectoral	(3) Cross-sectoral regulatory agency (example: Federal Network Agency for Postal, Telecommunications, and Electricity Services in Germany)	(4) Cross-sectoral ministry (examples: electricity regulation by the Federal Ministry of Economics in Germany; railroad regulation by the French Ministry of Transport)

model, in which regulatory functions are assigned to a ministry with cross-sectoral competences, as, for instance, a ministry of economics or transport.

The overall picture of this institution-building process also shows distinct variations among individual countries and sectors within Europe. Even though in the telecommunications sector the model of a sector-specific, independent regulatory agency is dominant, we have found highly differing forms of institutionalization in other sectors. Moreover, institutional reforms, as they have taken place during the past years in the German electricity sector and the British railway sector, indicate that the process of institutionalizing regulatory functions in Europe is far from complete. It seems that European countries are still in the middle of a search process that may not necessarily end in a model of sector-specific, independent regulatory agencies.[6]

As a look at the typology of different modes of regulation in the EU, developed by Christoph Knill and Andrea Lenschow (2004), shows, this state-centered form of regulation corresponds to a specific instrument of governance. In the field of public infrastructures, regulatory policy is primarily based on legal regulatory standards. Basically, they contain detailed and mandatory rules and instructions and concede only a minor (if at all) scope for their own decisionmaking to the addressees of regulation. New, less hierarchical instruments of governance, which concede a more extensive scope of discretion to the objects of public regulation as well as procedural forms of control and coordination, play an insignificant role in the regulation of public infrastructures on the national level. The same holds for the delegation of regulatory functions to private actors, that is, the type of private self-regulation in the shadow of the state.

The (Weak) Role of Private Actors

The new regulatory regimes in the area of public infrastructures are state-centered in yet another respect. The state was, and still is, the central actor in regulating public infrastructures. In all countries examined, the necessity of regulating public infrastructures has resulted in a reconstruction of the state and not in a shifting of public authority to private actors. With regard to regulatory functions, private actors on the whole play only a subordinated, in most cases even insignificant, role.[7] In our sample, there is only one case, the regulation of the German electricity sector, in which regulatory functions have partly been taken over by private actors, with dubious outcomes.

We also found no indications that such functions are being assigned to private institutions or that such an assignment might be useful to improve the efficiency of regulation. On the contrary, the example of German electricity regulation points in exactly the opposite direction, that is, toward a disempowerment of (business) associations and a transition from self-regulation toward an agency-based public regulation (see Eberlein 2001). This finding is in marked contrast to those studies stating an increasing importance of "private interest governments" and "private authorities" (Streeck and Schmitter 1985; Cutler, Haufler, and Porter 1999; Hall and Biersteker 2002; Cutler 2003) in a great variety of public policies and at both the national and transnational level. Interpreted in this context, the regulation of public infrastructures has obviously been excluded from this development.

How can we explain this anomaly? In our opinion, this is mainly due to the fact that many regulatory decisions, in particular in the transitory phase from (public) monopolies toward (private) competition, have far-reaching redistributive consequences. These redistributive consequences tend to exceed the capacity for cooperation and consensus of private actors without authoritative sanctioning power. For a better understanding of this argument, we have systematized the various distributive constellations of regulatory decisions in Table 13.2.[8] Here, we distinguish between the temporal dimension of regulatory impacts (short-term versus long-term) and their distributive consequences (concentrated versus diffuse).

This table shows that the field examined by us, the regulation of technical infrastructures (cell 1), and the area in which private interest governments are to be found most frequently, that is, technical regulation (cell 4) (see Voelzkow 1996), often represent entirely different problem constellations. As a consequence, they offer different opportunity structures for the involvement of private actors in public decisionmaking. The economic and social regulation of public infrastructures frequently has far-reaching redistributive consequences that directly affect a small group of regulated companies, for example, the operators of public telecommunications networks. Decisions as to fixing user fees for public networks, network access, requirements for the provision of services, and so on may result in a significant short-term redistribution of costs and benefits among competing providers. In comparison, the typical distributive constellation in the field of technical regulation is

Table 13.2 Redistributive Patterns and Regulatory Decisions

	Temporal Dimension	
Social Dimension	Short-Term	Long-Term
Concentrated	(1) High redistributive consequences (examples: user fees for public networks, network access)	(2) Medium-high redistributive consequences (example: licenses for new competitors)
Diffuse	(3) Medium-high redistributive consequences (example: tariffs)	(4) Low redistributive consequences (example: technical regulation)

fundamentally different. Its direct material consequences will often only become visible in the long run, and the group of persons concerned appears to be diffuse at the time of decisionmaking.

As a matter of fact, the problem constellations in regulatory decisionmaking are often much more complex. Nevertheless, our typological simplification might contribute to an explanation of the different actor constellations in various fields of public regulation and decisionmaking. This finding might be of importance well beyond the regulation of public infrastructures. Basically, it touches upon the fundamental question of possibilities and limits of a delegation or, respectively, a transfer of public functions to private actors; and it indicates that an answer to this question is much more challenging and complicated than often assumed by political scientists and economists.

Institutional Complexity:
Regulatory Regimes in Public Infrastructures

In all cases examined, regulatory functions and competences have been distributed across a number of public institutions and several levels of decisionmaking. They are not concentrated in one single organization—for example, an independent regulatory agency—as is maintained by the "agency approach" in research on public regulation (see, in place of many others, Thatcher 2002b). The institutional complexity of regulating public infrastructures might best be captured by the concept of a regulatory regime (see Eberlein and Grande 2003, 2005). The notion of a regulatory regime refers to the entity of actors, procedures, instruments, norms, and rules that influence the process and the outcome of public regulation in a specific sector. Regulatory regimes can be analyzed in various dimensions, two of which are of particular importance in our context: first, the degree of concentration or, respectively, fragmentation of regulatory competences, and, second, the modes of interaction between the relevant actors.

The first crucial aspect is the allocation of formal decisionmaking powers in a regulatory regime. The regulatory bodies, whether they are independent agencies or ministries, as a rule, are obliged to act within a system of shared competences. On the national level they have to share their formal regulatory powers with at least two other institutions: the national competition authorities and (other) public ministries. In all cases examined by us, national competition authorities—the Federal Cartel Office in Germany, the Monopolies and Mergers Commission in the UK, and the Conseil de la Concurrence in France—are involved in the regulation of public infrastructures by statutory defined rights and obligations to cooperate with sectoral regulators and to consult them. In addition, national ministries (ministries of economics, industry, and finance in particular) maintain a number of regulatory competences, even in cases in which the day-to-day business of regulation is organized according to the agency model and separated from government. Thus, as a rule, sectoral regulation has to be processed within a tri-polar structure of power and authority, and the strength of the individual poles—regulatory agency, competition authority, ministry—may vary considerably between countries and sectors. Formal rights of parliaments and, in federal systems, of subnational actors may add to this institutional complexity of regulatory regimes.[9]

This formal structure of authority has been partly superimposed by actors whose importance has been increasing considerably in the national regulatory state: the courts. Formally, regulatory decisions are administrative acts that can be taken to the courts in all three countries examined by us. The importance of courts varies significantly across these countries, however. This is due to differing formal restrictions against legal actions on the one hand, and the result of varying market structures and actor constellations in regulated sectors on the other hand. In Germany, formal obstacles against legal actions are lowest. As a consequence, there was hardly any regulatory decision in the German telecommunications sector that had not been contested at the administrative courts. A similar pattern can be observed in the electricity sector, whereas the railway sector is characterized by the absence of legal actions, not least because of the dominant market position of the public railway operator (Deutsche Bundesbahn), which discouraged competitors from filing suits against problematic regulatory decisions (van Riesen 2007). Compared to Germany, the role of courts in France and the UK has been much more limited. In the UK, legal actions against regulatory agencies are only accepted by the courts if their decisions can be identified unequivocally as being unfair, unreasonable, in contrast to the legal situation, or exceeding the agency's legal competences (cf. Bock 1995). As a result, legal actions against regulatory decisions have been very rare. The same holds for France, where judicial powers generally concede more discretion to administrative bodies. Altogether, it has become clear that regulatory governance of public infrastructures at the national level takes place within highly fragmented regulatory regimes with multipolar power and actor constellations. Within these regulatory regimes, regulatory agencies may assume a prominent role, but they are not in the position to dominate them.

This leads us directly to the second dimension in which we can examine regulatory regimes: the relationship between focal actors in such a multipolar actor constellation and the modes of interaction between them. In this context, we can in principle distinguish between at least four different modes of interaction: competition, cooperation, coordination, and hierarchical control. When analyzing the horizontal distribution of regulatory competences, we have already shown that among the cases examined by us, there is none in which an actor (ministry, competition authority, regulatory agency) has succeeded in controlling a regulatory regime by hierarchical means. It is interesting and by no means self-evident, however, that even competitive, conflict-ridden relations between main actors are rather an exception. This is even more remarkable since in most cases new agencies were established that had to find their role in a newly emerging field of public activity and that have to act in a system of fragmented and overlapping competences. In such a constellation, we would have expected many more interorganizational conflicts about competences and domains than we actually found. An example of such conflicts was the start-up phase of telecommunications regulation in Germany, during which there were fierce, partly public conflicts between the newly established regulatory agency and the Federal Cartel Office on the proper scope of regulation. In this case (as in most others), the coordination of activities and the cooperation between agencies have become the rule. As a result, national regulatory regimes are operating remarkably smoothly. This does not mean that regulatory governance functions efficiently in all cases, and we do not suggest that there are no (political) conflicts and controversies on regulatory decisions, but it is evident that the intensity of conflicts *within* regulatory regimes—as opposed to between regulators and regulated parties or among regulated parties—is remarkably low.

The Constitution and Construction of the European Regulatory Space in Public Utilities

What about the EU, then? It would be a gross mistake to conclude that because the institution-building process in infrastructure regulation took place exclusively at the national level, it means that the EU (or international organizations such as the World Trade Organization [WTO][10]) is completely irrelevant in this field. As we will show in the following, the EU has also gained in importance in the regulation of public utilities; however, this power is based neither on its own regulatory competences nor on its own regulatory institutions. The EU merely disposes indirect and implicit regulatory competences for regulating public utilities, particularly in the area of competition law. Regarding administrative capacities, it hitherto failed to establish its own supranational agencies to regulate public utilities. This is not to say that the European Commission has not made efforts to establish such capacities. In the telecommunications sector, for example, there have been repeated attempts by the Commission to create a European regulatory agency; however, these efforts have thus far proved ineffective.

How was it possible, then, that a multilevel system of regulation emerged under such circumstances? Which mechanisms have been conducive to the constitution of a cosmopolitan regulatory space in Europe? In order to answer these questions, we begin by examining the formal competences of the EU in the area of infrastructure regulation more closely. On this basis, we then proceed to identify the mechanisms by which the European space of interaction has been constituted in this field.

Bringing Europe Back In: Formal Competences of the EU in the Area of Infrastructure Regulation

The foremost importance of member states regarding the regulation of public infrastructures corresponds with marginal formal competences of the EU in this area. At first sight, this may sound astounding, since the EU has been the object of numerous studies on the liberalization of public utilities in Europe (see in particular Schmidt 1998; Levi-Faur 1999; Eising 2000). In a debate on the role of the EU in the transition from the positive state to the regulatory state in Europe, however, two aspects have to be distinguished clearly: first, the EU's contribution in enforcing and implementing the liberalization and privatization of public infrastructures in Europe, and, second, its role in the subsequent regulation of these sectors. Concerning market-making liberalization, the evidence available from the literature is rather mixed. On the one hand, there are accounts in which the EU has been accredited a decisive role (Schmidt 1998; Sandholtz 1998; Eising 2000; Renz 2001; Häge and Schneider 2004); on the other hand, there are also studies in which the EU has been considered as "not causative" for the "liberalization boom" since 1988 (Levi-Faur 2002; Jordana, Levi-Faur, and Puig 2006). In this context, the timing of reforms, the institutional framework for reforms, and the national and supra-national actor constellations have obviously been of considerable importance too. In any case, the role of the EU in the regulation of these sectors must be clearly distinguished. And here, the findings, at least as far as formal regulatory competences are concerned, are unequivocal: hitherto, in any of the sectors examined, the EU has failed to acquire sector-specific regulatory competences of its own. EU law is to a very large extent confined to meta-requirements regarding the organization of national regulatory institutions and to some basic aspects of sector-specific regulation.

If we examine the EU's legal framework in regulating public utilities in more detail, it immediately becomes apparent that primary legal provisions are almost completely missing. The only exception is the transport sector. The Treaty on the European Economic Community in 1957 included a specific chapter on transport, in which the objective of developing a joint transport policy was formulated. It was not used, however, to create a liberalized market for the supply of railway services. For the remaining two sectors (telecommunications and electricity), no specific primary legal provisions exist.

A European secondary law was created in all three areas in the mid-1980s, developed on the basis of the Community authorization with the aim of creating a single European market and initially concentrated on establishing market-opening regulations. The definition of the regulatory framework for the liberalized national markets, however, was left to national legislators. This allowed circumventing the structural problem identified by Fritz W. Scharpf (1999) regarding the EU's single European market project, that is, that member states were able to agree on market-making but not on market-correcting rules at the European level. In the area of utility regulation, the task of regulating markets was entirely left to the member states, and as we have seen, this formed the legal basis for establishing national governance regimes within the liberalized sectors. The EU's reticence did not last for long, however. The stronger the liberalization process became (as in the telecommunications sector) or the more difficult the opening of national markets turned out to be (as in the case of railways and the electricity sector), the more detailed supranational provisions regarding national regulation have become. In the aftermath, these provisions developed into a first mechanism by which the EU has become an integral part of a Europeanized regulatory space: the supranational regulation of national regulation.

The Construction of a Multilevel Regulatory System: Supranational Regulation of National Regulation

Supranational regulation of national regulation operates in various ways and at varying scopes of precision. A first, constitutive provision under European law, which was implemented at an early stage in all three sectors, stipulates an organizational separation of service provision from market supervision and control. This separation was regarded as a prerequisite for avoiding discrimination against new service providers in the liberalized utilities markets. The establishment of independent regulatory agencies and the privatization of public service providers, however, had initially been left at the member states' discretion.

Another key area in which European law intervenes in the regulation of public utilities is the regulation of network access. In all three sectors examined, services can only be provided on the basis of an (investment-intensive) physical network, which in most cases has remained the property of the former monopolist. As a result, access to the existing network or respectively an interconnection of networks of new market entrants with this network is an indispensable prerequisite for the development of competition. Therefore, at a very early stage of the liberalization and privatization process, the EU formulated legal principles for network access and specified technical as well as regulatory requirements that were supposed to allow such access in a transparent and nondiscriminatory manner. The extent of network access enforced by European law varied significantly between the sectors. It was most extensive in the telecommunications sector (the so-called free network access); in the case of the railways, however, it was restricted to international companies and railway carriers dealing with specific types of transborder goods traffic.

In the electricity sector, the stipulations under directive 96/92/EEC particularly affected the operators of transmission networks. Whether the scope of this network access would be authoritatively defined by state agencies (regulated network access), whether the parties involved arrived at an agreement among each other (negotiated network access), or whether the so-called single-customer system was chosen was initially left to the discretion of the member states.[11]

At the same time, the regulation of network access is an excellent example to show that the depth of intervention of European "framework regulation" has increased continuously and that the boundaries between framework regulation and detailed, mandatory regulatory standards have become blurred. As competition in the electricity sector, despite these stipulations, has developed only very sluggishly, a new directive on the single market for electricity now obliges member states to implement a regulated network access and to establish an independent national regulatory agency with clearly defined competences.[12] Similar rules apply to the railway sector, in which, since March 2003, a comprehensive free network access to a precisely defined trans-European railway network for goods is in force (directive 2001/12/EC, Article 10). In addition, rules for route allocation, rate collection, and safety regulation (which are of particular importance in the railway sector) have become more detailed and more compulsory. The establishment of a regulatory agency independent from national ministries for transport or economics was still not stipulated; however, the rules concerning the independence of service providers, customers, and public authorities responsible for the allocation of routes were tightened. Moreover, the EU has established rules concerning information authorizations of national regulatory agencies, basic principles for regulating cost calculation procedures (the so-called long incremental costs approach), and time limits for passing regulatory decisions in all three sectors, although there are considerable variations across sectors regarding the depth of intervention into national regulatory frameworks.

To sum up, regulatory governance on a European level basically means *framework regulation*. It formulates minimum requirements for an institutional design of national regulation, its procedures, and its objectives. Formally speaking, the result is a "two-tiered system of regulation" (McGowan and Wallace 1996) in which the EU is restricted to the definition of framework regulations for national liberalization, deregulation, and reregulation processes, and the task of materializing these framework regulations and the implementation of respective rules is left to national authorities.

Within this "regulation of regulation," the European Commission has increasingly aimed at influencing the definition and execution of national regulation. It acts as the "regulator of regulators" and has meanwhile succeeded in securing limited access to national regulatory processes. This is exemplified by the new consultation requirements in the telecommunications sector.

Here, national regulatory agencies are obliged to consult the European Commission and regulatory agencies of other countries when defining regulated markets and market-leading enterprises since the enactment of the "reform package" decided in December 2002. In the subsequent proceedings, the Commission may even request national regulatory agencies to refrain from planned measures (Article 7 of Directive 2002/21/EC on a common regulatory framework). So far, this is not linked to a formal right to veto; in recent reform debates, however, the Commission repeatedly proposed such a right.[13] In the railway sector, too, Article 10 of Directive 2001/12 EC gives the Commission the right to correct national regulatory decisions; however, this is strictly controlled by a committee of member states (van Riesen 2007: 65).

Multilevel Integration by Formation of Informal Regulatory Networks

From a European perspective, the governance mode of framework regulation raises a number of problems because it cannot be taken for granted that the member states will use their regulatory powers according to European objectives. Restricting this power by means of a supranational process governance (Padgett 2001) is one possibility of reacting to a decentralized regulatory structure. In the area of public utilities, however, we observe yet another mechanism for the Europeanization of national regulation, namely, the establishment of informal networks and forums. In these informal settings, some of those transnational regulatory problems are dealt with for which formal institutions could not be established on a European level (see Eberlein 2003; Eberlein and Grande 2003, 2005). Moreover, it might be of equal importance that these networks and forums make it possible to consolidate and institutionalize the interactions and communications between the national and the European levels of governance. When analyzing such networks and forums, it is useful to distinguish between "transgovernmental" and "transnational networks."[14] Transgovernmental networks are composed of public actors, "exchanging information, co-ordinating national policies, and working together to address common problems" (Slaughter 2004c: 122). In contrast, transnational networks are characterized by the involvement (or even the predominance) of nonstate actors—for instance, interest groups or companies. Both types of networks may be of a formal nature, established by official decisions, with regular meetings and explicit responsibilities vis-à-vis the instituting bodies. These networks may also be informal institutions, rather loosely connected, holding ad hoc meetings, and without formal obligations.

Transgovernmental networks are prevalent in the area of infrastructure regulation.[15] They exist in the form of comitology committees, as, for example, the old open network provision (ONP) committee and the "authorization committee" in telecommunications, whose contribution to the solving of regulatory decentralization problems, however, was not adequate from the Commission's point of view.[16] In this case, more or less informal regulatory networks have proved to be more efficient. These networks make it possible to identify problems of regulatory practice and to draft common concepts and best practice solutions. With regard to the instruments of regulation, these regulatory networks therefore are similar to the methods of soft governance practiced in the open method of coordination. The Independent Regulators Group (IRG), an informal consortium of the presidents of national regulatory agencies in the telecommunications sector, formed in 1998, is a good example to demonstrate this point. The IRG's main purpose is the exchange of experience between national regulatory agencies that has led, among other things, to efforts to harmonize the agencies' approaches in regulatory procedures. In the electricity sector, the Council of European Energy Regulators (CEER), founded in 2000, plays a similar role. Both IRG and CEER are closed administrative networks (Dehousse 1997), based on functional cooperation (Maurer, Mittag, and Wessels 2000: 30). This functional orientation is, for instance, manifested in jointly developed "principles of best practice." The harmonizing effect of these principles is in fact considerable, as national regulatory authorities orient themselves strongly according to these standards. At the same time, these informal networks offer some specific advantages for regulatory authorities: by cooperating, they jointly acquire the authority to define and interpret the relevant topics of regulation. Against the cumulative expert knowledge represented by these networks of regulatory authorities, neither the political principals (tempted to intervene) nor the objects of regulation (prepared to resist) have much to offer. Thus, apart from a reduction of decentralization problems, these informal networks of regulators also contribute to coping with typical challenges of the regulation process such as the protection of independence and authority vis-à-vis the objects of regulation.

In the electricity sector, in which liberalization as well as market regulation proved to be considerably more difficult than in the telecommunications sector, the European Commission purposefully utilized the advantages of another type of regulatory network and, in 1998, created the European Forum of Electricity Regulators (the so-called Florence Forum) (see Eberlein 2003). This network was supposed to accompany the implementation of the first directive on the opening of electricity markets.[17] Contrary to the CEER, which was established later, the Florence Forum includes not only regulatory agencies but also national ministries and relevant market actors such as network operators, large industrial customers, and electricity traders. Hence, it represents the type of a transnational network.[18] The results of the Florence Forum's activities—for instance, rules for cross-border electricity trade or the utilization of transmission networks—often served as a basis for decisions taken by the respective Council of Ministers on energy and thus became part of an expanding sector-specific EU law. Therefore, due to its specific composition and its setting outside of official institutional structures, the forum has become one of the forces that have strengthened the dynamism of the liberalization process.

A successful coordination of national regulatory strategies by informal networks depends, however, on a number of prerequisites (Eberlein and Grande 2003: 437–438). Among them are, in particular, mutual trust and the willingness to cooperate, long-term common interests concerning the objectives and effects of the regulatory process, and a certain degree of independence from domestic political principals. These factors partly explain why we cannot find an institution similar to the Florence Forum in the railway sector, although the Commission established a working group organizing national "regulatory bodies" in 2001 (van Riesen 2007: 233). This working group, however, is part of a comitology committee, whose task it is to advance the international cooperation of mainly nationally oriented railway regulators, as required by the "infrastructure package" in the railway sector. Simultaneously, the Directorate General (DG) on competition policy, DG Competition, has made efforts to bring railway experts from national competition authorities together and to have them develop principles of best practice for the implementation of market controls in the railway sector. These working groups have neither the encompassing forum character of the Florence Forum nor the closed and intimate nature of the Independent Regulators Group. On the one hand, there is a lack of powerful market actors who support liberalization and could be integrated into the discursive processes; on the other hand, owing to strong political influence at the national level, adequately independent national regulators, who might provide for a dynamic development of regulation, are missing.

Multilevel Dynamics by Problem Shifting and Changes of Arenas

The creeping Europeanization of infrastructure regulation, however, is not only effected from above by supranational institutions such as the Commission; it is also enforced from below by national regulatory agencies or by the addressees of national regulation. The European multilevel system of governance provides opportunities to transfer regulatory issues to the European level if these issues cannot be handled satisfactorily within national regulatory regimes. Such a change of the regulatory arenas might strengthen the position of regulatory agencies or companies in two ways: on the one hand, a shift of arenas will change actor constellations, and on the other hand, a change of the decisionmaking arena might bring about an extension of competences and regulatory instruments available. In any case, the consequence of this problem shifting is that regulatory decisions are transformed by domestic (public or private) actors into "cosmopolitan" multilevel games in order to enhance their "chances to win" (which primarily means the enforcement of their interests). The strategic potential of a change of the regulatory arena and the multilevel dynamics resulting from it are particularly striking in the case of the European Commission's competences in the field of competition law.

The European multilevel system in general improves the possibilities of responding to weaknesses in sector-specific liberalization and regulation by transferring the regulatory problem from the regulatory arena to the arena of competition policy and competition law. This possibility is available not only at the national level by involving national competition authorities but also in the vertical dimension by appealing to the European Commission's DG Competition. Particularly in the electricity sector, the Commission has repeatedly made use of the instruments of competition law at its disposal under Articles 81 and 82 ECT in order to advance competition in national regulatory arenas in spite of lacking provisions in the single market directive. Examples have been the approval of mergers in Germany or the approval of the shareholding of the French state-owned corporation EDF in the German utility company EnBW.

In the telecommunications sector as well, the Commission has applied the instruments of European competitive law, in this case, however, mostly to increase pressure on national agencies to correctly implement existing rules or regulatory decisions. Changing the actor constellation in the regulatory arena by involving DG Competition has frequently resulted in national regulatory authorities' intensifying their activities. This can partly be explained by the fact that the appearance of a supranational actor well known for its market-creating objectives will encourage national regulatory agencies to take a more rigorous course of action against the objectives of national regulation, for example, the former state-owned public network operators. However, the very existence of the possibility of arena shifts may change the behavior of national regulators by sheer institutional self-interest, because they are eager to offer EU institutions as little cause as possible for interventions into their domain. In this context, it has become apparent that a cooperative relationship between the various DGs—expressed, for example, by a mutual exchange of information and similar regulatory approaches—significantly increases the EU's potential for influencing the behavior of national regulatory regimes.

On the whole, the effect of these three mechanisms—the regulation of regulation, the establishment of informal networks, and the strategy of problem shifting and the change of arenas—has been that a transnational, cosmopolitan space of interaction has emerged in the field of infrastructure regulation. This space is not constituted by formal competences; it is shaped by the dynamic interaction of national and supranational, public and private actors. Its institutional center of gravity is at the national level, but national regulatory institutions are embedded in an ever closer web of European rules. This arrangement can most suitably be called "state-centred multi-level governance" (Levi-Faur 1999: 201). In this dynamic interaction, political power is continuously transformed and transferred between levels and actors so that formal competences of an institution are only of limited use if we want to get a clear idea of its real regulatory power. This is particularly true for national regulatory agencies. Not least, these findings show that an analysis of regulatory governance that is still focused on the regulatory state and its agencies increasingly fails to grasp the mechanisms of policymaking in this area and its dynamics.

The Dynamics of Regulatory Multilevel Policy and Its Consequences

From an institutional perspective, the results of our comparative case studies show a widely differing picture of regulatory governance in the European multilevel system. The transformation of state functions has resulted in the constitution of new institutional architectures of political decision-making and implementation in Europe in which national and transnational policy arenas are integrated in complicated ways. This kind of institutionalization of the regulatory state in the European multilevel system exemplifies a general pattern of the transnationalization of politics in which public decisionmaking competences and institutional capacities still largely remain with the nation state but are increasingly being embedded in ever closer, formal and informal networks of transnational cooperation and coordination (see Grande and Pauly 2005).

In the case of regulatory governance in the EU, the three basic modes of governance are combined in a peculiar manner. Although hierarchical, law-based regulatory standards dominate at the national level, the supranational regulation of public infrastructures is based on instruments of framework regulation; the integration of both levels rests primarily on communicative, network-based mechanisms of soft governance. For a proper assessment of the governance regimes that have emerged in the European multilevel system, it is crucial that they are not simply hard or soft forms of governance— and that their development cannot be characterized as a transition from one to the other. Their distinguishing trait is that they combine both modes, hard and soft governance, in variable ways. Unlike many other areas, in which an increasing importance of private actors has been observed, such forms of private governance, of private self-regulation "in the shadow of hierarchy" are rarely to be found in the economic regulation of public utilities. Regulatory governance in this area is state-centered in two ways: regulatory functions are not only performed mostly at the (nation) state level, they also remain exclusively in the state's sphere of competence.

This peculiar combination and configuration of different modes of governance has been the prerequisite for the emergence of an open, dynamic regulatory space between the various levels of regulatory governance. Characteristic of this dynamic interaction space is its high degree of variability and flexibility. The actor constellations are marked by a changeable and changing composition. Depending on the intensity of regulatory conflicts and the course of a regulatory process, entirely different public authorities, levels of action, and decisionmaking arenas are involved. The regulatory regimes thus constituted all have a (variable) institutional core that is formed by national regulatory authorities, competition agencies, and national ministries; apart from this core, however, they all display considerable flexibility. Regulatory governance in the European multilevel system is constituted and reconstituted with every single regulatory event in a specific institutional configuration (see Hartenberger 2007).

What about the performance of these cosmopolitan regulatory regimes? The problem-solving capacity of regulatory governance in public utilities must be examined in a differentiated way. On the one hand, multilevel systems of governance have some properties that can improve the effectiveness and efficiency of governance. Most obvious and important, the possibilities of "capturing" a regulatory agency in such a networked, interactive system are very limited, if they exist at all. The same holds true for the problem of "agency drift," in which regulatory agencies become too independent from their political principals. In our case studies, obvious examples for these problems have not been found. It seems that multilevel systems provide institutional solutions for two of the most intensely discussed problems of regulatory governance. Moreover, there are indications that cosmopolitan spaces of interaction create favorable conditions for policy learning, which have actually been used by the actors, in particular by regulatory agencies. On the other hand, it is evident that multilevel systems of governance also have some negative features. In the case of utility regulation, this holds true in particular for the problem of policy implementation. It is worth mentioning that in the sectors examined by us, most of the negative consequences of privatization and liberalization that were anticipated by many in the 1980s and 1990s failed to materialize. We can nevertheless observe considerable differences in the performance of these sectors and in the effectiveness and efficiency of regulation. This becomes evident if we distinguish between economic (market-creating) regulation on the one hand, and the supply of public infrastructures, which is part of market-correcting regulation, on the other hand (see Table 13.3).

This table clearly shows that the very constellation that critics of liberalization and privatization of public utilities have considered the most probable did not materialize in the three sectors examined by us: the combination of intensive competition and poor supply of public infrastructures. Instead,

Table 13.3 The Performance of European Regulatory Regimes in Public Utilities

	Competition	
Supply of Infrastructure	Low	High
Poor	Railways	
Good	Electricity	Telecommunications

three other constellations have emerged in these sectors. Among them, the telecommunications sector represents the most positive example. In this sector, in spite of shortcomings in details, regulation has by and large managed to achieve both goals (a high degree of competition and a satisfactory supply of public infrastructures) simultaneously. We should concede, however, that technological innovations (particularly in the area of switching and transmission technologies) have substantially contributed to this positive result. In contrast, the negative example is represented by the railway sector, which tends to miss both regulatory objectives simultaneously (see Hartenberger and van Riesen 2003; van Riesen 2007). The most striking example here was the failed railway privatization in the UK. In the electricity sector, public criticism of regulatory performance mostly emphasizes insufficient competition, which results in excessive electricity prices, and to a lesser extent the quality of public infrastructures. In view of these considerable differences between the sectors, the issue of regulatory performance in public utilities will have to remain on our research agenda. As this chapter has shown, such analyses should in particular focus on the dynamic interactions of different modes of governance and different types of actors in the European multilevel system.

Notes

1. The "interactive aspect" of European multilevel politics was emphasized in particular by Kohler-Koch (1998).

2. On the external dynamics of the European space of political authority, see Beck and Grande (2007a: chap. 3).

3. In this context, we use the term *cosmopolitism* in its new sociological, and analytical understanding and not in the traditional normative, philosophical meaning. Interpreted in this way, the concept of cosmopolitism refers to overcoming the division between the national and the global (i.e., international and European) levels of social activity (see Beck and Grande 2007a, 2007b; Grande 2006a)

4. Our contribution is based on the updated findings of an empirical research project, "The Regulatory State in Europe," which was directed by Edgar Grande from 2000 until 2004. This project was organized in three sectoral studies on telecommunications (Ute Hartenberger), the electricity sector (Burkard Eberlein), and the railway sector (Olivia van Riesen). The project was funded by Deutsche

Forschungsgemeinschaft (DFG) in the context of its special research program on "European Governance."

5. It must be noted, however, that US regulatory authorities, unlike the newly established regulatory agencies in Europe, also dispose of legislative competences. Hence, the model of an independent regulatory agency was not simply adopted by European countries from the United States; rather, it was reinvented in the context of their respective national governance systems and legal traditions.

6. Tenbücken and Schneider (2004), in their analysis of regulatory institutions in the Organization for Economic Cooperation and Development (OECD), also found a high institutional diversity. They, however, interpreted this as a "diverging convergence."

7. This applies particularly to the area of economic regulation. In the field of technical, but also social, regulation, there have also been examples of private actor involvement (i.e., user groups and consumer associations) in public infrastructures.

8. This typology differs in an important aspect from the well-known typology developed by Frank Q. Wilson (see Wilson 1980: 364–366) on distributive consequences of regulatory decisionmaking. Wilson contrasts the various distributive possibilities of costs and benefits of regulatory decisions in the social dimension, whereas we distinguish the costs of these decisions in both a temporal and a social dimension.

9. In the German railway sector, for instance, economic ministries of the federal states hold formal regulatory competences.

10. The WTO gained some importance in the telecommunications sector, in particular by the "Agreement on Basic Telecommunications Services" that was concluded in 1997 under the General Agreement on Tariffs and Trade (GATT). This agreement established not only general principles of a free market access concerning basic services but also basic principles for national regulatory practices.

11. On these types of network access, see Schneider (1999: 421–430).

12. Directive 2003/54/EC concerning common rules for the internal market in electricity.

13. See the Commission's communication on an examination of the EU's legal framework for electronic communication networks and services (COM [2006] 334, 29 June 2006). Reactions to this demand from member states have been negative so far, however (see *Financial Times Deutschland,* 2 April 2008).

14. On the distinction between transgovernmental and transnational activities, see Keohane and Nye (1971) and, for a more recent account, see the survey on the development of the phenomenon of transnationalism in the social sciences by Anne-Marie Slaughter (2004c: 124–129).

15. Following Slaughter (2004c), we subsume transnational networks composed of public regulatory agencies under the category of "transgovernmental" networks even if they are independent from national governments, because they all have the status of public institutions.

16. See the Commission's so-called Communications Review 1999 (COM [1999] 537, 11/11 1999).

17. Directive 96/92/EEC concerning common rules for the internal market in electricity.

18. It is worth mentioning in this context that the Commission has also established European Regulators Groups in these sectors. As far as their members are concerned, these groups practically duplicate the IRG and the CEER and their meetings are mostly held in parallel. It seems as if the Commission has created these committees to prevent national regulatory authorities and their informal networks from becoming too independent.

14

Extended Governance: Implementation of EU Social Policy in the Member States

Miriam Hartlapp

Since the beginning of European integration—and certainly since the mid-1980s—there has been a demand for a European social dimension. Not responding to this demand could endanger the integration project. Indeed, the 2005 referenda in France and the Netherlands, which rejected the Constitutional Treaty, have been widely interpreted as the demand by people of these countries that a greater social dimension be included in the European project. One dimension of social Europe, the regulatory output under the Community method, has significantly increased. European Union (EU)[1] directives could today guarantee important social standards.[2] The impact of EU social policy is constrained, however, by a lack of timely and correct implementation in the member states. This chapter takes the rather poor and sluggish performance of member states in the implementation of EU standards as the starting point for an analysis of limits and extensions of a hierarchical governance mode used by the Commission during the implementation phase.[3] As outlined in Chapter 1, implementation politics can be characterized as a specific governance process—far from being an automatic enactment of commonly agreed upon rules. Instead, member states and the European Commission (supported by the European Court of Justice [ECJ] and subnational actors) are understood to pursue their specific interests in this process. The central question addressed in this chapter is whether interactions in this governance process are guided by hierarchy as a governance mode. One could expect a hierarchical mode of governance, given that directives are "hard" policy instruments that originate in a legislative process and for which the European Commission is endowed with clear powers of enforcement that allow for exerting pressure on member states to comply.

It needs to be pointed out, however, that specific features of the EU system leave room for a continuation of policymaking during the implementation phase to a greater extent than comparable processes at the national level do. First, the EU is highly dependent on member states when it comes to implementation. Regulation is adopted at the central level, whereas implementation is left to decentralized actors (Scharpf 1985: 325). In the case of directives, national political and administrative structures are first entrusted with transposition and then with application of commonly agreed upon standards. Hence, there is an additional level that complicates the implementation task. Second, decisionmaking competences of the Council in collaboration with Parliament are restricted by the need to reach a majority or even unanimity among diverging interests and positions. Under these constraints, side payments are frequent and legislation tends to be based on compromise; as a result, the wording is often ambiguous. Vagueness and legal uncertainty (Schmidt 2004b) are the grounds on which actions by the Commission and the ECJ can lead to the emergence of a specific governance process during implementation.

Implementation processes for directives are assumed to be characterized by hierarchy as the governance mode, given that the directives are part of a regulatory framework over which the supranational level (ECJ, Commission, etc.) has supervisory powers that ensure that they can enforce compliance in transposition and application. Thus, with respect to governance modes, they are generally believed to contrast with negotiation and coordination as dominant modes under the soft and innovative instrument of the open method of coordination. This chapter looks at the instruments and procedures invoked by the European Commission and the ECJ for assuring the proper transposition and application of EU legislation and asks whether this assumption is correct. Is hierarchy indeed the prevalent governance mode in supranational implementation politics? Or can a governance mix be observed? And, if so, how can it be explained?

I argue that the development and use of different instruments in supranational implementation politics is constrained and motivated by the struggle over power and influence between member states and the European Commission. There are multiple reasons why member states oppose the implementation of a commonly adopted directive, for example, because it runs against the ideological orientation of the political party in government or because it imposes high costs. At the same time the governments of the day are aware that broad defection would endanger the integration project. I would expect them to be interested in other member states' compliance with the commonly agreed upon rules, for example, in order to remain competitive in the single market. Moreover, decentralized enforcement would carry the risk of "forum shopping" or uneven implementation (Majone 2000: 282). At the supranational level, the European Commission as guardian of the treaties has an interest in correct and timely implementation, since "its destiny and prestige are connected to the promotion of advances in European integration"

(Ross 1995: 14). Yet, implementation control is resource demanding and politically costly and might at times contradict other interests of the European Commission, for example, concerning parallel decisiontaking processes or different policy arenas or levels. I will lay out these rationales in more detail in the course of the chapter to explain why I see a mix of governance modes rather than an exclusive use of hierarchy in supranational implementation politics. These details will also provide evidence for the argument that in the multilevel system, implementation is subject to a specific governance process in which—far from automatic enactment of prior agreed rules—actors with diverging interests try to shape policies.

The remainder of this chapter is structured as follows. First, I will present a summary on the output of incremental social policymaking under the Community method. These are the grounds on which to quantify member states' reluctance to follow commonly agreed upon rules. I will then present supervision and enforcement policies enacted to counter this reluctance. It can be shown that member states have not only at times agreed to transfer competences for hierarchical control to the European level, but that the European Commission has skillfully extended these competences by recurring to other instruments and processes characterized by governance modes of competition and cooperation. It did so in interplay with the ECJ and was substantially supported by subnational, decentralized actors. Finally I will conclude on the specific governance mix used for policymaking during the implementation phase of EU social policy.

The Output of Incremental Social Policymaking

Since the founding of the EU, treaty reforms have resulted in a progressive extension of formal EU competences regarding social issues.[4] The capacity for action of the European Communities has been "incrementally increased in day-to-day politics" (Falkner et al. 2005: 41). The output of social policy over time allows us to trace this incremental policymaking. By the end of 2005 there were 88 social directives (63 individual social directives, 7 geographical extensions, and 18 amendments to existing directives). The most active field was health and safety at work, with 29 directives. Minimum standards on working conditions outside this area follow with 25 new directives. Finally, 9 directives belong to the field of nondiscrimination and gender equality policy (numbers from Falkner et al. 2005: 41–55, updated by my own calculations).

A rather slow takeoff in the first two decades resulted from very limited policymaking competences. In the Rome Treaty, regulatory competences on social policy had been transferred only for equal pay (Falkner 1998: 57) and for social protection to assure the free movement of workers (Leibfried and Pierson 1995). It was not deemed necessary to make further steps in European social policy provisions, as the thinking at the time was that economic growth would in itself provide sufficient improvements in welfare for all (Kohler-Koch 1997). During the late 1960s and early 1970s, European social policy started to gain momentum. This change was largely motivated by the desire to improve social issues in the wake of increased economic integration and of any negative consequences resulting from economic integration that might not be automatically resolved through regular market principles or by individual member state policies (Barnard 1999). Most important, a number of legislative measures proposed by the ensuing Social Action Programme (1974) were adopted by the Council as recently as the early 1980s. In this context the European Commission played an important role as a policy entrepreneur when undertaking studies, delivering opinions, and arranging for consultation where no regulatory competences existed (Cram 1997).

In the late 1980s and in the 1990s major progress was reached in the area of European social policy. When the Single European Act came into force in 1987, qualified majority voting (QMV) was introduced for minimum harmonization of health and safety provisions (Article 137 of the Treaty Establishing the European Communities [TEC]). On other issues less closely connected to the single market, member states still proved reluctant to give the EU a broader role. Arguing that an improvement of general working conditions would ensure the occupational safety and health of workers (OSH), the European Commission opened a path to adopt a wider range of social policy directives with QMV (using Article 137 to adopt measures only loosely related to OSH in a move to profit from QMV that has been called a "treaty base game"; Rhodes 1995: 100). A peak was reached in 1992 with six new directives, paralleling activities to accomplish the Common Market program under Commission president Jacques Delors.

Following the adoption of the Maastricht Treaty, also in 1992, QMV was extended to many more issues, including general working conditions, worker information, and consultation as well as gender equality for the labor force. This move went along with important innovations in procedural terms. Under the Social Protocol, social partners can independently negotiate agreements that are then framed into a directive by the Council (Falkner 1998: 78–96). In the following years three such agreements were negotiated and adopted without changes by the Council: parental leave (96/34/EC), part-time work (97/81/EC), and fixed-term work (99/70/EC). The Amsterdam Treaty (1997) as well as the Nice Treaty (2001) saw a progressive extension of social policy issues covered by regulatory competences.

Since then there seems to have been a declining trend in the number of newly adopted directives in the area of social policy. An explanation for this declining trend might be that some activities are being shifted to new areas of social policy, where legal or functional constraints suggest the use of the open method of coordination (e.g., social protection or employment), resulting not in the adoption of directives but of activity through different modes of governance. It is still unclear whether the observed mix of traditional legislative and new, softer modes of governance in social policy is complementary, thereby adding to the Community method, or whether it follows a logic of replacement (see Falkner 2004; Trubek and Trubek 2005). Overall, I find that one dimension of social Europe, the regulatory output under the Community method, has incrementally increased, and today could guarantee important social standards to EU constituents. Yet, these findings are confronted with implementation success and failure of EU social policy regulation, to be discussed in the next section.

Member States' Failure to Implement EU Social Policy

Member states are often reluctant to follow commonly agreed upon EU directives.[5] This reluctance does not need to be based on explicit political opposition (Falkner et al. 2004). Rather one can discern three "worlds" with different typical modes of treating implementation duties and thus different factors explaining noncompliance: a world of law observance, a world of domestic politics, and a world of neglect. The specific results of particular examples of (non)compliance tend to depend on different factors within each of the various worlds: the compliance culture in the field can explain most cases in the world of law observance, whereas in the world of domestic politics the specific fit with political preferences in each case plays a much larger role, and in the world of neglect this is true for administrative nonaction. These patterns seem to be rather stable over time and to outlive governments of opposing ideological orientation (Falkner et al. 2005: chap. 15).[6]

One possible way to quantify member state reluctance to implement is to look at infringement procedures initiated by the European Commission against noncompliant member states. In the 2002–2005 period, the European Commission initiated an annual average of 136 social policy infringement procedures (Commission of the European Communities 2003, 2004a, 2005b, 2006b). Most of them address failure to transpose EU standards into national legislation. A smaller, but increasing, number of infringement procedures concerns incorrect transposition. It is rare to find cases issued in reaction to an incorrect application, however. If one takes this method as a proxy for the transposition deficit, one may miss a considerable amount of the action. Obviously, the Commission only responds to a small minority of all failures and delays in implementation. In other words, this method only offers "the tip of the iceberg" of noncompliance (Hartlapp 2005: 191–197).

To provide a better account of (non)compliance, our research team looked in more detail at implementation processes and outcomes of six labor law directives in fifteen member states. The directives concern written information on employment conditions (91/533/EEC), parental leave (96/34/EC), working time (93/104/EC), and the protection of pregnant (92/85/EEC),

young (94/33/EC), and part-time workers (97/81/EC). They cover all important EU social policy directives from the 1990s that supersede national regulation (thus excluding transnational issues such as European works coun-
cils) and that are not too closely related to some other EU laws to be
studied individually.

We find that the discipline of the member states in implementing labor
law directives agreed upon in the Council is very weak. In more than two-
thirds of the cases, the adaptation was delayed by two years or more beyond
the transposition deadline set in the directive. Only 11 percent of the transposition cases were both on time and fully correct, and only 19 percent were
either on time or not more than six months delayed. Let us now turn to how
the European Commission dealt with this resistance of member states to implement regulative EU social policy (even though the Commission may not
have been necessarily aware of the full degree of noncompliance).

Implementation Politics Part One: The Commission's Powers in Putting Social Policy into Practice

In the EU, the implementation management of commonly agreed upon rules
lies with the European Commission as the guardian of the treaties (Article
211 TEC). Given member states' reluctance to implement commonly agreed
upon standards, the European Commission has different instruments and
strategies at its disposal to monitor and enforce transposition and application
of EU social policy. Here I will focus on the development of these instruments in the interplay of the European Commission's interest in increasing
leverage when executing its powers and member governments' reservations
about losing their grip over control and enforcement processes that might
drop back on national interests.

The European Commission can start an infringement procedure when a
member state does not follow commonly agreed upon rules (Articles 226
and 228 TEC). The procedure consists of four different steps, including a
judgment of the ECJ. In cases of remaining opposition to the ECJ judgment,
the procedure can be started over again, possibly leading to financial sanctions. Over time and for all policy areas, the numbers of procedures initiated
rose from an average of 670 in 1978 to 2,653 in 2005 (Commission of the
European Communities 2004a: annex 1, 2006b: annex 1). Similar developments can be traced for social policy (Commission of the European Communities 2003, 2004a, 2005b, 2006b), and in this area, financial sanctions have
been demanded by the European Commission in three cases.[7] But so far no
sanctions have been imposed in this area. Member states normally come into
line soon after sanctions are announced.

Member states delegated enforcement rights to the European Commission in the founding treaties. Their extension and practical use has developed

over time, driven both by member states' interest in mutual application of rules and the European Commission's interest in increasing its power when facing noncompliance. Until 1977 the use of the infringement procedure followed a diplomatic logic, and reluctant member states only rarely became the subject of enforcement (Audretsch 1986: 279–283). In the 1980s, as an increasing number of directives had to be implemented in light of the plan to complete the single market, the European Commission became more active and infringement procedures became more common. Tallberg (2003) shows how in 1991 it was in member states' interest to extend enforcement competences in order to counter an implementation deficit presumed to endanger the single market project.[8] Following this proposal, Maastricht saw the introduction of financial sanctions, and rules for calculations were published in 1997.[9] In 2005 the European Commission extended its leverage to punish defection of common regulation when proposing financial sanctions. Article 228 TEC merely adheres to the European Commission's right to "specify the amount of the lump sum *or* penalty payment to be paid by the Member State" (emphasis added). However, the ECJ—upon the proposal of the European Commission—ruled that both penalty *and* lump sum could be imposed in one case, thereby stretching an unclear treaty provision despite the criticism of some member states (C-304/02).[10]

In parallel and even when member states no longer showed specific motivation to put the single market into place,[11] the European Commission expanded its enforcement capacity along informal paths and by recurring to competition as a governance mode. It further depoliticized and streamlined internal procedures (Sécretariat Général 1998), systematically used informal means to exert pressure by issuing press releases for all infringement cases unless explicitly decided differently (Sécretariat Général 1996: 7), and shamed implementation laggards: "I urge all those Member States who are lagging behind, particularly Luxembourg, Greece, Italy, Belgium, France and Portugal to take appropriate action immediately or face the legal consequences" (Commissioner Flynn cited in Commission of the European Communities 1997). In 2001 the European Commission introduced the use of scoreboards to directly compare member states' performance when they notify transposition of social policy directives and to create a framework for more competition.[12]

Summarizing, this overview of enforcement politics shows that the European Commission has strong powers and is willing to use them. At the same time I have mentioned that infringement procedures only cover the "tip of the iceberg" of member states' noncompliance. To gain analytical leverage as to the logic of the European Commission in opening infringement proceedings, I differentiate between the European Commission's capacity to enforce infractions and its willingness to do so when facing potentially political costs.

With respect to capacity, the European Commission could be either unaware of infractions or it could lack the means to pursue them. In the EU system, monitoring of compliance is specifically difficult. The distance between supervisors in Brussels and addressees (in social policy enterprises and individual workers) is greater than at the national level. In addition, the transposition of directives allows for national diversity in the way the commonly agreed upon standards are assured. Allowing for member states' freedom to maintain regulatory traditions and to keep national specifics in legislation intact results in increased complexity of the control task. These systemic conditions are aggravated by limited resources. With a staff of 922 persons as of early 2006[13] and only a fraction of them dedicated to labor law regulation,[14] the Directorate General for Employment, Social Affairs, and Equal Opportunities (DG EMPL) is simply not in a position to follow up systematically on all cases of incorrect transposition. Thus, it seems logical to pick cases of higher political relevance and to concentrate on directives with greater visibility and impact. Looking at our ninety in-depth case studies and comparing cases of noncompliance and European Commission enforcement, I see indeed a bias toward prioritizing some directives (that is, the pregnant workers and work-time directives got higher priority) over others. Moreover, in 2002 the European Commission made such prioritization an explicit goal of enforcement policy (Commission of the European Communities 2002).

Following a different logic, the European Commission might simply prefer not to enforce noncompliance. One rationale is that it is more interested in the production of new "rules . . . than in the thankless and politically costly task of implementing existing ones" (Majone 2002a: 329). Member states are not only the addressees of rules—they are at the same time those who decide about (further) Community activity. If the European Commission wants to reach an agreement for a new initiative—or social policy or in a separate policy area—continuing an infringement procedure or proposing financial sanctions against a noncompliant member state risks being counterproductive (cf. Spencer 1994: 111). By the same token, not starting an infringement could be used as a side payment in negotiations.[15] Are these constraints on the European Commission's capacity to enforce infractions and its will to do so when potentially facing political costs simply accepted? To what extent do the strategies and mechanisms employed by the European Commission to counter these constraints lead to a specific mix of governance modes in implementation politics?

Implementation Politics Part Two: Interaction with Subnational Interests to Put Social Policy into Practice

It is well known that the European Commission has involved subnational interests in the run-up to negotiations of EU regulations (cf. Kohler-Koch

1997). I argue that in social policy implementation subnational interests are used in a similar fashion.

In many EU member states there is a long tradition of peak associations, both for trade unions and employers' associations. Moreover, during the 1980s, under the Delors presidency of the Commission, the role of EU-level social partners was systematically strengthened and enshrined in the treaties (Falkner 1998). A comparative analysis of different policy areas shows that DG EMPL has more contacts with interest representatives from industry, trade unions, and consumer groups than most other DGs.[16] Since the 1990s the European Commission has extended "lobby sponsoring" (Bauer 2002: 388) to other, nongovernmental social interest organization under the social platform. In a more concrete step, it made support in implementation and "monitoring transposition" an explicit requirement for Brussels-based nongovernmental organizations (NGOs) to receive funding under the Community Action Programme 2001–2006 to Combat Discrimination.[17] Here interests organized at the EU level function as transmission belts to raise awareness at subnational levels and as channels to upload information to the EU level. Overall, DG EMPL is in a good position to stimulate and receive information concerning implementation from organized interests at the European or national level.

By drawing on the delegation literature, we can characterize two different mechanisms of implementation politics—whistle blowing and preliminary rulings—the European Commission uses to build on subnational interest organizations or individuals. Both instruments respond to the constraints imposed by the limited capacity for systematic enforcement by following a cooperative governance mode. The latter also allows the European Commission to avoid political costs of direct enforcement. Initially the European Commission itself favored decentralized forms of implementation management as a prime avenue of enforcement in the EU multilevel system (Ehlermann 1987). During the negotiations of the Maastricht Treaty, it proposed to offer explicit guarantees to individuals to redress consequences of nonimplementation (Commission of the European Communities 1991c: 131). But member states refused to enshrine these powers in the treaties and opted for the more direct and hierarchical possibility of imposing financial sanctions. In the same year, however, the ECJ established that the fundamental principles of direct effect (*Van Gend & Loos,* C-26/62) and supremacy (*Costa v. ENEL,* C-6/64) could be exercised against the state. Under certain conditions, member states could be liable for nonimplementation (*Francovich,* C-6/90). Thus, the European Commission's implementation capacity was extended along indirect paths by the ECJ, its "primary ally in [the] implementation process" (Peters 1997: 193), thereby overruling member states that criticized "judge-made law and judicial activism" (Tallberg

2003: 105). This discussion leads into the next two sections, in which I examine whistle-blowing and preliminary rulings.

Whistle-Blowing to Prepare the
Ground for Hierarchical Enforcement

Whistle-blowing by decentralized actors provides valuable information to the European Commission at comparatively low costs (this mechanism is referred to as "fire-alarm" by McCubbins and Schwartz 1984). Individuals or organized interests can directly address the European Commission when they believe their government to be in breach of Community legislation. Although in principle information exchange between subnational actors and the European Commission existed before, the European Commission started to make systematic use of this channel in 1989. To facilitate this information exchange, a complaint form was published in the *Official Journal* (C-26, 1 February 1989, 7–8).[18] The systematic use of whistle-blowers helps the European Commission broaden its information base and counter the information deficit in order to efficiently target the use of hierarchical enforcement instruments. The extensive use of claimants was criticized by the European ombudsman as treating them as information providers "to be deployed as and when the Commission chooses" (Rawlings 2000: 13). The European Commission defended this action as essential to its role as guardian of the treaties and as necessary to guarantee efficiency of enforcement (Commission of the European Communities 2001b) but was forced to keep individual claimants informed throughout the whole procedure.

As for the quantitative use of the mechanism over all policy sectors, individual complaints are more often at the roots of infringement procedures than recognition of implementation failure by the European Commission. In social policy, complaints from the subnational level are the main source for detecting infringements. In 2004, almost half of the infringements were based on whistle-blowing.[19]

From our case studies on the implementation of six directives, I will provide here one key example of whistle-blowing. It concerns the transposition of the parental leave directive in Ireland. After having lost a battle during implementation at the national level, the Irish Congress of Trade Unions blew the whistle. The position they fought for was that parents of children born before the cutoff date set by government should benefit equally from the new right of three-month parental leave. The European Commission, after consultation with the European trade unions, quickly initiated an infringement procedure. Under such pressure, the Irish government brought the legislation into line (Treib 2004: 229–230). Whistle-blowing is an important example showing how the limited capacity to know about all cases of member states' reluctance to implement regulatory policies is partly compensated for by the adroit interaction with subnational actors.[20]

Preliminary Rulings as Enforcement at
Low Costs and as Stepwise Policymaking

Often individuals seek to enforce their (EU-based) right against their own government by demanding that a national court address the ECJ to request how to interpret a particular European directive or regulation. Implementation failure can, but must not necessarily, be the cause. The ECJ then lays out the meaning of a specific standard in a preliminary ruling (Article 234 TEC).[21]

With respect to supranational policymaking during implementation, preliminary rulings are interesting from two perspectives. First, they are an indirect enforcement instrument against member states' reluctance to implement EU legislation. Building on the legal principles of direct effect, supremacy, and state liability, they empower individuals and organized interests to actively support the European Commission in its role as guardian of the treaties (cf. the mechanism of "deck stacking" in McCubbins, Noll, and Weingast 1987). Second, they can earmark cases in which the ECJ judgment substantially alters a specific standard of a directive; in this way, policymaking continues beyond the adoption of a directive under the classical Community method.

To find out more about the indirect enforcement capacity of preliminary rulings, it is reasonable to look at their numbers together with ECJ rulings as part of infringement procedures. Both present supranational means to exert pressure on defecting member states. Their development is quantified in Figure 14.1.

The preceding section has shown that the EU was slow in adopting social policy directives. Thus it should come as no surprise that the first judgment referring to a directive stems only from 1977. From then on until the late 1990s there was an increasing trend of preliminary rulings. In the most recent years, numbers for ECJ judgments increased while numbers of preliminary rulings showed an unstable and overall declining tendency. These developments have to be seen in the light of the growing numbers of directives potentially invoked and the growing numbers of potential claimants due to enlargements.

Whether preliminary rulings are raised also depends on national legal culture and the legal system (Alter and Vargas 2000). The European Commission actively encourages the rise in preliminary rulings. It does so in the area of Community law in general by financial support for the training of national judges and through exchange programs of lawyers (the Robert Schuman project, the Grotius program, or the Technical Assistance Information Exchange [TAIEX] with new member states). In the area of social policy, it does so by organization and financing of seminars to explain legal implementation aspects of recently adopted directives to national legal

Figure 14.1 ECJ Judgments on Social Policy Directives

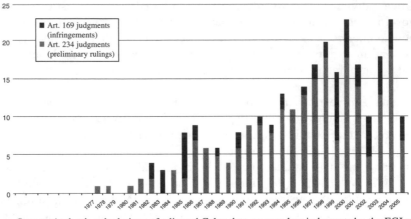

Source: Author's calculations of adjusted Celex data on case-law judgments by the ECJ on social provisions.

Note: Joint cases are counted as one entry. Judgments that refer to regulations or the treaty base only are excluded.

actors.[22] Thus, from the perspective of the European Commission, preliminary rulings are a means by which to indirectly enforce Community regulations without carrying potential political costs. Yet, besides whistle-blowing, the European Commission has little discretion in influencing the selection of cases or their substantive outcomes (but see Mattli and Slaughter 1998 on the pro-integrationist stance of the ECJ).

Preliminary rulings are also of interest for supranational policymaking during implementation because of their potential to substantially alter the contents of a directive. Specification through case law is a common feature of any legal system (Everling 2000: 218). But it is more important in the EU system because of greater legal uncertainty (Schmidt 2004b). Ambiguous wording of a directive is often a consequence of the negotiation dynamics prevailing at the European level at the time of adoption. In other words, unclear wording sometimes serves as an instrument to make proposals agreeable to the Council of Ministers. In addition, the overlap between national legal systems and supreme EU legislation often requires a fresh interpretation of a clause that had earlier been clearly defined.

To gain empirical insight into the use of preliminary rulings as an indirect means of enforcement and as an instance of policy alteration, we need again to look at the various cases. Of our ninety in-depth studies, there are fourteen preliminary rulings prior to 2005 dealing foremost with one of the six directives.[23] Of these, four cases can be characterized as depicting the indirect enforcement mechanism. Most clearly visible (and successful) is the mechanism in a case in which the dismissal protection of pregnant workers as prescribed in the EU directive was only transposed by the Spanish government after a preliminary ruling (C-438/99) had proven prior Spanish legislation to fall short of EU requirements (Hartlapp 2005: 95). The other cases concern the pregnant workers directive (C-356/03), the working-time directive (C-397/01-C403/01), and the directive on written employment information (C-253/96-C258/96). Moreover, in one case, concerning the implementation of the pregnant workers directive in Portugal, the simple threat of initiating a number of related preliminary rulings as expressed by trade unions and broadly announced in the media sufficed to force the Portuguese government into legislation that would retrospectively extend maternity leave to fourteen weeks (Falkner et al. 2005: 87). In a similar fashion, the British Trade Union Congress withdrew a case from the ECJ after having successfully used a preliminary ruling to alert the European Commission to incorrect implementation of a cut-off date for drawing on newly established rights during parental leave (Treib 2004: 200–201).

Cases from our sample in which I can clearly link observed policy alteration to difficult negotiations concern the working time directive. The directive was one of the most contentious social policy proposals of the 1990s because it touched upon politically and ideologically highly salient terms and was, economically speaking, a potentially very costly issue. Moreover, the European Commission played the "treaty base game" (Rhodes 1995) to adopt the directive by qualified majority voting, thereby increasing opposition of certain member states. During the negotiations the British government pressed for as many exemptions as possible and, what was most important, succeeded in pushing through the opportunity for individual workers to opt-out of the forty-eight-hour week. Other standards, especially the many derogation possibilities, saw tough negotiations among member states, too.

Since its adoption, the substance of the directive has been altered in many ways that governments had obviously not envisaged during negotiations (on unintended consequences, see Pierson 1996: 136–139). In the *SIMAP* case (C-303/98; similar cases were *Jaeger* C-151/02 and *Dellas* C-14/04), the ECJ decided that on-call duties were an integral part of working time and stepwise enlarged the scope of its judgments. Most countries hitherto had treated such duties (partly) as rest periods and would have to bear considerable direct economic costs resulting from the new definition—this was especially true of (public) hospitals (Commission of the European Communities 2004b: 34–39). Taking into account the fact that the original directive foresaw a revision of parts of the directive and following these ECJ rulings, the European Commission opened renegotiations in 2003. It initially proposed to stick to the ECJ working-time definition (interim directive 2003/88/EC). Facing fierce opposition from member states and increasing use of the individual opt-out to escape the effect of the ECJ working-time definition (Luxembourg, Spain, France, and Germany), the European Commission changed its position in its legislative proposal and added a new category of "inactive part of on-call time." Adopted in June 2008 this allows member states to save high direct economic costs. To sum up, this is a case in which compromise and vagueness in the text of the directive created much room for EU policymaking in implementation through alteration. Yet, it is also one of the rare cases in which—given the specific conditions of prior envisaged renegotiation combined with ECJ rulings perceived as having a costly impact—member states put a hold to supranational policymaking during implementation.

Conclusion

Over time and through incremental policymaking, a substantial social dimension of Europe has developed in the form of EU directives. But member states show rather great reluctance when it comes to implementing them correctly and in a timely manner. To counter this resistance, different instruments and procedures are invoked by the European Commission. Even though hierarchy is looked at as being the classical Community method, this chapter challenged that view as being the exclusive governance mode in implementation politics in the EU. I showed that there are a substantial amount of instruments involved that follow nonhierarchical governance modes. The development and use of instruments other than the well-known infringement procedures can be understood as resulting from the constraints of the EU system. Member states' reservations about transferring additional powers, as well as the political costs of enforcement and the limited capacity of the European Commission to systematically follow up on all cases, have been driving forces to enlarge room for maneuver by instruments that can be categorized as competitive in their governance mode (e.g., benchmarking). Interaction with subnational actors in the form of whistle-blowing increases the amount of information available to the Commission and hence increases the ability of the Commission to enforce compliance with the directives. Empowerment of individuals and organized interests to use preliminary rulings increased indirect pressure capacity. Thus, I found the European Commission to avail itself of a mix of governance modes whereby the powerful hierarchical mode of enforcement is complemented by competition as well as cooperation. Somewhat ironically, this mix seems to even extend the leeway of the European Commission in implementing policy goals vis-à-vis member states.

A second and more general conclusion to be drawn from the analysis of implementation instruments and procedures, and their development and use, is that implementation politics can be characterized as a specific governance process. This process is far from being an automatic enactment of

Community provisions; rather, actors actively engage in it in order to pursue their specific interests. This active role for various actors became clearly visible in the alteration of social policy standards in preliminary rulings. Case law is common at the national level, but its relevance is increased in the EU, where ambiguous wording of a directive is often a built-in consequence of the negotiation dynamics prevailing at the European level. Even though lacking clear channels to influence a specific outcome, the European Commission overall aims at stimulating preliminary rulings to specify contested standards for which negotiation at times has proved difficult. Instead of a separation of rule making and implementation, in these instances I see a blurring of the two and can thus conclude that here implementation can be considered a continuation of policymaking (even after the policy has been adopted) along the lines of a specific governance process.

Notes

I wish to thank the editors as well as the participants of the international conference, "Governance, Policy-making, and System-building of the European Union," at the University of Victoria, BC, Canada (2–4 March 2006) and at the University of Osnabrück (3 November 2006) for valuable comments. An earlier version of this chapter was published as Hugo Sinzheimer Institute Discussion Paper 2007-04.

1. Although strictly speaking it would be correct to use the term *European Communities* (EC) when referring to the first pillar, I employ the more general notion of European Union (EU), as is customary today.

2. The point here is not to state that regulation of social standards at the EU level embraces a similar range of issues as at the nation-state level, nor to claim that social Europe is sufficient to balance the existing liberalization tendencies.

3. By highlighting the importance of the supranational level, I do not wish to challenge the crucial role of member states during the implementation phase. Rather I simply take a perspective that differs from most EU research, in which the implementation phase has been addressed with respect to the national level (Héritier, Knill, and Mingers 1996; Duina and Blithe 1999; Haverland 2000; Green Cowles, Caporaso, and Risse 2001).

4. For more details, see "EU Social Policymaking over Time: The Role of Directives," in Falkner et al. (2005: chap. 3).

5. Here I draw on the work of a collaborative research project. Many thanks to my colleagues Gerda Falkner, Simone Leiber, and Oliver Treib (for more detailed results see Falkner et al. 2005).

6. Note that these country clusters are not based on geographical criteria and that hence there is no southern bloc (Hartlapp and Leiber 2006).

7. A demand for sanctions was issued in 1998 against Luxembourg concerning medical treatment on-board vessels and in 1999 against France for discrimination of women in access to night work and against Italy concerning work equipment.

8. Great Britain especially, as an advocate of the single market program, pushed for financial sanctions (Tallberg 2003)—possibly also because Britain itself showed a relatively good compliance record.

9. A standard flat rate (currently 600 euro) is multiplied by the member state's ability to pay and its weight in the Council (25.4–0.58), a coefficient for seriousness

(1–20, based on the importance of the violated norm and the effect of the violation), and a coefficient for duration (1–3).

10. Interview with a former member of the European Commissions Legal Service, Luxembourg, 22 February 2006.

11. An attempt of the European Commission to expand enforcement powers at the 1996–1997 intergovernmental conference (IGC) failed (Tallberg 2003).

12. Scoreboards had initially been introduced in 1997 for the Common Market and environmental issues.

13. This information is available at http://europa.eu.int/comm/budget/budget_detail/policy_areas_en.htm#4 (accessed 5 January 2006).

14. Interview with a former member of the European Commissions Legal Service, Luxembourg, 22 February 2006.

15. Yet, empirical analysis reveals that political costs of enforcement do not translate into a systematic favoritism of some countries over others, for instance, because they have more political weight or because their population is more euroskeptic (Falkner et al. 2005; Hartlapp 2005).

16. See the online register of expert groups provided by the European Commission, available at http://ec.europa.eu/secretariat_general/regexp/search.cfm. Unfortunately this source is based on the voluntary initiative of the interest groups and is thus not fully representative (but cf. Hooghe 2001).

17. Interview with official from the Directorate General for Employment, Social Affairs, and Equal Opportunities, Brussels, 20 February 2006; interview with European Older People (NGO), Brussels, 21 February 2006.

18. The complaint form can be downloaded from the Secretariat General's home page http://ec.europa.eu/secretariat_general/index_en.htm.

19. There were 100 infringement cases based on whistle-blowing. An additional 74 were initiated quasi-automatically for noncommunication of transposition legislation at the deadline, and another 33 cases were detected by the European Commission's own offices (Commission of the European Communities 2005b). For 2002 the respective numbers were 98, 11, and 28 (Commission of the European Communities 2003), and for 2003 the numbers were 88, 8, and 46 (Commission of the European Communities 2004a).

20. At first glance, whistle-blowing might seem like an attractive instrument for subnational interests to use to systematically shift the national balance of power. Yet preliminary rulings allow for relatively greater influence on the process and are thus a more attractive avenue for systematic use.

21. Article 234 TEC was installed so as to ensure uniform interpretation of Community law through member states.

22. Interview with official from the Directorate General for Employment, Social Affairs, and Equal Opportunities, Brussels, 20 February 2006.

23. This comprises six preliminary rulings for the working-time directive, five for the pregnant workers directive, two for written information on the working relationship, and one for the part-time directive. Rulings where one of our six directives is mentioned, but does not form the central piece of EU regulation the judgment refers to, are excluded.

15

Tackling the Regulatory Dilemma: The Rise of Incorporated Transgovernmental Networks

Burkard Eberlein and Abraham Newman

The European Union (EU) as a system of governance faces the double challenge of effectiveness and legitimacy (Scharpf 1999). In the complex policy cnvironment of a larger and more diverse European Union, the effectiveness of the classical blueprint, uniform Community legislation, is increasingly being called into question. Also, the legitimacy reservoir for further delegation of regulatory powers to the EU is rapidly depleting. The resounding rejection of the draft European Constitution by the Dutch and French electorate has underscored the thin legitimacy of "an ever closer union." Yet, short of accepting the negative externalities arising from diverging national approaches, the need for European coordination has increased rather than diminished.

In response to this dilemma, research on new modes of governance has exploded (e.g., Scott and Trubek 2002; Héritier 2003; Radaelli 2003a; Borrás and Greve 2004; Eberlein and Kerwer 2004). Departing from the "old" Community method of binding legislation through directives and regulations and relying instead on nonhierarchical coordination of member state policies, new modes of governance offer a potential escape to either the legitimacy or coordination demands. The open method of coordination (OMC) in particular has received extraordinary attention since the 2000 Lisbon European Council codified this coordination mechanism as a new and broadly applicable instrument of EU governance.[1] The underlying new governance idea is not to impose rigid regulatory standards but to share experience about national "experiments that are adapted to local circumstances, while fostering policy improvement, and possibly policy convergence, through institutionalized mutual learning processes" (Eberlein and Kerwer 2004: 123). Against this background, the OMC was touted as the "third way" in EU governance, to be used when "harmonisation is unworkable but mutual recognition and the resulting regulatory competition may be too risky" (Trubek and Mosher

237

2001: 21). Scholars began to identify implicit patterns of OMC-style new governance in a large number of policy areas, well beyond the OMC core of economic policy coordination, employment, and social policy: examples are immigration, the environment, research and innovation, and taxation. The initial excitement surrounding the OMC and new governance, however, has made room for a sober and often skeptical assessment of its merits and limits in empirical practice (e.g., Borrás and Greve 2004; but see also Zeitlin, Pochet, and Magnusson 2005).

On a conceptual level, new governance is now being analyzed in the context of more sophisticated typologies of different modes of governance. Many adopt a Europeanization perspective, distinguishing between different degrees of "bindingness" in policy formulation on the one hand and different degrees of discretion in policy implementation on the other hand. New governance is typically associated with nonbinding or low-obligation types of policies that give actors a high degree of discretion or flexibility in implementation (e.g., Knill and Lenschow 2004). The stylized juxtaposition of old versus new governance is being replaced by a continuum of governance that locates different practices along a common variable such as the degree of supranational coordination (NEWGOV 2005). Closer analysis reveals that some practices that are considered as new in one area might have been "long-established practices in other areas" (Treib, Bähr, and Falkner 2005: 4). Most important, it is recognized that in practice, "old" and "new" modes are selected and combined in various ways (embedded, sequentially ordered, and so on) and that they need to be studied in their shifting interaction and development, not in artificial isolation or dichotomy (e.g., see Chapter 5).

Notwithstanding these sophistications in the scholarly conversation on EU governance innovations,[2] the debate focuses predominately on patterns that are nonregulatory and eschew formal authority. The emphasis is very much on cooperative, negotiated, or deliberative techniques of decisionmaking (as depicted by the dashed oval in Figure 15.1) that are contrasted with the use of legal, formal authority (e.g., Börzel, Guttenbrunner, and Seper 2005: 6).

The central argument of this chapter is that the prevailing focus on nonbinding, deliberative, OMC-style types of new governance tends to overlook an alternative and, in practice, increasingly important exit from the regulatory dilemma: *incorporated transgovernmental networks*. This governance strategy falls within the dashed oval depicted in Figure 15.2. In a range of sectors from financial services to utilities, the EU has formally incorporated organized groups of national regulators through European law into a novel, network-type of regulatory process. In contrast to informal transgovernmental cooperation among substate actors, these networks have been recognized by law and placed within the hierarchy of EU decisionmaking. These incorporated transgovernmental networks take on critical roles in defining and enforcing European rules. They produce binding rules while resting on a complex web of multilevel authority. As these networks confront the challenges of harmonizing diverse European markets, network participants enjoy significant domestic regulatory authority. They may then simultaneously leverage both supranational and national authority to coordinate European projects.

The goal of this chapter is to offer an initial window into this innovative governance technique. As such, it is organized around three sections. The first

Figure 15.1 Current Focus of New Governance Research

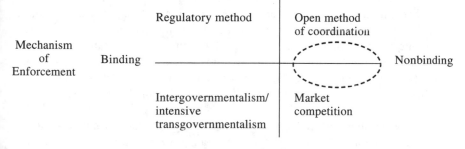

Locus of Coordination

Supranational

	Regulatory method	Open method of coordination	
Mechanism of Enforcement	Binding		Nonbinding
	Intergovernmentalism/ intensive transgovernmentalism	Market competition	

National

Figure 15.2 Incorporated Transgovernmentalism

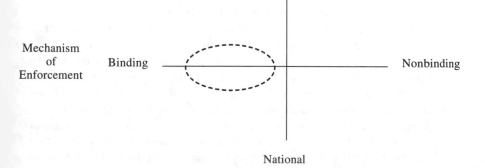

Locus of Coordination

Supranational

Mechanism of Enforcement   Binding   Nonbinding

National

presents a thorough description of incorporated transgovernmental networks and its main components, specifically who the key actors are and why these incorporated networks emerge. The next offers detailed case studies in two critical sectors, data privacy and energy. The cases are chosen so as to flesh out the analytic category, building a more robust theoretical typology of European governance (George and Bennett 2005). Although data privacy offers the earliest and most developed example of incorporated transgovernmentalism, the energy sector represents a host of policy domains for which the ongoing rise of incorporated transgovernmentalism is closely tied to the recent expansion of the regulatory state in Europe. The final section concludes by addressing the implications of this new governance mode for policymaking legitimacy and the distribution of power within multilevel governance.

The Second Escape: Incorporated Transgovernmentalism

In an effort to manage the dilemmas posed by the regulatory method, the European Union has experimented recently with innovative governance tools. Although the academic literature has actively investigated self-enforcing techniques that flatten supranational hierarchy—most notably the open method of coordination—additional innovative mechanisms emphasizing binding enforcement have also been created. Incorporated transgovernmentalism provides a critical example of this new tool in the European regulatory palette.

This strategy officially incorporates transgovernmental networks into the supranational governance process. Transgovernmental networks comprise subnational actors (such as independent regulatory authorities) that meet and interact with their counterparts from other nations (Slaughter 2000; Raustiala 2002; Newman 2008a). The *primary actors,* then, are networks of national regulatory agencies. In incorporated transgovernmentalism, these networks, whose existence often predated incorporation, are integrated through European law into the supranational policymaking process. European legislation establishes new formal cooperative bodies with dedicated secretariats, funded and supported by the European Union. These networks are then granted the authority to participate in EU rule making, enforcement, and implementation. Specifically, they serve to advise the Commission, draft implementing legislation, coordinate national enforcement, promote information exchange among national regulators, and make recommendations to the public on emerging regulatory issues. This means that these regulatory groups organize and interact with sectoral stakeholders as supranational legislation is developed and at the same time devise on-the-ground strategies for implementation. In many sectors, such networks have been layered on top of traditional comitology procedures, raising the stature of national regulators vis-à-vis other EU actors, such as the European Parliament. Distinct from intensive transgovernmentalism (see Chapter 16), the actors in these networks have considerable autonomy in their domestic political settings and have statutory authority at the domestic level to sanction noncompliance and regulate behavior. In other words, European institutions have formally delegated supranational authority to networks of subnational actors.

The move to integrate transgovernmental networks into the formal supranational regulatory process is a logical, yet a unique, extension of traditional transgovernmental efforts in Europe. National expert networks have long played an active role in European politics (Dehousse 1997). They advise the various European institutions and constitute the substructure of many of the European regulatory agencies. Pan-European agencies active in areas ranging from discrimination to the environment serve as central nodes in information exchange among national experts. European political institutions can leverage the expertise in these networks to fill information gaps, and the networks offer to inject transparency into supranational politics. This "governance by information," as coined by Majone, focuses on highlighting differences and disparities across member states but rarely delves into issues of regulatory enforcement or development (Majone 1997a: 274). In the case of incorporated transgovernmentalism, such networks are not only information warehouses but become independent political institutions with the authority to shape rule making and rule enforcement. To be sure, these networks, too, use informal policy mechanisms such as information sharing in their day-to-day practice. Yet, we argue that their distinctive character lies in the fact that they simultaneously wield power over rules as national regulators vested with domestic authority and formally coordinate the supranational regulatory framework.

Incorporated transgovernmentalism has become a fast growing governance mechanism in the European Union. Many major sectors, including financial securities, banking, insurance, energy, and data privacy, now have a transgovernmental network that is officially embedded in the supranational policymaking process. These networks are most often composed of member state national regulatory authorities.

Why, then, do we see the emergence of this governance mechanism? The shift toward incorporated transgovernmentalism has been deeply tied to the development of the regulatory state in Europe since the 1980s (Majone 1996). The regulatory state is characterized by a shift from direct government intervention into economic and business affairs toward a focus on arm's-length oversight of markets. Governments have moved from owning and running companies to setting the terms by which companies compete. With sectors ranging from telecommunications to energy liberalized and state industries privatized, arm's-length regulations that enforce and manage market competition have replaced direct command and control state intervention (Héritier 2002b). Independent, "nonmajoritarian" regulatory agencies have been created to oversee such markets (Gilardi 2002). Although this form of government was first popularized during the New Deal and Great Society periods in the United States, it started to gain widespread attraction in Europe in the 1970s. European Union legislation has actively encouraged this development in a host of sectors by adopting legislation that requires all member states to create independent regulatory agencies. As a result, implementation and enforcement at the national level have increasingly shifted away from executive ministries to independent regulatory agencies. This regulatory revolution at the national level has then facilitated the rise of incorporated transgovernmentalism as national regulators have been appointed and become available to coordinate a viable supranational governance strategy.

The incorporation of transgovernmental actors exemplifies the diversity of governance modes possible in a system of multilevel governance (Hooghe and Marks 2001). These networks have been delegated authority at the supranational level to coordinate policy development and implementation at the same time that they rely on domestically delegated authority to enforce their decisions. Independent regulators in these sectors simultaneously act to enforce national rules and to develop and coordinate supranational policy.

Incorporated Transgovernmental Networks in Practice

In order to extrapolate on the depiction of incorporated transgovernmental networks as a significant governance mechanism, we present two case studies that identify their origins, structure, and day-to-day operations (George and Bennett 2005). The cases represent the two temporal extremes, with data privacy as the first example of incorporated transgovernmentalism and energy as the most recent. The cases offer a useful contrast, highlighting how the governance mode has evolved over time. Moreover, the two cases cover both economic regulation (of market access and conditions in energy) and social regulation (consumer protection and control of negative externalities in data privacy). The case of privacy exemplifies a bottom-up process whereby the network was then incorporated into supranational policymaking, whereas the energy case demonstrates a much more active role by the Commission and the EU in constructing the network, its members, and the final incorporation.

Data Privacy

Starting in the late 1960s, governments and businesses across the advanced industrial societies began investing in large mainframe computer systems. Proposals emerged to construct large consumer and citizen databases in order to increase efficiency, better target services, and minimize fraud. These initiatives hoped to rationalize operations by linking a wide range of personal data ranging, for example, from welfare receipts to consumer purchases. Such organizational optimism, however, quickly confronted a powerful set of interests that opposed such efforts under the banner of protecting personal privacy (Hondius 1975).

An alliance formed between groups that feared the expansion of executive authority and those concerned with the concentration of power in big business. Legislators across Europe sought expert advice from committees to examine the effects of computers on personal freedom. A group of socially active lawyers interested in the interaction between law and technology worked in these groups to devise comprehensive rules to govern this new policy area (Newman 2008b). By the end of the 1970s, a core set of countries, including France, Germany, and Sweden, had adopted comprehensive data privacy legislation. These laws established a clear set of rules for the collection, processing, and exchange of personal information for the public and private sectors (Bennett 1992). In addition, they created new independent regulatory institutions—data privacy authorities—that were empowered to monitor and enforce the new regulations. Although the exact powers vary somewhat across the member states, generally, these agencies have the authority to advise their governments on issues pertaining to data privacy, maintain registries of databanks, investigate and sanction violations of the law, and communicate publicly on critical issues in the field. Concerned that large multinational corporations might transfer personal information to countries with lower regulatory standards, many of these data privacy authorities were also delegated the authority to regulate interstate information exchanges.[3]

These young regulatory bodies quickly took up the transnational issues associated with cross-border information exchanges. It was clear that both multinational businesses and European governments would share information across jurisdictions. Regulators from nations with comprehensive rules feared that this would place their citizens' privacy at risk and jeopardize their newly acquired regulatory authority (Hondius 1975). In order to meet this transnational challenge, the regulators formed a transgovernmental association, which met annually at the International Data Protection Commissioners' Conference starting in Berlin in 1979.[4] Multiple working groups were formed to examine critical cross-border issues such as telecommunications, and data privacy authorities worked through multiple international organizations to formulate a coherent set of international norms.[5] Early efforts included a set of fundamental data privacy principles, which were agreed upon in 1980 by the Organization for Economic Cooperation and Development (OECD), and a Council of Europe convention on the processing of personal information in 1981 (OECD 1980; Council of Europe 1981). Although these agreements codified a set of fundamental privacy principles and confirmed the international dimension of the issue, they failed to solve the problem of regulatory arbitrage. Both relied on national implementation legislation, and by the end of the 1980s a third of the European Community had not yet adopted comprehensive rules. European data privacy authorities, then, began working to develop concrete proposals for a European Community proposal.[6]

Prodded by the demands of the European data protection authorities, the European Union adopted a directive for the protection of personal information in 1995.[7] The directive requires that all member states implement comprehensive regulations, supervised by an independent regulatory authority. The directive also includes an extraterritorial clause that prevents the transfer of personal information to countries outside of Europe that have failed to adopt adequate protections.

In addition to requiring member state action, the directive formally established the first incorporated transgovernmental network within the European Union. Article 29 of the directive calls for the creation of a working group of national data privacy authorities. The Article 29 Working Party is empowered to advise the Commission on emerging data privacy concerns facing the EU, make recommendations regarding the implementation and enforcement of the directive, and evaluate the adequacy of levels of protection in countries outside of the EU. The Commission supports a secretariat for the Working Party in Brussels, which has greatly enhanced transgovernmental cooperation. The Working Party, which is run collectively by the members and is steered by a chair elected from the national privacy authorities, has an annual work plan. Subgroups of officials from the various agencies meet regularly on topics ranging from biometric data to Internet cookies. These efforts are supported by the financial, technical, and linguistic resources of the Commission-sponsored secretariat.

Since its formation in 1997, the Working Party has actively engaged supranational rule enforcement and development in the area of data privacy. It has released more than 100 opinions on a wide range of topics, setting guidelines for national implementation of the directive, calling for or evaluating new European legislation, and determining the adequacy of protection levels in foreign countries.

These opinions have had far-reaching effects for national enforcement within Europe, shaping the implementation of the directive. The Working Party's opinions have been interpreted by courts as part of the directive's legislative intent and have been enforced (UNICE 2002). The Working Party has set diverse standards, from the use of Internet cookies to biometric data. Business practices determined unacceptable by the Working Party face potential punishment by national regulators (who conveniently comprise the Working Party). The Working Party then relies on regulatory authority delegated in the national context to coordinate policy across Europe.

Internationally, the Working Party has played a major role in shaping the external enforcement of the directive. The Working Party has evaluated foreign country efforts, releasing a set of adequacy rulings. Threatened with being excluded from the European market, countries ranging from Albania to Argentina have modeled European rules (Newman 2008b). Those countries deemed inadequate, such as Australia and the United States, have been forced to engage the European Union in international negotiations (Farrell 2003; Heisenberg 2005; Bach and Newman 2007). The Commission relies on the argumentation of the Working Party to constrain its bargaining position with delegates from other countries and improve the resulting international settlement.

In the area of rule development, the Working Party actively advises the European political institutions on new areas affecting privacy. Even though these opinions are not binding, they have played a significant role in European policymaking. In a recent debate over the retention of telecommunications data, the Working Party warned that initial proposals from the Council would violate the European Human Rights Convention (Article 29 Data Protection Working Party 2004). These warnings were then taken up by the European Parliament in its effort to scale back the initial Council proposal. Not only was the argumentation of the Working Party integrated into the debate, but a committee consisting of parliamentarians, industry, data protection, and law enforcement monitors the implementation of the new legislation. The Working Party has taken up a host of other issues in its work plan where rule development is in progress, including on-line authentication, spam, and biometric data in passports.

Data privacy offers the earliest example of incorporated transgovernmentalism in the EU. As one of the first sectors in Europe to experiment with independent regulators (the French data privacy authority, for example, was one of the first independent regulators to be created in France), it has been at the cutting edge of the development of the European regulatory state. This long tradition of delegation in the area combined with the natural transnational character of cross-border data flows made data privacy a logical case to expect transgovernmental cooperation. As the EU moved to enter the sphere of data privacy regulation in the 1990s in order to facilitate the integration of the internal market, it is interesting to note that it relied on the expertise and domestically delegated authority of national regulators to guide implementation and harmonization in the issue area. The Article 29 Working Group has then actively participated in managing the implementation of the directive and promoting harmonization within the member states at the same time that it has shaped the future course of privacy policy at the supranational level.

Energy

Whereas transgovernmental networking between national agencies has a long history in data privacy, it is a nascent phenomenon in the energy (electricity and gas) sector. The emergence of incorporated transgovernmentalism is closely linked to the recent transformation of the industry and the rise of the regulatory state in the utility sector (e.g., Coen and Thatcher 2001; Coen and Héritier 2006).

Until the early 1990s, the European electricity and gas industries were essentially organized as public utilities in a closed national context. Since the supply of electricity and gas depends on network infrastructures involving specific, capital-intensive assets, the entire sector was regarded as a natural monopoly. The industries were mostly held in public ownership, or heavily regulated, with executive ministries, not independent agencies, as key players. Sector governance was deeply entrenched in the broader political economy of individual countries. Cross-border exchanges in electricity were very limited and only technical in nature.

Although European integration originated in the energy sector (the European Coal and Steel Community and the European Atomic Energy Community), earlier attempts to develop a supranational energy policy invariably failed.[8] The dual perception of energy as an essential public service and as a strategic national resource prevailed and blocked market reforms. In addition, the vast differences between national power sectors, in terms of the mix of energy inputs, the degree of import dependence, and of ownership structures, undermined attempts at European-level harmonization.

This picture only changed in the early 1990s when two developments intersected: globally, the liberalization movement seized the realm of infrastructure and utilities; and the energy sector in Europe was successfully incorporated into the single market agenda by an activist and skillful Commission. Technological change and global competition drove reform much less than in the telecommunication sector, where the digital revolution undermined natural monopoly features (Bartle 2005). Moreover, the advocates of liberalization were opposed by a powerful alliance of incumbent utilities and national governments. Hence, the success of liberalization hinged considerably on the skills of the Commission to pull the energy sector into the single market mold and to reframe energy as amenable to the powerful market norm (Jabko 2005). The apparent success of electricity liberalization in Britain (1990), the first major country to implement industry restructuring, served as an important "anchor" and provided a welcome reform template that was "uploaded" to the EU level (Padgett 2003).

The road toward liberalization and EU-level policies, launched in 1988 with the Working Paper on the Internal Energy Market, was protracted and slow. The decisive breakthrough was achieved with the Electricity Directive (96/92/EC) in 1996 (followed by the Gas Directive, 98/30/EC, in 1998). The deadlock in Council negotiations was broken by a Franco-German agreement that accepted the principle of market opening and regulatory reform (e.g., Eising and Jabko 2001).

Given the political resistance to liberalization and European harmonization, the legislation prescribed only incremental and moderate market opening, however, and it left member states a large margin of discretion regarding crucial regulatory issues such as the regime of access, for new market entrants, to the monopoly networks. The directives also failed to establish rules for cross-border trade between individual markets. The result was a European patchwork of national rules, not a level playing field. Yet, the idea of open energy markets gained ground, and many member states went beyond the requirements of the directive and opted for faster and more comprehensive liberalization and regulatory reform. Following the British template, many countries created new regulatory agencies, the future building blocks of regulatory networks. To varying degrees, these agencies acquired some regulatory powers that would otherwise have been held by executive ministries.[9]

The Commission built on this momentum, and on the Lisbon Agenda drive for competitiveness, pressed for further legislation. The 2003 Directives for Electricity (2003/54/EC) and Gas (2003/55/EC) delivered a more robust EU framework. A firm date for full market opening (July 2004 for nonhousehold customers, July 2007 for all customers) was set, and stricter rules for national network access regimes and unbundling (of noncompetitive and competitive industry segments) were put into place. Yet, the common rules still allow for "considerable scope for diversity in implementation among the member states" (Cameron 2005: 8). Politically, it was not an option to require full harmonization or to delegate formal regulatory powers to the Commission, let alone to establish a new EU energy regulator. Instead, the EU framework relies on national regulatory authorities to enforce existing EU-level rules, to develop new ones, and to coordinate national implementation (Eberlein 2005).

Crucially, the 2003 directives made it mandatory for member states to have independent regulatory authorities with a minimum set of functions and competences to regulate national energy markets. This was to ensure that regulatory laggards, such as Germany, would fall into line with the agency model of market regulation and move away from ministerial or self-regulatory patterns. Also, the legislation required regulators to cooperate with each other and the Commission in order to develop a level playing field.[10] These measures laid important foundations for networking between national regulators.

Early on in the process, in the aftermath of the 1996 Electricity Directive, the Commission's strategy was to compensate for the lack of full regulatory powers by establishing alternative governance mechanisms of coordination between member state policies. Transgovernmental networks in the energy sector originated in this context (Eberlein 2008).

The most prominent avenues were the Florence Forum for electricity and the Madrid Forum for gas, set up in 1998 and 1999 respectively.[11] These informal forums, set up by Directorate General (DG) Energy and Transport, meet biannually and bring together national regulators and ministries and important market actors and stakeholders—such as network operators and representatives of the electricity or gas industries—as well as industry consumers and traders. As informal bodies, they develop best-practice rules and procedures for sector regulation, based on professional standards and industry expertise. The practical challenge was to develop a system of cross-border trade, the linchpin of an integrated energy market. The process was slow and at times had to be prodded by casting the shadow of new legislation or competition law. Yet, under Commission leadership and with industry input, the Florence and Madrid processes successfully produced rules for cross-border trade (rules for the use of transmission networks and of scarce interconnection capacities). These voluntary rules were later incorporated into binding EU regulations on cross-border trade as part of the 2003 legislative package.[12]

The forum formula also played a crucial role in building institutions to federate national regulators in EU-level networks. In March 2000, the Council of European Energy Regulators (CEER) was constituted, based on a memorandum of understanding.[13] It brings together the energy regulators from all EU member countries (except Luxembourg) plus Norway and Iceland. The main purpose is to facilitate the creation of an internal energy market by fostering cooperation between national regulators and with EU institutions. Operating out of a small office in Brussels and organized around issue-specific working groups and task forces, its mission is to help develop an EU energy regulatory framework. The Commission encouraged this regulatory institution building by mandating CEER, a body without formal regulatory powers, to develop a system for cross-border trade within the forum context, thus promoting CEER as a single regulatory voice on the EU level. CEER, in concert with the Commission, was the main driver of the forum process.

CEER provided the organizational foundation for the recent incorporation of transgovernmentalism into the energy sector. In November 2003, the Commission created the European Regulators Group for Electricity and Gas (ERGEG), to give informal cooperation between national regulators a more formal status. Formalization and incorporation were to address the drawbacks of the informal and more inclusive forum process, which lacked regulatory teeth and appeared cumbersome, particularly in view of the approaching EU-25 context.

The purpose of this advisory group is "to advise and assist the Commission in consolidating the internal energy market."[14] In particular, the group's objective is to facilitate "consultation, coordination, and cooperation of national regulatory authorities, contributing to a consistent application" of

Community legislation.[15] The ERGEG is run collectively by the members and is steered by a chair. The Commission provides funding for some ERGEG activities, and a high-level member of the Commission attends group meetings. The group is organized in subgroups of national officials from the various agencies that meet regularly on topics such as cross-border tarification and regional electricity markets.

CEER continues to co-exist with the ERGEG, and the two bodies essentially represent two faces of one network: CEER prepares material for ERGEG and continues to facilitate informal cooperation, and ERGEG provides formal advice to the Commission.[16]

In substance, therefore, much of CEER's work on regulatory harmonization in the internal market, initiated under the forum process, continues under a different label. A crucial point is that the incorporation of the network into the supranational regulatory framework, however, allows the Commission to draw more effectively on the domestic regulatory authority of national agencies, whereas the group's formal status helps national regulators to assert their position in the domestic arena. Since the growth of the regulatory state is a very recent phenomenon in both the energy and in other sectors, most agencies, with the exception of those in Britain, are young regulatory bodies—they still need to establish themselves, jockeying for influence with established ministries and competition authorities.

Compared to the well-established agencies and regulatory networks in data privacy, the regulatory state and incorporated transgovernmentalism in the energy sector are at an early stage of development. In a politically difficult context, regulatory reform and transnational networking so far owe more to skillful Commission engineering than to bottom-up self-organization by well-entrenched agencies. In the energy case, agencies are just emerging as "new kids on the block" in a nascent regulatory state, bolstered and enlisted by the Commission in an effort to advance harmonization.

Implications and Conclusions

As the tasks managed by and the members participating in the European Union expand, European leaders face the daunting challenge of maintaining an efficient and legitimate system of governance. Scholars of the European Union have rightly recognized that, in terms of policy modes, a palette of options exists, each with its respective fields of application, and advantages and disadvantages (Wallace 2005). Attention here has focused on the regulatory method, intergovernmentalism, and new governance patterns such as the open method of coordination. Although all of these strategies will no doubt persist in the coming decades, we hope to have spurred a discussion about a new and innovative mode of governance that is emerging as a viable strategy for a range of sectors within Europe. We have labeled this strategy *incorporated transgovernmentalism.* In this concluding section, we argue for the distinctiveness of this new strategy, and we discuss how incorporated transgovernmentalism relates to two critical issues that face any governance mechanism within Europe: legitimacy, and power.

A Distinct Governance Strategy?

In this new governance strategy, transgovernmental networks comprising substate actors are consciously embedded in the supranational policymaking process. Explicitly granted the authority to assist in rule development and enforcement, incorporated transgovernmental actors oversee the harmonization process and guide further integration. They combine supranational coordination within the transgovernmental body with national delegated authority. Their decisions then simultaneously inform EU policy and actual enforcement on the ground.

What is distinctive about incorporated transgovernmentalism compared to other policy modes? This mode is different, on the one hand, from OECD-style "policy coordination" (Wallace 2005) and OMC processes in that it does not exclusively rely on deliberative mechanisms and peer pressure but can bring delegated authority to bear. In this sense, it borrows from the traditional regulatory method but on the basis of domestic, horizontally delegated authority. On the other hand, it is also different from "intensive transgovernmental" cooperation that is often practiced in areas that are not subject to supranational authority. Incorporated transgovernmental networks, by contrast, are exactly that—firmly incorporated in a supranational framework and mode of operation while resting on domestic, governmental authority.

Incorporated transgovernmentalism is on the rise. Since the early 1990s, the EU has been experimenting with this form of governance, and it is currently at work in seven sectors ranging from banking to energy. We believe that such networks—although not an option available in all policy domains—are particularly attractive in sectors where there has been a significant expansion of the regulatory state. This then brings us to the critical questions of legitimacy and power.

A Legitimate Mode of Governance?

Although incorporated transgovernmentalism may help to resolve the efficiency concerns raised by European governance challenges, it has a more complicated relationship to legitimacy. Composed of independent regulatory agencies, these networks derive less legitimacy than those modes sponsored by directly elected officials. In transgovernmental networks, nonelected officials exercise substantial regulatory powers. More often than not, these networks are effective in cases in which they are deliberately isolated from electoral-political pressures. Even though this situation helps to increase "output legitimacy," which rests on expertise and policy efficacy, it poses a serious problem for "input legitimacy" and accountability (Dahl 1994; Scharpf 1999). Furthermore, regulatory networks can be criticized for introducing substantive policy bias. Technical expertise and professionally defined best practices are not neutral. They privilege certain worldviews and interests over others. In the case of the energy regulatory community, for example, the economic training of many regulators has resulted in much greater attention to issues of market making than to environmental protection or security of supply.

By contrast, each agency is appointed by an elected national government and therefore enjoys a marginal amount of procedural legitimacy. In contrast to many EU institutions that have little direct contact with national constituencies, members of incorporated transgovernmentalism have a multitude of relationships with sector participants. They may then leverage these relationships to get input on critical policy areas, embedding a diverse set of interests into the transgovernmental rule-making and rule-enforcing processes. Obviously, access to and influence on regulatory decisions is not equally available to all citizens. This type of "stakeholder participation" may produce some level of input legitimacy, but it clearly does not confer democratic legitimacy. Yet, although limiting participatory inclusion (especially when compared to some new governance strategies such as OMC) to those active in the sector, the incorporated transgovernmental network approach may surpass traditional technocratic governance by better integrating national constituencies.

Network participants are not always endowed with equal voice within such networks (Padgett and Ansell 1993). National decisions limiting domestically delegated authority circumscribe the resources an individual regulator brings to the network, affecting their influence within the network. Regulators with similar national regulatory systems may also form coalitions within the network that exclude the policy preferences of those with idiosyncratic domestic regulatory structures. In short, the distribution of power and influence among the players in the transgovernmental network will shape the ability of such networks to obtain legitimacy within the European policymaking process.

What about the "nonmajoritarian" escape from the dilemma of democratic legitimacy that is advanced by some scholars in the regulatory state debate? This avenue proposes to limit the powers of independent, nonelected regulators to nondistributive, Pareto-optimal decisions that can be assessed and legitimated based exclusively on their technical quality. Political, distributive decisions, by contrast, remain in the realm of majoritarian, representative politics (Majone 1999, 2000). It is difficult to see how technical issues can be unequivocally separated from distributive or political issues. Also, this route would require a high degree of US-style formalization of agency decisionmaking, so that procedural standards of reason and transparency are effectively observed. It seems unlikely that the often informal operation of transgovernmental networks could be successfully subjected to this type of procedural control and transparency. Hence, the conundrum of democratic legitimacy remains unresolved.

Incorporated Transgovernmentalism as a Shift of Institutional Power?

Following our approach, we find that at the supranational level both the Commission and the Parliament must relinquish some power in order for transgovernmental networks to function. By implicitly delegating some rule making and rule enforcing to national regulatory agencies, the European institutions have forfeited direct control over a policy area. Losing some control does not mean that these European institutions are no longer significant actors. Instead, the dynamics of interaction between the institutions has changed: the Commission loses some of its agenda-setting authority and the Parliament some of its oversight power. As a result, the Commission and the Parliament must struggle to monitor the activities of transgovernmental networks in order to protect against mission creep. The Parliament's recent concerns over the authority of the Committee of European Securities Regulators (CESR) in the area of financial services demonstrate the real institutional implications of this strategy. At the same time, the networks can provide the Commission or the Parliament with invaluable technical information, which either body may then use in debates with member state governments. In addition, EU institutions may come to rely on the networks as a means of mobilizing national constituencies, thereby increasing policy buy-in. In short, such networks have a Janus-faced effect on the distribution of power at the supranational level. From a member state perspective, the rise of incorporated transgovernmentalism may have a paradoxical boomerang effect. Member states have in most areas resolutely resisted the formal delegation of regulatory powers to EU agencies in order to retain national control. Now they may find that horizontal delegation to domestic regulators might result in a similar loss of control as national regulators collectively leverage domestic authority to advance supranational harmonization.

In sum, the addition of incorporated transgovernmental networks into European governance may have dramatic implications for the future of European integration, serving both to respond to needed policy challenges and to add a host of new actors to supranational politics.

Notes

1. The OMC is a procedure designed to foster iterative processes of mutual learning by way of joint target setting and peer review as well as benchmarking of

member state experiences under broad and unsanctioned European guidance. There has been a bourgeoning literature on the OMC. The most comprehensive and updated literature overview is provided by the OMC Research Forum at the EU Center of Excellence, University of Wisconsin–Madison (http://eucenter.wisc.edu/OMC/). For discussion of the OMC as a governance instrument, see, for example, Borrás and Jacobsson (2004); de Burca (2003); Radaelli (2003a).

2. Much of this debate takes place within the context of the EU FP6 Integrated Project "New Modes of Governance" (available at www.eu-newgov.org).

3. Although these agencies were universally independent, their exact regulatory powers differed somewhat across Europe. Some had clear powers to investigate and sanction; others were granted an ombudsperson status, focusing on mediating complaints. For a detailed explication of the regulatory structure and delegated authority of these institutions, see Flaherty (1989). These powers, however, have been equalized to a degree through the passage of the European directive in 1995.

4. For a description of the first conference, see "European Data Production Chiefs to Meet in Bonn," *Transnational Data Report,* 1 March 1979, 1.

5. The International Working Group on Data Protection in Telecommunications (IWGDP) was established in 1983 under the auspices of the International Conference of Data Protection Commissioners. It meets biannually and comprises data protection organizations; it invites participation from industry and independent specialists. The group's work is available at http://www.datenschutz-berlin.de/doc/int/iwgdpt/index.htm.

6. For the position of the transgovernmental network see "Data Protection Essential to EC 1992" (1990).

7. For the political history of the directive see Newman (2008b). See also Council of the European Union and the Parliament (1995).

8. Energy policy has thus been considered as "one of the weakest policy areas of the EU" (Matlary 1997: 13). The key reason is that member states have been keen to keep tight control over a sector they consider of strategic economic importance (Padgett 1992).

9. The directive had only required member states to "create appropriate and efficient mechanisms for regulation, control and transparency so as to avoid any abuse of a dominant position" (Article 22).

10. Article 23, Directive 2003/54/EC (electricity), and Article 25, Directive 2003/55/EC (gas).

11. The official terms are European Electricity Regulation Forum and European Gas Regulatory Form. Florence and Madrid are the two cities where the two forums began to meet. For details on the forum processes, see Eberlein (2005).

12. Regulation (EC) No. 1228/2003 of 26 June 2003 on conditions for access to the network for cross-border exchanges in electricity; Regulation (EC) No. 1775/2005 on access conditions to the gas transmission networks.

13. In 2003 CEER adopted the status of a not-for-profit association under Belgian law. For details, see www.ceer-eu.org.

14. "Commission Decision of 11 November 2003 on Establishing the European Regulators Group for Electricity and Gas" (2003/7 96/EC), Art. 1, par. 2 (OJ L 296/35.

15. Ibid.

16. See ERGEG Work Programme 2006, 3n1, available at http://www.ergeg.org. In essence, the establishment of the ERGEG formalizes the informal regulatory role played by CEER in the forum process. To be sure, the CEER remains a distinct body with a slightly broader membership base (not restricted to EU member states).

And it does play a larger role, for example, in international networking and in providing training courses for regulators through the Florence School of Regulation. Yet, it is quite clear that in terms of activities and leadership in the EU context, there is broad overlap between the ERGEG and the CEER. It is significant that ERGEG is housed at the CEER Secretariat in Brussels.

16

Transgovernmentalism in the Area of Freedom, Security, and Justice

Sandra Lavenex

There is probably no other policy area in the European Union (EU) in which the tension between European integration and national prerogatives—between supranationalism and intergovernmentalism—is as pronounced and pervasive as in the Area of Freedom, Security, and Justice (AFSJ). The label AFSJ was created with the Amsterdam Treaty to suggest coherence in a range of very diverse areas of justice and home affairs cooperation that evolved in an incremental, decentralized manner. These areas (asylum, migration, border controls, judicial cooperation in civil matters, police cooperation and judicial cooperation in criminal matters), although diverse in substance and institutionally spread over distinct pillars of the European Union, all share a particular resistance toward supranational or hierarchical modes of governance. Their emergence on the European agenda was justified with the need to develop compensatory measures for the safeguarding of internal security after the realization of the single market and was dominated by intergovernmental forms of cooperation. Over time, however, the patterns of governance in the AFSJ have become more diversified, reflecting variation in domestic interests and the degree to which the member states were willing to concede competences to the European level.

Whereas some policy areas, such as visa policy or asylum determination procedures, are gradually moving toward more supranational structures, others see a mix of minimalist harmonization with an emphasis on mutual recognition (e.g., criminal law), and still other areas are only addressed through open coordination (migrant integration) or predominantly operational horizontal cooperation among member states' authorities (police cooperation). Nevertheless, even if some areas are moving more toward the Community method of integration than others, there is not a single official "common policy" in any of the areas so far, and the tension between supranational and national competence is omnipresent. What the different AFSJ domains namely have in common is that they touch upon core aspects of state sovereignty. Control over the territory and providing security and justice to citizens are not only central prerogatives of the modern nation state but also essential elements of its reason of being and legitimacy (Mitsilegas, Monar, and Rees 2003; Jachtenfuchs et al. 2006; Wagner 2007). Therefore, it would amount to a major transformation of statehood for the member states and of the political system of the EU if we were to observe important sovereignty transfers in these areas. As a consequence, a peculiar mix of governance modes has developed that may best be described as intensive transgovernmentalism (Wallace 2005).

This chapter aims at elaborating the specificities of European governance in the areas of policymaking covered by the AFSJ and thereby at contributing to our understanding of how the "incomplete European polity" governs in core areas of statehood. In order to highlight path-dependencies in these modes of governance, the chapter starts with a short historical overview of the emergence of European cooperation in these areas. After introducing the main actors at both the supranational and national level, the main section identifies seven characteristics of current governance structures through intensive transgovernmentalism. The conclusion recapitulates the reasons for the specific constellation of actors and governance modes in the AFSJ and asks whether these are likely to be a transitory phenomenon in the evolution toward supranational governance or whether they are likely to persist.

Origins of Intensive Transgovernmentalism

The first steps toward cooperation in asylum, immigration, criminal, and penal matters were made in the framework of the Council of Europe and, for police cooperation, in Interpol, the international police organization. In the 1970s the lead was taken over by new transgovernmental groups composed of representatives from national home ministries, partly with the participation of non-EU countries (Bigo 1996: 79ff). In contrast to intergovernmental forms of cooperation, these networks were composed of governmental actors below the level of heads of state and government, such as members of national administrations, police forces, and other law enforcement agencies.

The most influential forum became the so-called Trevi Group founded in 1975 by the Rome European Council. This network of home affairs officials to a considerable degree shaped the development of what became later the third pillar, including the Europol Convention. Starting with the problem of terrorism, Trevi's mandate was subsequently widened to include the issues of international (organized) crime, drugs, external borders, fraud, immigration, and asylum. This evolution corresponded with the conjuncture of internal security preoccupations in influential member states and was marked by the proliferation of informal consultation forums among them. In this context the reinvigoration of the single market project in the Single European Act (SEA) provided an opportunity for linking domestic internal security concerns with the broader project of European integration and in particular the free movement of persons (Lavenex 2001). The coupling of existing transgovernmental cooperation in Justice and Home Affairs (JHA) with the questions of freedom of movement and European integration became most explicit in the Schengen group, founded originally by five member states in 1985 (the Benelux countries, France, and Germany), which framed its cooperation as "compensatory" for the realization of free movement of persons.[1] This logic was taken over by the Maastricht Treaty, which formalized the existing structures of transgovernmental cooperation in its third pillar.

More important steps bringing JHA to the center of EU "governance" were made with the Amsterdam Treaty. The Schengen Agreement was included in the EU framework. Parts of what used to be the third pillar were transferred into the Community pillar (asylum, immigration, external borders, and judicial cooperation in civil law matters; Title IV of the Treaty Establishing the European Community [TEC]). At the same time, this transfer broke with the Community orthodoxy, since intergovernmental decisionmaking procedures were maintained for a transitory period of five (de facto: seven) years. It was not until the completion of the Amsterdam work program with the adoption of the last outstanding directive, the refugee procedures directive in December 2005, that the normal decisionmaking procedures were introduced: exclusive instead of shared right of initiative for the Commission, decisionmaking by qualified majority voting in the Council, and the right of codecision for the European Parliament (EP). Yet, important exceptions prevail for legal immigration, which is still subject to unanimimous voting, and on the powers of the European Court of Justice (ECJ). What was left of the new third pillar was renamed "police and judicial cooperation in criminal matters" (PJCCM; Title VI of the Treaty on European Union [TEU]). Issues with important overlap with Community competence, such as financial fraud and customs cooperation, were given a legal basis in the "mainstream" EC Treaty. Although implying a diversification between policy areas that would eventually come under full Community competence and those maintained under intergovernmental procedures, the Amsterdam Treaty gave these issues a certain symbolic unity as constituents of an Area of Freedom, Security, and Justice.

The opposition to the introduction of European decisionmaking procedures that would allow for hierarchical modes of governance, in the terminology of this book, did not prevent JHA cooperation from becoming "booming business" (den Boer 1999: 319), prompting some commentators to compare the dynamism of the AFSJ with that of the single market program (Monar 2001). Although home ministry officials—the "policemen of sovereignty," in the words of a former member of the European Parliament (van Outrive

1995: 395)—were the least internationalized parts of national bureaucracies, by the end of the 1990s an extensive set of transgovernmental networks had developed. Acting both outside and under the overall structure of the European Union, these operate on several political and executive levels, ranging from the responsible ministers through directors-general of the relevant ministries to middle-ranking civil servants and representatives of police forces and other agencies.

Ministries of justice were drawn in more slowly. It was not until the revival of the concept of a European Judicial Area, after the Treaty of Amsterdam, that a similar European network began to emerge. With the decision of the Tampere European Council of 1999 to introduce the principle of mutual recognition as a cornerstone of judicial cooperation in both civil and criminal matters within the EU, direct communication between judicial authorities has become one of the most dynamic aspects of JHA cooperation.

Characteristics of Intensive Transgovernmentalism

The term *intensive transgovernmentalism* was first introduced by Helen Wallace to describe a new form of network governance in the EU that rests "mainly on interaction between the relevant national policy-makers, and with relatively little involvement by the EU institutions" (Wallace 2000: 33). In contrast to the use of the term *intergovernmentalism,* the term *transgovernmental* refers to the activities of governmental actors below the level of heads of state and government, such as ministerial officials, law enforcement agencies, and other bureaucratic actors. These officials act with a certain degree of autonomy from chief executives and develop their own policy agenda (Keohane and Nye 1974; Slaughter 2004a). In the context of the EU, transgovernmental cooperation may occur both outside the treaty framework and within, and the impetus for cooperation comes from the transgovernmental networks rather than from supranational or governmental actors. A second difference from the intergovernmentalist approach to European integration is that transgovernmentalism does not limit the notion of integration to interest-driven bargaining between state representatives. In contrast to the classical modes of governance in the EU, hierarchy and negotiation (see Chapter 2), intensive transgovernmentalism stresses the role of horizontal network governance that interacts in different ways with more hierarchical governance modes in the EU.

Apart from the particular role played by lower executives, the special characteristics of intensive transgovernmentalism in JHA are the following: the relative weakness of supranational actors compared to governmental ones; the relative weakness of legislative instruments in the balance between legislative versus operational cooperation; the preference for mutual recognition rather than a harmonization relationship between vertical (supranational) versus horizontal (transgovernmental) integration; the role of flexible arrangements of cooperation and the experimentation with open modes of coordination; the prevalence of operational cooperation; the pervasiveness of differential modes of participation; and the blurring distinction between internal and external cooperation in these fields. The next sections discuss these points in detail.

The Relative Weakness of Supranational Actors

Traditionally, the process of European integration has been based on a supranational setting for the liberalization of the common market and the development of common rules approximating the legislation of the member states. The central actors in this legislative arena are (according to the Community method of integration) the Commission, with the exclusive right of initiative; the Council of Ministers, deciding by qualified majority voting; the European Parliament, with the right of codecision; and the ECJ, with jurisdictional powers. In JHA cooperation, the legislative level is characterized by a strengthened role of the Council of Ministers vis-à-vis the supranational actors and an emphasis on operational cooperation that is only loosely coupled with legislative approximation. As a result of this constellation, the output of legislation in JHA tends to be rather "soft," with a lower degree of legalization than in other areas of European integration (see below).

The stronger role of governmental versus supranational elements at the legislative level is backed by a particular division of resources between the participating actors and the pervasiveness of intergovernmental decisionmaking procedures. Both aspects privilege the position of the Council of Ministers toward the Commission. In the Commission, a Directorate General (DG) on JHA, later renamed into Justice, Freedom, and Security (JFS), has only existed since October 1999. By then, it was widely recognized that its predecessor, the task force on JHA, which counted only forty-six full-time employees in 1998, had been desperately overworked and understaffed and therefore had been very restricted in its abilities to influence third pillar developments. With the creation of the new DG under the lead of Portuguese Commissioner António Vitorino, the number of personnel was significantly increased, to 283 in 2002 and 443 in 2005. Its budget also saw a steep increase, from 42 million euros in 1999 to 124 million euros in 2002 and 600 million in 2005, with roughly 60 percent being spent for the strengthening of the external borders (see European Union Financial Reports, 1999–2005).[2] Nevertheless, compared to older DGs dealing tangentially with related issues, such as social affairs, DG JFS remains one of the smaller units in the Commission, both in terms of staff and its budget.

With its limited resources, the Commission has always been challenged vis-à-vis its counterparts in the Council Secretariat. The responsible unit of the Council, DG H (Justice and Home Affairs), was more generously staffed than the Commission Task Force on JHA during the 1990s, with additional staff recruited in 1998–1999. The Treaty of Amsterdam furthermore provided for the separate Schengen Secretariat, which had been co-located with the Benelux Secretariat in Brussels, to be integrated into DG H. Permanent representations of the member states in Brussels were also drawn in, adding legal advisers and officials seconded from interior ministries to their staff.

In addition to budget and staff, the specific structure of the JHA Council gives particular weight to national JHA officials. Between the Permanent Representatives Committee (Coreper)[3] and the working groups, the JHA structure has an additional intermediary level composed of special coordinating committees that bring together in Brussels senior officials from national ministries, usually meeting once a month (the Article 36 Committee; the Strategic Committee on Immigration, Frontiers, and Asylum [SCIFA]; and the Committee on Civil Law Matters). Although these committees of senior national officials were set up for a transitional period, they have not been phased out. Rather, in summer 2002 a new "external borders practitioners' common unit," the "SCIFA+," was created. It regroups the members of the SCIFA with the heads of national border control authorities.

From a procedural point of view, these committees of senior officials share a certain rivalry with their colleagues in Coreper, who monitor the cycle of working group meetings week by week and prepare agendas for the JHA Council. This allows them to act as a gateway between the collective gathering of senior officials and ministerial council sessions at which all the strands of policy are supposed to be brought together. The coordinating committees have often been slower to clear dossiers because of their less frequent meetings and their close ties to their national ministries, which limits their room for maneuver in negotiations. The seconding of staff from interior and justice ministries to the permanent representations in Brussels has mitigated this rivalry and further strengthened the role of JHA officials.

In practice, two additional intergovernmental levels of policymaking are relevant and have even been gaining importance. The first is composed of various "horizontal" or "high-level" groups linking together relevant negotiations within the different working groups in asylum and migration matters, drugs, or organized crime. The second level is the European Council, which has played an increasingly influential political role in JHA. The ground was laid with the first European Council focused specifically on JHA held under the Finnish Presidency in Tampere in 1999, which set out far-reaching objectives.

Compared to the Commission and the Council, the role of the European Parliament has remained limited. Even in those issues falling under the first pillar, the EP was not granted any powers to amend or block legislation by the Council—until the end of the transition period in December 2005. Prior to the introduction of the codecision procedure, the EP had merely consultative powers, which it still has in third pillar matters. Yet in practice, even this minimum level of involvement has often been violated by the Council. Either the EP's often excessive amendment proposals were not taken into consideration, or the EP was not properly consulted, prompting several infringement procedures before the ECJ.[4] For matters under the third pillar, the Nice Treaty introduced a deadline of at least three months for the consultation of the EP in order to allow it a real opportunity to examine and, where necessary, to propose amendments to proposed measures.

The Weakness of Legislative Output

Apart from the distribution of resources and decisionmaking procedures, the opposition toward supranationalism is also salient in the kind of output produced in JHA legislation. The effects of intensive transgovernmentalism on the adoption of supranational policies that might result in "positive integration" (Scharpf 1999) are twofold. First, by privileging governmental actors' respective interests over a comprehensive vision of a policy area, not all relevant aspects of a policy become subject to approximation, but only those where actors' interests converge. Second, if a legal text is finally adopted, it will usually reflect the lowest common denominator and reserve to the member states a large degree of discretion in implementation. The lack of consistency in approximation is well reflected in the area of criminal law, in which most of the approximation has concerned substantive criminal law and, in particular, the definitions of offenses. By contrast, the areas of criminal sanctions and of criminal procedure, which are at the core of national sovereignty, have been largely neglected (Weyembergh 2005: 1585). Furthermore, the types of crime covered by this substantive approximation tend to reflect political conjunctures rather than objective criteria in terms of severity or cross-border nature of crimes.[5] The second characteristic of positive integration measures in JHA is the weakness of obligations implied. Definitions are often formulated in a vague manner, so as to rule out substantial adjustment of domestic legislation; the legal texts contain many exemption clauses; and the member states retain a high margin of discretion in the interpretation and application. This can be retraced in both third (Weyembergh 2005) and first pillar legislation (Lavenex 2006a).

It seems that the Commission noticed this lack of political will when it conceded—in its report on the implementation of the Hague program on JHA cooperation of June 2006—that results in legal approximation both in asylum and criminal law matters had remained behind expectations. A good example of the limits of positive integration in first pillar issues is the directive on minimum standards in asylum procedures adopted after multiple delays in December 2005. Fraught with exemption clauses and vague formulations and providing for minimum standards below those usual in national legislation, the directive has been criticized by the European Parliament for constituting a threat to human rights and refugee law principles and for containing too many exceptions.[6] In the case of third pillar legislation, the Commission Report of 2006 notes that "major delays . . . sadly arose with the adoption of two flagship measures: political agreement on the Framework Decision on the evidence warrant was reached only in June 2006, and the one relating to certain procedural rights is still under discussion. Neither of them was adopted in 2005 as planned in the Hague programme" (COM[2006] 333 final §51). The Commission proposal for a framework decision on procedural rights applying in proceedings in criminal matters throughout the EU constitutes an attempt at legal approximation in procedural law. Defensive in its wording, the Commission proposal has been criticized by the European Parliament and the United Kingdom (UK) House of Lords for being too vague and noncommittal (European Parliament 2005; House of Lords 2005: §42). Indeed, its support among the member states can be questioned. Whereas some argue that the European Convention on Human Rights provides enough protection, others are concerned that such a measure would impose constraints on their domestic criminal justice systems and would thus infringe on the subsidiarity principle (Morgan 2004). Citing the lack of progress in Council negotiations, a number of observers have voiced the concern that without a shift to qualified majority voting, it would become nearly impossible to agree on common provisions. An attempt by the European Commission and the Finnish Presidency to realize this shift through the application of the so-called *passerelle* (gateway) provision of Article 42 TEU, which allows for majority voting, was however rejected by the informal JHA Council in September 2006.

Pending the introduction of supranational procedures, which is foreseen in the Constitutional Treaty, it seems that rather than hierarchical modes of governance focusing on supranational legislative integration, a majority of member states prefers more horizontal, less legally binding, and more sovereignty-friendly avenues of integration: mutual recognition and operational cooperation.

The Appeal of Mutual Recognition

Rather than focusing on common policies and the harmonization of national laws or, in the words of Fritz Scharpf, "positive integration" (see, e.g., Scharpf 1999: 32f) governance in the AFSJ has privileged forms of "negative integration." The cornerstone of negative integration is the principle of mutual recognition. This principle was officially introduced in JHA with the Tampere European Council of 1999 for judicial cooperation in both civil and criminal matters. Before, it had been realized in the system of state responsibility for the examination of asylum claims, the 1990 Dublin Convention, and later turned into a European Community (EC) regulation. In a nutshell, the implementation of this principle removes a major obstacle to cross-border law enforcement because different national standards with regard to refugee law or criminal codes no longer obstruct judicial cooperation and extraditions between member states. At a first glance, the motives for adopting the principle in market integration and the AFSJ are similar: it allows for coordination despite the impossibility of agreeing on the harmonization of rules and a fully supranational integration.

The apparent safeguarding of national sovereignty under the principle of mutual recognition, in contrast to supranational harmonization, was a major motive in the eyes of its promoters in the run-up to the Tampere summit, in particular the UK government. The idea that mutual recognition would allow for cooperation despite the many obstacles to harmonization and thus would represent a more realistic and easily achievable alternative to the latter permeates the earliest to the latest documents dealing with the issue. Although not completely denying the interplay between the two modes of coordination, the Commission noted in a 2000 communication that "not always, but often, the concept of mutual recognition goes hand in hand with a certain degree of standardization of the way states do things. Such standardization indeed often makes it easier to accept results reached in another state. On the other hand, mutual recognition *can to some degree make standardization unnecessary*" (Commission of the European Communities 2000: 4, emphasis added). In a similar vein, the relevant article of the (stalled) Constitutional Treaty reads: "The Union shall endeavor to ensure a high level of security through . . . the mutual recognition of judgments in criminal matters and, *if necessary,* through the approximation of criminal laws" (Article III-257[3], emphasis added). On the surface, the adoption of mutual recognition appears easier than harmonization or the adoption of minimum standards, since it does not imply the creation of supranational rules and thus appears less compromising for state sovereignty. Yet, as Kalypso Nicolaïdis suggests, mutual recognition "is meant to respect sovereignty on the one hand," by forgoing the option of total harmonization and centralization, "while radically reconfiguring such sovereignty on the other," by delinking the exercise of authoritative power "from the territorial anchor of sovereignty" (Nicolaïdis 2005: 3). From this perspective, the exercise of mutual recognition constitutes "a reciprocal allocation of jurisdictional authority to prescribe and to enforce" (Nicolaïdis 2005: 4), or a horizontal transfer of sovereignty (see also Schmidt 2005: 190; Chapter 9). The implications of mutual recognition for states' prerogatives in the process of European integration are very salient in the first measure to officially introduce this principle in JHA cooperation, the European Arrest Warrant. Under the European Arrest Warrant, the member state issuing the warrant delegates the act of arresting a suspect to another. The latter, by arresting the suspect, puts its monopoly of force into the service of the former (Jachtenfuchs et al. 2006: 24). The underlying assumption is that the requesting state's judicial decisions are both legal and legitimate in the light of shared standards of human rights and procedural safeguards.

The framing of mutual recognition as the "easier" and less demanding way to achieve coordination not only underestimates the importance of legal harmonization and approximation for the realization of mutual recognition in the single market as complementary mechanisms of integration (Majone 1994a: 83; Nicolaïdis 1993; Schmidt 2005: 192) but also fails to see that for a number of institutional reasons outlined above, these complementary mechanisms are more difficult to achieve in JHA than in economic cooperation (see also Lavenex 2007; Chapter 9).

The Experimentation with Open Modes of Coordination

Faced with the member states' reluctance toward supranational legislation, the Commission has started to experiment with the introduction of softer forms of cooperation inspired by the open method of coordination (OMC) first developed in the areas of social policy and employment (see, e.g., De la Porte and Pochet 2002). This is especially the case in the area of legal immigration, which comprises both economic immigration (for which the member states have repeatedly opposed the introduction of supranational decisionmaking procedures) and immigrant integration (see Caviedes 2004).

The proposal for an OMC on legal migration was issued in the same year as a Commission proposal for a directive on the conditions of admission and stay of third country workers. Both proposals failed: the proposed admission directive was rejected in first reading in the Council, and the proposal on the introduction of OMC was not even decided upon. As a consequence, the Commission took two steps back. In 2005, it relaunched the debate on the need for common rules for the admission of economic migrants with a Green Paper on an EU approach to managing economic migration (COM [2004] 811), which led to the adoption of a non–legally binding "Policy Plan on Legal Migration" in December 2005. A somewhat weaker simulation of the OMC was then retained for the less controversial area of immigrant integration. A network of National Contact Points on Integration has been set up and meets regularly to exchange and discuss best practices. The first output of this network was its participation in the preparation of the Commission's *Handbook on Integration,* published in November 2004, and the Commission's annual reports on migration and integration, which provide an overview of national migration policies. So far, these activities have not yielded additional legislative action. Rather, the Commission seems to be further following the promotion of "soft law," as through the communication "A Common Agenda for Integration— Framework for the Integration of Third-Country Nationals in the European Union," adopted in September 2005 (COM [2005] 389). Rather than proposing common measures, this communication encourages member states to strengthen their efforts with a view to developing comprehensive national integration strategies while new ways of ensuring consistency between actions taken at the EU and national level are proposed.

The Importance of Operational Cooperation

Operational cooperation formed the basis of JHA integration from the 1970s onward and continues to play an important role along with the legislative integration process. The clear distinction between operational and legislative integration in the draft Constitutional Treaty suggests that the former is seen as an alternative to legal approximation.

Operational networks of law enforcement officials are created for exchanging information, conducting joint investigations to enforce the law, and setting standards of cooperation in the form of memorandums of understanding. Originally developed "bottom-up" between the relevant authorities of the member states (horizontal networks), such operational networks have been complemented by more vertical structures created on the European level to spur their operations (on vertical networks, see den Boer 2005).

The proliferation of such vertically structured networks in the form of semiautonomous special agencies and bodies is a special characteristic of governance in the AFSJ. The multiplication of actors over the past few years has been impressive and illustrates the dynamism of this area of cooperation. Some of the earliest were agencies established on the basis of first pillar secondary legislation: the European Monitoring Centre on Drugs and Drug Addiction (EMCDDA) set up in 1993 in Lisbon and the European Monitoring Centre on Racism and Xenophobia (EUMC) established in 1997 in Vienna. Most developments, however, took place in the framework of the third pillar. Here the earliest was the Task Force for the Coordination of Fraud Prevention, the predecessor of the European Anti-Fraud Office (OLAF), the now communitarized European Anti-Fraud Office. The Europol Convention had been adopted in 1995, but it was not until 1998 that it entered into force, after lengthy national ratification procedures, and Europol became operational only one year later. In 1998, the European Judicial Network was launched, an initiative pushed forward by the Belgian Presidency, supporting the proposal of Élisabeth Guigou, then the French minister of justice, for the creation of a European Judicial Area. Following the model of the European Judicial Network in Criminal Matters, a network on civil and commercial matters was set up in 2001.

The European Council in Tampere in 1999 proposed the creation of three new bodies: the European Police College (CEPOL), the European Police Chiefs' Task Force (PCOTF), and Eurojust. The Tampere conclusions provided for the creation of CEPOL, established in Denmark in 2000, to develop cooperation between the national training institutes for senior police officers in the member states. PCOTF, created the same year, was set up to develop personal and informal links among the heads of the various law-enforcement agencies across the EU and to promote information exchange. Eurojust, which became operational in 2002, was the "college" of senior magistrates, prosecutors, and judges, set up to coordinate cross-border prosecutions. The immediate reaction of the urgent European Council on Terrorism meeting after the terrorist attacks in Madrid in March 2004 was to create an additional post: the EU Anti-Terrorism Coordinator. Acting under the EU High Representative for Foreign and Security Policy, the coordinator was intended to promote effective counter-terror coordination and intelligence sharing. The most recent JHA agency is the Border Management Agency Frontex in Warsaw, which took over the work of the Common Unit of external border practitioners created in June 2002. The Commission envisages this agency as the core of a future European Border Guard. With these new common bodies, the number of common databases has also proliferated; the data of EU and third country nationals are stored and scrutinized, partly under Commission supervision (Eurodac), but mostly monitored by a special joint supervisory authority within the Council Secretariat (the Europol and Eurojust databases and the Customs Information System [CIS]). The most recent developments are the establishment of a Visa Information System (VIS), a database with personal information (including biometrics) on every visa application, and a revamped Schengen Information System (SIS) or "SIS II" that, in the words of the European Commission, will transform the SIS "from a reporting system to a reporting and investigation system" (European Commission 2001d: 7).

This proliferation of actors indicates the strong impetus for more intensive cooperation in internal security, but it also reflects the tension between, on the one hand, the case for tighter collective policy management by the EU institutions and, on the other hand, the persistence of looser transgovernmental coordination. It also shows the interplay between practitioners' preference for flexibility and the pressures for greater transparency and accountability. For instance, most of these agencies created since the end of the 1990s lack a clear legal base in the treaties. PCOTF remains an ad hoc forum with no legal base, no formal rules of procedure, and no mechanism for scrutiny. Now that they are institutionalized, both Europol and Eurojust have seen a rapid expansion of their mandates. Europol was originally set up to put pressure on the national agencies responsible for combating terrorism, and its objectives were to improve the effectiveness of, and cooperation among, the competent authorities in the member states. Its mandate was expanded—even before the agency became operational in 1998—to include "crimes committed or likely to be committed in the course of terrorist activities" (European Council 2002). After 11 September 2001, the Council added a long list of serious international crimes requiring collective action, such as murder, kidnapping, hostage taking, racism, corruption, unlawful drug trafficking, smuggling illegal immigrants, trafficking in human beings, motor vehicle crime, and so forth. In 2002, Europol's budget was increased by almost 50 percent in order to address these additional tasks.

Originally conceived of exclusively as coordinating bodies, both Europol and Eurojust have also gradually gained operational powers. Representatives of both agencies are allowed to participate in a "supporting capacity" in joint investigation teams. Furthermore, Europol and Eurojust have been granted the right to request EU member states to start or to abstain from an investigation or prosecution in specific cases, a request that can only be turned down by giving good reasons.

Overall, therefore, JHA is based on a complex pattern of governance. This proliferation of agencies and bodies not only poses an increasing challenge of coordination but also bears deficits regarding transparency or democratic and judicial accountability. Thus, for example, based as it is on an intergovernmental convention, Europol's activities are subject neither to the supervision of the EP nor to judicial control by the ECJ. Under the present system, the Council acts not only as initiator and legislator but also as executive and supervisor (in the form of the Article 36 Committee), thereby defying the principle of separation of powers.

The Pervasiveness of Differentiation

The sixth characteristic of intensive transgovernmentalism is its high degree of flexibility, allowing for differentiated forms of participation both within and outside the treaties. The cautious transfer of selected issue areas toward supranational decisionmaking structures in the first pillar through the Amsterdam Treaty prompted three member states to seek à la carte solutions. Denmark, for example, participates in the free movement area and may adopt relevant European provisions as international law (avoiding the direct effect of EC law and ECJ jurisdiction). Ireland and the UK maintain their opt-out from lifting internal frontier controls but, on a selective basis, adhere to the flanking measures of the JHA acquis such as PJCCM and the SIS (Kuijper 2000: 354). Another element of flexibility accompanies the "rolling ratification" of conventions in the third pillar, according to which conventions shall, once adopted by at least half of the member states, enter into force for those member states. Another à la carte solution was found for the ECJ's role under the third pillar: it is up to the member governments to decide on the viability of preliminary ruling procedures. At present, the UK, Ireland, and Denmark do not allow for preliminary rulings by the ECJ, and Spain permits only final courts to refer cases. Procedures to permit enhanced cooperation further add to the fragmented institutional framework of JHA cooperation.

Yet, even in the light of these generous provisions, the formalization of flexibility has not prevented individual member states from engaging in selective forms of intergovernmental cooperation outside the provisions of the treaties. This was demonstrated in May 2003 with the creation of the so-called G-5, an intergovernmental group bringing together the five interior ministers from France, Italy, Spain, Germany, and the UK. In 2006, Poland joined the group, now called G-6. Seeking to speed up the move toward operational goals and to circumvent the lengthy decisionmaking processes of the Council of Ministers, the group is working to conclude a series of bilateral agreements that should then form the basis of future EU-wide laws and measures. Among the issues on the table are cooperation to combat terrorism, illegal immigration, establishing a list of "safe" countries of origin whose citizens would not be entitled to make refugee applications, establishing financial criteria for issuing visas for entry to the EU, making it compulsory for airlines to communicate passenger data to the law enforcement agencies, and EU biometric passports. The first important output of this cooperation is the Prüm Treaty signed on 27 May 2005 between seven member states to step up cross-border cooperation, particularly in combating terrorism, cross-border crime, and illegal migration.[7] Named after the German city in which it was signed, the treaty (sometimes also called "Schengen III") enables the signatories to speed up the exchange of information. The official objective of the Prüm Treaty is to "further development of European cooperation, to play a pioneering role in establishing the highest possible standard of cooperation especially by means of exchange of information, particularly in combating terrorism, cross-border crime and illegal migration, while leaving participation in such cooperation open to all other Member States of the European Union."[8] As pointed out by Balzacq et al. (2006), however, the revitalization of the traditional form of intergovernmental cooperation outside the treaties weakens the prospects for supranational integration in two ways. First, it allows a small number of member states to create new standards of cooperation on a multilateral basis, which put other states under adaptation pressure without giving them the possibility of shaping the contents of these standards. Second, by reverting to an intergovernmental arena, the Commission and European Parliament are ignored precisely at a time when they are achieving an increasingly central role in lawmaking in this area. Finally, the ECJ is also excluded from jurisdiction—as long as the Prüm Treaty is not integrated into EC/EU law.

The External Dimension of JHA Cooperation

The different quality of governance in the AFSJ compared to more "hierarchical" or supranational modes of governance is also reflected in its greater permeability toward the involvement of third countries. This openness is a salient manifestation of the more transgovernmental or "international" rather than supranational, and by definition territorially bound, mode of integration.

The association of nonmember states exacerbates the variable geometry of the "area of freedom, security, and justice." Norway and Iceland, as members of the preexisting Nordic common travel area, have been included within the Schengen area and are fully associated with the Schengen and Dublin conventions. The situation for Switzerland is different. Entirely surrounded by Schengen members, but (unlike Iceland and Norway) not a member of the wider European Economic Area, Switzerland has negotiated a corresponding bilateral agreement. Under their respective agreements, these three non-EU European countries share an unusual degree of legal and institutional association. The Schengen/Dublin association agreements with Norway and Switzerland imply their full harmonization with the relevant EU acquis, including the newly developing elements. This dynamic legal association is accompanied by a far-reaching opening of organizational structures that exceeds the degree of participation offered in other sectors. Norway and Switzerland have an explicit right to decision shaping in the elaboration of the new acquis through participation not only in comitology but also through participation in the formal legislative procedure in the JHA Council and its working groups. In this so-called Comité-Mixed procedure, which deals with all Schengen/Dublin-relevant legislation, associated countries enjoy the full right of speech but no voting rights (Wichmann 2006). In addition, they are full members in all relevant information systems such as the SIS, Eurodac, and VIS.

On the other side of the Atlantic, the United States has been actively pursuing access to shared data and networks of cooperation since the early 1990s. The terrorist attacks of September 2001 led to a redoubling of its efforts, leading to a series of agreements on transatlantic association in this area, some of them very controversial. An example of such a controversial agreement is the Europol-US agreement that was signed in December 2002, despite concerns expressed by national parliaments in EU countries regarding safeguards for the exchange of personal data. Before it was signed, in June 2003, the text of the proposed EU-US Judicial Cooperation Agreement was submitted for national scrutiny only on a confidential basis, until a strong protest from the British House of Lords led the Greek Presidency to declassify it (Mitsilegas 2003). The secrecy under which negotiations with the United States have been conducted, and concerns over lack of reciprocity in exchange of information and over the protection of personal data, have made transatlantic cooperation in this sphere a source of unease for civil liberties groups and parliamentarians.

Finally, the diminishing distinction between internal and external security has prompted the development of an external JHA dimension that increasingly involves the EU's new neighbors to the east and the south in the governance of the AFSJ (Lavenex and Uçarer 2002, 2004; Lavenex 2004, 2006b). JHA has gained a prominent place in relations not only with the Balkan countries and Turkey but also with Russia, Ukraine, Moldova, and the Maghreb countries. In short, this variable geometry reflects not only the transnational nature of the preoccupations that underlie the development of JHA but also the continual need to reinforce transgovernmental mechanisms both within and beyond the circle of the member states.

Conclusion

Notwithstanding the differences between the various policy areas covered by the AFSJ and between the institutional modes of interaction formalized in the different pillars of the EU, this chapter has highlighted a number of characteristics that substantiate a particular mode of governance in the AFSJ, namely intensive transgovernmentalism. These characteristics include a particular division of resources that favors the role of the Council of Ministers and its working groups in the legislative process; limitations on the full realization of the Community method of decisionmaking; the weakness of legislative outputs in terms of substantive scope and legal stringency; the focus on less compromising forms of integration such as mutual recognition and, although very hesitantly, open coordination; the importance of operational coordination; and the prevalence of differentiated forms of participation both inside the Union and toward third countries. In a nutshell, this mode of governance privileges integration through the promotion of personal, communicative, and operational linkages between member states' administrations and law enforcement authorities while keeping the role of common hierarchical, supranational rules to a minimum. Whereas this pattern of governance reflects the preferences of the majority of member states in these sensitive areas of domestic politics, it has also become institutionalized in the structures of cooperation in JHA. Examples of this institutionalization are the Commission's own decision to promote soft modes of coordination rather than binding legislation as well as the proliferation of semiautonomous agencies to assist such coordination both in the realization of mutual recognition and the enforcement of operational cooperation. Furthermore, differentiation has become a pervasive element of JHA cooperation, and there have been few attempts to reduce the degree of discretion resulting from the various opt-outs and opt-ins within the treaties or the recently reinvigorated intergovernmental cooperation outside the treaties. With the EU's rapid enlargement to twenty-seven plus member states, these looser structures of cooperation are likely to prevail.

There are also limits, however, to what can be achieved through transgovernmental networks, mutual recognition, and operational cooperation. In order to be efficient, these horizontal forms of integration require not only the active support of responsible state agencies in providing the information requested, for example, for the functioning of a database or the mutual recognition of asylum decisions or arrest warrants issued by another state. They also require a certain degree of approximation of substantive norms—be it on data protection standards, asylum determination criteria, or the definition of criminal offenses[9]—as well as mutual trust in each other's systems of laws and professional practices. Apart from their functional efficiency, these modes of governance also raise important questions with regard to their legitimacy. It is now well documented in the literature that the seclusiveness of transgovernmental networks dominated by home ministries and internal security agencies has favored a securitarian approach with serious drawbacks for civil liberties and liberal values. This substantive challenge to legitimacy is exacerbated by the procedural deficits with regard to the transparency and the parliamentarian and judicial scrutiny of intensive transgovernmentalism. Therefore, these horizontal forms of coordination are likely to coexist with a pressure for more vertical integration—not in major legislative steps, but incrementally, through the daily interaction between EU institutions and agencies, transgovernmental networks, and national bodies involved.

Notes

1. After the signature of the second Schengen Agreement in 1990, which lays down the compensatory measures for abolishing internal border controls, all member states with the exception of Ireland and the UK joined the Schengen group.

2. The Financial Reports are available at http://europa.eu/generalreport/en/welcome.htm.

3. As stipulated in Article 207 of the Treaty Establishing the European Community, Coreper is responsible for preparing the work of the Council of the European Union. It consists of the member states' ambassadors to the European Union (i.e., the Permanent Representatives) and is chaired by the member state that holds the Council Presidency.

4. In issues falling under the first pillar, this was the case for the asylum procedures directive of 2005 and the directive on the right to family reunification of 2003.

5. Examples are the Joint Action of 24 February 1997 concerning action to combat trafficking in human beings and sexual exploitation of children, adopted in the aftermath of the Belgian *Dutroux* case; the Framework Decision and Directive of 28 November 2002 concerning the facilitation of unauthorized entry, transit, and residence, adopted after the death of fifty-eight illegal immigrants in a container lorry at Dover; or the Framework Decision of 13 June 2002 on combating terrorism in the aftermath of 11 September 2001. See Weyembergh (2005: 1585ff).

6. See the European Council on Refugees and Exiles (ECRE), *ECRAN Weekly Update* of 17 March 2005, available at http://www.ecre.org/Update/Index.shtml. Similar criticisms have also been raised with regard to the minimum standards directives adopted in the area of legal migration.

7. The signatory states to the Prüm Treaty are Belgium, Germany, Spain, France, Luxembourg, the Netherlands, and Austria.

8. Preamble to the Treaty of Prüm, p. 3.

9. On the functional pressure for harmonization deriving from such horizontal forms of cooperation in the area of asylum and immigration, see Lavenex (2006a).

17

Weak Process, Strong Results: Cooperation in European Higher Education

Barbara G. Haskel

Within less than a decade, one major state's proposal to three European counterparts to create " a common architecture" for their individual higher education systems became a highly elaborated cooperation and coordination process, resembling the open method of coordination (OMC), and extended to forty-six countries. In this process not only did the objectives expand but instruments for and measurements of achievement were agreed by the participants. Although begun as strictly intergovernmental and outside the European Union, within three years the European Commission had been recognized as a full participant (not an observer) of what became known as the Bologna Process.

The professed aim of the effort was a European Higher Education Area (EHEA) in which students and researchers could have their work recognized and therefore have access to the whole of Europe's higher education. Four original countries (France which took the initiative, Germany, Italy, and the United Kingdom) wished to obtain legitimacy and allies for internal reforms of their individual university systems, systems they deemed ineffective and costly as well as highly resistant to change. Recent comparative European reports assess that there has been substantial implementation, even if uneven, both within and between countries.

The major question of the chapter is how such a weak governance process could lead astonishingly fast to hard policy changes within states. In the language of this book, what modes of governance were used? Two subsidiary issues are what accounts for the speed with which this initiative spread and how it was sustained and institutionalized. How did the European Commission become an integral, if not leading, part of the process? Does this case tell us anything about the conditions under which such governance is likely to be created and sustained?

My argument is that the Bologna Process, a voluntary endeavor and therefore characterized by a predominantly cooperative mode of governance, began as a strictly intergovernmental process but that this quickly proved ineffective, creating an implicit "demand" for leadership. The Commission, which especially in the education area had had long experience with the constraints of the Treaty on European Union (TEU), worked together with the association representing European universities in crafting a catalytic and coordinative role—the policy and leadership "supply"—even though this process was not initiated or formally driven by the EU. Especially because of the "softness" of the governance process, a "driver" was necessary. Put another way, once the team comprising the Commission and the universities' association became an institutionalized player, the whole seemingly intergovernmental process became institutionalized. I account for the rapidity with which the number of member states increased by what I call "the coordination imperative."

The Surprisingly Rapid Spread of the European Higher Education Area

French minister of higher education Claude Allegre, in 1998, using the occasion of the eight hundredth anniversary of the founding of the Sorbonne, invited his counterparts in Germany, Italy, and, as an afterthought, the United Kingdom to agree to a "Joint Declaration on the Harmonization of the Architecture of the European Higher Education System." The story has been recounted by several authors (Corbett 2005; Ravinet 2005; De Wit 2003; Naeve 2003; Keeling 2006). In 1999, at Bologna, the ministers of twenty-nine countries signed the Bologna declaration, calling for the creation of a European Higher Education Area by 2010. The countries were the fifteen members of the EU, the then eleven accession states—Cyprus joined a little later—and the three members of the European Economic Area. The group established a process of biannual ministerial meetings, with rotating venue, chair, and secretariat. Preparation for these meetings included information circulation, meetings, and workshops to compare information about their higher education systems. Six operational objectives or "action lines" were specified: (1) adoption of a system of easily readable and comparable degrees; (2) adoption of a system essentially based on two cycles; (3) establishment of a system of credits; (4) promotion of academic mobility; (5) promotion of European cooperation in quality assurance; (6) promotion of a European dimension in higher education.

In the ensuing eight years the policy areas increased to ten, by adding (7) lifelong learning; (8) involvement of higher education institutions and students as "active partners"; (9) enhancement of the "attractiveness" of EHEA;

and (10) doctoral studies as a third cycle and synergy between EHEA and the European Research Area (ERA). The Bologna strategy was melded with the larger EU Lisbon strategy, and the number of participant states increased radically, to forty-six.

Institutionally, nonstate and expert actors were made observers, the key one being the European Universities' Association (EUA). Others were its vocational education counterpart (the European Association of Institutions in Higher Education, EURASHE) and the National Unions of Students in Europe (ESIB) as well as international organizations long active in gathering information and offering policy prescriptions on education, the Council of Europe and the Organization for Economic Cooperation and Development (OECD). A crucial part of the process, the Bologna Follow-Up Group (BFUG), which was the between-ministerial-meetings group and its steering committee, was institutionalized in 2001. At the same time the European Commission was formally included as a member (not just as an observer) both in ministerial meetings *and* in BFUG. By 2003 the European Network for Quality Assurance (ENQA) was a participant as well as one of the European-level social partners, the European Employers Federation (UNICE). UNICE and Education International (EI), a worldwide organization of academic trade unions (from preschool to university), were brought in as "consultative members" of BFUG. This elaborate consultative and policy-promoting process revolves around biannual meetings of education ministers.[1]

The reform that has been emblematic for Bologna is the 3-year first degree plus the 2-year second degree, later complemented with a notionally 3- to 4-year doctoral degree (three "cycles"). This reform allows for ease in attending other universities, even one in another country, to pursue second or third degrees. It replaces the continental template of a 5-year first degree from which there were many dropouts and under which those who completed it tended to do so in 7 to 8 years.

Recent studies taking stock of the program concluded that the change had been adopted by "almost all signatory countries" in "almost all fields" (except medicine) and that there were fewer "structural barriers between cycles."[2] A credit system, the so-called European Credit Transfer System (ECTS), is in use in most countries and used both for credit transfer and credit accumulation. Over half the countries will provide a diploma supplement (DS) for all institutions and study programs. The DS serves some of the purposes of a North American transcript, which had had no European equivalent. The change in the structure of degrees, ECTS, and the DS comprise the original "mobility Bologna." More demanding, but meant to fulfill the same overarching purpose, is the call for a National Qualifications Framework, "certified against the overarching Framework for Qualifications of the EHEA," to which ten countries have committed themselves. Related is the Lisbon Recognition Convention (ratified by thirty-six of the forty-five Bologna countries by 2005) that shifts the burden of proof in any denial of recognition of qualifications to the institution denying them.

Reform within a university program included the introduction of "research training," that is, organized courses taught by faculty, as opposed to just writing a thesis for the doctorate. Virtually all signatory countries either recommended or required this reform.

Even if one qualifies the findings of the recent reports,[3] and even if we understand that there are (and are bound to be) disparities in implementation and performance among institutions within states, still, by any measure, the movement since 1999 has been remarkable.

An Explanation of the Pace:
The Coordination Imperative

One can only be impressed by the success of the coordination aspect (Hardin 1995; Schelling 1971; Krasner 1991) of the early Bologna Process. I would argue that the fact that the four largest member states agreed to "something" worked as a critical mass. The agreement of the four largest states gave strong incentives for others to join. Why? The only potential cost was being left out when many and important others were in; the sanctions would be having one's students' education not recognized in what was to be a process importantly aimed at recognition by each other and by outsiders, recognition not only of individual students but of one's universities, one's attractiveness as an educational and scientific center. Being out would stymie one's students' and faculty members' mobility *in the new context,* one in which, unlike the past, others would be mobile. Thus one significant incentive to join the dominant group is not to be left out and left behind. The prospect of competition under the new conditions created incentives to cooperate.

The two-cycle, 3 plus 2 pattern provided a focal point for the states (Garrett and Weingast 1991). At the time different models were being thought about by the ministers in France and Germany. Now the discussion was crystallized around 3-year bachelor's and 2-year master's degrees.[4] The focal point idea helps us understand the looseness with which the 3 plus 2 idea has been interpreted: the first cycle is 3–4 years; the second cycle is 1–2 years, but the two cycles together should not be more than 5 years. This permits the British 3-year first degree or 4-year (first) honors degree plus a 1-year master's (Becker 2004). In this whole process, without overt sanctions and with a desire to allow for national educational traditions, leeway is important and the question is the tolerability of the leeway for the objective of mutual recognition, within a roughly similar pattern.

The context of enlargement also makes the coordination argument plausible. Accession countries were eager to join "European" and "Western" networks. Academically they wanted and needed recognition for their educational systems in the aftermath of ideological inheritances and needed technical assistance to catch up. Some countries had great ancient universities with long and illustrious traditions, and they wanted recognition for that.

Of course coordination is only one dimension of this process. Countries could hardly be indifferent to the characteristics of the system with which they were to "coordinate" and for which they would be obliged to make technically and politically expensive changes. This does not, however, vitiate the point that there was in addition a coordination aspect—and in this case, it seems to have outweighed reservations about substance astonishingly quickly. An "education specialist-diplomat-entrepreneur," when asked how the smaller countries were brought along in the year between Sorbonne (four countries in 1998) and Bologna (twenty-nine countries in 1999), said that the argument was "It's going to happen."[5] That, I would maintain, is exactly the argument likely to elicit the "if so, we had better be in" response— what I call the perceived "coordination imperative."

The Incentives for States and Universities to Cooperate

For states, the consequences of the status quo had become very visible in an era of increased student mobility and worldwide scientific and economic competition. In many European countries (Germany and Italy were the models), mass education had been superimposed on university structures, which had changed little from the time of very small elite cohorts. This was not only straining resources but was both cost inefficient and cost ineffective. Graduates were not clearly employable. In general, universities were extremely underfunded. The number of students going from Europe to North America and from Asia to North America far outnumbered those coming to Europe for higher education. When a Shanghai ranking of universities put European universities far down, Europeans were shocked.

The exception was the United Kingdom, which attracted international students, for both academic and language reasons, and charged substantial foreign fees; higher education was one of the UK's "export industries." Others aspired to attract foreign students for scientific, industrial, economic, and cultural reasons.

A related issue, the role of knowledge in the economy, focused attention upon research generation as a weapon in the "economic competitiveness" battle. Comparative information showed that national levels of funding for research in the United States, and then Canada and Japan, were far higher than those in most of Europe. In the United States, a much greater proportion of the funding came from private, mostly industry, sources and also from tuition. Connected with this, and with underfunded universities, was clearly the issue of attracting the best researchers and advanced students.

The European Union's Lisbon agenda (2000), for example, had emphasized the role of knowledge in its diagnosis of the lagging economies of

Europe. It found the economic problems to be "structural," exacerbated but not caused by the radically intensified global trade and investment competition. The new requirements were economic restructuring and increased "flexibility." The universal nostrums were education and training, investing in human capital, upgrading skills, and lifelong learning for "employability." Science was seen as part and parcel of innovation, and close ties between research and industry were to be promoted. Knowledge creation had become part of economic potential. In this context Huisman and van der Wendt's observation (2004) that "the presumed lack of national governments' acceptance of international or supranational interference in higher education is not as deep as expected" is less surprising than it might be.

What were the incentives for universities to participate in the process? The Bologna Process was, in important ways, a "bottom-up" process, although it seems impossible that anything like this could have taken off without the "top-down" agreement of the states. In what sense, if any, did it emerge from the universities?

First of all and symbolically, a decade earlier than the Sorbonne declaration had come the Magna Charta Universitatum of 1988, a statement by the rectors of European universities. It stressed first the autonomy of the universities and the inseparability of research and teaching. It called for encouragement of mobility of teachers and students and policies of equivalence for diplomas. These important desiderata were picked up and operationalized a decade later at Bologna (1999). In 2001, in a more significant move, these rectors and universities formed the EUA from two prior organizations. EUA claimed to represent more than 750 universities. High up on its agenda was influencing the Bologna Process "through collective action" and including the universities in the policy discussions on the ERA (EUA 2005). In fact, EUA has met and produced declarations before each ministerial meeting since Bologna; it participates in the BFUG and in the drafting of the ministerial communiqués; it publishes "responses" to Commission statements.

The Commission has contracted with EUA to produce, prior to each ministerial meeting, the major biannual comparative descriptive report (published under the series title *Trends*). The Commission and others make use of these reports in policy documents. One of the EUA's principal specialists, Guy Haug, who was involved in the Bologna meetings from the outset, has at other times been on contract to the Commission.[6] Together with the striking policy consonance of the two organizations, this suggests a rather blurred line between the Commission and the universities' organization and between the Commission and expert groups, the establishment of several of which it helps sustain.

Many of the key elements of Bologna—such as several levels of university education with "bridges" between them, some form of credit transfer system, independent assessment, and accountability based upon learning outcomes—have become part of the accepted aims of specialists in education at every level. Pedagogues, the educational "epistemic community" (Haas 1992), provided much of the mutually accepted information as well as similar *diagnoses* and generally similar *prescriptions*.[7]

The educational objectives of those international organizations that have long produced cross-national research on education—OECD, the United Nations Educational, Scientific, and Cultural Organization (UNESCO), and the Council of Europe—are largely the same. They have been part of the creators of the epistemic understanding and part of the prehistory of Bologna; they have been reinforcing regimes, contributing data, ideas, and framing. They have participated in Bologna as observers from the start.[8]

Michel Crochet, rector of the University of Louvain, argues that academics, especially the rectors, were the motor of change (Crochet 2004). Claude Allegre, the French education minister, was a scientist, Crochet an engineer; scientists and engineers were particularly attuned to worldwide standards of excellence, to the consequences of low funding, to ties to the economy, to issues of the job market. Luigi Berlinguer, the Italian minister of higher education in 1998, was a jurist, not a scientist (in the North American sense of the word), but had been the president of the rectors' conference in Italy. To adduce quite different evidence, in 2005, when a vice rector at Université Libre de Bruxelles was asked about the reception of Bologna changes in the university, he volunteered that it was "good for the managers."[9] I would argue that what we see here is an entrepreneurial alliance between EUA, which represents universities' administrations, and the Commission. This alliance created drive, what is usually called leadership, as well as developed the policy and information that aided largely willing states' administrations. These state ministries then, in de facto alliance with some rector teams, instituted changes in the universities. It has been commented perceptively that what has resulted is a form of differentiated integration, but this time not a core-periphery model.[10] Several of the EU founding states (Germany, Italy, France) "went to Europe" to get allies or legitimation for change; they were not the sources of models for diffusion to others. They were the source of demand for reform and the Commission-EUA alliance the source of policy supply. Other countries responded largely to the "coordination imperative."

Crochet's view that academics were seminal might apply to the rectors whose organization was one of the two components of the new EUA, but university academics as such were not part of the Bologna Process. Although by the turn of the twenty-first century both universities and student organizations were organized on the European level, there was no such European organization of professors. To understand how the Bologna Process elaborated new objectives, instruments, and measures so rapidly it helps to know that the category of actors who might be expected to have opinions or reservations about changes—changes to external judgments of "quality," to conditions of funding, and in university governance—was missing.[11]

How Did the Commission Acquire a
Role in the Bologna Process?

If the initiative for the Sorbonne/Bologna Process was in both form and authority strictly intergovernmental, how did the Commission acquire a substantial role in the process? There are three elements to the answer: (1) the clumsiness of a strictly intergovernmental process (generating implicit *demand*); (2) the Commission's honed techniques of influence, developed under the constraints of a treaty in which it had a very small and delimited role in the area of education (*supply*); and (3) a new political context.

Clumsy Intergovernmentalism?

By the first ministerial meeting after Bologna, the Commission was made a regular participant. Why? Anne Corbett, who wrote a history of the Commission's activities in higher education, thought that by Prague (2001) the process needed policy development and "they brought in the Commission and EUA."[12] The point is that the intergovernmental process by itself was probably "clumsy," that is, ineffective or inefficient or both, giving incentives to the member states or the Presidency to look to the Commission. This is supposition. But it does imply that the states were generally speaking "in cahoots" with the entrepreneurial team.

Continuity of Techniques Developed
Within Delimited Treaty Scope

The Treaty of Rome leaves the central area of education to the member states. How then did the Commission become so deeply involved in it? The Commission did have some treaty authority. "Vocational education and training" had been put within the Commission's authorized scope by virtue of its connection to the single market. The Commission had had some help as well from the European Court of Justice, which in 1985 had defined "vocational education" so broadly that almost *all university education* would be considered "vocational" (Corbett 2005: 123–125). The Commission was also given some treaty authority over research (TEU Article 189). In hindsight, we can see that the sentence in the Maastricht Treaty stipulating that the Commission should "encourage" quality in higher education was neither an exclusive nor shared jurisdiction, but it could be used as authority to be a chivier; it is permission to herd cats. The Commission used the "encourage quality" formulation to claim treaty-based authority in the education area.[13]

Corbett (2005) traces the Commission's efforts over nearly forty years to find a strategy in the educational sector. A key point in 1976 was an institutional innovation, when an Education Committee was established in which the European Commission participated *as a member* in what otherwise looked like a comitology group, that is, a gathering of national civil servants under the European Council (Corbett 2005: chap. 7; European Commission 2006: 88–89). Today we see parallels in several such arrangements in areas of the open method of coordination.

The kinds of techniques that the Commission developed, given the treaty constraints, are relatively well known, and I shall just briefly note them here. First, a crucial technique is direct and indirect capacity creation. Directorate General (DG) Education and Culture and its Schools and Higher Education Unit have used funding to create and support organizations (for example, Eurydice, the information network on education in Europe [Brussels], or the *European Journal of Education* [Paris]). Over time these created the information, statistics and comparative analysis, academic knowledge, and policy discussion on which both the member states and the Commission then drew.

Some of the institutions that the Commission created exemplify what Susanne Schmidt (in Chapter 9) calls "support structures," needed because "mutual recognition" (which, *grosso modo,* is what Bologna aims at) shifts transaction costs from decisionmaking to the implementation stage.[14] Thus the important information and credential evaluations centers such as the European Network of Information Centres (ENIC) in the European region or National Academic Recognition Information Centres (NARIC) and the European Network for Quality Assurance (ENQA) agencies, for example, are intended to establish the "trust" among universities that will allow them to recognize, credit, and accept students and scholars from other institutions, especially from other Bologna countries.

Indirectly, the Commission contracts out, as in the case of the important *Trends* series, mentioned earlier. For example, *European Universities Implementing Bologna: Trends IV Report,* published by EUA, provided implementation information for BFUG and descriptive analysis for more general availability, especially to make comparisons to peers (Reichert and Tauch 2005).

Second, the Commission has also sought out interlocutors—"stakeholder" groups, such as the ESIB, the organization representing national unions of students in Europe, or, as we have seen, the EUA itself. It looks sometimes as if the Commission has had a hand in, if not taken the initiative for, creating such groups. For example, in 2000 (the year of the adoption of the Lisbon agenda) three European student organizations—ESIB, Association des États Généraux des Étudiants de l'Europe (AEGEE), and the Erasmus student network—were constituted as what was called a European liaison group; this group then participated in the consultative meeting organized by the European Commission on Socrates and higher education, together with representatives of universities and other higher education institutions. Later ESIB alone won recognition as the representative of students (Klemencic 2007). In a second example, after the Lisbonization of Bologna, the Commission also called in noneducational but interested stakeholders such as the highly influential European Round Table of Industrialists (which brings together some of the largest and most successful transnational firms), with whom other parts of the Commission had worked on other issues.

Third, the Commission may use its formal position within the EU legislative process to formulate and propose recommendations to the Council and Parliament. If the Commission's recommendation becomes that of the European Parliament and Council, then the substance of the recommendation can be brought to the next Bologna ministerial meeting with considerable expectation of passing; if passed there it will represent agreement by the forty-six.

Perhaps most important, the role of the Commission in framing educational issues is now well documented. It may reconceive the use of standard EU resources, for example, proposing that the states reorient the EU structural funds toward improving states' support for research and human capital (thus framing education and research issues as an ingredient in economic growth).[15] Related to this, the Commission often seeks to give technical issues a public face. For example, it proposed an ECTS label for the diplomas of universities that have instituted ECTS throughout all their programs, or a diploma supplement label for universities that provide a DS with all diplomas, automatically, without cost, and in a major European language.

How does the Commission itself see its role? Guy Haug argues that in 1999 most ministers and universities were aware of internal issues but not, for example, of the growth of transnational education, of the challenges of privatization, of the "decreasing attractiveness" of European higher education to the rest of the world.[16] To increase this awareness was what he and the Commission-EUA collaboration had set out to do. Consciousness-raising is therefore a Commission role. In a 2006 communication, "Delivering on the Modernisation Agenda for Universities: Education, Research, and Innovation," the Commission, after diagnosing the challenges to European universities and the changes required, included a page headed "and what the Commission can and should do": "The Commission is not a direct actor in the modernisation of universities, but it can play a catalytic role, providing political impetus and targeted funding in support of reform and modernisation" (European Commission, COM 2006, 208 final, 1). This quote provides a good summary of the examples above. It gives no idea, however, of the ingenuity and persistent entrepreneurship with which they are used.[17]

New Political Conditions

The change in the political conditions was not directly connected to education per se. It was a product of the EU's Lisbon agenda, which was decided upon in 2000. In this connection the European Council "invited" the ministers of education to cooperate. "Now the Commission has the EU institutions behind it," related Guy Haug.[18] The Bologna Process was intellectually assimilated to the Lisbon agenda, thus putting it squarely in an area where the Commission had authority (vis-à-vis EU members) (Keeling 2006) and connecting it to the main preoccupation of the member states, the amelioration of the condition of their economies. Seen from the vantage point of the Lisbon agenda, research and innovation, and the education that contributes to them, are viewed as a deployable resource.

Ruth Keeling (2006) elaborates astutely on the "European Commission's expanding role in higher education discourse," showing how it made Bologna and Lisbon a hybrid Bologna/Lisbon agenda that creates higher education as a European policy domain. But the framing changed in another way. From a focus on individual students (focus on the micro level, student mobility, student preparation for the labor market), the issues have been reframed to emphasize society. Education is now being dealt with primarily as in the service of society.

The change was made clear not only by the Commission's being brought into the Bologna Process in 2001 but also by its work program of 2002, "Education and Training 2010," which was adopted by the ministers of education. It was indicated as well by the efflorescence of Commission policy papers. The title of one document tells it all: "Mobilising the Brainpower of Europe" (European Commission 2005c). A hard-hitting critique, it calls for "enabling universities to make their full contribution to the Lisbon Strategy" and recommends a "core modernisation agenda": "attractiveness, governance, and funding," now revealing its view that universities must be differentiated and must have "diversified" (i.e., not solely public) sources of funding. The Lisbon agenda itself has not been the catalytic force that was envisioned by its creators. But the Lisbonization of Bologna raised the priority of higher education policy by centering on its role in the economy; in this way it confronted the "why are they horning in on a strictly national area?" argument, legitimating the involvement of the Commission.

How was it possible that the Commission, a weak player at the outset, could generate strong results? One can discern three phases in the Bologna Process, and in each phase the Commission took on a different role. In Phase 1, from Sorbonne (1998) to Bologna (1999), neither the EU nor the Commission is mentioned in either declaration. The Commission-EUA network works for the broad acceptance of the declaration of the four countries. It picks up the ball. During Phase 2, from Bologna to Prague (2001), the Commission moves from being marginalized at Bologna to being invited to be a full participant by Prague (or at its Tampere preparatory meeting), although given no special role. In Phase 3, from Prague (via Berlin, 2003) and Bergen (2005) through London (2007), the system of a rotating secretariat and chair came under attack. A BFUG report before the Berlin meeting argued for a change in the "steering structures," in which the country hosting the meeting provides the secretariat and the chair. There had been an extensive internal debate within BFUG on proposals for a permanent secretariat or permanent chair,[19] but this was not approved by the ministers in Berlin. Had the intention been for the Commission to be the secretariat? Or had the Council of Europe, which was encouraging the extension to and beyond Eastern European members, been in mind? Whichever it was, the question was raised again two years later at Bergen[20] (at which the number of countries increased to forty-five) and once again it was not accepted by the ministers, that is, by the states. From the present standpoint, the Bologna intergovernmental system, now supplemented informally by Commission-aided information and policy capabilities, seems quite stable, even with a rotating secretariat. If one thinks of phases not in terms of organizational characteristics but of political mandate, then the Commission is now empowered in its mandate to encourage quality, by the Education and Training 2010 Program authorized by the Bologna education ministers, and by the convergence of Bologna with the Lisbon agenda.

Clearly, compared to the Monnet method, the Commission has no exclusive right of initiative in this policy area. Since before the Bologna declaration, however, the alliance of the Commission and the EUA has been evident in the diagnoses made, areas and proposals selected, and the kind of operationalization and review procedures, that is, persistent initiatives. Clearly also the Commission lacks sanctions. Guy Haug, when asked whether he then considered the Bologna method "a weak method," responded "It *is* a weak method" but it is operating "in the context of great awareness."[21] What has changed is *not* the subsidiarity constraint but the political mandate for what some analysts call the Commission's "leading role"[22] and what I would call the leadership role of the Commission-EUA alliance. In other words, over time the Commission's role has been strengthened.

Conclusion

This chapter has discussed the coordinative-diplomatic process of governance by cooperation that has led to such a surprising spread not only of goals but also of courses of action and instruments in the area of higher education. The Bologna Process has been predominantly based on a strategy that implies that "a rising tide lifts all boats." It has had a dual-track (diplomatic/epistemic) sponsor of initiatives, a driver that has been able to use its "hub" position not just to coordinate but to lead. That driver has created concepts and uniform operationalizations, assembling, classifying, and analyzing the comparative information it requires of the states. It has used joint "commitment" and jointly agreed upon instruments,[23] together with "support structures" that supply "templates" for reform.

An implicit governance mode has been competition, focused overtly, until now, upon universities from other regions of the globe. Benchmarking, however, is implicitly competitive, and now the Commission is working toward a "European ranking" to answer the Shanghai ranking.[24]

Where have these soft law processes met obstacles? It is difficult sometimes to distinguish cases of problem solving (changes agreed upon after unsatisfactory experience) from cases of bargaining (proposed reforms meeting national obstacles). Hard bargaining probably accounts for the loosening of the 3 plus 2 model or, more recently, for the alteration of the original proposal for a single European register of quality assurance agencies, able to be selected by any university from any country, into a text permitting national authorities to accord recognition only to those QAAs they will permit their universities to use.[25] This last form of compromise (really potentially an opt-out) is a familiar form of EU joint decision. Problem solving and bargaining are undoubtedly both present.

What kind of issues might be amenable to such a soft process? Peter Leslie, pondering the open method of coordination to which Bologna bears a strong resemblance, suggested that such a process helps "to identify and advance common interests on those issues in which all have the same interests and no one can be advantaged by cheating."[26] Restructuring national higher education systems would seem to be such a case. When, then, can weak processes create strong results? This case study of the Bologna Process suggests that it is (1) when there is at a minimum a permissive consensus among the states (at a maximum, of course, a joint mandate); (2) when there are several interested parties who, for quite different reasons, want changes but might not, by themselves, be able to create the strategy around which an alliance can be built (i.e., a collective action problem);[27] and (3) when there is a body in a "hub" position that, by itself or in alliance, has incentives to provide the strategy and act as the "driver" to "herd the cats."

Notes

The author is grateful for the opportunities and support extended by the following: Deutscher Akademischer Austausch Dienst (German Academic Exchange Service) Study Trip on Europe's Higher Education and Research (2004); La Chaire internationale d'enseignement et de la recherche, Université Libre de Bruxelles (2005); a librarian at Sciences Po, Paris, who went out of her way for a researcher beginning in a new area; the European Education Policy Network; and, among others, the following individuals in Paris and Brussels who took time from busy schedules: Chantal

Barry, Youri Devuyst, Guy Haug, Christine Musselin, and Noël Vercruysses. Martin Spiewak of *Die Zeit* was kind enough to read a draft.

1. "Communiqué of the Conference of European Ministers Responsible for Higher Education," Bergen, 19–20 May 2005, 1 (known as the Bergen Communiqué). See also the most recent official Bologna website, http://www.dfes.gov.uk/bologna/, which has a link to historical material put together on the Bergen website and lists BFUG meetings and BFUG-sponsored "seminars" structured to end in recommendations to the next ministerial meeting.

2. Based on Eurydice (2005: 5). See also Reichert and Tauch (2005).

3. The comparative reports on implementation are significant but difficult to interpret. A report by Eurydice, a European information network on education, warned that it was reporting data "on the intentions of policy-makers" (Eurydice [European Unit] 2005: 5). Eurydice's 2007 *Focus* used general quantitative terms such as "most." For academic analyses of what had been accomplished at the halfway point (to 2010) see "The Bologna Process: A Mid-term Review," *European Journal of Education* (special issue) 39:3 (September 2004) and "Le processus de Bologne a mi-parcours," *Politiques d'Education et de Formation* 12:3 (2004).

4. Ravinet (2005: 29–30n57) argues that "coagulation" around the "3+2" idea at the Sorbonne meeting, given its stability in later years, is like the famous QWERTY keyboard. See also David (1985). I would add that the QWERTY analogy warns that an early decision may or may not be best (most efficient). Bologna, for example, has run into problems with having graduates of three-year degrees accepted in many US institutions.

5. Guy Haug, interview, Brussels, 29 November 2005.

6. In 2005 the Commission itself had only a few people in its unit on schools and higher education within Directorate General (DG) Education and Culture, and only one other, as far as I could find out, who followed the Bologna Process.

7. Although one should note that this community's diagnoses and prescriptions were aimed at, and justified as, what is effective and efficient for the individual student.

8. UNESCO and the Council of Europe sponsored the 1997 Lisbon recognition convention that, much as mutual recognition had done for the single market within the EU, reversed the burden of proof in the recognition of academic credentials.

9. Interview, Brussels, 28 November 2005. I take "managers" to mean "administrators." See also Musselin (2004) for a description of 1998 changes in "steering" in French universities. The Dutch university model has appointed deans, and an attempt was made by key Flemish rectors at Leuven and Ghent in Belgium to institute this model. (Interview, Noël Vercruysse, Ministry of Education, Flemish Community, 29 November 2005.)

10. Remarks by Katharina Holzinger at the conference on "Governance and Policy-Making in the European Union," University of Osnabrück, 2–4 November 2006.

11. The only organization representing faculty members as observers was Education International, which is an organization of trade unions of teachers from preschool to university, and from 160 countries, not limited to Europe, although they have a European division. It was they who commissioned the sole work I found on the reactions of faculty members, a survey called "The Role of Academics in the Bologna Process." Note that Huisman and van der Wendt (2004: 354) argue that the level of support for change by both academics and students is key to the variation in implementation. They also expect greater turmoil as quality assurance issues, brain drain, minority language protection, and GATS come to the fore. My main point is

about both efficacy and legitimacy. Unintended testament to this lack of input from university faculty comes from a student of the EU, Ian Bache, who studied a different educational issue, the EU-funded network in European studies (Bache 2006). What is important for our purposes is that he raises the analogous question of whether there are significant and appropriate channels through which academics, worried about disciplinary, or more broadly, intellectual consequences of an EU-sponsored process, can be heard at the European level.

12. Anne Corbett, interview, London, 6 November 2005.

13. Haug, interview. The treaty source is Chapter 3, Article 126 (Keeling 2006).

14. Susanne K. Schmidt at the conference on "Governance and Policy-Making in the European Union," University of Osnabrück, 2–4 November 2006.

15. Haug, interview.

16. Guy Haug, keynote speech, "Visions of a European Future: Bologna and Beyond," presented at the Eleventh European Association for International Education (EAIE) Conference, Maastricht, 2 December 1999, 2.

17. For the origin of the concept of "political entrepreneurship" see Frohlich, Oppenheimer, and Young (1971). Corbett emphasizes the "policy entrepreneurship" of key Commission individuals in the history of EU efforts in higher education. Derek Beach (2004, 2005) argues generally that EU *institutions* can be thought of as "informal entrepreneurs" and that they face a strategic choice of either "agenda setting" or "brokering." His major point germane to our case is that "governments are not fully in control even in the most intergovernmental fora" (in his case, intergovernmental conferences [IGCs]) (2005: 245).

18. Haug, interview.

19. Zgaga (2003: 52–54). This so-called Zgaga report, after its rapporteur, was commissioned by BFUG to be presented at the Berlin ministerial meeting in 2003.

20. Haug, interview. One thinks of the "third pillar question": Would the intergovernmental system put in place persist? Or—as happened in the area of EU asylum policy, where member states took such care in the Maastricht Treaty to isolate the whole domain of Justice and Home Affairs from the Commission and from "normal" EU policymaking—would the states find in the longer run that they were too hampered by the ineffectiveness of the system? Hix (2005: 370) notes that during the time of the isolated third pillar, the Commission strengthened its ability to develop policy ideas, wrote "think pieces, funded independent research and established internal organization," what Hix calls a "long term strategy." The techniques sound familiar.

21. Haug, interview.

22. Huisman and van der Wendt (2004: 352).

23. On the power of "instruments," see Bruno, Jacquot, and Madin (2006).

24. The ministers at both the Berlin and Bergen meetings commissioned a "stocktaking" report and appointed a Working Group to report to the next ministerial meeting. The word "stocktaking" is an unthreatening word. But the chair of the Stocktaking Working Group, Andrejs Rauhvargers, commented that the "purpose of stocktaking was analysis of where we stand, *not* races between countries" (his emphasis). This alludes to the fact that the "drivers" of Bologna are being suspected of transforming the purpose of the data collection to a competitive one. But compare European Commission (2005b: 5, 19) and the Commission's support and funding for devising an "alternative" European ranking.

25. "Applications for inclusion on the Register should be evaluated on the basis of substantial compliance with the ESG [adopted at the 2005 ministerial meeting] evidence through an independent review process *endorsed by national authorities, where this endorsement is required by those authorities,*" London Communiqué, 18

May 2007, point 2.14, my emphasis. See also "Recommendation of the European Parliament and of the Council of 15 February 2006 on Further European Cooperation in Quality Assurance in Higher Education" (2006/147/EC).

26. Comments at Roundtable, Institute for European Studies, Montreal, 11 February 2005.

27. I am indebted for this observation to Andrew Martin, Center for European Studies, Harvard University.

PART 4

Conclusion

18

Innovative Governance in the European Union: What Makes It Different?

Ingeborg Tömmel and Amy Verdun

The objective of this book was to provide insights into how governance evolves in a range of policymaking areas. We sought to identify the various modes of governance that are adopted in various areas. When reviewing the modes of governance, the authors have explicitly or implicitly assessed a number of key questions: Who are the actors? What modes of governance are dominant? What is the institutional setting in which actors operate? Has there been a change over time? With regard to who the actors are, various chapters have examined the level of government at which the dominant actors operate and what level of importance one would need to assign to these actors. In addition, some chapters have examined the relationship between nonstate actors versus governmental actors. Insofar as the modes of governance are concerned, the various chapters have assessed the extent to which one of four modes of governance was dominant and to what extent one could observe a combination of modes of governance. With regard to the institutional setting, chapters examined the existing institutional structure and what additional institutions were set up or restructured in order to make European governance work. Finally, the authors of the chapters have assessed whether there has been a change over time as to the dominant actors, the modes of governance, and the institutional setting in the respective policymaking areas. The authors have also endeavored to find an explanation for any shift over time (or lack thereof) in modes of governance, dominant actors, and institutional structures in those areas. This concluding chapter revisits the core questions raised in the introductory chapter and offers some general conclusions.

Let us first revisit our four main objectives. Our first aim was to contribute to a further clarification of the governance approach and its application to European Union (EU) research. The governance approach enables us to analyze the policymaking process in different terms. It offers us tools with which to examine the modes of governance used to develop policies, also in the absence of hierarchy and of clear competences for EU institutions, in particular, the European Commission. The framework developed for this book, with four ideal types of modes of governance—hierarchy, negotiation, competition, cooperation—has enabled us to analyze how various actors make use of certain mechanisms of coordination for developing policymaking in different institutional settings. We have shown that these modes of governance are mostly used in specific combinations and in hybrid forms. As such, this book has provided building blocks for further application of the governance approach in EU research.

Our second aim was to identify the nature of governance in a number of European policymaking areas. The case studies of this book have shown that a wide range of modes of governance, in varying combinations, is used in different policymaking areas. A number of policies have moved from one mode of governance to another, for example, from cooperation to hierarchy or vice versa, or from hierarchy or cooperation to negotiation or competition. Not all policymaking areas are going through the same sequence of development, but they actually all converge around combinations of modes of governance. There is also a wide variety of actors involved: supranational, national, and in some cases subnational actors, thus increasing the demand for coordination. Most areas of European policymaking witness a strong role of public actors, and nonstate actors are only important players in some cases.

Our third aim was to strive to compare these case studies so as to identify common characteristics of, as well as divergences among, the different areas of European policymaking and the respective forms of governance. The previous chapters have shown a more general characterization of how the areas of policymaking discussed here are similar and different in adopting modes of governance and even whether they moved from hard modes of governance (hierarchy and partly competition) to softer modes (negotiation, competition, and cooperation) or vice versa. Also, we found that in each area of policymaking shifts occurred over time in the use of modes of governance, leading to a certain degree of convergence and, in most cases, to an increasing complexity. We observed the wide variety of innovative modes of governance used more recently. In most cases we concluded that these innovative modes of governance are not necessarily "new" in the way they work (i.e., which mechanisms or actors played an important role); rather they are "new" as they increasingly complement and further advance policymaking in some areas. In some cases, softer modes of governance are used if member states do not want to transfer competences to the EU even though they are keen to make further progress in that particular area of policymaking.

Our fourth aim was to generate insights into the interrelation between European modes of governance and the institutional structure of the EU.

What the studies have clearly shown is that the whole evolution of the EU and the modes of governance chosen are intricately linked. Because the institutional setting of the EU enables, even requires, a role for both the supranational institutions and the actors to play at the national level, which in turn requires finding compromises between the actors involved, seemingly nonhierarchical modes of governance emerge and are used more widely. At the same time, more hierarchical modes of governance are used in policy areas in which a consensus about deeper integration has emerged. In other words, the EU is not only generating a range of ever softer modes of governance; we also see the EU moving in some policy areas from softer toward harder modes of governance. In the following sections we examine these conclusions in more detail.

Lessons from the Case Studies

When drawing more detailed conclusions with regard to the case studies brought together in this book, we can first conclude that the EU system is characterized by a steadily growing variety of modes of governance that evolve together with increasing differentiations in European policymaking. Apart from hierarchical modes of steering, generally enacted through hard law and authoritative decisions, increasingly differentiated patterns of negotiation and cooperation occur, encompassing harder as well as softer modes of governance. In addition, competitive mechanisms and arrangements play an important role, putting actors under pressure to conform to more or less clearly defined requirements.

A closer look at European modes of governance across policy sectors shows that the four ideal types identified in Chapter 2 evolve in combination with each other and in hybrid forms. Combinations may emerge synchronically; in many cases, however, they evolve in a sequence, either from harder to softer modes of governance or in the reverse direction. Thus single market regulation was initially based on hard law constituting the basic framework for creating a European-wide market. Since such regulation remained incomplete and ineffective, additional regulatory measures evolved: mutual recognition of national regulations; embedded self-regulation, as for example norms and standards setting by stakeholders or various forms of voluntary cooperation, often in the framework of transnational networks (see Chapters 9 and 11). Similar processes characterize competition policy. Although this policy has a strong treaty base, complemented by additional regulations and guidelines, binding decisions of the Commission are regularly accompanied by extensive negotiations among all actors involved, resulting rather in compromises than in "hard" implementation of competition law. In addition, parts of European competition policy have recently been decentralized to national regulatory agencies. Fine-tuning of competition law is achieved through cooperation among national regulatory agencies in transnational networks, which define additional rules, norms, and standards of procedure. Finally, private actors are involved in the enforcement of competition law through courts and in procedures of arbitration between the conflicting parties (see Chapter 8).

Environmental policy is another case that initially was steered through hard law—first in the framework of single market regulations, later under specific regulations of the Single European Act (SEA). The effectiveness of environmental legislation remained limited, however. Therefore, the policy was complemented with additional instruments of the softer spectrum: economic instruments, voluntary agreements, and other forms of cooperation. Although hierarchy as a mode of governance continues to dominate the field, a significant shift toward negotiation, competition, and cooperation is taking place (see Chapter 4).

Monetary policy, in contrast, is characterized by a reverse sequence. European endeavors in this field started in the form of voluntary cooperation among member states in a limited number of fields and issue areas. It was only after a longer process of convergence between national policies that hierarchy was established by transferring competences in monetary affairs to the European level. An independent agency, the European Central Bank (ECB), was entrusted to take binding decisions in this field. But also after this far-reaching step, cooperative modes of governance, in particular for coordinating budgetary and macroeconomic policies of the member states, remain in place in order to complement monetary policy at the European level (see Chapter 6).

Other policy areas are characterized from the very beginning by a combination of modes of governance, where hierarchy often provides the shadow (Scharpf 1994) that triggers softer modes of governance or indirect means of steering to evolve. This is most obvious in the case of enlargement policy, which is dominated by extensive negotiations between the EU and the accession states, whereas hierarchy, exercised by the EU in the form of strong conditionality, plays an important, if not the decisive, role in the background (see Chapter 12). Combinations also characterize direct tax policy, in which softer modes of governance, usually in the form of cooperation, emerge in the shadow of hard modes, although the latter are still very limited at the European level in this field (see Chapter 5).

In some cases, hierarchy functioned as a catalyst for the emergence of other modes of governance. Sport policy is an example. Although this policy was not a deliberately chosen area of European endeavors, it is nevertheless increasingly being (co-)regulated by the EU because case law of the European Court of Justice (ECJ) resulted in unintended consequences, that is, disproportionate interventions into the sector. Therefore the Commission embarked on intensive negotiations with nonstate actors, the sport organizations. Their cooperation with the European level is triggered by a massive threat emanating from competition law to treat sport as an economic business. This threat is particularly effective because the ECJ judged in most cases that sport issues fall under economic regulations (see Chapter 10).

A combination of hard law and voluntary forms of cooperation prevails in social policy. It is interesting to note that voluntary cooperation can be used both to extend the realm and scope of European social policy (see Chapter 7) and also to reinforce pressures on member states to conform to European law (see Chapter 14). Additional pressure is being exercised in this field by mobilizing nonstate actors for formulation and due implementation of such policies (see Chapter 7). As far as hard law at the European level exists in this field, the Commission co-opts nonstate actors who support its surveillance of transposition of European law into national legal systems (see Chapter 14).

Finally, some policy fields are predominantly or even exclusively governed by more or less voluntary forms of cooperation. This is most obviously the case with the so-called Bologna Process, which aimed at developing common standards and procedures of quality control in higher education (Chapter 17). It also applies to different forms of transnational cooperation in Justice and Home Affairs (see Chapter 16). Furthermore, it can be observed in some newly emerging regulatory policy fields, as, for example, the regulation of public utilities and the data privacy sector (see Chapters 13 and 15). In all these cases, cooperation among actors from the member state level prevails: central governments, specialized regulatory agencies, upper-level civil servants, sectoral experts, and sometimes also nonstate actors. What differs is the degree of institutionalization of these forms of transnational cooperation. In some cases, highly formalized networks—established on the basis of Council regulations—prevail, often presided over by the European Commission, as is the case in the regulation of public utilities and the data privacy sector, but also in competition policy. Such networks provide an umbrella in order to define common objectives or to set informal rules and standards (see Chapters 8 and 15). In other cases, the European Commission is officially excluded but nevertheless plays an important role in the background through shaping and structuring discourse and debate: by defining the nature of the problem, by presenting basic policy objectives, and by proposing potential solutions for the perceived problems (see Chapters 16 and 17). In all these policy areas, transnational cooperation is initiated, supported, and sometimes structured by actors from the European level. A further mechanism that enhances such forms of voluntary cooperation is strong competitive pressures, often intensified through market liberalization, as is the case in the public utilities sector (see Chapters 13 and 15) and also in higher education (see Chapter 17). Even cooperation in Justice and Home Affairs is—although indirectly—triggered by market liberalization, since open borders have eroded national policies, that is, those regarding immigration or organized crime (see Chapter 16). Thus, policy areas that at first glance seem to be exclusively governed by voluntary cooperation among member states are often also subject to governance activities initiated or exercised at the European level. In addition, it has to be borne in mind that in all these cases hierarchy exercised at the national level is indispensable in order to make such policies work.

Turning to hybrids of modes of governance, the most important case referred to in this volume is mutual recognition, forming a hybrid of hierarchy and cooperation. This mode, triggered by the famous judgment of the ECJ in the *Cassis de Dijon* case (1979), is increasingly playing a crucial role in the governance of the EU. Besides enormously accelerating the evolution of the single market, it has actually also been transferred to the Justice and Home Affairs field (in particular with the European Arrest Warrant) (see Chapters 9 and 16). This mode of governance forms a creative, though not always effective, solution to the fundamental dilemma of EU governance: the fragmentation of sovereignty between member states and its lack at or insufficient transfer to the European level.

In sum, when looking at European policymaking from a governance perspective, we can see a wide variety of combinations of harder and softer, traditional and more recently emerged modes of governance. Softer modes of governance are increasingly pervading existing policy fields and thus softening them up, but the reverse process also occurs: a sequence from softer to harder modes of governance. In addition, softer modes of governance can be used to render hard modes more effective. Hard modes, in particular hierarchy and competition, are being used similarly to make soft modes more effective. Thus, on the whole, it is the combination of modes of governance, aimed at rendering European policymaking more effective, that constitutes the innovative aspect of governance in the EU (see Chapter 3).

If we look at the actors that promote the evolution of European governance and in particular its innovative forms, we find that the Commission stands out. The Commission often initiates shifts in governance, in particular toward the softer spectrum, in those cases in which hierarchy alone does not result in effective policymaking (see the chapters in Part 2). Furthermore, the Commission is most keen to exploit hierarchy as a catalyst to initiate experiments in governance. Thus, the Commission often uses a treaty base, existing legislation, or an ECJ ruling to initiate new policies or to restructure existing ones. In all these cases, hierarchy is used to put pressure on actors to cooperate or compromise with EU institutions, as represented by the Commission (see chapters in Part 2). In some cases, the Commission also makes use of competition as an indirect means of putting pressure on actors to conform. Also in those cases in which member states are keen to keep the Commission at a distance, the Commission nevertheless succeeds in creating a role for itself (see chapters in Part 3). Such a role may be exercised in a more informal way, for example, by structuring discourses on policy issues. But it can also be exercised in a more organized way, by playing a major role in establishing and managing transnational networks, composed of delegates or representatives of the member states.

The Commission is also willing to share competences with national actors and sometimes with nonstate actors. Sharing competences occurs especially when the Commission has clearly hierarchical means at its disposal, as it has for example in competition policy (see Chapter 8). This case shows that the Commission alone does not have the authority to direct processes of policymaking. It is always the permissive or restrictive consensus—or the absence of any consensus—between member states that shapes the process of policymaking and the configuration of governance modes. Thus, governments of the member states often reject clear transfers of powers to the European level, and sometimes they even try to undermine competences that they have transferred in earlier stages of the integration process. But they often accept proposals to deliberate on procedures and institutions that give them or their delegates a major role in continuously exerting influence on European policymaking, as is the case with many transnational networks that have been recently created (see Chapters 9, 13, and 15).

The Characteristics of European Governance

Comparing Policy Areas

What are the characteristics of European governance across policy areas? As the case studies in this book illustrate, there is much variety across policy fields at first sight. What all European policies have in common, at least in the longer run, however, is the innovative combination of hard and soft governance modes. These features become visible especially when examining them in historical perspective. From such a perspective, European policies increasingly converge in their combinations of modes of governance. Sectors that were initially exclusively governed by law are successively complemented with softer modes of governance and vice versa. This convergence can first be interpreted as an indication of a maturing EU polity, which has evolved into a fully fledged system of policymaking. Yet at second glance, it can also be seen as the expression of the specific structure of the EU. Governance in this system always occurs in the form of co-governance (Kooiman 2003: 96–114), at least between the European and the national level. Therefore, legislation at the European level is often less effective because it is superimposed on mature national legal systems. In order to render such legislation workable, complementary modes of governance are required: the pressure of competition, the consensus-building impact of negotiation, or the coordinative effect of (voluntary) cooperation. But the opposite is also true:

soft modes of governance alone, in particular in the form of voluntary co-operation, are insufficient to trigger compliance or conforming behavior of the member states (see Chapter 3). Additional, harder modes of governance are needed in order to achieve coordination.

Comparing European vs. National-Level Governance

To what extent do European modes of governance differ from those at the national level and in which sense can they be characterized as innovative or specific? Modes of governance, as they are conceptualized in this book, are seen as ideal types. The typology used here refers primarily to the process dimension of governance. At this level of abstraction, it is not possible to elaborate on relevant distinctions between the EU and its member states. We can only state that innovative modes of governance seem to prevail in quantitative terms and that they also seem to have gained in importance over time. Significant differences between European and national modes of governance can be found, however, in the structural dimension of governance, that is, the actor structure, the corresponding patterns of interaction, and the institutional structure underlying these interactions. Analyzing these dimensions of governance also allows for drawing conclusions with regard to the importance of different governance modes in the context of EU policymaking.

Actor Constellations

By looking, first, at the actors, the same categories of actors play a role in the European as well as in the national context: public or state actors, private actors, and representatives of civil society. There are significant differences, however, in the respective roles that these actors play, in the resources at their disposal, and in the constellation of combining or aggregating them in governance processes. Since all three categories of actors are often, in the European context, representatives or delegates of the member states, a strong need of horizontal coordination arises between them and within each category. If different categories of actors combine their efforts in European governance processes, horizontal coordination has to be complemented with cross-actor coordination. It is the diversity among member states and the multitude of actors involved that poses an enormous challenge of complexity to European governance. To manage this complexity, transnational networks have been created in nearly every policy field (see, in particular, Chapters 6, 8, 13, 15–17).

When looking at the respective roles of actors, and the power resources at their disposal, differences become particularly obvious with regard to public actors. In national governance constellations, they can rely on the power resources of the state: national sovereignty, hierarchical rule or intervention, and financial resources. When acting in the context of European governance, these power resources can only be used by national actors as far as they are able successfully to aggregate or pool them. Pooling resources is severely hampered by the well-known constraints to collective action and therefore requires specific coordinative efforts.

Public actors of the European institutions, by contrast, have less explicit power resources at their disposal. Although they often take the lead in coordinating national agents and actors, they are severely constrained in this exercise. The Council itself mirrors the divergences between member states and therefore is hampered in its role as the ultimate decisiontaker. The Commission has only "procedural powers" (Tömmel 2008) at its disposal, which enable it to set the agenda and to shape coordination but not its outcomes; and the European Parliament, together with the Council, is at best a colegislator in certain, but not all, policy fields. Only the ECJ has a strong and in particular a comparatively independent power position. In addition, power distribution is highly fragmented between the European institutions, and the EU altogether is by no means superimposed onto the member states.

This complex and, to a certain degree, inverse actor constellation in European governance as compared to national governance implies, first, an exponentially increased demand for coordinative efforts and, second, a certain tendency toward relying less on hierarchy but more on negotiation, competition, and cooperation as modes of governance. This is not only the case for horizontal and vertical coordination among public actors in the European context, but it also applies to coordination between public and private or other nonstate actors on and across all levels and sectors. In sum, the actor constellation in European governance is more complex, less clearly based on explicitly defined or assigned power resources, and more dependent on actors' redefining their roles in the European context. This complexity is due to the enormous diversity between member states and the ensuing governance challenges and to the fragmented and constrained power resources at the European level.

Interactions

When looking at interactions, three types can be distinguished. Following Kooiman (2003: 20–25), interactions can be categorized according to their degree of formalization: interference, interplay, and intervention. Kooiman relates interference to self-governance, interplay to co-governance, and intervention to hierarchical governance, even though he emphasizes that all three types of interaction might occur in each mode of governance. Although these types of interaction clearly play a role at both the national and the European level, it can be assumed that interplay is the dominant type in European governance, since interplays have, as Kooiman defines them, "a typical 'horizontal' character. In principle, there is no formal authority, domination or subordination within them. Interplays aim to reach goals by engaging actors in collective, rather than interdependent action and on a general equal basis" (Kooiman 2003: 21–22).

Such a constellation is typical for the EU, where explicit relationships of domination and subordination lack or only play a minor role. In particular it applies to those cases in which transnational policy networks, composed of representatives or delegates of the member states, play a decisive role. Actors in those networks have, at least in formal terms, an equal standing. But even when European actors, in particular the Commission, are directly involved, that is, in coordinating policy networks, it is predominantly interplay that characterizes interactions with other public or nonstate actors of all levels, since European actors are not superior to those of the member states. A distinctive role is played by the ECJ and the ECB, which can take binding decisions and thus make use of intervention as a mode of interaction. Interplay as a type of interaction is closely connected to negotiation and cooperation as governance modes, which both presuppose more or less equal participants.

Institutional Structures

In turning to the institutional structures underlying modes of governance, we can conclude that, in the European case, as compared to national states, hierarchy is based on a comparatively weaker institutional structure whereas negotiation, competition, and cooperation are embedded into a more organized and formalized institutional framework. Hierarchy in the EU, as was mentioned in Chapter 2, is based not on sovereignty of the European level but on a selective and conditional transfer of powers from the member states and thus on delegated or "pooled sovereignty" (Keohane and Hoffmann 1991). At the same time, member states continue to be sovereign in the framework of the EU—although this sovereignty is, to a certain degree, constrained—and thus form an additional barrier to the use and effectiveness of hierarchy. This constellation results in malfunctioning of hierarchical rules, as is the case in single market competition, environmental, social, and many other European policies (see, e.g., Chapters 4, 8, 9, 11, and 14); in weakening of hierarchical rule, as in the sluggish transposition of regulations into national law (social policy; see Chapter 14); and, generally, in fragmentary and defective European legislation, which affects more or less all policy fields of the EU.

By contrast, when looking at the institutional structure underlying negotiation, competition, and cooperation, it is obvious that the respective governance modes are embedded into more organized and formalized institutional structures than is usually the case at the national level. Thus, the EU is in itself already a "negotiated order" *(Verhandlungssystem)* (Scharpf 1992b), providing an institutional framework for facilitating forms of negotiation between all actors involved in governance processes, for example, enlargement policy (see Chapter 12) and sport policy (see Chapter 10). Furthermore, the EU is also a competitive order, since creating a European single market sets not only private actors but also the member states under competitive pressures (see Chapters 8, 9, 11, 12, and 17)

In addition to those basic institutional structures of the EU that facilitate negotiation and competition, further institutions have been created in order to enable coordination under conditions of complexity. Thus, transnational policy networks beyond the formalized institutions of intergovernmental bargaining (the Council and its substructure) have been established in nearly all policy fields of the EU (see, in particular, Chapters 8, 13, and 15–17). They are in general more institutionalized and formalized—in most cases by Council regulations or directives—than policy networks at the national level, which often rely on self-organization (Rhodes 1997). Moreover, actors in such networks, in particular those delegated from national governments, are less dependent on the exchange of resources; instead they cooperate in order to pool their resources. This implies, on the one hand, that exchange of resources as a glue binding networks together plays a minor role in European policymaking, whereas, on the other hand, more binding institutional provisions are needed—and enacted—in order to stabilize networks and in particular to enable pooling of resources. Against this background, it is not so surprising that many transnational policy networks are regulated by legal provisions and thus embedded into hierarchically determined governance structures at the European level (see Chapters 8, 13, and 15).

Even hybrid and seemingly informal modes of governance, as for example the open method of coordination (OMC), are embedded into highly formalized institutional structures, which are partly the basic structures of the EU, partly newly created institutions (see Chapter 3). Thus the OMC is not merely a process of mutual learning between member states, as is widely suggested in the literature, but also a carefully designed procedure, underpinned by strong institutions. In addition, these procedures are institutionalized in such a way that they often entail strong competitive pressures on the actors involved (see Chapter 3).

Those networks constituting transnational cooperation without being explicitly embedded into European rules or modes of procedure, as is the case with Justice and Home Affairs and the Bologna Process, are nevertheless well institutionalized (see Chapters 16 and 17). In these cases, institutional settings rely more on the authority of national states, whereas the European level gives an important input into policymaking through structuring debates and discourses on problem definitions and possible ways toward solutions.

What all the case studies of this book confirm is that European modes of governance, in particular those on the nonhierarchical side of the spectrum, are not predominantly informal procedures, caused and implemented simply to circumvent the weaknesses and deficiencies of the EU system. Instead, they are embedded into well-defined institutional structures, partly the basic structures of the EU system itself, partly carefully designed and well-organized institutions created in particular for purposes of governance and policymaking under conditions of divergence among member states and complexity of governance challenges. Thus European governance is not limited to managing interactions geared to achieving certain policy goals but also includes institution building and institutional transformation for enabling and facilitating governance or, as Kooiman (2003: 153–169) defines it, establishing second-order governance.

To sum up, European governance does not differ from that at the national level because of significant differences in the process dimension of governance but rather because of its structural dimension: the actor constellation, the predominant type of interaction, and the underlying institutional setting. The latter is in part due to the nature of the EU, but in part it is also created so that European policies can work. The actor constellation can generally be characterized as more complex and diverse compared to national political systems. More important, however, is that actors in many constellations are more or less equal or that inequalities between them play only a secondary role. As a result, the type of interaction is predominantly a horizontal one, characterized as interplay and aimed at achieving common objectives; interdependence is not absent but plays a background role. The institutional foundations of European governance are comparatively weaker in the case of hierarchy; in the case of negotiation, competition, and cooperation, they are more strongly organized and formalized.

Conclusion

In this book we have presented various policymaking areas and analyses thereof and offered a look at the developments through a governance lens. We developed a systematic framework that distinguishes between basic governance modes and elaborates on the interrelation between governance modes and the institutional structure of the EU. This framework served as a basis for the analyses of policymaking and innovative governance in the case studies. We have seen complex and intensive interactions between the EU institutions and those of the member states and in some cases nonstate actors. Furthermore, we have found dynamic changes in the modes of governance adopted in response to institutional constraints and incentives in the process of policymaking. Even though we have characterized governance processes and the underlying institutional structures in a wide range of areas of policymaking, it should be clear that European governance is still very much in flux at the present time. It would be worthwhile doing the exercise again in ten years to see where we will be at that point.

Abbreviations and Acronyms

AFSJ	Area of Freedom, Security, and Justice
ASEAN	Association of South East Asian Nations
BEPG	Broad Economic Policy Guidelines
BFUG	Bologna Follow-Up Group
BSI	Business Information (the British Standards body)
CCCTB	Common Consolidated Corporate Tax Base
CEDEFOP	European Centre for the Development of Vocational Training
CEER	Council of European Energy Regulators
CEN	European Committee for Standardization
CENELEC	European Committee for Electro-technical Standardization
CEPOL	European Police College
CESR	Committee of European Securities Regulators
CFI	Court of First Instance
CIS	Customs Information System
CONCORD	European NGO Confederation for Relief and Development
Coreper	Permanent Representatives Committee
CSCG	Civil Society Contact Group
DAAD	Deutscher Akademischer Austausch Dienst (German Academic Exchange Service)
DG	Directorate General
DG Comp	Directorate General for Competition
DG EMPL	Directorate General for Employment, Social Affairs, and Equal Opportunities
DG H	Directorate General Justice and Home Affairs (of the Council)
DIN	Deutsches Institut für Normung (the German Standards body)
DS	diploma supplement

EAP	environmental action program
EAPN	European Anti-Poverty Network
EASA	European Aviation Safety Authority
EC	European Community
ECB	European Central Bank
ECJ	European Court of Justice
ECN	European Competition Network
ECOFIN	Council of Ministers of Economic and Financial Affairs
ECOSOC	Economic and Social Committee
ECPR	European Consortium of Political Research
ECRE	European Council on Refugees and Exiles
ECSC	European Coal and Steel Community
ECTS	European Credit Transfer System
EDA	European Defence Agency
EEA	European Economic Area
EEA	European Environment Agency
EEB	European Environment Bureau
EEC	European Economic Community
EES	European employment strategy
EFAH	European Forum for Arts and Heritage
EFSA	European Food Safety Authority
EFTA	European Free Trade Association
EHEA	European Higher Education Area
EI	Education International
EMCDDA	European Monitoring Centre on Drugs and Drug Addiction
EMI	European Monetary Institute
EMS	European Monetary System
EMSA	European Maritime Safety Authority
EMU	Economic and Monetary Union
ENIC	European Network of Information Centres
ENQA	European Network for Quality Assurance
EP	European Parliament
ERA	European Research Area
ERGEG	European Regulators Group for Electricity and Gas
ESCB	European System of Central Banks
ESG	European Standards and Guidelines
ESU	European Students Unions
ETSI	European Telecommunications Standards Institute
ETUC	European Trade Union Confederation
EU	European Union
EUA	European Universities' Association
EUMC	European Monitoring Centre on Racism and Xenophobia
EU-OSHA	European Agency for Safety and Health at Work

EURASHE	European Association of Institutions in Higher Education
EUSA	European Union Studies Association
EWL	European Women's Lobby
FEANTSA	European Federation of National Organizations Working with Homeless
FIA	Fédération Internationale d'Automobile
FIBA	International Basketball Federation
FIFA	Fédération Internationale de Football Association
FIFPro	Fédération Internationales des Associations de Footballeurs Professionels
FIGC	Italian Football Federation
GATT	General Agreement on Tariffs and Trade
GDP	gross domestic product
HELIOS	Handicapped People in the EC Living Independently in an Open Society
HRDN	Human Rights and Democratization Contact Group
ICFA	Independent Court for Football Arbitration
IGC	intergovernmental conference
IOC	International Olympic Committee
IRG	Independent Regulators Group
IWGDP	International Working Group on Data Protection in Telecommunications
JFS	Justice, Freedom, and Security
JHA	Justice and Home Affairs
MEP	Member of the European Parliament
NARIC	National Academic Recognition Information Centres
NATO	North Atlantic Treaty Organization
NGO	nongovernmental organization
NOC	National Olympic Committees
OAS	Organization of American States
OAU	Organization of African Unity
OECD	Organization for Economic Cooperation and Development
OLAF	Office de Lutte Antifraude
OMC	open method of coordination
ONP	open network provision
OSH	occupational health and safety
PCOTF	European Police Chiefs' Task Force
PJCCM	police and judicial cooperation in criminal matters
QAA	quality assurance agencies
QMV	qualified majority voting
SCIFA	Strategic Committee on Immigration, Frontiers, and Asylum
SEA	Single European Act

SGP	Stability and Growth Pact
SIS	Schengen Information System
SSHRC	Social Sciences and Humanities Research Council of Canada
TAIEX	Technical Assistance Information Exchange
TCA	Trade and Cooperation Agreement
TEC	Treaty Establishing the European Community
TEU	Treaty on European Union
UEFA	Union of European Football Associations
UK	United Kingdom
UN	United Nations
UNESCO	United Nations Educational, Scientific, and Cultural Organization
UNICE	European Employers Federation
VIS	Visa Information System

References

ABA (2005), "The European Competition Network: What It Is and Where It Is Going," American Bar Association Section of Antitrust Law Brown Bag Program. Available at: http://www.abanet.org/antitrust/at-source/05/07/Jul05-ECNBrBag7=28f.pdf.

Abbott, Kenneth, and Duncan Snidal (2000), "Hard and Soft Law in International Governance," *International Organization,* 54, no. 3, 421–456.

Adonnino Committee (1985), "A People's Europe," *Bulletin of the European Communities,* Supplement 7, 18–30.

Agence Europe (1994), number 6348, 31 October, p. 14.

Ahrens, Joachim, Herman Hoen, and Renate Ohr (2005), "Deepening Integration in an Enlarged EU: A Club-Theoretical Perspective," *Journal of European Integration,* 27, no. 4, 417–439.

Aldestam, Mona (2004), "Soft Law in the State Aid Policy," in Ulrika Mörth (ed.), *Soft Law in Governance and Regulation* (Cheltenham: Edward Elgar), 11–36.

Allen, David (1996), "Competition Policy: Policing the Single Market," in Helen Wallace and William Wallace (eds.), *Policy-making in the European Union* (Oxford: Oxford University Press), 157–183.

Alter, Karen J., and Sophie Meunier-Aitsahalia (1994), "Judicial Politics in the European Community: European Integration and the Pathbreaking Cassis de Dijon Decision," *Comparative Political Studies,* 26, 535–561.

Alter, Karen J., and Jeannette Vargas (2000), "Explaining Variation in the Use of European Litigation Strategies: European Community Law and British Equality Policy," *Comparative Politics,* 33, no. 4, 452–482.

Amato, Giuliano, and Judy Batt (1999), *Final Report of the Reflection Group on the Long-Term Implications of EU Enlargement: The Nature of the New Border* (Florence: Robert Schuman Centre).

Armony, Ariel C., and Hector Schamis (2005), "Babel in Democratization Studies," *Journal of Democracy,* 16, no. 4, 113–128.

Armstrong, Kenneth (2002), "Rediscovering Civil Society: The European Union and the White Paper on Governance," *European Law Journal,* 8, no. 1, 102–132.

——— (2006), "Inclusive Governance? Civil Society and the Open Method of Coordination," in Stijn Smismans (ed.), *Civil Society and Legitimate European Governance* (London: Edward Elgar), 42–68.

Article 29 Data Protection Working Party (2004), "Opinion 9/2004 on a Draft Framework Decision on the Storage of Data Processed and Retained for the Purpose of

Providing Electronic Public Communications Networks with a View to the Prevention, Investigation, Detection, and Prosecution of Criminal Acts, Including Terrorism," Brussels, European Community.

Audretsch, H.A.H. (1986), *Supervision in European Community Law: Observance by the Member States of Their Treaty Obligation—A Treatise on International and Supra-National Supervision* (Amsterdam: Elsevier Science).

Auel, Katrin (2003), *Regionalisiertes Europa—Demokratisches Europa? Eine Untersuchung am Beispiel der europäischen Strukturpolitik* (Baden-Baden: Nomos).

Auel, Katrin, and Arthur Benz (2006), "Politics of Adjustment—The Europeanization of National Parliamentary Democracy," *Journal of Legislative Studies,* 11, no. 3–4, 372–393.

Aujean, Michel, et al. (2005), "La fiscalité des sociétés en Europe: Développements et perspectives. Rapport pour le Conseil des Impôts," typescript, Brussels.

Ayres, Ian, and John Braithwaite (1992), *Responsive Regulation: Transcending the Deregulation* (Oxford: Oxford University Press).

Bach, David, and Abraham L. Newman (2007), "The European Regulatory State and Global Public Policy," *Journal of European Public Policy,* 16, no. 6, 827–848.

Bache, Ian (2006), "The Europeanization of Higher Education: Markets, Politics or Learning?" *Journal of Common Market Studies,* 44, no. 2, 231–248.

Bache, Ian, and Matthew Flinders (eds.) (2004), *Multi-level Governance* (Oxford: Oxford University Press).

Bailey, David (2007), "Damages Action Under the EC Merger Regulation," *Common Market Law Review,* 44, 101–139.

Balzacq, Thierry, Didier Bigo, Sergio Carrera, and Elspeth Guild (2006), "Security and the Two-Level Game: The Treaty of Prüm, the EU and the Management of Threats," CEPS Working Document 234, Brussels.

Bardach, Eugene (1977), *The Implementation Game: What Happens After a Bill Becomes a Law* (Cambridge, MA: MIT Press).

Barnard, Catherine (1999), "EC 'Social' Policy," in Paul Craig and Gráinne De Burca (eds.), *The Evolution of EU Law* (Oxford: Oxford University Press), 479–516.

Bartle, Ian (2005), *Globalisation and EU Policy-making: The Neo-liberal Transformation of Telecommunications and Electricity* (Manchester: Manchester University Press).

Bartolini, Stefano (2005), *Restructuring Europe, Centre Formation, System Building, and Political Structuring Between the Nation State and the European Union* (Oxford: Oxford University Press).

Bauer, Michael W. (2002), "Limitations to Agency Control in EU Policy-Making—The Commission and the Poverty Programmes," *Journal of Common Market Studies,* 40, no. 3, 381–400.

Baun, Michael J. (2000), *A Wider Europe: The Process and Politics of European Union Enlargement* (Lanham, MD: Rowman and Littlefield).

Beach, Derek (2004), "The Unseen Hand in Treaty Reform Negotiations: The Role and Influence of the Council Secretariat," *Journal of European Public Policy,* 11, no. 3, 408–439.

——— (2005), *The Dynamics of European Integration: Why and When EU Institutions Matter* (New York: Palgrave Macmillan).

Beck, Ulrich, and Edgar Grande (2004), *Das kosmopolitische Europa: Gesellschaft und Politik in der Zweiten Moderne* (Frankfurt: Suhrkamp).

——— (2007a), *Cosmopolitan Europe* (Cambridge: Polity Press).

——— (2007b), "Cosmopolitanism—Europe's Way out of Crisis," *European Journal of Social Theory,* 10, no. 1, 67–85.

Becker, Mattias (2004), "Out of Step," *The Guardian,* 6 July.

Beger, Nicolas (2004), "Participatory Democracy: Organised Civil Society and the 'New' Dialogue," paper presented to the Federal Trust and UACES Conference "Towards a European Constitution," London.

Beloff, Nora (1963), *The General Says No: Britain's Exclusion from Europe* (Harmondsworth: Penguin).

Bennett, Colin (1992), *Regulating Privacy: Data Protection and Public Policy in Europe and the United States* (Ithaca, NY: Cornell University Press).

Benz, Arthur (2000), "Entflechtung als Folge von Verflechtung: Theoretische Überlegungen zur Entwicklung des Europäischen Mehrebenensystems," in Edgar Grande and Markus Jachtenfuchs (eds.), *Wie problemlösungsfähig ist die EU? Regieren im europäischen Mehrebenensystem* (Baden-Baden: Nomos), 141–163.

———— (2003), "Mehrebenenverflechtung in der Europäischen Union," in Markus Jachtenfuchs and Beate Kohler-Koch (eds.), *Europäische Integration,* 2. Aufl (Opladen: Leske und Budrich), 327–361.

———— (ed.) (2004a), *Governance—Regieren in komplexen Regelsystemen* (Wiesbaden: VS Verlag für Sozialwissenschaften).

———— (2004b), "Governance—Modebegriff oder nuetzliches sozialwissenschaftliches Konzept?" in Arthur Benz (ed.), *Governance—Regieren in komplexen Regelsystemen* (Wiesbaden: VS Verlag für Sozialwissenschaften), 11–28.

———— (2004c), "Multilevel Governance—Governance in Mehrebenensystemen," in Arthur Benz (ed.), *Governance—Regieren in komplexen Regelsystemen* (Wiesbaden: VS Verlag für Sozialwissenschaften), 125–144.

———— (2005), "Governance in Mehrebenensystemen," in Gunnar F. Schuppert (ed.), *Governance-Forschung: Vergewisserung über Stand und Entwicklungslinien* (Baden-Baden: Nomos), 95–120.

———— (2006), "Eigendynamik von Governance in der Verwaltung," in Jörg Bogumil, Werner Jann, and Frank Nullmeier (eds.), *Politik und Verwaltung,* PVS-Sonderheft 37 (Wiesbaden: VS Verlag für Sozialwssenschaften).

———— (2007), "Accountable Multilevel Governance by the Open Method of Coordination?" *European Law Journal,* 13, no. 4, 505–522.

Benz, Arthur, Susanne Lütz, Uwe Schimank, and Georg Simonis (eds.) (2007a), *Handbuch Governance: Theoretische Grundlagen und empirische Anwendungsfelder* (Wiesbaden: VS Verlag für Sozialwissenschaften).

———— (2007b), "Einleitung," in Arthur Benz, Susanne Lütz, Uwe Schimank, and Georg Simonis (eds.), *Handbuch Governance: Theoretische Grundlagen und empirische Anwendungsfelder* (Wiesbaden: VS Verlag für Sozialwissenschaften), 9–25.

Beunderman, Mark (2005), "Member States Seek Tougher Text on Turkey Talks," *EU Observer,* September 26.

———— (2006), "Dutch Want Break on EU Enlargement," *EU Observer,* April 11.

Bigo, Didier (1996), *Polices en Réseaux* (Paris: Presses de la Fondation Nationale des Sciences Politiques).

Binder, K. G. (1999), *Grundzüge der Umweltökonomie* (Munich: Vahlen).

Blanke, Gordon (2006), *The Use and Utility of International Arbitration in EC Commission Merger Remedies: A Novel Supranational Paradigm in the Making?* (Groningen: European Law Publishing).

Blanpain, Roger (1996), *L'affaire Bosman: La fin de l'ère des transferts?* (Leuven: Peters).

Blatter, Joseph (2001), "Letter of Blatter to Monti," 5 March. Available at http://www.fifa.com/download/BlatterLetter.pdf.

Blessing, Marc (2003), *Arbitrating Antitrust and Merger Control Issues* (Basel: Helbig and Lichtenhahn).

Bock, Matthias (1995), *Die Regulierung der britischen Telekommunikationsmärkte* (Baden-Baden: Nomos).

Bomberg, Elizabeth, and Alexander Stubb (eds.) (2003), *The European Union: How Does It Work?* (Oxford: Oxford University Press).

Borrás, Susana, and Bent Greve (2004), "The Open Method of Coordination in the European Union," *Journal of European Public Policy* (special issue), 11, no. 2, 329–336.

Borrás, Susana, and Kerstin Jacobsson (2004), "The Open Method of Co-ordination and New Governance Patterns in the EU," *Journal of European Public Policy,* 11, no. 2, 185–208.

Bort, Eberhart (2003), "EU Enlargement: Policing the New Borders," *International Spectator,* 38, no. 1, 51–68.

Börzel, Tanja (2005), "European Governance—nicht neu, aber anders," in Gunnar F. Schuppert (ed.), *Governance-Forschung. Vergewisserung über Stand und Entwicklungslinien* (Baden-Baden: Nomos), 72–94.

——— (2007), "European Governance—Verhandlungen und Wettbewerb im Schatten der Hierarchie," in Ingeborg Tömmel (ed.), *Die Europäische Union: Governance und Policy-Making,* PVS-Sonderheft 40 (Wiesbaden: VS Verlag für Sozialwissenschaften), 61–91.

Börzel, Tanja A., Sonja Guttenbrunner, and Simone Seper (2005), *Conceptualizing New Modes of Governance in EU Enlargement* (NEWGOV project deliverable ref. 12/D1). Available at http://www.eu-newgov.org/.

Braithwaite, John, and Peter Drahos (2000), *Global Business Regulation* (Cambridge: Cambridge University Press).

Brenton, Paul (2001), "What Are the Limits to Economic Integration?" CEPS Working Document 177, Brussels.

Breyer, Stephen (1982), *Regulation and Its Reform* (Cambridge, MA: Harvard University Press).

Brodley, Joseph F. (1995), "Antitrust Standing in Private Merger Cases: Reconciling Private Incentives and Public Enforcement Goals," *Michigan Law Review,* 94, no. 1, 1–108.

Bruno, Isabelle, Sophie Jacquot, and Lou Madin (2006), "Europeanisation Through Its Instrumentation: Benchmarking, Mainstreaming and the Open Method of Coordination . . . Toolbox or Pandora's Box?" *Journal of European Public Policy,* 13, no. 4, 519–536.

Bureau of European Policy Advisors and DG for Economic and Financial Affairs (2006), "Enlargement, Two Years After: An Economic Evaluation," *European Economy,* Occasional Papers 24. Available at http://www.europa.eu.int/comm/economy_finance/publications/occasionalpapers_en.htm.

Büthe, Tim (2007), "The Politics of Competition in the European Union: The First 50 Years," in S. Meunier and K. McNamara (eds.), *The State of the European Union* (Oxford: Oxford University Press), 175–194.

Cameron, Peter D. (2005), "Completing the Internal Market in Energy: An Introduction to the New Legislation," in Peter D. Cameron (ed.), *Legal Aspects of EU Energy Regulation* (Oxford: Oxford University Press), 7–39.

Caporaso, James A., and Joerg Wittenbrinck (2006), "The New Modes of Governance and Political Authority in Europe," *Journal of European Public Policy,* 13, no. 4, 471–480.

Cave, Martin, and Robert W. Crandall (2001), "Sports Rights and the Broadcast Industry," *The Economic Journal,* 111 (February), 4–26.

Caviedes, Alexander (2004), "The Open Method of Co-ordination in Immigration Policy: A Tool for Prying Open Fortress Europe?" *Journal of European Public Policy,* 11, no. 2, 289–310.

Chatham House (2003), *Unfinished Business: Making Europe's Single Market a Reality* (London: RIIA).

Chiti, Edoardo (2002), "Decentralised Integration as a New Model of Joint Exercise of Community Functions? A Legal Analysis of European Agencies," Arena Working Paper WP 02/3, Oslo.

Cini, Michelle (2001), "The Soft Law Approach: Commission Rule-making in the EU's State Aid Regime," *Journal of European Public Policy,* 8, no. 2, 192–207.

"Les Citoyens de l'Union Européenne et le Sport" (2003), special issue, *Eurobaromètre,* 197. Available at http://ec.europa.eu/public_opinion/archives/ebs/ebs_197_fr_summ.pdf.

Coen, David, and Adrienne Héritier (eds.) (2006), *Refining Regulatory Regimes in Europe: The Creation and Correction of Markets* (Cheltenham: Edward Elgar).

Coen, David, and Mark Thatcher (eds.) (2001), *Utilities Reform in Europe* (Huntington, NY: Nova Science).

—— (2005), "The New Governance of Markets and Non-Majoritarian Regulators," *Governance,* 18, no. 3, 329–346.

—— (2008), "Network Governance and Delegation: European Networks of Regulatory Agencies," *Journal of Public Policy,* 28, no. 1, 49–71.

Cohen, Joshua, and Charles Sabel (1997), "Directly-deliberative Polyarchy," *European Law Journal,* 3, no. 4, 313–342.

Coleman, James S. (1988), "Social Capital in the Creation of Human Capital," *American Journal of Sociology,* 94, 95–120.

Collier, Ute (1998), "The Environmental Dimensions of Deregulation: An Introduction," in Ute Collier (ed.), *Deregulation in the European Union: Environmental Perspectives* (London: Routledge), 3–24.

Collins, Doreen (1975), *The European Communities: The Social Policy of the First Phase* (London: Martin Robertson).

Commission of the European Communities (1962), *Fifth General Report* (Luxembourg: Office for Official Publications).

—— (1963a), *Bulletin of the European Communities,* 2/1963.

—— (1963b), *Bulletin of the European Communities,* 12/1963.

—— (1991a), "First Report on the Application of the Union Charter of the Fundamental Social Rights of Workers," COM (91) 511 final, Brussels, 27 June.

—— (1991b), "The European Community and Sport: Communication from the Commission to the Council and the European Parliament," SEC (91) 1438 final, 31 July. Available at http://aei.pitt.edu/3153/.

—— (1991c), "Initial Contributions by the Commission to the Intergovernmental Conference on Political Union SEC (91) 500," *Composite Working Paper* (Brussels: Commission of the European Communities).

—— (1993), "European Social Policy: Options for the Union Green Paper," COM (93) 551 final, Brussels, 17 November.

—— (1994), "European Social Policy: A Way Forward for the Union White Paper," COM (94) 333 final, Brussels, 27 July.

—— (1995), "Medium-term Action Programme 1995–1997," COM (95) 134 final, Brussels 12 April.

—— (1996), "Working on European Social Policy: A Report on the Forum," Brussels, 27–30 March.

—————— (1997), "Commission to Bring Infringement Proceedings Against 14 Member States in the Social Field," Press Release IP/97/1126, Brussels.

—————— (1999a), "The Helsinki Report on Sport," *Report of the Commission to the European Council,* COM 644, 10 December. Available at http://europa.eu/ eurlex/en/com/rpt/1999/com1999_0644en01.pdf.

—————— (1999b), "Mutual Recognition in the Context of the Follow-up to the Action Plan for the Single Market," Communication from the Commission to the Council and the European Parliament, COM (99) 299 final, 16 June.

—————— (2001a), "European Governance: A White Paper," COM (2001) 428 final, 25 July.

—————— (2001b), "Recommendations for the Improvement of the Application of Community Law by the Member States and Its Enforcement by the Commission," Commission Staff Working Paper, Brussels. Available at http://europa .eu.int/comm/governance/white_paper/recommendations_en.pdf.

—————— (2002), "Better Monitoring of the Application of Community Law," COM (2002) 725 final/4 16 May.

—————— (2003), "Twentieth Annual Report on Monitoring the Application of Community Law," COM (2003) 669 final, 21 November.

—————— (2004a), "Twenty-first Annual Report on Monitoring the Application of Community Law," COM (2004) 839 final, Brussels, 30 December.

—————— (2004b), "Proposition de directive modifiant la directive 2003/88/CE du Parlement européenne et du Conseil du 4 novembre 2003 concernant certains aspects de l'amenagement du temps de travail."

—————— (2004c), "Report on the Implementation of the Community Notice on the Application of the State Aid Rules to Measures Relating to Direct Business Taxation," COM (2004) 434, 9 February.

—————— (2005a), "Communication from the Commission on the Social Agenda," COM (2005) 33 final, 9 February.

—————— (2005b), "Twenty-second Annual Report on Monitoring the Application of Community Law (2004)," COM (2005) 570 final, 23 December.

—————— (2006a), "Green Paper on the Role of Civil Society in Drugs Policy in the European Union," COM (2006) 316 final, 26 June.

—————— (2006b), "Twenty-third Annual Report on Monitoring the Application of Community Law (2005)," COM (2006) 416 final.

—————— (2007a), "White Paper on Sport," COM 391. Available at http://ec.europa .eu/sport/whitepaper/wp_on_sport_en.pef.

—————— (2007b), "The EU and Sport: Background and Context," SEC 935. Available at http://ec.europa.eu/sport/whitepaper/dts935_en.pdf.

—————— (2007c), "Action Plan 'Pierre de Coubertin,'" SEC 934. Available at http://ec .europa.eu/sport/whitepaper/sec934_en.pdf.

Committee for the Study of Economic and Monetary Union (1989), *Report on Economic and Monetary Union in the European Community* (Delors Report) (Luxembourg: Office for Official Publications of the European Communities).

Corbett, Anne (2005), *Universities and the Europe of Knowledge: Ideas, Institutions and Policy Entrepreneurship in European Union Higher Education Policy, 1955–2005* (Basingstoke: Palgrave).

Council of Europe (1981), *Convention for the Protection of Individuals with Regard to Automatic Processing of Personal Data* (Strasbourg: Council of Europe).

Council of the European Union and the Parliament (1995), "The Directive on the Protection of Individuals with Regard to the Processing of Personal Data and on the Free Movement of Such Data," *Official Journal of the European Community* (L 281), 31.

Cowles, Maria Green (1995), "Setting the Agenda for a New Europe: The ERT and EC 1992," *Journal of Common Market Studies*, 33, no. 4, 501–526.

Cowles, Maria, James Caporaso, and Thomas Risse (eds.) (2001), *Transforming Europe: Europeanization and Domestic Change* (Ithaca, NY: Cornell University Press).

Cram, Laura (1993), "Calling the Tune Without Paying the Piper: Social Policy Regulation: The Role of the Commission in European Union Social Policy," *Policy and Politics*, 21, 135–146.

——— (1994), "The European Commission as a Multi-Organization: Social Policy and IT Policy in the European Union," *Journal of European Public Policy*, 1, no. 2, 195–217.

——— (1997), *Policy-Making in the European Union: Conceptual Lenses and European Integration* (London: Routledge).

——— (2001), "Governance 'to Go': Domestic Actors, Institutions and the Boundaries of the Possible," *Journal of Common Market Studies*, 39, no. 4, 595–618.

Crespo Pérez, Juan de Dios (1998), "Análisis de los ultimos conflictos juridicos en la era post-Bosman del fútbol profesional," *Revista General de Derecho*, 642, March. Available at http://www.iusport.es/opinion/crespo97.htm.

Crochet, Michel (2004), "Le processus de Bologne: L'aboutissement d'un long cheminement," *Etudes: Revue de Culture Contemporaine*, 401, 461–472.

Croci, Osvaldo, and John Forster (2005), "Sport e politica: La questione della legittimità delle organizzazioni sportive internazionali," in Paolo Dell'Aquila and Paolo Zurla (eds.), *Sport e Società: Contributi multidisciplinary* (Cesena: Il Ponte Vecchio), 85–102.

Crozier, David (2007), "Universities Shaping the European Higher Education Area," Trends V Report, European Universities Association.

Cutler, Claire (2003), *Private Power and Global Authority* (Cambridge: Cambridge University Press).

Cutler, Claire, Virginia Haufler, and Tony Porter (1999), *Private Authority and International Affairs* (Albany: SUNY Press).

Dahl, Robert A. (1994), "A Democratic Dilemma: System Effectiveness Versus Citizen Participation," *Political Science Quarterly*, 109, 23–34.

"Data Protection Essential to EC 1992" (1990), *Transnational Data and Communications Report*, May, 5–10.

David, Paul A. (1985), "Clio and the Economics of QWERTY," *American Economic Review*, 75, no. 2, 332–337.

Davies, John L. (n.d.), "The Dialogue of Universities with Their Stakeholders: Comparisons Between Different Regions of Europe," a project of CRE, the European Commission, and the European Round Table.

De Búrca, Gráinne (2003), "The Constitutional Challenge of New Governance in the European Union," *European Law Review*, 28, 814.

Deganis, Isabelle (2006), "The Politics Behind Consensus: Tracing the Role of the Commission Within the European Employment Strategy," *Journal of Contemporary European Research*, 2, no. 1, 21–40.

De Grauwe, Paul (1991), "Is the European Monetary System a DM-Zone?" in Alfred Steinherr and Daniel Weiserbs (eds.), *Evolution of the International and Regional Monetary Systems* (London: Macmillan), 207–227.

Dehousse, Renaud (1997), "Regulation by Networks in the European Community: The Role of European Agencies," *Journal of European Public Policy*, 4, 246–261.

——— (2002), "Misfits: EU Law and the Transformation of European Governance," Jean Monnet Paper 02/02, Jean Monnet Center, New York University School of Law.

De la Porte, Caroline, and Patricia Nanz (2004), "The OMC—A Deliberative-democratic Mode of Governance? The Case of Employment and Pensions," *Journal of European Public Policy,* 11, no. 2, 267–288.

De la Porte, Caroline, and Philippe Pochet (eds.) (2002), *Building Social Europe Through the Open Method of Co-ordination* (Brussels: PIE-Peter Lang).

De La Rochefoucauld, Estelle (n.d.), "Collection of Sports-related Case-law," prepared for the Sport and Law Commission of the IOL. Available at http://multi media.olympic.org/pdf/en_report_264.pdf.

Demaret, Paul (1996), "Quelques observations sur la signification de l'arrêt Bosman," *Revue du Marché Unique Européen,* 1, 11–15.

"Democracy, Governance and European NGOs: Building a Stronger Structured Social Dialogue" (2001), Platform of European Social NGOs, March.

Den Boer, Monica (1999), "An Area of Freedom, Security and Justice: Bogged Down by Compromise," in David O'Keeffe and Patrick Twomey (eds.), *Legal Issues of the Amsterdam Treaty* (Oxford: Oxford University Press), 493–519.

—— (2005), "Cobweb Europe—Venues, Virtues and Vexations of Transnational Policing," in Wolfram Kaiser and Peter Starie (eds.), *Transnational Europe— Towards a Common Political Space* (London: Routledge).

De Wit, Kurt (2003), "The Consequences of European Integration for Higher Education," *Higher Education Policy,* 16, 161–178.

Dezalay, Yves, and Bryan Garth (1996), *Dealing in Virtue: International Commercial Arbitration and the Construction of a Transnational Legal Order* (Chicago: University of Chicago Press).

Diedrichs, Uwe, and Wolfgang Wessels (2003), "Will Widening Paralyze the EU?" *Internationale Politik* (Atlantic edition), 4, no. 2, 37–42.

Dierx, Adriaan, and Fabienne Ilzkovitz (2007), "Making the Most of the EU Internal Market in a Changing Economic Environment." Paper presented at EUSA Biennial Conference, Toronto, May.

Dolmans, Maurits, and Jacob Grierson (2003), "Arbitration and the Modernization of EC Antitrust Law: New Opportunities and New Responsibilities," *ICC International Court of Arbitration Bulletin,* 14, no. 2, 37–51.

Drolet, Jean-Christian (2006), "Extra Time: Are the New FIFA Transfer Rules Doomed?" *International Sports Law Journal,* 5, no. 1–2, 66–73.

Dubey, Jean-Philippe (2002), *La libre circulation des sportifs en Europe* (Berne: Staempfli).

Duina, Francesco G., and Frank Blithe (1999), "Nation-States and Common Markets: The Institutional Conditions for Acceptance," *Review of International Political Economy,* 6, no. 4, 494–530.

Dupont, Jean-Louis (1996), "Le droit communautaire et la situation du sportif professionnel avant l'arrêt Bosman," *Revue du Marché Unique Européen,* 1, 65–77.

Dyson, Kenneth (ed.) (2002), *European States and the Euro* (Oxford: Oxford University Press).

Dyson, Kenneth, and Kevin Featherstone (1999), *The Road to Maastricht: Negotiating Economic and Monetary Union* (Oxford: Oxford University Press).

Easton, David (1965), *A Framework for Political Analysis* (Englewood Cliffs, NJ: Prentice Hall/Harvester Wheatsheaf).

Eberlein, Burkard (2001), "To Regulate or Not to Regulate: Explaining the German Sonderweg of Electricity Regulation," *Journal of Network Industries,* 2, no. 3, 1–32.

—— (2003), "Formal and Informal Cooperation in Single Market Regulation," in Thomas Christiansen and Simona Piattoni (eds.), *Informal Governance in the European Union: An Introduction* (Cheltenham: Edgar Elgar), 150–172.

—— (2005), "Regulation by Cooperation: The 'Third Way' in Making Rules for the Internal Energy Market," in Peter D. Cameron (ed.), *Legal Aspects of EU Energy Regulation* (Oxford: Oxford University Press), 59–88.

—— (2008), "The Making of the European Energy Market: The Interplay of Governance and Government," in "The Shadow of Hierarchy and New Modes of Governance: Sectoral Governance and Democratic Government," special issue, *Journal of Public Policy*, 28, no. 1, 73–92.

Eberlein, Burkard, and Edgar Grande (2003), "Die Europäische Union als Regulierungsstaat: Transnationale Regulierungsnetzwerke und die Informalisierung des Regierens in Europa," in Markus Jachtenfuchs and Beate Kohler-Koch (eds.), *Europäische Integration*, 2nd ed. (Opladen: Leske und Budrich), 417–447.

—— (2005), "Beyond Delegation: Transnational Regulatory Regimes and the EU Regulatory State," *Journal of European Public Policy*, 12, no. 1, 89–112.

Eberlein, Burkard, and Dieter Kerwer (2004), "New Governance in the European Union: A Theoretical Perspective," *Journal of Common Market Studies*, 42, no. 1, 121–142.

Eberlein, Burkard, and Abraham Newman (2008), "Escaping the International Governance Dilemma? Incorporated Transgovernmental Networks in the European Union," *Governance*, 21, no. 1, 25–52.

Economic and Social Committee (1999), "The Role and Contribution of Civil Society Organisations in the Building of Europe," Economic and Social Committee Opinion, *Official Journal of the European Communities* (C 329), 30–38.

EEB (2004), *Annual Report on the Activities of the European Environmental Bureau 2004* (Brussels: European Environmental Bureau).

—— (2005), *Annual Report on the Activities of the European Environmental Bureau 2005* (Brussels: European Environmental Bureau).

EEC (1963), "Report of the Fiscal and Financial Committee (Neumark Report)," Brussels, 1963, available in English in IBFD (ed.), *The EEC Reports on Tax Harmonization* (Amsterdam: International Bureau for Fiscal Documentation).

Egan, Michelle (1998), "Regulatory Strategies, Delegation and European Market Integration," *Journal of European Public Policy*, 5, no. 3, 485–506.

—— (2001), *Constructing a European Market: Standards, Regulation and Governance* (Oxford: Oxford University Press).

—— (forthcoming), "Political Economy," in Michelle Egan, Neill Nugent, and William Patterson (eds.), *Future of EU Studies* (Basingstoke: Palgrave Macmillan).

Ehlermann, Claus-Dieter (1987), "Ein Plädoyer für die dezentrale Kontrolle der Anwendung des Gemeinschaftsrechts durch die Mitgliedstaaten," in Francesco Capotorti (ed.), *Du droit international au droit de l'intégration: Liber Amicorum Pierre Pescatore* (Baden-Baden: Nomos), 205–226.

Ehlermann, Claus-Dieter, and Isabela Atanasiu (eds.) (2004), *European Competition Law Annual 2002: Constructing the EU Network of Competition Authorities* (Oxford: Hart Publishing).

Eising, Rainer (2000), *Liberalisierung und Europäisierung: Die regulative Reform der Elektrizitätsversorgung in Großbritannien, der Europäischen Gemeinschaft und der Bundesrepublik Deutschland* (Opladen: Leske and Budrich).

Eising, Rainer, and Nicolas Jabko (2001), "Moving Targets: National Interests and Electricity Liberalization in the European Union," *Comparative Political Studies*, 34, no. 7, 742–767.

Eising, Rainer, and Beate Kohler-Koch (1999), "Introduction: Network Governance in the European Union," in Beate Kohler-Koch and Rainer Eising (eds.), *The Transformation of Governance in the European Union* (London: Routledge), 3–13.

Eising, Rainer, and Andrea Lenschow (2007), "Governance in der Europäischen Union," in Arthur Benz et al. (eds.), *Handbuch Governance* (Wiesbaden: VS Verlag für Sozialwissenschaften), 325–338.

Eisner, Marc Allen, Jeff Worsham, and Evan J. Ringquist (2000), *Contemporary Regulatory Policy* (Boulder: Lynne Rienner).

Elgie, Robert (2006), "Why Do Governments Delegate Authority to Quasi-Autonomous Agencies? The Case of Independent Administrative Authorities in France," *Governance*, 19, no. 3, 207–227.

Endres, Alfred (2000), *Umweltökonomie* (Stuttgart: Kohlhammer).

Engsig Sørensen, Karsten (2006), "Abuse of Rights in Community Law: A Principle of Substance or Merely Rhetoric?" *Common Market Law Review*, 43, no. 2, 423–459.

Ennis, Darren (2007), "Top Sport Bodies Back EU Treaty and Claim Victory," Reuters, 20 October. Available at http://in.reuters.com/article/idINIndia30076220071020.

EUA (2005), "Building One Association for Europe's Universities: Report of the EUA President and Board 2001–2005," in "New Trends in German and European Higher Education," a compendium of materials by Deutscher Akademischer Austausch Dienst (DAAD) prepared for *Germany Today*.

European Commission (1984), *Zehn Jahre Umweltpolitik der Europäischen Gemeinschaft* (Brussels: Office for Official Publications).

—— (1995), *Report of the Independent Group of Experts on Legislative and Administrative Simplification* (Brussels: Commission of the European Union).

—— (1998a), "The Development and Prospects for Community Action in the Field of Sport," Directorate General X, Commission Staff Working Paper, 29 September. Available at http://ec.europa.eu/sport/action_sports/historique/docs/doc_evol_en.pdf.

—— (1998b), "The European Model of Sport," Consultation Document of Directorate General X. Available at http://www.sportin.Europe.com/SIU/HTML/PDFFiles/EuropeanModelofSport.pdf.

—— (2000a), "Upgrading the Investment Services Directive," COM (2000) 729 final, Brussels, 16 November.

—— (2000b), "Communication on Mutual Recognition of Final Decisions in Criminal Matters," COM (2000) 495 final, Brussels, 26 July.

—— (2000c), "Economic Reform: Report on the Functioning of Community Product and Capital Markets." Available at http://ec.europa.eu/internal_market/economic-reports/docs/cardiff99en.pdf.

—— (2001a), "Tax Policy in the European Union, Priorities for the Years Ahead," COM (2001) 260 final, Brussels, 23 May.

—— (2001b), "Towards an Internal Market Without Tax Obstacles: A Strategy for Providing Companies with a Consolidated Tax Base for Their EU-wide Activities," COM (2001) 582 final, Brussels, 23 October.

—— (2001c), "The Elimination of Tax Obstacles to the Cross-border Provision of Occupational Pensions," COM (2001) 214 final, Brussels, 19 April.

—— (2001d), "Communication on the Development of the Schengen Information System II," COM (2001) 720 final, Brussels, 18 December.

—— (2003), "Dividend Taxation of Individuals in the Internal Market," COM (2003) 810 final, Brussels, 19 December.

—— (2005a), "The Contribution of Taxation and Customs Policies to the Lisbon Strategy," COM (2005) 532 final, Brussels, 25 October.

—— (2005b), "From Berlin to Bergen: The Contribution of the European Commission to the Bologna Process," Directorate General Education and Culture.

—— (2005c), "Mobilising the Brainpower of Europe: Enabling Universities to Make Their Full Contribution to the Lisbon Strategy," COM (2005) 152.

——— (2006), *The History of European Cooperation in Education and Training: Europe in the Making—An Example.*

——— (2007), *From Bergen to London: The Contribution of the European Commission to the Bologna Process.*

——— (2008), "Refining the Present Coverage of Council Directive 2003/48/EC on Taxation of Income from Savings," SEC (2008) 559, 29 April.

European Commission and Council (2004), "Education and Training 2010: The Success of the Lisbon Strategy Hinges on Urgent Reforms," in "The Bologna Process: A Mid-term Review," special issue, *European Journal of Education,* 39 (September), no. 3, 261–377.

European Communities-Commission (1963), "The EEC Reports on Tax Harmonization (Neumark Report): The Report of the Fiscal and Financial Committee and the Reports of the Sub-groups A, B, and C." Unofficial translation by H. Thurston (Amsterdam: International Bureau of Fiscal Documentation).

European Convention (2002), "Session of the European Convention: List of Speakers," Secretariat, Brussels, CONV 126/02, 19 June.

European Council (2000), "Lisbon European Council, Presidency Conclusion" (23–24 March). Available at http://www.europarl.europa.eu/summits/lis1_de.htm.

——— (2002), "Council Framework Decision of 13 June 2002 on Combating Terrorism," (2002/475/JHA) of 22.6.2002, § 5.

European Parliament (2005), *Report on the Proposal for a Council Framework Decision on Certain Procedural Rights in Criminal Proceedings Throughout the European Union.* Rapporteur: Kathalijne Maria Buitenweg, A6-0064/2005, 1 March.

European Social Policy Forum (1998), "Summary Report," Brussels, 24–26 June.

European Union (1997), "Agenda 2000—Summary and Conclusions of the Opinions of Commission Concerning the Application for Membership to the European Union by the Candidate Countries," Doc/97/8, Strasbourg/Brussels, 15 July.

——— (2002), *Consolidated Version of the Treaty on European Union.* Available at http://www.dpt.gov.tr/abigm/abib/Antlasmalar/Consolidated%20Version%20of%20the%20EU%20Treaty%20(En).pdf.

Eurydice (European Unit) (2005), *Focus on the Structure of Higher Education in Europe 2004/05: National Trends in the Bologna Process* (Brussels: European Commission).

Everling, Ulrich (2000), "Richterliche Rechtsfortbildung in der Europäischen Gemeinschaft," *Juristenzeitung,* 55, no. 5, 217–227.

Everson, Michelle (1995), "Independent Agencies," *European Law Journal,* 1, 180–204.

——— (2002), "Adjudicating the Market," *European Law Journal,* 8, no. 1, 152–171.

——— (2005), "Good Governance and European Agencies: The Balance," in Damien Geradin, Rodolphe Munoz, and Nicolas Petit (eds.), *Regulation Through Agencies in the EU: A New Paradigm of European Governance* (Cheltenham: Edward Elgar), 138–161.

Falkner, Gerda (1998), *EU Social Policy in the 1990s: Towards a Corporatist Policy Community* (London: Routledge).

——— (2000), "EG-Sozialpolitik nach Verflechtungsfalle und Entscheidungslücke: Bewertungsmaßstäbe und Entwicklungstrends," *Politische Vierteljahresschrift,* 41, no. 2, 279–301.

——— (2004), "Kontinuität und/oder Wandel? Zahlen und Fakten zur EU-Sozialpolitik," IHS Working Paper, Political Science Series 100 (Vienna: Institute for Advanced Studies).

Falkner, Gerda, Miriam Hartlapp, Simone Leiber, and Oliver Treib (2004), "Opposition Through the Backdoor? The Case of National Non-Compliance with EU Directives," *West European Politics,* 27, no. 3, 452–473.

Falkner, Gerda, Oliver Treib, Miriam Hartlapp, and Simone Leiber (2005), *Complying with Europe: EU Harmonisation and Soft Law in the Member States* (Cambridge: Cambridge University Press).

Faludi, Andreas, and Bas Waterhout (2002), *The Making of the European Spatial Development Perspective: No Masterplan!* (London: Routledge).

Farmer, Paul, and Richard Lyal (1994), *EC Tax Law* (Oxford: Clarendon).

Farrell, Henry (2003), "Constructing the International Foundations of E-commerce: The EU-US Safe Harbor Arrangement," *International Organization,* 57, no. 2, 277–306.

FEANTSA (1993), *Annual Report: Homeless in the Single Market* (Brussels: FEANTSA).

Featherstone, Kevin, and Claudio Radaelli (eds.) (2003), *The Politics of Europeanization* (Oxford: Oxford University Press).

Fierke, Karin, and Antje Wiener (1999), "Constructing Institutional Interests: EU and NATO Enlargement," *Journal of European Public Policy,* 6, no. 5, 721–742.

Flaherty, David (1989), *Protecting Privacy in Surveillance Societies* (Chapel Hill: University of North Carolina Press).

Flockhart, Trine (1996), "The Dynamics of Expansion: NATO, WEU, EU," *Security Studies,* 5, no. 2, 196–218.

Franklin, Michael (1990), *Britain's Future in Europe* (London: Pinter for the RIIA).

Frey, Bruno S. (1972), *Umweltökonomie* (Göttingen: Vandenhoeck and Ruprecht).

Friis, Lykke (1998), "And Then They Were 15: The EU's EFTA-Enlargement Negotiations," *Cooperation and Conflict,* 33, no. 1, 81–107.

—— (2003), "EU Enlargement—And Then There Were 28?" in Elizabeth Bomberg and Alexander Stubb (eds.), *The European Union: How Does It Work?* (Oxford: Oxford University Press), 177–194.

Friis, Lykke, and Anna Jarosz-Friis (2002), *Countdown to Copenhagen: Big Bang or Fizzle in the EU's Enlargement Process?* (Copenhagen: Danish Institute of International Affairs).

Frohlich, Norman, Joe A. Oppenheimer, and Oran R. Young (1971), *Political Leadership and Collective Goods* (Princeton, NJ: Princeton University Press).

Gammie, Malcolm (2003), "The Role of the ECJ in the Development of Direct Taxation in the European Union," *Bulletin for International Fiscal Documentation,* 57, no. 3.

Garrett, Geoffrey (1998), *Partisan Politics in the Global Economy* (Cambridge: Cambridge University Press).

Garrett, Geoffrey, and Barry A. Weingast (1991), "Ideas, Interests, and Institutions: Constructing the European Community's Internal Market," in Judith Goldstein and Robert O. Keohane (eds.), *Ideas and Foreign Policy: Beliefs, Institutions, and Political Change* (Ithaca, NY: Cornell University Press), 173–206.

Genschel, Philipp, and Thomas Pluemper (1997), "Regulatory Competition and International Co-operation," *Journal of European Public Policy,* 4, no. 4, 626–642.

George, Alexander, and Andrew Bennett (2005), *Case Studies and Theory Development in the Social Sciences* (Boston: MIT Press).

George, Stephen (1990), *An Awkward Partner: Britain in the European Community* (Oxford: Oxford University Press).

Geradin, Damien (2005), "The Development of European Regulatory Agencies: Lessons from the American Experience," in Damien Geradin, Rodolphe Munoz, and Nicolas Petit (eds.), *Regulation Through Agencies in the EU: A New Paradigm of European Governance* (Cheltenham: Edward Elgar), 214–244.

Geradin, Damien, Rodolphe Munoz, and Nicolas Petit (eds.) (2005), *Regulation Through Agencies in the EU: A New Paradigm of European Governance* (Cheltenham: Edward Elgar).

Gilardi, Fabrizio (2002), "Policy Credibility and Delegation to Independent Regulatory Agencies," *Journal of European Public Policy,* 9, no. 6, 873–893.

—— (2005), "The Institutional Foundations of Regulatory Capitalism: The Diffusion of Independent Regulatory Agencies in Western Europe," *Annals of the American Academy of Political and Social Science,* 598, 84–101.

Gordon, Roger H. (1992), "Can Capital Income Taxes Survive in Open Economies?" *Journal of Finance,* 47, no. 3, 1159–1180.

Goyder, D. G. (2003), *EC Competition Law,* 4th ed. (Oxford: Oxford University Press).

Grabbe, Heather (2003), "Europeanization Goes East: Power and Uncertainty in the European Accession Process," in Kevin Featherstone and Claudio Radaelli (eds.), *The Politics of Europeanization* (Oxford: Oxford University Press), 303–327.

Grande, Edgar (1993), "Entlastung des Staates durch Liberalisierung? Zum Funktionswandel des Staates im Telekommunikationssektor," in Rüdiger Voigt (ed.), *Abschied vom Staat—Rückkehr zum Staat?* (Baden-Baden: Nomos), 373–394.

—— (1994), "The New Role of the State in Telecommunications," *West European Politics,* 17, no. 3, 138–157.

—— (1997), "Vom produzierenden zum regulierenden Staat: Möglichkeiten und Grenzen von Regulierung bei Privatisierung," in Klaus König and Angelika Benz (eds.), *Privatisierung und staatliche Regulierung* (Baden-Baden: Nomos), 576–591.

—— (2000), "Multi-Level-Governance: Institutionelle Besonderheiten und Funktionsbedingungen des europäischen Mehrebenensystems," in Edgar Grande and Markus Jachtenfuchs (eds.), *Wie problemlösungsfähig ist die EU? Regieren im Europäischen Mehrebenensystem* (Baden-Baden: Nomos), 11–32.

—— (2006a), "Cosmopolitan Political Science," *British Journal of Sociology,* 57, no. 1, 87–111.

—— (2006b), "Entscheidet Europa alles Wesentliche? Der Regulierungsstaat im europäischen Mehrebenensystem," in Hermann Hill (ed.), *Die Zukunft des öffentlichen Sektors* (Baden-Baden: Nomos), 81–90.

Grande, Edgar, and Burkard Eberlein (1999),"Der Aufstieg des Regulierungsstaates im Infrastrukturbereich: Zur Transformation der politischen Ökonomie der Bundesrepublik Deutschland," in Roland Czada and Helmut Wollmann (eds.), *Von der Bonner zur Berliner Republik—10 Jahre deutsche Einheit* (Wiesbaden: Westdeutscher Verlag), 631–650.

Grande, Edgar, and Markus Jachtenfuchs (eds.) (2000), *Wie problemlösungsfähig ist die EU? Regieren im Europäischen Mehrebenensystem* (Baden-Baden: Nomos).

Grande, Edgar, and Louis W. Pauly (eds.) (2005), *Complex Sovereignty: Reconstituting Political Authority in the Twenty-first Century* (Toronto: University of Toronto Press).

Granell, Francisco (1995), "The European Union's Enlargement Negotiations with Austria, Finland, Norway and Sweden," *Journal of Common Market Studies,* 33, no. 1, 117–141.

Gray, Virginia (1973), "Innovation in the States: A Diffusion Study," *American Political Science Review,* 67, 1174–1185.

Green Cowles, Maria, James Caporaso, and Thomas Risse (eds.) (2001), *Transforming Europe: Europeanization and Domestic Change* (Ithaca, NY: Cornell University Press).

Grimwade, Nigel (2005), "Developments in the Economies of the 'Fifteen,'" *Journal of Common Market Studies,* 43, Annual Review, 181–199.

Gusy, Christoph (ed.) (1998), *Privatisierung von Staatsaufgaben: Kriterien—Grenzen—Folgen* (Baden-Baden: Nomos).

Haas, Peter M. (1992), "Introduction: Epistemic Communities and International Policy Coordination," *International Organization,* 46, no. 1, 1–35.

Häge, Frank, and Volker Schneider (2004), "Hauptachsen staatlicher Redimensionierung: Die Rolle von Europäisierung und Globalisierung," in Volker Schneider and Marc Tenbücken (eds.), *Der Staat auf dem Rückzug: Die Privatisierung öffentlicher Infrastrukturen* (Frankfurt: Campus), 275–313.

Haigh, N. (2005), *Manual of Environmental Policy: The EU and Britain.* Institute for European Environmental Policy (Leeds: Maney).

Haigh, Nigel (ed.) (2000), *The Manual of Environmental Policy: The EC and Britain* (London: Catermill Publishing).

Hall, Rodney Bruce, and Thomas J. Biersteker (eds.) (2002), *The Emergence of Private Authority in Global Governance* (Cambridge: Cambridge University Press).

Hallerberg, Mark (1996), "Tax Competition in Wilhelmine Germany and Its Implications for the European Union," *World Politics,* 48, no. 3, 324–357.

Hancher, Leigh, and Michael Moran (1989), *Capitalism, Culture and Economic Regulation* (Oxford: Clarendon Press).

Hantrais, Linda (1995), *Social Policy in the European Union* (London: Macmillan).

Hardin, Russell (1995), *One for All: The Logic of Group Conflict* (Princeton, NJ: Princeton University Press), chap. 2.

Hartenberger, Ute (2007), "Auf dem Weg zum transnationalen Regulierungsregime? Eine Analyse am Beispiel des Telekommunikationssektors," Universität Bremen, TranState Arbeitspapiere Nr. 52/2007.

Hartenberger, Ute, and Olivia van Riesen (2003), "Zur Problemlösungsfähigkeit von Regulierungsregimen in Deutschland: Wettbewerbsregulierung im Eisenbahn- und Telekommunikationssektor," in Edgar Grande and Rainer Prätorius (eds.), *Politische Steuerung und neue Staatlichkeit* (Baden-Baden: Nomos), 189–208.

Hartlapp, Miriam (2005), *Die Kontrolle der nationalen Rechtsdurchsetzung durch die Europäische Kommission* (Frankfurt: Campus).

——— (2006), "Über Politiklernen lernen: Überlegungen zur Europäischen Beschäftigungsstrategie," WZB discussion paper, Berlin, Wissenschaftszentrum Berlin für Sozialforschung. Available at http://www.wzberlin.de/ars/ab.

Hartlapp, Miriam, and Simone Leiber (2006), "Europeanization of Policy and Politics: Changing the Social Dimension in Southern Europe?" conference paper, 15th International Conference of the Council for European Studies, Chicago, 29 March–2 April.

Harvey, Brian (1992), *Networking in Europe* (London: National Council for Voluntary Organizations and Community Development Foundation).

Hatzopoulos, Vassilis, and Thien Uyen Do (2006), "The Case Law of the ECJ Concerning the Free Provision of Services," *Common Market Law Review,* 43, 923–991

Haverland, Markus (2000), "National Adaptation to European Integration: The Importance of Institutional Veto Points," *Journal of Public Policy,* 20, no. 1, 83–103.

Hedström, Peter, and Richard Swedberg (eds.) (1998), *Social Mechanisms: An Analytical Approach to Social Theory* (Cambridge: Cambridge University Press).

Heipertz, Martin, and Amy Verdun (2004), "The Dog That Would Never Bite? On the Origins of the Stability and Growth Pact," *Journal of European Public Policy*, 11, no. 5, 773–788.

———— (2005), "The Stability and Growth Pact— Theorizing a Case in European Integration," *Journal of Common Market Studies*, 43, no. 5, 985–1008.

Heisenberg, Dorothee (2005), *Negotiating Privacy: The European Union, the United States, and Personal Data Protection* (Boulder: Lynne Rienner).

Héritier, Adrienne (1999), *Policy-Making and Diversity in Europe: Escape from Deadlock* (Cambridge: Cambridge University Press).

———— (2002a), "New Modes of Governance in Europe: Policy-Making Without Legislating?" in Adrienne Héritier (ed.), *Common Goods: Reinventing European and International Governance* (Lanham, MD: Rowman and Littlefield), 185–206.

———— (2002b), "Public Interest Services Revisited," *Journal of European Public Policy*, 9, no. 6, 995–1019.

———— (2003), "New Modes of Governance in Europe: Increasing Political Capacity and Policy Effectiveness," in Tanja A. Börzel and Rachel Cichowski (eds.), *The State of the European Union, 6—Law, Politics, and Society* (Oxford: Oxford University Press), 105–126.

Héritier, Adrienne, Christoph Knill, and Susanne Mingers (1996), *Ringing the Changes in Europe: Regulatory Competition and the Transformation of the State* (Berlin: de Gruyter).

Héritier, Adrienne, and Dirk Lehmkuhl (2008), "The Shadow of Hierarchy: Sectoral Governance and Democratic Government," in "The Shadow of Hierarchy and New Modes of Governance: Sectoral Governance and Democratic Government," special issue, *Journal of Public Policy*, 28, no. 1, 1–17.

Hix, Simon (1998), "The Study of the European Union II: The 'New Governance' Agenda and Its Rivals," *Journal of European Public Policy*, 5, no. 1, 38–65.

———— (2005), *The Political System of the European Union*, 2nd ed. (New York: Palgrave Macmillan).

Hodson, Dermot, and Imelda Maher (2001), "The Open Method as a New Mode of Governance: The Case of Soft Economic Policy Coordination," *Journal of Common Market Studies*, 39, no. 4, 719–746.

Hoffmann, Herwig C.H. (2006), "Negotiated and Non-negotiated Administrative Rule-making: The Example of EC Competition Policy," *Common Market Law Review*, 43, no. 1, 153–178.

Holloway, John (1981), *Social Policy Harmonization in the European Community* (Farnborough: Gower).

Holzinger, Katharina (1987), *Umweltpolitische Instrumente aus der Sicht der staatlichen Bürokratie*, Ifo-Studien zur Umweltökonomie 6 (Munich: Ifo-Institut für Wirtschaftsforschung).

———— (2002), "The Provision of Transnational Common Goods: Regulatory Competition for Environmental Standards," in Adrienne Héritier (ed.), *Common Goods: Reinventing European and International Governance* (Lanham, MD: Rowman and Littlefield), 57–79.

Hondius, Fritz (1975), *Emerging Data Protection in Europe* (New York: Elsevier).

Hooghe, Liesbet (2001), *The European Commission and the Integration of Europe: Images of Governance* (Cambridge: Cambridge University Press).

———— (2004), "Globalization and the European Union: Shared Governance on a Global Scale," in Harvey Lazar and Hamish Telford (eds.), *The Impact of Globalization on Federal Systems* (Montreal: McGill University/Queen's University Press), 283–327.

Hooghe, Liesbet, and Gary Marks (1997), "The Making of a Polity: The Struggle over European Integration," EIOP European Integration Online Papers, 1, no. 4. Available at http://eiop.or.at/eiop/texte/1997-004a.htmc.

———— (2001), *Multi-level Governance and European Integration* (Lanham, MD: Rowman and Littlefield).

———— (2003), "Unravelling the Central State, but How? Types of Multi-level Governance," *American Political Science Review*, 97, 233–243.

House of Lords (2005), "The Hague Programme: A Five Year Agenda for EU Justice and Home Affairs, Tenth Report of the House of Lords' Select Committee on the European Union, London, 23 March. Available at http://www.parliament .the-stationery-office.co.uk/pa/ld200405/ldselect/ldeucom/84/8402.htm.

Howarth, David J., and Peter H. Loedel (2003), *The European Central Bank: The New European Leviathan* (Baskingstoke: Palgrave).

Huber, John D., and Charles R. Shapin (2002), *Deliberate Discretion? The Institutional Foundation of Bureaucratic Autonomy* (Cambridge: Cambridge University Press).

Huisman, Jeroen, and Marijk van der Wendt (2004), "The EU and Bologna: Are Supra- and International Initiatives Threatening Domestic Agendas?" *European Journal of Education*, 39, no. 3, 349–357.

Husting, Alexandre (2001), "L'Union européenne, un cadre réglementaire pour l'activité sportive," in Jean-Michel De Waele and Alexandre Husting (eds.), *Sport et Union Européenne* (Brussels: Éditions de l'Université de Bruxelles).

Idema, Timo, and Daniel R. Kelemen (2006), "New Modes of Governance, the Open Method of Coordination and Other Fashionable Red Herring," *Perspectives on European Politics and Society*, 7, no. 1, 108–123.

Ifo-Institute for Economic Research (1989), *The Polluter Pays Principle and Environmental Impacts* (Munich: Ifo-Institut für Wirtschaftsforschung).

Infantino, Gianni (2006), "Meca-Medina: A Step Backwards for the European Sports Model and the Specificity of Sport?" UEFA Inf. 02.10.16. Available at http://www.uefa.com/MultimediaFiles/Download/uefa/KeyTopics/480391_ Download.pdf.

Jabko, Nicolas (2005), "The Reform of Energy Regulation in the EU: The Market as a Norm," paper prepared for delivery at the ECPR Conference, Budapest, 8–10 September. Available at http://regulation.upf.edu/ecpr-05-papers/njabko.pdf.

Jachtenfuchs, Markus (2001), "Theorizing European Integration and Governance: The Governance Approach to European Integration," *Journal of Common Market Studies*, 39, no. 2, 245–264.

Jachtenfuchs, Markus, Jörg Friedrichs, Eva Herschinger, and Christiane Kraft-Kasack (2006), "Policing Among Nations: Internationalizing the Monopoly of Force," paper presented at the UACES Annual Convention, Limerick, 31 August–2 September.

Jachtenfuchs, Markus, and Beate Kohler-Koch (eds.) (1996), *Europäische Integration* (Opladen: Leske and Budrich).

Jansen, Dorothea (2006), *Einführung in die Netzwerkanalyse: Grundlagen, Methoden, Forschungsbeispiele*, 3rd ed. (Wiesbaden: VS Verlag für Sozialwissenschaften).

Jarre, Dirk (2005), "The Third Sector and the European Multi-Level Process," presentation to TEPS workshop, Berlin, 1–2 April.

Jessop, Bob (2003a), *The Future of the Capitalist State* (Cambridge: Polity Press).

———— (2003b), "Governance and Meta-governance: On Reflexivity, Requisite Variety, and Irony," in Henrik P. Bang (ed.), *Governance, Governmentality and Democracy* (Manchester: Manchester University Press), 142–172.

Joerges, Christian (2004a), "What Is Left of the European Economic Constitution?" EUI Law Papers 2004/13. Available at http://hdl.handle.net/1814/2828.

——— (2004b), "The Challenges of Europeanization in the Realm of Private Law: A Plea for a New Legal Discipline," EUI Working Paper 2004/12. Available at http://www.iue.it/PUB/law04-12.pdf.

Joerges, Christian, and Christine Godt (2005), "Free Trade: The Erosion of National, and the Birth of Transnational, Governance," *European Review*, 13, no. 1, 93–117.

Joerges, Christian, and Jürgen Neyer (1997), "Transforming Strategic Interaction into Deliberative Problem-solving: European Comitology in the Foodstuffs Sector," *Journal of European Public Policy*, 4, no. 4, 609–625.

Joerges, Christian, Inger-Johanne Sand, and Gunther Teubner (eds.) (2004), *Transnational Governance and Constitutionalism* (Oxford: Hart Publishing).

Johnson, Stanley P., and Guy Corcelle (1989), *The Environmental Policy of the European Communities* (London: Graham and Trotman).

Jordan, Andrew (1999), "The Implementation of EU Environmental Policy: A Problem Without a Political Solution?" *Environment and Planning C: Government and Policy*, 17, no. 1, 69–90.

Jordan, Andrew, Rüdiger Wurzel, and Anthony Zito (eds.) (2003), *"New" Instruments of Environmental Governance? National Experiences and Prospects* (London: Routledge).

Jordana, Jacint, and David Levi-Faur (eds.) (2004), *The Politics of Regulation: Institutions and Regulatory Reforms for the Age of Governance* (Cheltenham: Edward Elgar).

Jordana, Jacint, David Levi-Faur, and Imma Puig (2006), "The Limits of Europeanization: Regulatory Reforms in the Spanish and Portuguese Telecommunications and Electricity Sectors," *Governance*, 19, no. 3, 437–464.

Kahler, Miles (2004), "Global Governance Redefined," paper presented at the Conference on Globalization, the State, and Society, Washington University School of Law, St. Louis, 13–14 November 2003 (revised October 2004; available at http://law.wustl.edu/Centeris/Papers/globalization/KAHLERMilesFINALPAPER.pdf).

Kahler, Miles, and David A. Lake (eds.) (2003), *Governance in a Global Economy: Political Authority in Transition* (Princeton, NJ: Princeton University Press), 199–225.

Kappelhoff, Peter (2000), "Der Netzwerkansatz als konzeptueller Rahmen für eine Theorie interorganisationaler Netzwerke," in Jörg Sydow and Arnold Windeler (eds.), *Steuerung von Netzwerken: Konzepte und Praktiken* (Opladen: Westdeutscher Verlag), 25–57.

Keeling, Ruth (2006), "The Bologna Process and the Lisbon Research Agenda: The European Commission's Expanding Role in Higher Education Discourse," *European Journal of Education*, 41, no. 2, 203–223.

Kelemen, R. Daniel, and Eric Sibbitt (2004), "The Globalization of American Law," *International Organization*, 58, no. 1, 103–136.

Keohane, Robert O., and Joseph S. Nye Jr. (eds.) (1971), *Transnational Relations and World Politics* (Cambridge, MA: Harvard University Press).

——— (1974), "Transgovernmental Relations and International Organizations," *World Politics*, 27, 39–62.

Keohane, Robert O., and Stanley Hoffmann (1991), "Institutional Change in Europe in the 1980s," in Robert O. Keohane and Stanley Hoffmann (eds.), *The New European Community: Decisionmaking and Institutional Change* (Boulder: Westview), 1–39.

Kerber, Wolfgang, and Martina Eckardt (2005), "Policy Learning in Europe: The 'Open Method of Coordination' and Laboratory Federalism," Thünen Series of Applied Economic Theory Working Paper 48, Rostock, University of Rostock, Lehrstuhl für Volkswirtschaftslehre.

Kingdon, John (1984), *Agendas, Alternatives and Public Policies* (New York: Harper Collins).

Kitzinger, Uwe (1973), *Diplomacy and Persuasion: How Britain Joined the Common Market* (London: Thames and Hudson).

Kjaer, Anne Mette (2004), *Governance* (Cambridge: Polity Press).

Klemencic, Manja (2007), "Analysis of Policies and Policy-making Regarding the European Educational Agenda by ESIB, the National Union of Students in Europe, the Representative Platform of European Students," paper presented at the European Education Policy Network Conference, "Defining the European Education Agenda," Cambridge University, 11 January.

Knill, Christoph, and Andrea Lenschow (eds.) (2000), *Implementing EU Environmental Policy: New Directions and Old Problems* (Manchester: Manchester University Press).

——— (2004), "Modes of Regulation in the Governance of the European Union: Towards a Comprehensive Evaluation," in Jacint Jordana and David Levi-Faur (eds.), *The Politics of Regulation: Institutions and Regulatory Reforms for the Age of Governance* (Cheltenham: Edward Elgar), 218–244.

——— (2005), "Compliance, Competition and Communication: Different Approaches of European Governance and Their Impact on National Institutions," *Journal of Common Market Studies*, 43, no. 3, 583–606.

Kohler-Koch, Beate (1997), "Organized Interests in European Integration: The Evolution of a New Type of Governance?" in Helen Wallace and Alasdair Young (eds.), *Participation and Policy-Making in the European Union* (Oxford: Oxford University Press), 67–107.

——— (ed.) (1998), *Interaktive Politik in Europa: Regionen im Netzwerk der Integration* (Opladen: Leske and Budrich).

——— (1999), "The Evolution and Transformation of European Governance," in Beate Kohler-Koch and Rainer Eising (eds.), *The Transformation of Governance in the European Union* (London: Routledge), 14–35.

Kohler-Koch, Beate, and Rainer Eising (eds.) (1999), *The Transformation of Governance in the European Union* (London: Routledge).

Kohler-Koch, Beate, and Berthold Rittberger (2006), "The 'Governance Turn' in EU Studies," *Journal of Common Market Studies*, 44, annual review, 27–49.

Komninos, Assimakis P. (2001), "Arbitration and the Modernisation of European Competition Law Enforcement," *World Competition*, 24, no. 2, 211–238.

König, Klaus, and Angelika Benz (eds.) (1997), *Privatisierung und staatliche Regulierung: Bahn, Post und Telekommunikation, Rundfunk* (Baden-Baden: Nomos).

Kooiman, Jan (ed.) (1993), *Modern Governance: New Government-Society Interactions* (London: Sage).

——— (2003), *Governing as Governance* (London: Sage).

Krämer, Ludwig (1996), "Defizite im Vollzug des EG-Umweltrechts und ihre Ursachen," in Gertrude Lübbe-Wolff (ed.), *Der Vollzug des europäischen Umweltrechts* (Berlin: Erich Schmidt Verlag), 7–36.

Krasner, Steven (1991), "Global Communications and National Power: Life on the Pareto Frontier," *World Politics*, 43, no. 3, 336–366.

——— (1999), *Sovereignty: Organized Hypocrisy* (Princeton, NJ: Princeton University Press).

Kreher, Alexander (1997), "Agencies in the European Community: A Step Towards Administrative Integration in Europe," *Journal of European Public Policy*, 4, no. 2, 225–245.

Kruse, D. C. (1980), *Monetary Integration in Western Europe: EMU, EMS and Beyond* (London: Butterworths).

Kuijper, Pieter J. (2000), "Some Legal Problems Associated with the Communitarization of Policy on Visas, Asylum and Immigration Under the Amsterdam Treaty and Incorporation of the Schengen Acquis," *Common Market Law Review*, 37, 345–366.

Laffan, Brigid, and Colin Shaw (2005), "Classifying and Mapping OMC in Different Policy Areas," report prepared for NEWGOV New Modes of Governance, "Integrated Project Priority 7: Citizens and Governance in the Knowledge-based Society." Available at http://eucenter.wisc.edu/OMC/Papers/laffanShaw.pdf.

Lange, Stefan, and Uwe Schimank (2004), "Einführung," in Stefan Lange and Uwe Schimank (eds.), *Governance und gesellschaftliche Integration* (Wiesbaden: Verlag für Sozialwissenschaften), 9–44.

Laurent, Pierre-Henri, and Marc Maresceau (eds.) (1998), *The State of the European Union 4: Deepening and Widening* (Boulder: Lynne Rienner).

Lavenex, Sandra (2001), *The Europeanisation of Refugee Policies: Between Human Rights and Internal Security* (Aldershot: Ashgate).

—— (2004), "EU External Governance in Wider Europe," *Journal of European Public Policy*, 11, no. 4, 680–700.

—— (2006a), "Towards a Constitutionalization of Aliens' Rights in the European Union?" *Journal of European Public Policy*, 13, no. 8, 1284–1301.

—— (2006b), "Shifting Up and Out: The Foreign Policy of European Immigration Control," *West European Politics*, 29, no. 2, 329–350.

—— (2007), "Mutual Recognition and the Monopoly of Force: Limits of the Single Market Analogy," special issue, *Journal of European Public Policy*, 14, no. 5, 762–779.

Lavenex, Sandra, and Emek Uçarer (eds.) (2002), *Migration and the Externalities of European Integration* (Lanham, MD: Lexington Books).

—— (2004), "The External Dimension of Europeanisation," *Cooperation & Conflict*, 39, no. 4, 417–443.

Lax, David A., and James K. Sebenius (1986), *The Manager as Negotiator: Bargaining for Cooperative and Competitive Gain* (New York: Free Press).

Lehmkuhl, Dirk (2003), "Structuring Dispute Resolution in Transnational Trade: Competition and Co-evolution of Public and Private Institutions," in Marie-Laure Djelic and Sigrid Quack (eds.), *Globalisation and Institutions—Redefining the Rules of the Economic Game* (Cheltenham: Edward Elgar), 278–301.

—— (2007), *Overlapping Authorities in Transnational Governance: Four Case Studies in Dispute Resolution* (Zurich: Institute of Political Science at the University of Zurich).

Leibfried, Stephan, and Paul Pierson (eds.) (1995), *European Social Policy: Between Fragmentation and Integration* (Washington, DC: Brookings).

Lenschow, Andrea (1999), "Transformation in European Environmental Governance," in Beate Kohler-Koch and Rainer Eising (eds.), *The Transformation of Governance in the European Union* (London: Routledge), 39–60.

—— (ed.) (2002), *Environmental Policy Integration: Greening Sectoral Policies in Europe* (London: Earthscan).

—— (2007), "Political Instruments Designed for Learning: What Makes Them Effective?" Paper presented at the European Union Studies Association (EUSA) Biennial Conference, Montreal, 17–19 May.

Lenschow, Andrea, and Katja Rottmann (2005), "Privatizing EU Governance: Emergence and Characteristics of Voluntary Agreements in European Environmental Policy," paper presented at the Connex Workshop "Soft Modes of Governance and the Private Sector," Darmstadt, 2–3 November. Available at http://www.mzes.uni-mannheim.de/projekte/typo3/site/index.php?id=476.

"Le processus de Bologne a mi-parcours" (2004), *Politiques d'Education et de Formation,* special issue, 12, no. 3, 5–116.

Levi-Faur, David (1999), "The Governance of Competition: The Interplay of Technology, Economics, and Politics in European Union Electricity and Telecom Regimes," *Journal of Public Policy,* 19, 175–207.

―――― (2002), "On the 'Net Impact' of Europeanization: The EU's Telecoms and Electricity Regimes Between the Global and the National," *European Integration Online Papers,* 6, no. 7.

―――― (2005), "The Global Diffusion of Regulatory Capitalism," *The Annals of the American Academy of Political and Social Science,* 598, 12–32.

Levy, Brian, and Pablo T. Spiller (1996), *Regulations, Institutions, and Commitment: Comparative Studies of Telecommunications* (Cambridge: Cambridge University Press).

Lobjakas, Ahto (2006), "EU: Constitutional Impasse Threatens Enlargement," *RFE/RL Features,* June 15.

Lowe, Philip (2005), "Chairman's Closing Remarks," in *Anti-Trust Reform in Europe: A Year in Practice* (Brussels: International Bar Association/European Commission Conference).

Ludlow, Peter (1982), *The Making of the European Monetary System: A Case Study of the Politics of the European Community* (London: Butterworth).

Magnette, Paul (2005), "The Politics of Regulation in the EU," in Damien Geradin, Rodolphe Munoz, and Nicolas Petit (eds.), *Regulation Through Agencies in the EU: A New Paradigm of European Governance* (Cheltenham: Edward Elgar), 3–23.

Mahoney, Honor (2006), "German Government and Parliament Wrestle over Enlargement," *EU Observer,* 15 June.

Majone, Giandomenico (1984), "Science and Trans-science in Standard Setting," *Science, Technology and Human Values,* 9, 15–22.

―――― (1989), *Evidence, Argument and Persuasion in the Policy Process* (New Haven, CT: Yale University Press).

―――― (ed.) (1990), *Regulatory Reform in Europe and the United States* (London: Pinter).

―――― (1992), "Ideas, Interests and Policy Change," European University Institute Working Paper 92/21, Florence.

―――― (1993), "The European Community Between Social Policy and Social Regulation," *Journal of Common Market Studies,* 31, no. 2, 153–168.

―――― (1994a), "Mutual Recognition in Federal Type Systems," in Anne Mullins and Cheryl Saunders (eds.), *Economic Union in Federal Systems* (Sydney: Federation Press), 69–84.

―――― (1994b), "The Rise of the Regulatory State in Europe," in Wolfgang C. Müller and Vincent Wright (eds.), *The State in Western Europe: Retreat or Redefinition?* (Ilford: Frank Cass), 77–101.

―――― (1995), "Mutual Trust, Credible Commitments and the Evolution of Rules for a Single European Market," EUI Working paper. EUI RSC 1995/01.

―――― (1996), *Regulating Europe* (London: Routledge).

———— (1997a), "The New European Agencies: Regulation by Information," *Journal of European Public Policy,* 4, no. 2, 262–275.

———— (1997b), "The Agency Model: The Growth of Regulation and Regulatory Institutions in the European Union," *Archive of European Integration.* Available at http://aei.pitt.edu/786/01/scop97_3_2.pdf.

———— (1999), "The Regulatory State and Its Legitimacy," *West European Politics,* 22, 1–24.

———— (2000), "The Credibility Crisis of Community Regulation," *Journal of Common Market Studies,* 38, no. 2, 273–302.

———— (2002a), "Delegation of Regulatory Powers in a Mixed Polity," *European Law Journal,* 8, no. 3, 319–339.

———— (2002b), "The European Commission: The Limits of Centralization and the Perils of Parliamentarization," *Governance,* 15, no. 3, 375–392.

———— (2005), *Dilemmas of European Integration: The Ambiguities and Pitfalls of Integration by Stealth* (Oxford: Oxford University Press).

———— (2006), "The Common Sense of European Integration," *Journal of European Public Policy,* 13, no. 5, 607–626.

Maresceau, Marc (ed.) (1997), *Enlarging the European Union: Relations Between the European Union and Central and Eastern Europe* (London: Longman).

Marks, Gary (1993), "Structural Policy and Multilevel Governance in the European Community," in Alan Cafruny and Glenda G. Rosenthal (eds.), *The State of the European Community* (Boulder: Lynne Rienner), 491–511.

Marks, Gary, and Liesbet Hooghe (2001), *Multi-Level Governance and European Integration* (Lanham, MD: Rowman and Littlefield).

Marks, Gary, Liesbet Hooghe, and Kermit Blank (1996), "European Integration and the State: Multi-level Versus State-Centric Governance," *Journal of Common Market Studies,* 34, no. 3, 341–378.

Marks, Gary, Fritz W. Scharpf, Philippe C. Schmitter, and Wolfgang Streeck (1996), *Governance in the European Union* (London: Sage).

Matlary, Janne Haaland (1997), *Energy Policy in the European Union* (New York: St. Martin's Press).

Mattli, Walter (2001), "Private Justice in a Global Economy: From Litigation to Arbitration," *International Organization,* 55, no. 4, 919–948.

———— (2003), "Public and Private Governance in Setting International Standards," in Miles Kahler and David Lake (eds.), *Governance in a Global Economy: Political Authority in Transition* (Princeton, NJ: Princeton University Press).

Mattli, Walter, and Anne-Marie Slaughter (1998), "Revisiting the European Court of Justice," *International Organization,* 52, no. 1, 177–210.

Maurer, Andreas, Jürgen Mittag, and Wolfgang Wessels (2000), "Theoretical Perspectives on Administrative Interaction in the European Union," in Thomas Christiansen and Emil Kirchner (eds.), *Committee Governance in the European Union* (Manchester: Manchester University Press), 23–44.

Mayhew, Alan (1998), *Recreating Europe: The European Union's Policy Towards Central and Eastern Europe* (Cambridge: Cambridge University Press).

Mayntz, Renate (2002), "Common Goods and Governance," in Adrienne Héritier (ed.), *Common Goods: Reinventing European and International Governance* (Lanham, MD: Rowman and Littlefield), 15–27.

———— (2004), "Governance im modernen Staat," in Arthur Benz (ed.), *Governance—Regieren in komplexen Regelsystemen: Eine Einführung* (Wiesbaden: VS Verlag für Sozialwissenschaften), 65–76.

────── (2005), "Governance Theory als fortentwickelte Steuerungstheorie?" in Gunnar F. Schuppert (ed.), *Governance-Forschung: Vergewisserung über Stand und Entwicklungslinien* (Baden-Baden: Nomos), 11–20.

Mayntz, Renate, and Fritz W. Scharpf (1995), "Der Ansatz des akteurzentrierten Institutionalismus," in Renate Mayntz and Fritz W. Scharpf (eds.), *Gesellschaftliche Selbstregelung und politische Steuerung* (Frankfurt: Campus), 39–72.

Mazey, Sonia, and Jeremy Richardson (1993), "Policy Coordination in Brussels: Environmental and Regional Policy," EPPI Occasional Papers 93/5, Warwick University.

────── (1994), "EC Policy-Making: An Emerging European Policy Style?" EPPI Occasional Papers 94/2, Warwick University.

McAfee, Randolph P., Hugo M. Mialon, and Sue H. Mialon (2006), "Private v. Public Antitrust Enforcement: A Strategic Analysis," Emory Law and Economics Research Paper 05-20. Available at http://ssrn.com/abstract=775245.

McAuley, Darren (2002), "They Think It Is All Over . . . It Might Be Now: Unravelling the Ramifications for the European Football Transfer System," *European Competition Law Review,* 23, no. 7, 331–340.

McCubbins, Mathew D., Roger G. Noll, and Berry R. Weingast (1987), "Administrative Procedures as Instruments of Political Control," *Journal of Law, Economics, and Organization,* 3, no. 2, 243–277.

McCubbins, Mathew D., and Thomas Schwartz (1984), "Congressional Oversight Overlooked: Police Patrols Versus Fire Alarm," *American Journal of Political Science,* 28, no. 1, 165–197.

McGowan, Francis, and Helen Wallace (1996), "Towards a European Regulatory State," *Journal of European Public Policy,* 3, 560–576.

McGowan, Lee (2007), "Theorising European Integration: Revisiting Neofunctionalism and Testing Its Suitability for Explaining the Development of EC Competition Policy?" *European Integration Online Papers,* 11, no. 3. Available at http://eiop.or.at/eiop/texte/2007-003a.htm.

McGowan, Lee, and Michelle Cini (eds.) (1998), *Competition Policy in Europe* (Basingstoke: Macmillan).

────── (1999), "Discretion and Politicization in EU Competition Policy: The Case of Merger Control," *Governance,* 12, no. 2, 175–200.

McGowan, Lee, and Stephen Wilks (1995), "The First Supranational Policy in the European Union," *European Journal of Political Research,* 28, 141–169.

Metcalfe, Les (1996), "The European Commission as a Network Organization," *Publius: The Journal of Federalism,* 26, no. 4, 43–62.

────── (1999), "Reforming the Commission," *EIPASCOPE,* 3–9.

────── (2000), "Reforming the Commission: Will Organizational Efficiency Produce Effective Governance?" *Journal of Common Market Studies,* 38, no. 5, 817–841.

Miège, Colin (2001), "Le sport et la Cour de Justice des Communauté européennes," *Revue du Marché Commun et de l'Union Européenne,* 452, 631–636.

Miles, Lee, and John Redmond (1996), "Enlarging the EU: The Erosion of Federalism?" *Conflict and Cooperation,* 31, no. 3, 285–309.

Miller, Fiona, and Steve Redhead (1994), "Do Markets Make Footballers Free?" in John Bale and Joseph Maguire (eds.), *The Global Sports Arena: Athletic Talent Migration in an Interdependent World* (London: Frank Cass), 141–152.

Mitsilegas, Valsamis (2003), "The New EU-US Cooperation on Extradition, Mutual Legal Assistance and the Exchange of Police Data," *European Foreign Affairs Review,* 8, no. 4, 515–536.

Mitsilegas, Valsamis, Jörg Monar, and Wyn Rees (2003), *The European Union and Internal Security: Guardian of the People?* One Europe or Several Series (Houndmills: Palgrave).

Moe, Terry (2005), "Power and Political Institutions," *Perspectives on Politics,* 3, no. 2, 215–233.

Mol, Arthur P., Volkmar Lauber, and Duncan Liefferink (eds.) (2000), *The Voluntary Approach to Environmental Policy* (Oxford: Oxford University Press).

Monar, Jörg (2001), "The Dynamics of EU Justice and Home Affairs," *Journal of Common Market Studies,* 39, no. 4, 747–764.

Monti, Mario (2001), "Competition and Sport: The Rules of the Game," speech presented at the Conference on "Governance in Sport," Brussels, 26 February. Available at http://europa.eu/rapid/pressReleasesAction.do?reference=SPEECH/01/84&format=HTML&aged=0&language=EN&guiLanguage=en.

—— (2004a), "The EU Gets New Competition Powers for the 21st Century: Interview with Mario Monti, Commissioner Responsible for Competition," *Competition Policy Newsletter,* special edition, 1. Available at http://ec.europa.eu/comm/competition/publications/special/interview_monti.pdf.

—— (2004b), "Private Litigation as a Key Complement to Public Enforcement of Competition Rules and the First Conclusions on the Implementation of the New Merger Regulation," Speech at IBA—Eighth Annual Competition Conference, Fiesole, 17 September.

Moran, Michael (2002), "Review Article: Understanding the Regulatory State," *British Journal of Political Science,* 32, 391–413.

Moravcsik, Andrew (1998), *The Choice for Europe: Social Purpose and State Power from Messina to Maastricht* (Ithaca, NY: Cornell University Press).

Morgan, Caroline (2004), "The European Arrest Warrant and Defendants' Rights: An Overview," in Robert Blekxtoon (ed.), *Handbook on the European Arrest Warrant* (Cambridge: Cambridge University Press), 195–208.

Morgan, Eleanor J. (1998), "EU Merger Control Reforms: An Appraisal," *European Management Journal,* 16, no. 1, 110–120.

—— (2001), "A Decade of Merger Control," *International Journal of the Economics of Business,* 8, no. 3, 451–473.

Mosher, James (2000), "Open Method of Coordination: Functional and Political Origins," *ECSA Review,* 13, no. 3, 6–7.

Mosher, James, and David Trubek (2003), "Alternative Approaches to Governance in the EU: EU Social Policy and the European Employment Strategy," *Journal of Common Market Studies,* 41, no. 1, 63–88.

Müller, Wolfgang C., and Vincent Wright (eds.) (1994), *The State in Western Europe: Retreat or Redefinition?* (Ilford: Frank Cass).

Musselin, Christine (2004), *The Long March of French Universities* (London: Routledge).

Naeve, Guy (2003), "The Bologna Declaration: Some of the Historic Dilemmas Posed by the Reconstruction of the Community in Europe's Systems of Higher Education, *Educational Policy,* 17, no. 1, 141–164.

NEWGOV (2005), "The Scientific Objectives of the NEWGOV Project: A Revised Framework," first presented by Martin Rhodes at the NEWGOV Consortium Conference, 30–31 May, Version 3, EUI, Florence. Available at http://www.eu-newgov.org/database/PUBLIC/P11000-06-DESC06_Scientific_Objectives_revision_September_2005.pdf

Newman, Abraham L. (2008a), "Building Transnational Civil Liberties: Transgovernmental Entrepreneurs and the European Data Privacy Directive," *International Organization,* 62, no. 1, 103–130.

—————— (2008b), *Protectors of Privacy: Regulating Personal Data in the Global Economy* (Ithaca: Cornell University Press).

Nicolaïdis, Kalypso (1993), "Mutual Recognition Among Nations: The European Community and Trade in Services," PhD diss. (Cambridge, MA: Harvard University).

—————— (1996), "Mutual Recognition of Regulatory Regimes: Some Lessons and Prospects," in OECD (ed.), *Regulatory Reform and International Market Openness* (Paris: OECD), 171–203.

—————— (2005), "A World of Difference: Exploring the Dilemma of Mutual Recognition," mimeo.

Nicolaïdis, Kalypso A., and Susanne K. Schmidt (2007), "Mutual Recognition on Trial: The Long Road to Services Liberalization," *Journal of European Public Policy,* 14, no. 5, 717–734.

Nyssen, Laszlo, and Xavier Denoël (1996), "La situation des ressortissants de pays tiers à la suite de l'arrêt Bosman," *Revue du Marché Unique Européen,* 1, 119–133.

OECD (1980), *Guidelines on the Protection of Privacy and Transborder Flows of Personal Data* (Paris: OECD).

—————— (1981a), *An Assessment of the Implementation of the Polluter-Pays-Principle, Environment Committee, Group of Economic Experts* (Paris: OECD).

—————— (1981b), *The Implementation of the Polluter-Pays-Principle: A Review of Member Countries' Practices (A Summary of the Replies and the Replies from Member Countries)* (Paris: OECD).

—————— (1994), *Managing the Environment: The Role of Economic Instruments* (Paris: OECD).

—————— (1997), *Evaluating Economic Instruments for Environmental Policy* (Paris: OECD).

—————— (1998), *Harmful Tax Competition: An Emerging Global Issue* (Paris: OECD).

—————— (1999), *Economic Instruments for Pollution Control and Natural Resources Management in OECD Countries: A Survey* (Working Party on Economic and Environmental Policy Integration) (Paris: OECD).

—————— (2005), *Competition Law and Policy in the European Union* (Paris: OECD).

Oliver, Peter (1999), "Some Further Reflections on the Scope of Articles 28–30 (Ex 30–36) EC," *Common Market Law Review,* 36, 783–806.

Oliver, Peter, and Wulf-Henning Roth (2004), "The Internal Market and the Four Freedoms," *Common Market Law Review,* 41, 407–441.

Opschoor, Johannes B., and Hans B. Vos (1989), "The Application of Economic Instruments for Environmental Protection in OECD Countries," final report, Paris.

Padgett, John, and Chris Ansell (1993), "Robust Action and the Rise of the Medici," *American Journal of Sociology,* 98, no. 6, 1259–1319.

Padgett, Stephen (1992), "The Single European Energy Market: The Politics of Realization," *Journal of Common Market Studies,* 30, no. 1, 53–75.

—————— (2001), "Market Effects and Institutions in Transnational Governance Formation: European Regulatory Regimes in Telecommunications and Electricity," paper presented at the ECPR, Joint Sessions, Grenoble, 6–11 April.

—————— (2003), "Between Synthesis and Emulation: EU Policy Transfer in the Power Sector," *Journal of European Public Policy* 10, no. 2, 227–246.

Parrish, Richard (2003), *Sports Law and Policy in the European Union* (Manchester: Manchester University Press).

Pelkmans, Jacques (2002), "Mutual Recognition in Goods and Services: An Economic Perspective," College of Europe Working Paper Series 2, Bruges.

—— (2006), "Functioning of the Internal Market," paper presented at the College of Europe Conference on Interdisciplinary Perspectives on the Single Market, Bruges, Belgium, 1–2 May.

—— (2007), "From Promising Design to Better Delivery: On Mutual Recognition in EU Goods Markets," *Journal of European Public Policy,* 14, no. 4, 699–716.

Pelkmans, Jacques, Ellen Vos, and Luca Di Mauro (2000), "Reforming Product Regulation in the EU: A Painstaking, Iterative Two-level Game," in Giampaolo Galli and Jacques Pelkmans (eds.), *Regulatory Reform and Competitiveness in Europe* (Cheltenham: Edward Elgar), 238–291.

Peters, B. Guy (1997), "The Commission and Implementation in the European Union: Is There an Implementation Deficit and Why?" in Neill Nugent (ed.), *At the Heart of the Union: Studies of the European Commission* (Houndmills: Macmillan), 187–202.

Peterson, John (1995), "Decision-Making in the European Union: Towards a Framework for Analysis," *Journal of European Public Policy* 2, no. 1, 69–93.

Picciotto, Sol (2000), "North Atlantic Cooperation and Democratizing Globalism," in George Bermann, Matthias Herdegen, and Peter L. Lindseth (eds.), *Transatlantic Regulatory Cooperation* (Oxford: Oxford University Press), 459–519.

—— (2002), "Introduction: Reconceptualizing Regulation in the Era of Globalization," *Journal of Law and Society,* 29, no. 1, 1–11.

Pierre, Jon (ed.) (2000), *Debating Governance* (New York: Oxford University Press).

Pierre, Jon, and B. Guy Peters (2000), *Governance, Politics and the State* (Basingstoke: Macmillan).

—— (2005), *Governing Complex Societies: Trajectories and Scenarios* (Basingstoke: Palgrave Macmillan).

Pierson, Paul (1996), "The Path to European Integration: A Historical Institutionalist Analysis," *Comparative Political Studies,* 29, no. 2, 123–163.

Platform of European Social NGOs (1999–2000), *Annual Report* (Brussels: Platform of European Social NGOs). Available at http://www.socialplatform.org/AboutUs.asp?DocID=8151.

Pons, Jean-François (1999), "Sport and European Competition Policy," paper presented at the 26th Annual Conference on International Antitrust Law and Policy, New York, Fordham Corporate Law Institute, 14–15 October. Available at http://ec.europa.eu/comm/competition/speeches/text/sp1999_019_en.pdf.

Porro, Nicola (1997), "Politics and Consumption: The Four Revolutions of Spectator Football," in Roberto D'Alimonte and David Nelken (eds.), *Italian Politics: The Center-Left in Power* (Boulder: Westview), 183–197.

Puetter, Uwe (2006), *The Eurogroup: How a Secretive Circle of Finance Ministers Shape European Economic Governance* (Manchester: Manchester University Press).

Quack, Sigrid, and Marie-Laure Djelic (2005), "Adaptation, Recombination, and Reinforcement: The Story of Antitrust and Competition Law in Germany and Europe," in Wolfgang Streeck and Kathleen Thelen (eds.), *Beyond Continuity: Institutional Change in Advanced Political Economies* (Oxford: Oxford University Press), 255–281.

Radaelli, Claudio M. (1997), *The Politics of Corporate Taxation in the European Union: Knowledge and International Policy Agendas* (London: Routledge).

—— (1999), *Technocracy in the European Union* (Harlow: Longman).

—— (2003a), "The Open Method of Coordination: A New Governance Architecture for the European Union?" Sieps Report 1, Stockholm.

—— (2003b), "The Code of Conduct Against Harmful Tax Cooperation: Open Method of Coordination in Disguise?" *Public Administration,* 81, no. 3, 513–531.

———— (2005), "Diffusion Without Convergence: How Political Context Shapes the Adoption of Regulatory Impact Assessment," *Journal of European Public Policy*, 12, no. 5, 723–747.

Radnege, Keir (2000), "Blatter: The Millennium Interview," *World Soccer* (January), 32–33.

Raustiala, Kal (2002), "The Architecture of International Cooperation: Transgovernmental Networks and the Future of International Law," *Virginia Journal of International Law*, 43, 1–92.

Ravinet, Pauline (2005), "The Genesis of the Bologna Process: What the Empirical Data Teach Us About Europeanization," paper presented at Third ECPR Conference. Budapest, 8–10 September.

Rawlings, Richard (2000), "Engaged Elites: Citizen Action and Institutional Attitudes in Commission Enforcement," *European Law Journal*, 6, no. 1, 4–28.

Reding, Viviane (2001), "The European Community and European Sport," address by Viviane Reding, member of the European Commission with responsibility for education and culture to the 9th Sports Forum of the Konrad Adenauer Foundation, Eichholz, 3 May. Available at http://ec.europa.eu/sport/action_sports/historique/docs/200105-reding-ad_en.pdf.

Redmond, John, and Glenda Rosenthal (eds.) (1998), *The Expanding European Union: Past, Present and Future* (Boulder: Lynne Rienner).

Rehbinder, Eckard, and Richard Stewart (1985), *Environmental Protection Policy: Integration Through Law* (Berlin: de Gruyter).

Reichert, Sybille, and Christian Tauch (2005), *European Universities Implementing Bologna: Trends IV Report* (Brussels: European Universities Association).

Renz, Thomas (2001), *Vom Monopol zum Wettbewerb: Die Liberalisierung der deutschen Stromwirtschaft* (Opladen: Leske and Budrich).

Rettman, Andrew (2006), "Time for Pause in Enlargement, Top Commission Official Says," *EU Observer*, 23 February.

Rhodes, Martin (1995), "A Regulatory Conundrum: Industrial Relations and the Social Dimension," in Stephan Leibfried and Paul Pierson (eds.), *European Social Policy: Between Fragmentation and Integration* (Washington, DC: Brookings Institution), 78–122.

Rhodes, Ron A.W. (1997), *Understanding Governance: Policy Networks, Governance, Reflexivity and Accountability* (Buckingham: Open University Press).

———— (2007), "Understanding Governance: Ten Years On," *Organization Studies*, 28, 1243–1264.

Riley, Alan (2003a), "EC Antitrust Modernisation: The Commission Does Very Nicely—Thank You! Part Two: Between the Idea and the Reality: Decentralisation Under Regulation 1," *European Competition Law Review*, 24, 657–672.

———— (2003b), "EU Antitrust Reform: Does It Deliver?" *European Policy Analyst*, March, 63–75.

Rittberger, Berthold, and Jeremy J. Richardson (2003), "Old Wine in New Bottles? The Commission and the Use of Environmental Policy Instruments," *Public Administration*, 81, no. 3, 575–606.

Rodrik, Dani (1997), *Has Globalization Gone Too Far?* (Washington, DC: Institute for International Economics).

Rosenau, James N. (1992), "Governance, Order and Change in World Politics," in James N. Rosenau and Ernst-Otto Czempiel (eds.), *Governance Without Government: Order and Change in World Politics* (Cambridge: Cambridge University Press), 1–29.

Rosenau, James N., and Ernst-Otto Czempiel (eds.) (1992), *Governance Without Government: Order and Change in World Politics* (Cambridge: Cambridge University Press).

Rosenthal, Glenda Goldstone (1975), *The Men Behind the Decisions: Cases in European Policy-Making* (Lexington, MA: Lexington Books, D.C Heath).

Ross, George (1995), *Jacques Delors and European Integration* (Cambridge: Polity Press).

Ross, Stephen F. (1991), "Break Up the Sport League Monopolies," in Paul D. Staudohar and James A. Magan (eds.), *The Business of Professional Sport* (Urbana: University of Illinois Press), 152–174.

Roth, Wulf-Henning (1988), "The European Economic Community's Law on Services: Harmonisation," *Common Market Law Review*, 25, 35–94.

Ruding, Onno (2005), "The Past and the Future of EU Corporate Tax," *EC Tax Review*, 14, no. 3, 2–3.

Ruggie, John G. (1972), "Collective Goods and Future International Collaboration," *American Political Science Review*, 66, 874–893.

Sabatier, Paul (1998), "The Advocacy Coalition Framework: Revisions and Relevance for Europe," *Journal of European Public Policy*, 5, no. 1, 98–130.

Sabel, Charles F., and Jonathan Zeitlin (2007), "Learning from Difference: The New Architecture of Experimentalist Governance in the European Union," European Governance Papers (EUROGOV) C-07-02.

Sandholtz, Wayne (1993), "Choosing Union: Monetary Politics and Maastricht," *International Organization*, 47, no. 1, 1–39.

——— (1998), "The Emergence of a Supranational Telecommunications Regime," in Wayne Sandholtz and Alec Stone Sweet (eds.), *European Integration and Supranational Governance* (Oxford: Oxford University Press).

Savage, Jim, and Amy Verdun (2007), "Reforming Europe's Stability and Growth Pact: Lessons from the American Experience in Macrobudgeting," *Review of International Political Economy*, 14, no. 5, 842–867.

Sbragia, Alberta (2000), "The European Union as Coxswain: Governance by Steering," in Jon Pierre (ed.), *Debating Governance: Authority, Steering and Democracy* (Oxford: Oxford University Press), 219–240.

Schäfer, Armin (2006), "A New Form of Governance? Comparing the Open Method of Coordination to Multilateral Surveillance by the IMF and the OECD," *Journal of European Public Policy*, 13, no. 1, 70–88.

Schamis, Hector (2006), "Corruption and Economic Reform," American University, unpublished manuscript.

Scharpf, Fritz W. (1985), "Die Politikverflechtungs-Falle: Europäische Integration und deutscher Föderalismus im Vergleich," *Politische Vierteljahresschrift*, 26, no. 4, 323–356.

——— (1992a), "Einführung: Zur Theorie von Verhandlungssystemen," in Arthur Benz, Fritz W. Scharpf, and Reinhard Zintl (eds.), *Horizontale Politikverflechtung: Zur Theorie von Verhandlungssystemen* (Frankfurt: Campus), 11–27.

——— (1992b), "Koordination durch Verhandlungssysteme: Analytische Konzepte und institutionelle Lösungen," in Arthur Benz, Fritz W. Scharpf, and Reinhard Zintl (eds.), *Horizontale Politikverflechtung: Zur Theorie von Verhandlungssystemen* (Frankfurt: Campus), 51–96.

——— (1993a), "Positive und negative Koordination in Verhandlungssystemen," in Adrienne Héritier (ed.), *Policy-Analyse*, PVS-Sonderheft 24 (Opladen: Westdeutscher Verlag), 57–83.

────── (1993b), *Games in Hierarchies and Networks: Analytical and Empirical Approaches to the Study of Governance Institutions* (Frankfurt: Campus Verlag).

────── (1994), "Games Real Actors Could Play: Positive and Negative Coordination in Embedded Negotiations," *Journal of Theoretical Politics,* 6, no. 1, 27–53.

────── (1997a), *Games Real Actors Play: Actor-Centered Institutionalism in Policy-Research* (Boulder, CO: Westview).

────── (1997b), "Introduction: The Problem-solving Capacity of Multi-level Governance," *Journal of European Public Policy,* 4, no. 4, 520–538.

────── (1997c), "Economic Integration, Democracy and the Welfare State," *Journal of European Public Policy,* 4, no. 1, 18–36.

────── (1999), *Governing in Europe: Effective and Democratic?* (Oxford: Oxford University Press).

────── (2001), "Notes Toward a Theory of Multilevel Governing in Europe," *Scandinavian Political Studies,* 24, no. 1, 1–26.

Schelkle, Waltraud (2005), "Understanding New Forms of European Integration: A Study in Competing Political Economy Explanations," in Erik Jones and Amy Verdun (eds.), *Political Economy Approaches to the Study of European Integration* (London: Routledge), 149–169.

Schelling, Thomas (1971), "On the Ecology of Micromotives," *The Public Interest,* 25, 59–98.

Schepel, Harm (2005), *The Constitution of Private Governance* (Oxford: Hart Publishers).

Schimank, Uwe (2003), "Theoretische Modelle sozialer Strukturdynamiken: Ein Gefüge von Generalisierungsniveaus," in Renate Mayntz (ed.), *Akteure—Mechanismen—Modelle* (Frankfurt: Campus), 151–178.

────── (2007), "Elementare Mechanismen," in Arthur Benz et al. (eds.), *Handbuch Governance* (Wiesbaden: VS Verlag für Sozialwissenschaften), 29–45.

Schimmelfennig, Frank (2003), *The EU, NATO and the Integration of Europe: Rules and Rhetoric* (Cambridge: Cambridge University Press).

Schmidt, Susanne (1998), *Liberalisierung in Europa: Die Rolle der Kommission* (Frankfurt: Campus).

────── (2003), "Das Projekt der europäischen Marktschaffung: Die gegenseitige Anerkennung und der Binnenmarkt für Dienstleistungen," in Roland Czada and Reinhard Zintl (eds.), *Politik und Markt,* PVS-Sonderheft 34 (Wiesbaden: VS Verlag für Sozialwissenschaften), 83–106.

────── (2004a), *Rechtsunsicherheit statt Regulierungswettbewerb: Die nationalen Folgen des europäischen Binnenmarkts für Dienstleistungen Habilitationsschrift* (Hagen: Fern Universität Hagen).

────── (2004b), "Rechtsunsicherheit als Folge der bizephalen Struktur der EU," in Patricia Bauer and Helmut Voelzkow (eds.), *Die Europäische Union—Marionette oder Regisseur?* (Wiesbaden: VS Verlag für Sozialwissenschaften), 51–65.

────── (2005), "Notwendigerweise unvollkommen: Strukturprobleme des Europäischen Binnenmarktes," *Zeitschrift für Staats-und Europawissenschaften (ZSE)/ Journal of Comparative Government and European Policy,* 3, no. 2, 185–210.

────── (2007), "Mutual Recognition as a New Mode of Governance," *Journal of European Public Policy,* 14, no. 4, 667–681.

Schmidt, Vivien A. (2003), "The Europeanization of Governance in Larger European Democracies," paper presented at the European Union Studies Association (EUSA) Biennial Conference, 27–29 March, Nashville.

Schneider, Volker (1999), *Staat und technische Kommunikation* (Wiesbaden: Westdeutscher Verlag).

Schneider, Volker, and Marc Tenbücken (eds.) (2004), *Der Staat auf dem Rückzug* (Frankfurt: Campus).

Schout, Adriaan, and Andrew Jordan (2005), "Coordinated European Governance: Self-Organizing or Centrally Steered?" *Public Administration,* 83, no. 1, 201–220.

Schuppert, Gunnar Folke (ed.) (2005), *Governance-Forschung: Vergewisserung über Stand und Entwicklungslinien* (Baden-Baden: Nomos).

Scott, Colin (2002), "Private Regulation of the Public Sector: A Neglected Facet of Contemporary Governance," *Journal of Law and Society,* 29, 56–76.

Scott, Joanne, and David M. Trubek (2002), "Mind the Gap: Law and New Approaches to Governance in the European Union," *European Law Journal,* 8, no. 1, 1–18.

Sécretariat Général (1996), "Note à l'Attention de Mesdames et Messieurs les Directeurs Generaux," SEC (96) 1785, Brussels, European Commission.

——— (1998), "Amélioration des méthodes de travail de la Commission relatives aux procédures d'infraction," SEC (98) 1733, Brussels, European Commission.

Segal, Ilya, and Michael D. Whinston (2006), "Public vs. Private Enforcement of Antitrust Law: A Survey," Stanford Law and Economics Olin Working Paper 335. Available at http://ssrn.com/abstract=952067.

Seidman, Harold, and Robert Gilmour (1986), *Politics, Position and Power: From the Positive to the Regulatory State,* 4th ed. (Oxford: Oxford University Press).

Shaw, Jo (2000), *Social Law and Policy in an Evolving European Union* (London: Hart).

Siebert, Horst (1976), *Analyse der Instrumente der Umweltpolitik* (Göttingen: Otto Schwartz in cooperation with W. Vogt).

Sievers, Julia (2006), "Judicial Cooperation in Criminal Matters: The Potential of Mutual Recognition as a Mode of Governance," paper presented at the SECURINT Summer School, 17–21 July, Strasbourg.

Slaughter, Anne-Marie (2000), "Governing the Global Economy Through Government Networks," in Michael Byers (ed.), *The Role of Law in International Politics: Essays in International Relations and International Law* (Oxford: Oxford University Press), 177–205.

——— (2004a), *A New World Order* (Princeton, NJ: Princeton University Press).

——— (2004b), "Disaggregated Sovereignty: Towards the Public Accountability of Global Government Networks," *Government and Opposition,* 39, no. 2, 336–391.

——— (2004c), "Global Government Networks, Global Information Agencies and Disaggregated Democracy," in Karl-Heinz Ladeur (ed.), *Public Governance in the Age of Globalization* (Aldershot: Ashgate), 121–155.

Slaughter, Anne-Marie, and David Zaring (2007), "Networking Goes International: An Update," Washington & Lee Public Legal Studies Paper 12.

Smismans, Stijn (2003), "European Civil Society: Shaped by Discourses and Institutional Interests," *European Law Journal,* 9, no. 4, 473–495.

——— (2006a), "Civil Society and European Governance: From Concepts to Research Agenda," in Stijn Smismans (ed.), *Civil Society and Legitimate European Governance* (Cheltenham: Edward Elgar), 3–19.

——— (2006b), "Functional Participation in the EU," in Arthur Benz and Yannis Papadopolous (eds.), *Governance and Democracy: Comparing National, European and Transnational Experiences* (London: Routledge), 115–137.

Smith, Martin, and Graham Timmins (2000), *EU and NATO Enlargement in Comparative Perspective* (Aldershot: Ashgate).

Smith-Hillman, A. Vindelyn (2006), "EC Approach to Governance as Applied to the Modernization of Competition Policy," *European Business Review*, 18, no. 1, 33–49.

Sorensen, Georg (2004), *The Transformation of the State: Beyond the Myth of Retreat* (Basingstoke: Palgrave).

Spence, David (1994), "Structure, Functions and Procedures in the Commission," in Geoffrey Edwards and David Spence (eds.), *The European Commission* (London: Longman), 97–116.

Steinmo, Sven (1993), *Taxation and Democracy* (New Haven, CT: Yale University Press).

Strange, Susan (1996), *The Retreat of the State: The Diffusion of Power in the World Economy* (Cambridge: Cambridge University Press).

Streeck, Wolfgang (1998), "Vom Binnenmarkt zum Bundesstaat? Überlegungen zur politischen Ökonomie der europäischen Sozialpolitik," in Stephan Leibfried and Paul Pierson (eds.), *Standort Europa: Europäische Sozialpolitik* (Frankfurt: Suhrkamp), 369–421.

Streeck, Wolfgang, and Philippe Schmitter (eds.) (1985), *Private Interest Government: Beyond Market and State* (London: Sage).

Sugden, John, and Alan Tomlinson (1998), *FIFA and the Contest for World Football: Who Rules the People's Game?* (Cambridge: Polity Press).

Sun, Jeanne-Mey, and Jacques Pelkmans (1995), "Regulatory Competition in the Single Market," *Journal of Common Market Studies*, 33, no. 1, 67–89.

Swyngedouw, Erik (2005), "Governance Innovation and the Citizen: The Janus Face of Governance-Beyond-the-State," *Urban Studies*, 42, no. 11, 1991–2006.

Szyzsczak, Erica (2006), "Experimental Governance: The Open Method of Coordination," *European Law Journal*, 12, no. 4, 486–502.

Tallberg, Jonas (2003), *European Governance and Supranational Institutions: Making States Comply* (London: Routledge).

Teague, Paul (1989), *The European Community: The Social Dimension* (London: Cranfield School of Management and Kogan Page).

Tenbücken, Marc, and Volker Schneider (2004), "Divergent Convergence: Structures and Functions of National Regulatory Authorities in the Telecommunications Sector," in Jacint Jordana and David Levi-Faur (eds.), *The Politics of Regulation: Institutions and Regulatory Reforms for the Age of Governance* (Cheltenham: Edward Elgar), 245–272.

Thatcher, Mark (2002a), "Regulation After Delegation: Independent Regulatory Agencies in Europe," *Journal of European Public Policy*, 9, no. 6, 954–972.

—— (2002b), "Delegation to Independent Regulatory Agencies: Resources, Functions and Contextual Mediation," *West European Politics*, 25, no. 1, 125–147.

—— (2005), "Independent Regulatory Agencies and Elected Politicians in Europe," in Damien Geradin, Rodolphe Munoz, and Nicolas Petit (eds.), *Regulation Through Agencies in the EU: A New Paradigm of European Governance* (Cheltenham: Edward Elgar), 47–66.

Thatcher, Mark, and Alec Stone Sweet (2002), "Theory and Practice of Delegation to Non-Majoritarian Institutions," *West European Politics*, 25, 1–22.

Tison, Michael (2002), "Unravelling the General Good Exception: The Case of Financial Services," in Mads Andenas and Wulf-Henning Roth (eds.), *Services and Free Movement in EU Law* (Oxford: Oxford University Press), 321–381.

Tömmel, Ingeborg (1994), *Staatliche Regulierung und europäische Integration: Die Regionalpolitik der EU und ihre Implementation in Italien* (Baden-Baden: Nomos).

———— (2006a), "EU Structural Policy—More Than a Financial Transfer Between Rich and Poor?" *Foedus, Rivista Quadrimestrale*, 15, 3–10.

———— (2006b), *Das politische System der EU*, 2nd ed. (Munich: Oldenbourg).

———— (ed.) (2007), *Die Europäische Union: Governance und Policy-Making*, PVS-Sonderheft 40 (Wiesbaden: VS Verlag für Sozialwissenschaften).

———— (2008), *Das politische System der EU*, 3rd ed. (Munich: Oldenbourg).

Treib, Oliver (2004), *Die Umsetzung europäischer Sozialpolitik: Die Bedeutung der nationalen Parteipolitik für die Umsetzung europäischer Sozialrichtlinien* (Frankfurt: Campus).

Treib, Oliver, Holger Bähr, and Gerda Falkner (2005), "Modes of Governance: A Note Towards Conceptual Clarification," *EUROGOV*, no. N-05-02, 1–22.

———— (2007), "Modes of Governance: Towards a Conceptual Clarification," *Journal of European Public Policy*, 14, no. 1, 1–20.

Trubek, David, and James Mosher (2001), "New Governance, EU Employment Policy, and the European Social Model," Working Paper 15/01, New York University School of Law, Jean Monnet Chair.

Trubek, David, and Louise G. Trubek (2005), "The Open Method of Coordination and the Debate over 'Hard' and 'Soft' Law," in Jonathan Zeitlin, Philippe Pochet, and Lars Magnusson (eds.), *The Open Method of Coordination in Action: The European Employment and Social Inclusion Strategies* (Brussels: P.I.E.—Peter Lang), 83–103.

Tsoukalis, Loukas (1977), *The Politics and Economics of European Monetary Integration* (London: Allen and Unwin).

———— (1981), *The EC and Its Mediterranean Enlargement* (London: Allen and Unwin).

Twitchett, Carol Cosgrove (1981), *Harmonization in the EEC* (London: Macmillan).

UNICE (2002), "Implementation of Directive 95/46/EC on the Protection of Individuals with Regard to the Processing of Personal Data and on the Free Movement of Such Data of 24 October 1995," Brussels, 1–10.

Van den Brink, Jens Pelle (2000), "EC Competition Law and the Regulation of Football," *European Competition Law Review*, 21, no. 8, 359–368; and no. 9, 420–427.

Van Miert, Karel (1996), "L'arrêt Bosman: La suppression des frontières sportives dans le Marché unique européen," *Revue du Marché Unique Européen*, 1, 5–9.

Van Outrive, Lode (1995), "Commentary on the Third Pillar and the 1996 Intergovernmental Conference: What Should Be on the Agenda?" in Roland Bieber and Jörg Monar (eds.), *Justice and Home Affairs in the European Union: The Development of the Third Pillar* (Brussels: Interuniversity Press), 391–396.

Van Riesen, Olivia (2007), *Zur Leistungsfähigkeit des Regulierungsstaats im Bahnsektor: Eisenbahnregulierung in Europa im Spannungsfeld zwischen institutionellem Design und der politischen Ökonomie des Bahnsektors* (Münster: LIT Verlag).

Van Waarden, Frans, and Michaela Drahos (2002), "Courts and (Epistemic) Communities in the Convergence of Competition Policies," *Journal of European Public Policy*, 9, no. 6, 913–934.

Verdun, Amy (1996), "An 'Asymmetrical' Economic and Monetary Union in the EU: Perceptions of Monetary Authorities and Social Partners," *Journal of European Integration*, 20, no. 1, 59–81.

———— (1999), "The Role of the Delors Committee in the Creation of EMU: An Epistemic Community?" *Journal of European Public Policy*, 6, no. 2, 308–328.

——— (2000a), *European Responses to Globalization and Financial Market Integration: Perceptions of Economic and Monetary Union in Britain, France and Germany* (Basingstoke: Palgrave-Macmillan).

——— (2000b), "Governing by Committee: The Case of the Monetary Committee," in Emil Kirchner and Thomas Christiansen (eds.), *Committee Governance in the European Union* (Manchester: Manchester University Press), 132–145.

Voelzkow, Helmut (1996), *Private Regierungen in der Techniksteuerung* (Frankfurt: Campus).

Vogel, Steven K. (1996), *Freer Markets, More Rules: Regulatory Reform in Advanced Industrial Countries* (Ithaca, NY: Cornell University Press).

Vos, Ellen (2005), "Independence, Accountability and Transparency of European Regulatory Agencies," in Damien Geradin, Rodolphe Munoz, and Nicolas Petit (eds.), *Regulation Through Agencies in the EU: A New Paradigm of European Governance* (Cheltenham: Edward Elgar), 120–139.

Wagner, Wolfgang (2007), "Europäisches Regieren im Politikfeld Innere Sicherheit?" in Ingeborg Tömmel (ed.), *Die Europäische Union: Governance und Policy-Making,* PVS-Sonderheft 40 (Wiesbaden: VS Verlag für Sozialwissenschaften), 323–342.

Wallace, Helen (2000), "The Institutional Setting: Five Variations on a Theme," in Helen Wallace and William Wallace (eds.), *Policy-Making in the European Union* (Oxford: Oxford University Press), 3–36.

——— (2005), "An Institutional Anatomy and Five Policy Modes," in Helen Wallace, William Wallace, and Mark A. Pollack (eds.), *Policy-Making in the European Union,* 5th ed. (Oxford: Oxford University Press), 49–90.

Wallace, William (1976), "Wider but Weaker: The Continued Enlargement of the European Community," *The World Today,* 32, no. 3, 104–111.

——— (2000), "From the Atlantic to the Bug, from the Arctic to the Tigris? The Transformation of the EU and NATO," *International Affairs,* 76, no. 3, 475–493.

Weale, Albert, Geoffrey Pridham, Michelle Cini, and Dimitrios Konstadakopulos (2000), *Environmental Governance in Europe: An Ever Closer Ecological Union* (Oxford: Oxford University Press).

Weatherhill, Stephen (2003), "Fair Play Please! Recent Developments in the Application of EC Law to Sport," *Common Market Law Review,* 40, 51–93.

Werner Report (1970), "Report to the Council and the Commission on the Realization by Stages of Economic and Monetary Union in the Community," in Council and Commission of the EC, *Bulletin of the European Communities,* Supplement 11, Doc. 16. 956/11/70, 8 October. Available at http://ec.europa.eu/economy_finance/emu_history/documentation/chapter5/19701008en72realisationbystage.pdf.

Weyembergh, Anne (2005) "Approximation of Criminal Laws, the Constitutional Treaty and the Hague Programme," *Common Market Law Review,* 42, 1567–1597.

Wichmann, Nicole (2006), "The Participation of the Schengen Associates: Inside or Outside?" *European Foreign Affairs Review,* 11, no. 1, 87–107.

Wigger, Angela, and Andreas Nölke (2007), "Enhanced Roles for Private Actors in the EU Business Regulation and the Erosion of Rheinish Capitalism: The Case of Antitrust Enforcement," *Journal of Common Market Studies,* 45, no. 2, 487–513.

Wilks, Stephen (2005a), "Agency Escape: Decentralization or Dominance of the European Commission in the Modernization of Competition Policy?" *Governance,* 18, no. 3, 431–452.

—— (2005b), "Competition Policy: Challenge and Reform," in Helen Wallace, William Wallace, and Mark A. Pollack (eds.), *Policy-Making in the European Union,* 5th ed. (Oxford: Oxford University Press), 113–139.

—— (2007), "The European Competition Network: What Has Changed?" paper presented at the European Union Studies Association (EUSA) Biennial Conference, Montreal, 17–19 May.

Wilks, Stephen, and Ian Bartle (2002), "The Unanticipated Consequences of Creating Independent Competition Agencies," *West European Politics,* 25, no. 1, 148–172.

Wils, Wouter P.J. (2007), "The European Commission's 2006 Guidelines on Antitrust Fines: A Legal and Economic Analysis," *World Competition,* 30, no. 2, 197–229.

Wilson, Frank Q. (ed.) (1980), *The Politics of Regulation* (New York: Basic Books).

Wright, George (1999), "The Impact of Globalisation," *New Political Economy,* 4, no. 2, 268–273.

Yataganas, Xénophon (2001), "Delegation of Regulatory Authority in the European Union: The Relevance of the American Model of Independent Agencies," Jean Monnet Working Paper. Available at http://www.jeanmonnetprogram.org/papers/01/010301.html.

Young, Alasdair R. (2005), "The Single Market. A New Approach to Policy," in Helen Wallace, William Wallace, and Marc A. Pollack (eds.), *Policy-Making in the European Union,* 5th ed. (Oxford: Oxford University Press), 94–112.

Zeitlin, Jonathan (2003), "Introduction: Governing Work and Welfare in a New Economy: European and American Experiments," in Jonathan Zeitlin and David M. Trubek (eds.), *Governing Work and Welfare in a New Economy: European and American Experiments* (Oxford: Oxford University Press), 1–30.

Zeitlin, Jonathan, Philippe Pochet, and Lars Magnusson (eds.) (2005), *The Open Method of Coordination in Action: The European Employment and Social Inclusion Strategies* (Brussels: P.I.E.—Peter Lang).

Zgaga, Pavel (2003), "Bologna Process Between Prague and Berlin: Report to the Ministers of Education of the Signatory Countries," September, 52–54.

Zielonka, Jan (2001), "How New Enlarged Borders Will Reshape the European Union," *Journal of Common Market Studies,* 39, no. 3, 507–536.

Zürn, Michael (2005), "Global Governance," in Gunnar F. Schuppert (ed.), *Governance-Forschung: Vergewisserung über Stand und Entwicklungslinien* (Baden-Baden: Nomos), 371–469.

The Contributors

Arthur Benz is professor of political science at the University of Hagen (Germany). He taught at the Universities of Konstanz and Halle-Wittenberg and was visiting researcher at the Max-Planck Institute for the Study of Societies in Cologne. In 2007–2008 he worked as John G. Diefenbaker scholar at Carleton University Ottawa. He has published on government, federalism, and multilevel governance, and his articles have appeared in scholarly journals such as *European Journal of Public Policy, The European Law Journal, Public Administration, Publius, Regional and Federal Studies,* and *West European Politics.*

Laura Cram is reader in politics in the Department of Government of the University of Strathclyde (United Kingdom). She is author of *Policy-Making in the European Union: Conceptual Lenses and the Integration Process* (1997), coeditor of *Developments in the European Union* (1999) and of a special edition of the journal *Governance* on the Institutional Balance in the European Union (2001), and editor of a themed section of *Nations and Nationalism* (2008). She has published articles on the European Union in *Governance,* the *Journal of Common Market Studies, Journal of European Public Policy, Nations and Nationalism,* and *Policy and Politics.*

Osvaldo Croci is professor of political science, at Memorial University (St. John's, NL, Canada) where he teaches courses on the European Union as well as in international politics, foreign policy, and sport and politics. He has coedited (with Amy Verdun) two books on EU institutional and policy reforms and on transatlantic relations as well as a number of articles on Canadian and Italian foreign policy, transatlantic relations, and sport and politics.

Burkard Eberlein is assistant professor at the Schulich School of Business, York University (Toronto) and a faculty member of the Canadian Centre for German and European Studies. His research focuses on comparative public policy and international governance, with a special interest in EU policymaking, multilevel regulatory governance, and the domain of energy policy. His work has been published in journals such as *Governance, Journal of Common Market Studies, Journal of European Public Policy, Journal of Public Policy,* and in several edited volumes. He is coeditor with Bruce Doern of *Governing the Energy Challenge: Germany and Canada in a Multi-Level Regional and Global Context* (2009).

Michelle Egan is associate professor and Jean Monnet Chair in the School of International Service, American University, in Washington, DC. She has published several books on the European single market and transatlantic economic relations. She is currently completing two books titled *Studying the European Union: Current and Future Agendas* and *Single Markets: Economic Integration in Europe and the US.* She is the coeditor of the Palgrave EU Series and has received a number of fellowships from the German Marshall Fund, Howard Foundation, European Commission, and Bosch Foundation. She has been a research associate at the Center for European Policy Studies (CEPS) in Brussels, a nonresident associate at the Atlantic Council, and has worked with the State Department and European Commission on EU-related issues.

Edgar Grande is professor and chair of comparative politics at the Geschwister-Scholl Institute for Political Science of the University of Munich. He is also the director of the Munich Center on "Governance, Communication, Public Policy and Law." He currently directs two research projects on "Globalization and the Future of the Nation State" and on "Globalization of National Political Spaces," both funded by the German Research Association (DFG). His recent books include: *West European Politics in the Age of Globalization* (2008; coauthored with H. Kriesi et al.); *Cosmopolitan Europe* (2007; coauthored with Ulrich Beck), and *Complex Sovereignty* (2005; coedited with Louis W. Pauly).

Ute Hartenberger is senior researcher at the Department of Political Science, Technical University of Munich in Germany. She previously worked at the Max-Planck Institute for the Study of Society in Cologne. Her research concentrates on European integration, governance in multilevel political systems, social policymaking, and regulation of infrastructures.

Miriam Hartlapp heads the Independent Young Researcher Group "Position Formation in the EU Commission" at the Social Science Research

Center Berlin (WZB). She was a doctoral and postdoctoral researcher at the Max-Planck Institute for the Study of Societies, in Cologne. She is coauthor of *Complying with Europe: The Impact of EU Minimum Harmonisation and Soft Law in the Member States,* winner of the EUSA Best Book on Europe 2005–2006 prize. She has also published in scholarly journals such as *European Journal of Political Research, Journal of Common Market Studies, Journal of European Public Policy, Journal of European Social Policy, Journal of Social Policy, Politische Vierteljahresschrift,* and *West European Politics.*

Barbara G. Haskel recently retired from the Department of Political Science, McGill University (Montreal). Her current research focuses on the Bologna Process and creation of a European Higher Education Area. This work follows from her interest in the theory of political integration, the role of the Commission, and forms of EU governance. She has taught and written on international political economy and the political economies of industrialized states, particularly those of Scandinavia, and she has published articles in journals such as *Cooperation and Conflict, International Organization, International Studies Quarterly, Political Studies,* and *Scandinavian Studies.*

Katharina Holzinger holds the Chair of International Relations and Conflict Management at the University of Konstanz, Germany. She held research positions at the Social Science Research Center Berlin and the Max-Planck Institute for the Study of Collective Goods in Bonn before she became professor of government and director of the Centre for Globalization and Governance at Hamburg University (2004–2007). She has published in *European Union Politics, European Journal of Political Research, European Journal of International Relations, International Organization, Journal of European Public Policy, Political Communication,* and *Rationality and Society.* Her most recent book is *Environmental Policy Convergence in Europe* (2008, with Christoph Knill and Bas Arts).

Christoph Knill is Chair of Comparative Public Policy and Administration at the University of Konstanz. He was research associate at the Max-Planck Institute for the Study of Societies in Cologne, the European University Institute in Florence (1995–1998), and the Max-Planck Project Group for the Study of Common Goods in Bonn (1998–2000). Before joining the department, he was professor of political science at the University of Jena (2001–2004). He has published nine monographs and numerous articles in *Comparative Political Studies, Governance, European Journal of Political Research, International Organization, Journal of Common Market Studies, Journal of European Public Policy, Journal of Public Policy,* and *Public Administration.*

Ulrike Kraemer has been a Marie Curie Fellow at the Centre for European Studies at the University of Bradford and previously held the post of research assistant in the Department of Politics, University of Exeter. Her research interests lie in political economy and European studies, including European direct tax cooperation. Ulrike has published articles in the *Journal of Common Market Studies* and *Journal of Conflict Resolution*. She is currently working at the South West of England Regional Development Agency.

Sandra Lavenex is professor of international politics at the University of Lucerne, Switzerland. She has written and edited four books on EU asylum and immigration policies and EU internal security. Her articles have appeared in scholarly journals such as *Journal of Common Market Studies, Journal of European Integration, Journal of European Public Policy,* and *West European Politics.*

Dirk Lehmkuhl is professor of European politics at the University of St. Gallen in Switzerland. Previously he worked at the Universities of Konstanz and Bielefeld in Germany, the European University in Florence, the Max-Planck Institute for the Research of Collective Goods in Bonn, Germany, and the University of Zurich in Switzerland. His teaching and research portfolio includes themes of European integration and international relations, including comparative regional integration, the contribution of nonstate actors to global governance, and the legalization of transnational relations.

Andrea Lenschow is professor of European integration and politics and Jean Monnet Chair at Osnabrück University, Germany. She has edited several books and published on European governance, implementation, European and comparative environmental policy, and theories of EU policymaking in scholarly journals such as *Comparative Political Studies, European Environment, European Law Journal, Governance, Journal of Common Market Studies,* and *Journal of European Public Policy.*

Abraham L. Newman is assistant professor of international relations at the Edmund Walsh School of Foreign Service, Georgetown University, and a faculty member at the BMW Center for German and European Studies. His research focuses on transgovernmental politics, especially in the domain of data privacy. His work has appeared in journals such as *Governance, International Organization,* and the *Journal of European Public Policy.* He coedited with John Zysman, *How Revolutionary Was the Digital Revolution? National Responses, Market Transitions, and Global Technology* (2006).

Charles Pentland is professor of political studies and Director of the Centre for International Relations at Queen's University, in Kingston, Ontario, Canada, where he teaches courses on international organizations and global governance. Over the past years, his research and publications have focused on the external relations of the European Union, especially its eastward enlargement, its role in the Balkans, its relations with the former Soviet Union, and its Common Foreign and Security Policy. He has also written on Canadian foreign policy and transatlantic relations.

Claudio Radaelli is professor of political science and Jean Monnet Chair in EU Policy Analysis at the University of Exeter, where he directs the Centre for European Governance. He has published widely on the role of knowledge in the policy process, international taxation, regulatory reform, policy learning, and Europeanization.

Susanne K. Schmidt is professor of political science at the University of Bremen and is engaged in the Bremen International Graduate School of Sciences, funded by the German excellence initiative as well as in the collaborative research center "Transformations of the State," funded by the German Research Foundation. She edited in 2007 a special issue of the *Journal of European Public Policy* on mutual recognition as a new mode of governance.

Ingeborg Tömmel is professor in international politics, Jean Monnet Chair in European Politics and Policies, and director of the Jean Monnet Centre of Excellence at the University of Osnabrück. She held the John G. Diefenbaker Award in 2005–2006 to work at the University of Victoria. She has edited a special issue of PVS on "Die Europäische Union: Governance und Policymaking" (2007). In addition she is the author of six books, five edited volumes, numerous articles in academic journals, and book chapters on different aspects of European integration.

Amy Verdun is professor of political science, Jean Monnet Chair in European Integration Studies, and director of the Jean Monnet Centre of Excellence at the University of Victoria. She is author or editor of nine books and has published in scholarly journals such as *Acta Politica, European Union Politics, International Studies Review, Journal of Common Market Studies, Journal of European Integration, Journal of European Public Policy, Journal of Public Policy,* and *Review of International Political Economy.*

Index

347

About the Book

Do the traditional tools of governance make sense in the decidedly non-traditional political entity that is the European Union? Or are the realities of the unique EU system generating new, and sometimes eclectic, approaches to policymaking? Responding to these questions, *Innovative Governance in the European Union* explores the emergence and development of governance approaches in a wide range of policy areas.

The book's strong conceptual framework coupled with extensive empirical studies allows systematic comparison across EU policy areas. It also sheds light on the politics of policymaking in the context of the incentives and constraints set by the EU's institutional structure. Taken as a whole, it provides a comprehensive and authoritative overview of the forms of governance now emerging in the European Union.

Ingeborg Tömmel is professor of international politics and holds the Jean Monnet Chair in European Politics and Policies at the University of Osnabrück. **Amy Verdun** is professor of political science and holds the Jean Monnet Chair in European Integration Studies at the University of Victoria.